AF352716

Hybridity in Systemic Functional Linguistics

Hybridity in Systemic Functional Linguistics

Grammar, Text and Discursive Context

Edited by
Donna R. Miller and Paul Bayley

SHEFFIELD UK   BRISTOL CT

Published by Equinox Publishing Ltd.

UK: Office 415, The Workstation, 15 Paternoster Row, Sheffield, South Yorkshire
      S1 2BX
USA: ISD, 70 Enterprise Drive, Bristol, CT 06010

www.equinoxpub.com

First published 2016

British Library Cataloguing-in-Publication Data

A catalogue record for this book is available from the British Library.

ISBN-13 978 1 78179 064 9 (hardback)

Library of Congress Cataloging-in-Publication Data
Hybridity in systemic functional linguistics : grammar, text and discursive context
edited by Donna R. Miller and Paul Bayley.
    pages cm
  Includes bibliographical references and index.
    ISBN 978-1-78179-064-9 (hb)
1. Functional discourse grammar. 2. Systemic grammar. 3. Multiculturalism–
Social aspects. 4. Functionalism (Linguistics) I. Miller, D.R. (Donna R.) editor.
II. Bayley, Paul
P167.H93 2015
415–dc23
                          2015010870

Typeset by S.J.I. Services, New Delhi
Printed and bound by Lightning Source Inc. (La Vergne, TN), Lightning Source
UK Ltd. (Milton Keynes), Lightning Source AU Pty. (Scoresby, Victoria).

Contents

Acknowledgements   vii
List of Figures   ix
List of Tables   xi

1   Preliminaries: Hybridity & Systemic Functional Linguistics   1
     Donna R. Miller and Paul Bayley

Part I   Grammatical Hybridity   **19**

2   On the (non)necessity of the hybrid category behavioural process   21
     David Banks

3   Hybridity in TRANSITIVITY: Phraseological and metaphorically
     derived processes in the system network for TRANSITIVITY   41
     Gordon Tucker

4   Hybridity and process types   64
     Jorge Arús Hita

**Part II   Hybridity: Implications for pedagogy and professional
             practice**   **83**

5   Re-orienting semantic dispositions: The role of hybrid forms of
     language use in university learning   85
     Caroline Coffin

6   Teaching through English: Maximal input in meaning making   109
     John Polias and Gail Forey

7   The multilayeredness of hybridity in the written stylistic
     analysis argument   133
     Anne Isaac

8   Activity types, discourse types and role types: Interactional
     hybridity in professional-client encounters   154
     Srikant Sarangi

Part III   Registerial – and/or generic – hybridity   **179**

9   Hybridisation: How language users graft new discourses on
     old root stock   181
     Geoff Thompson

10   Registerial hybridity: Indeterminacy among fields of activity   205
     Christian M.I.M. Matthiessen and Kazuhiro Teruya

11   Woolf's lecture/novel/essay *A Room of One's Own*   240
     Carol Taylor Torsello

12   Genre and register hybridisation in an historical text   268
     Michael Cummings

13   Hybrid contexts and lexicogrammatical choices:
     Interpersonal uses of language in peer review reports in
     linguistics and mathematics   286
     Akila Sellami-Baklouti

14   The permeable context of institutional and newspaper
     discourse: A corpus-based functional case study of the
     European sovereign debt crisis   306
     Sabrina Fusari

Part IV   A closing statement: Hybridity – or permeability?   **335**

15   In the nature of language: Reflections on permeability
     and hybridity   337
     Ruqaiya Hasan

     Index   384

Acknowledgements

Thanks to Michael Halliday, copyright holder of Figures 4.1 and 4.2, for permission to reprint them. Thanks to Frances Pinter publishers for permission to reproduce Figure 4.3, and thanks also to Louise Ravelli for her cooperation in this matter.

Thanks to Sally Morgan for permission to reproduce, in Chapter 7, copyright material from 'The Letter' © 1988. In J. Davis (ed.) (1990) *Paperbark: A Collection of Black Australian Writing* 1–3. St Lucia, Queensland: University of Queensland Press. Thanks also to *Exploring style and meaning in language* (ESML), a one-semester stylistics-based EAP subject offered to L2 international undergraduates at an Australian university, for allowing the author of the chapter to use their writing in her study.

Thanks are also due to Teun van Dijk (editor of *Discourse Studies*) and Ali Baklouti (member of the editorial board of *Advances in Pure and Applied Mathematics*) for providing the author of Chapter 13 with the corpora used for her study.

The compilation of the IntUne corpus, used as one of the reference corpora in Chapter 14, was made possible by a grant from the INTUNE project (Integrated and United: A quest for Citizenship in an ever closer Europe) financed by the Sixth Framework Programme of the European Union, Priority 7, Citizens and Governance in a Knowledge Based Society (CIT3-CT-2005-513421).

List of Figures

Figure 2.1   Process types   35
Figure 2.2   Process types, incorporating voluntary and involuntary
              perception   36
Figure 2.3   Process types, incorporating projecting and non-
              projecting verbal process   36
Figure 3.1   *a brief hug* as a Main Verb Extension   55
Figure 3.2   *my heart* analysed as Emoter at Complement in the
              clause   58
Figure 3.3   Emoter conflated with *my* in *she broke my heart*   59
Figure 4.1   Metaphor seen from below (after Halliday 2008:91)   67
Figure 4.2   Metaphor seen from above (after Halliday 2008:91)   67
Figure 4.3   Compound semantics of metaphorical meaning
              (after Ravelli 1988:137)   68
Figure 6.1   A Teaching and Learning Cycle (adapted from
              Callaghan and Rothery [1988] and Custance, Dare
              and Polias [2011])   112
Figure 6.2   Mini-cycles within a larger Teaching and Learning
              Cycle (adapted from Custance, Dare and Polias [2011])   113
Figure 6.3   Scaffolding the responsibility of teaching and learning   115
Figure 6.4   Example of planning the TLC in a long jump lesson   117
Figure 6.5   Example of a 10-minute phase, itself acting as the
              Modelling and Deconstruction stage of a TLC of a long
              jump lesson   118
Figure 6.6   Teacher writes the process for calculating file size
              alongside the calculations so the visual representation
              of the steps can serve as a scaffold for the students   121
Figure 6.7   Slide 1 used in the music lesson, showing the drum and
              its name   125
Figure 6.8   Slide 4 used in the music lesson, showing the three
              major sounds produced   127
Figure 6.9   Slide 5 used in the music lesson, showing the clock
              face used to represent the drum   128
Figure 9.1   Yes/no question forms   184
Figure 10.1   The eight primary fields of activity and their subtypes   207
Figure 10.2   Simultaneous contexts of situation unfolding within
              the same material situational setting   213
Figure 10.3   Rhetorical-relational analysis of the last paragraph of
              Text 2   221

Figure 10.4 Example of a 'sponsored feature'   223
Figure 10.5 Examples of indeterminacy – ambiguities, overlaps,
             blends and neutralisations   231
Figure 13.1 CorpusTool scheme for corpus annotation   292

List of Tables

Table 2.1   Potential behavioural verbs   28

Table 3.1   A representative range of clause types associated with break X as a material and mental Process respectively   57

Table 4.1   Summary of hybrid types   78

Table 5.1   Data summary   88

Table 7.1   Comparative staging of the ESML model stylistic analysis and Aliénor's text   142

Table 7.2   Comparative staging of the ESML model stylistic analysis and Susanne's text   147

Table 9.1   The football data   186

Table 9.2   Speech functions in the football data   186

Table 9.3   Incomplete MUs in the football data   187

Table 9.4   Interactant reference in the football data   188

Table 9.5   The *Guardian* data   192

Table 9.6   Speech functions in the *Guardian* data   192

Table 9.7   Incomplete MUs in the *Guardian* data   193

Table 9.8   Interactant reference in the *Guardian* data   193

Table 10.1   Examples of registerial indeterminacy between pairs of fields of activity (field of activity 1 and field of activity 2)   211

Table 11.1   Contextual configurations of three genres   256

Table 12.1   Opening of *Sermo Lupi ad Anglos*   274

Table 12.2   The *Sermo Lupi* rises to a climax   278

Table 12.3   Conclusion of *Sermo Lupi ad Anglos*   282

Table 13.1   Corpus description   291

Table 13.2   Distribution of moves in the corpus   294

Table 13.3   Distribution of MOOD in the corpus   297

Table 13.4   Distribution of MOOD in the Recommendation move   297

Table 13.5   Distribution of MODALITY in the two sub-corpora   299

Table 13.6   Classification of Criticism clauses according to the ATTITUDE SYSTEM   301

Table 14.1   First 25 keywords (in order of keyness) in News Corpus   310

Table 14.2   First 25 keywords (in order of keyness) in Institutional Corpus   311

Table 14.3   Common keywords in News and Institutional Corpus   311

Table 14.4   Keywords exclusive to each corpus   312

Table 14.5   Collocations with *Eurozone* as a Classifier (News Corpus)   313

Table 14.6   Geographical/nationality Classifiers modifying *banks* (News Corpus)   317

Table 14.7   *Banks* in relational Processes (News Corpus)   319

Table 14.8   Examples of markers of objective Modality associated with *banks*   320

Table 14.9   Nominal group complexes with *growth* (Institutional Corpus)   321

Table 14.10   Epithets and Classifiers modifying *growth* as Thing (Institutional Corpus)   322

Table 14.11   Things modified by *growth* as Classifier (Institutional Corpus)   322

Table 14.12   Epithets and Classifiers modifying *growth* as Thing (News Corpus)   323

Table 14.13   Things modified by *growth* as Classifier (News Corpus)   324

Table 15.1   Conditioned uses of *give* type Process: grammar and meaning   364

Table 15.2   The permeability of Process *give* in operation   367

Table 15.3   Some ways of construing process   372

1

Preliminaries: Hybridity and Systemic Functional Linguistics

Donna R. Miller and Paul Bayley
University of Bologna

1.1   In the margins of hybridity

The term 'hybridity' has been around for a long time and, for most of its history of use, has been pressed into the most disparate – and often dubious – services. As Matthiessen and Teruya point out (this volume), it originated in the field of biology, where one finds its use was, exceptionally, 'neutral', to mean something that is neither more nor less than 'mixed'. But the evaluation it comes to enact over time is typically that of + or – appreciation: composition, and often, by extension, valuation (Martin and White 2005). Its genealogy has been traced through nineteenth-century racial theory and twentieth-century linguistics, prior to its post-colonial appropriation in the late twentieth century (cf., e.g., Young 1995), and, though it is neither our intention nor our brief to do any such comprehensive mapping, an example or two may be instructive of its burgeoning meaning potential and the roles it has played in the construction of new forms of knowledge and authority.

Racial theory argued the need for protecting the 'purity' of the White 'race' from the contamination of inferior impure ones; thus hybridity was negatively evaluated, while linguistic hybridity initially challenged the theory that language genesis could be adequately explained by means of a simple family tree system, thus hybridity was appreciated positively, as necessary complexity, and simplicity negatively invoked as inadequate.

Wikipedia notes that in contemporary times what has become known as 'hybrid talk', or the rhetoric of hybridity, has been getting more and more voluble and extending over an ever-wider expanse of disciplinary space, despite the fact that many scholars see it as resonating in a 'rhetorical cul-de-sac'.[1] As Matthiessen and Teruya also point out (this volume), the post-colonial turn in the use of the concept meant its most recent application to the study of social and semiotic systems, notably following upon the publication of *The Location of Culture* (1994) by Homi Bhabha, which theorised hybridity with reference to the ambivalent narratives of cultural imperialism and, subsequently, to the cultural politics of the 'migrant' in the modern metropolis. It then became more broadly associated to the flow and interactions of cultures, finding new applications in sociological theories of identity, multiculturalism, and (in)tolerance of 'the other'. And University cultural studies courses address the topic as well.[2] But the reach of hybridity's tentacles is seemingly limitless. The word reverberates in texts on contemporary visual, fine and applied arts. The novel use of industrial and/or recycled materials, the application of new technologies and digital media, are said to create brave new hybrid forms that dismantle traditional boundaries of expression.[3] And it is understood that 'Since the 1960s, the promulgation of hybridity constitutes a large facet of music'.[4]

Bakhtin's notion of 'polyphony', invariably positively appraised whatever the discipline appropriating it, is another typical grafting, likewise applied to investigating hybrid 'narratives and discourses, genres and identities, material forms and performances' in the fields of folklore, and cultural anthropology, but not only (Kapchan and Turner Strong 1999:239). Indeed, in their article on 'Hybridities in political media discourse', Fetzer and Johansson (2008) note that Bakhtin also features strongly in dialogue-centred approaches to the multilayeredness of political media discourse. They cite Fairclough (e.g.1995) as illustrative of the critical-discourse-analytic approach to contextualised text production and reception, in terms of relations between discourse and social practices, as well as the sociopragmatic slant of Lauerbach and Fetzer (2007), with an eye to identifying communicative strategies.

Within still another offshoot of post-colonial studies, current sociolinguistics research into World Englishes speaks of 'hybrid languages' (or, 'bilingual mixed languages'), which are seen to occur when a local language comes into contact with English, giving rise to code-mixing varieties such as Hinglish, Singlish, Spanglish, Japlish, etc., often serving – and praised – as highly-valued symbols of socio-cultural identity (Mesthrie and Blatt 2008). Increasingly, it has also become an essentially positive buzz word in discourse and genre studies as well. As Isaac observes (this volume), the poststructuralist perception of a text is not that it 'belongs to' a genre, but that it should be seen as a performance that 'participates' in several genres and continuously 'reconstitutes' them (Threadgold 1989). Indeed, as she also notes, Bawarshi and Reiff (2010: 21) repropose the notion of text itself as 'performance' that is able to refashion the genre it partakes in, 'Every textual performance repeats, mixes, stretches, and potentially reconstitutes the genre(s) it participates in.'

So, one might well ask, are we just riding the still catchable wave, trying to find room on the bandwagon while it still has momentum? No, we'd answer, we don't think so. Despite our perceptibly ironic critical stance up to this point towards the octopus hybridity, we realise that it's a fact of life that needs reckoning with and also a fitting metaphor for pondering and accounting for the heterogeneous and contradictory concerns of our post-colonial, globalised world. It provides a variegated take on reality that is far preferable to too-selective, and thus distorting, black and white positionings. And it was about time that Systemic Functional Linguistics (hereafter SFL) raised its voice on the subject – in a resounding chorus rather than a few solo vocals (e.g., Hasan 2000, more on which below, and Bartlett 2012). Hence the idea for the volume. But the idea wasn't revealed in a Damascus-like flash; rather it ripened over a few days of listening to academic papers – and savouring the warm winter Neapolitan sun.

1.2   Hybridity and SFL

A recent international conference in Naples at the end of 2009 was dedicated to the theme of 'Genre(s) on the Move: Hybridization and Discourse Change in Specialized Communication'. The plenary speakers included Srikant Sarangi and Norman Fairclough and debate on the meaning of the term 'hybridity' – but even more so on the intimately connected notion of 'context' – was lively, at times even heatedly exhilarating. It provoked much thought and can actually be said to have sowed the seeds of the projects that then bred this book.

Towards the end of Sarangi's excellent talk he cited Ruqaiya Hasan, with the following beguiling words:

> It is not simply that predetermined qualities of genres are being mixed, combined, hybridized: the fact of the matter is that by these devices people extend, elaborate and reclassify their discursive contexts. Derrida's celebrated claim that one cannot *not* mix genres should really be rephrased as contexts of life cannot but be permeable; the rest follows by the dialectic of language and discursive situation. (Hasan 2000:44)

The words stimulated us to dedicate the 23rd ESFLCW which we organised in Bertinoro, Italy in 2012 specifically to these interrelated issues: 'Permeable contexts and hybrid discourses'. The above quote then became publicised in the conference flyer and on the website.

Inevitably over-simplifying Hasan's keen perceptions, we might say that her focus in the cited article is on what she terms 'con/textual shift/ integration' taking place within the dialectic of language and discursive situation, or on how 'a discursive shift' is able to reset the values of contextual variables, thus redefining 'the frame within which the talk is embedded' (2000:43, passim). This mutual permeability is based on the powerful activation/construal dialectic between context and language, system and instance. Thus she rejects the assumption that weakly metaphorical terms such as 'hybridity' or 'genre combination' are able to adequately articulate the full complexity of what is really going on in discourse, which can (re) define, reclassify, the parameters of the context of situation incessantly, to the same extent and quite as significantly as the context defines the genre and/or register, etc., and so also the lexicogrammar of the discourse. In the paper, Hasan was arguing the case with reference to spontaneously unfolding spoken communicative encounters; although such a situation of context best illustrates her theories, the principle of dynamic language in use can clearly be applied to written text as well.

As a sort of aside, but not an irrelevant one, Fairclough did not agree with Sarangi's appreciative mention of Hasan's point of view. As Ventola noted in her presentation to ESFLCW 2012, Chouliaraki and Fairclough devoted a full chapter (in 1999) to criticising the conceptual and analytical powers of SFL, compared with those of Critical Discourse Analysis (CDA), yet failing to offer anything more than nebulous formulae in substitution (unpublished presentation). Ventola's assessment can be fully applied to his censure of Hasan and the SFL theory of context on the occasion of the conference 'Genre(s) on the Move ...'. That theory of context has of course also been critiqued as 'inadequate', 'incomplete' and 'disappointing' by another distinguished discourse analyst over the years – Teun van Dijk (e.g. 2004:343). Although our present remit does not include replaying the familiar arguments for and against these well-known evaluations, it's fair, if reductive, to say that for Fairclough SFL cannot have anything valid to say about hybridity since it lacks a system corresponding to the 'order of discourse', while the prime motive for van Dijk's dissatisfactions is what he pinpoints as a lack in SFL of an adequate cognitive element, or proper concern with the individual mind, in SFL.[5] In any event, we are confident that this volume demonstrates that SFL has quite a good deal to say perceptively on the question.

So then, it was Sarangi's quote from Hasan's paper which 'provoked' the theme of the Bertinoro conference and the conference in turn spawned the extant volume, the contents of both of which, however, quickly moved beyond addressing solely the implications of our own promptings, i.e., beyond Hasan's model of context and language as *mutually permeable* via instances of text. One might deduce that the time for speaking exclusively and directly to the topic of 'permeable contexts and hybrid discourses' – even in SFL circles – has not yet come, is not quite ripe, and 'that would be a perfectly reasonable conclusion' (Robin Fawcett p.c.); nonetheless, it may not be the whole story. We suggest one might also, less categorically and more positively perhaps, infer that the Classifier 'hybrid' in our conference title acted happily as a stimulant, a catalyst for articulating more extensive ideas for theorising and investigating concrete instances of hybridity in a wider SFL perspective.

For so it has apparently proved to be. Indeed, from the call for papers, again for both the conference and then the volume, we reaped a myriad of exciting eclectic proposals, focusing on diverse domains of observation, analysis, description and theory at the different phases of instantiation and levels of the hierarchy of stratification. This triggered a re-thinking of our overarching topic, which led to our engaging the metaphor of hybridity after all and refashioning the title of the volume to 'Hybridity in Systemic Functional Linguistics'. The metaphor may conceivably be 'weak', but we're confident the volume's own strengths will prove to go no short way towards firming it up by revealing the richly multifaceted complexity of the notion as well as its potential as a theoretical construct in SFL – so, hybridity being positively appreciated by us.

The sub-title of the volume reads: 'Grammar, Text and Discursive Context', mirroring the categories into which the accepted papers then by and large fell, to which we now turn.

1.3   The volume chapters

The first section gathers together papers addressing *Grammatical hybridity*, hybridity within the stratum of lexicogrammar itself. We like to think of it as illustrating what Halliday calls 'grammatics', '…a term for a specific view of grammatical theory, whereby it is not just a theory about grammar but also a way of using grammar to think with' (2002 [1996]:417).

In his provocative paper, David Banks takes issue with the neatness of the classification of process types as illustrated by the cover to IFG2

(Halliday 1994), maintaining that such neatness is illusory, whereas '… natural languages have the habit of being frustratingly untidy. They very rarely, if ever, fall into neat preprepared boxes'. Neatness is also not tantamount to correctness, or with the requisite clarity of status and definition that categories should have and the behavioural category does not. So he challenges the need for this too-'hybrid' ready-made 'box', admitting however that the phenomena it is meant to accommodate are indeed real and need to be dealt with. This he proposes can be done more satisfactorily at a greater level of delicacy, which would include networks providing the further choice between voluntary and involuntary perception and between projecting and nonprojecting verbal processes. Cases falling outside of these networks 'can be analysed either as material or as mental, depending on the particular clause in which they appear; or indeed as *both*' (our emphasis), meaning that process types can be seen as primary or secondary and that it is the context that will determine which, highlighting, for example, whether action in the physical world or a given mental state is of greater importance – which we might call a theory of permeable contexts and hybrid process types.

We're pleased to have at least one paper representing the alternative Cardiff Grammar (CaG) developed by Robin Fawcett and Gordon Tucker himself. Premising that lexicogrammatical hybridity is a problem for the design and organisation of the system network, Tucker's chapter investigates hybridity in the TRANSITIVITY SYSTEM, scrupulously probing the potential interaction of different transitivity types in clausal patterns featuring phraseological and metaphorically derived processes. This he does by putting forward for testing a twofold hypothesis concerning a verb's lexicogrammatical behaviour *vis-à-vis* its prototypical and metaphorical senses, after which he proceeds systematically to: (a) define the extent to which the process in a given expression is hybrid or not on the basis of its use of metaphor/metonymy; (b) apply various criteria tests for determining process type membership in any given expression; (c) try out a range of alternatives for modelling these in the system network representation of the meaning potential available to speakers of a language; and (d) contemplate the lexicogrammatical consequences of each alternative. As the SFL separation of the semantic and lexicogrammatical strata is not shared by CaG, the task of modelling metaphoricity is an even thornier one, which, however, Tucker negotiates admirably. In conclusion he notes, among other qualms, that 'It does appear that descriptions and procedures set up for prototypical cases strain under the weight of hybridity'. Nonetheless he would shun any solution that involved '[b]rushing the problem under the carpet'. Happily for us!

Jorge Arus Hita practises his grammatics at clause level as well, also aiming to account for what happens when a typically non-metaphorical lexical verb is used metaphorically. Hybrid processes, he suggests, undergo a transformation in meaning: the literal meaning – which he calls A – is transposed to a different area of the lexicogrammar – B – whereby the resulting hybrid meaning – C – is brought about. Accordingly, hybrid processes are seen as the intended product of literal plus metaphorical senses. Depending on the degree to which the metaphorical load is felt, three levels of hybridity are theorised. With processes whose metaphoricity is perceived as formidable, the A meaning is seen as more prominent than the B meaning in the interpretation of the resulting C meaning. Then there are those cases in which the metaphorical use is well-established and the weight of the A and B meanings fairly balanced. The third level occurs when the A and B meanings have so blended that they can no longer be felt as two distinct senses at all: 'In this case, we are in front of a new lexicalised meaning, no longer a hybrid but rather ... a highbred (as in 'highbred cattle') resulting from the previous process of hybridity'. Arùs Hita bolsters his argument by offering multiple analyses for each of these degrees of hybridity and exemplifying the distinctive semantic interplay taking place within each type of construction.

The second grouping of chapters deals with *Hybridity: implications for pedagogy and professional practice* – a set of papers which the number of stimulating proposals on these issues actually created. The first three chapters are sited in the classroom, be it physical or virtual, while the last is situated in professional environments.

In her chapter, Caroline Coffin considers how one's 'semantic disposition' (after Hasan 2009a) may be re-oriented (or not) through the process of institutionalised learning. As students appropriate and internalise concepts and perspectives from within and across different disciplines and apply these to personal and/or professional lived experience, they are learning to reconfigure the world. In so doing, their existing semantic dispositions are inevitably unsettled and re-formed – to a greater or lesser extent. So how does this occur? What role does language play? Coffin examines contexts of learning that activate meanings and wordings which can be seen as 'hybrid' from a number of perspectives. She argues that such contexts and discourses potentially enable students inhabiting a largely practical world constituted by specific lived experiences to enter into a predominantly theorised world constituted by abstract and generalised models of human behaviour, illustrating how, by expanding their semiotic resources, students become active agents in discursively extending, reclassifying and navigating between personal, professional and academic worlds.

John Polias and Gail Forey focus on language education and pedagogy in which the teacher uses various hybrid modes and resources. They discuss the value of SFL in teaching through English in different key learning areas (KLA's) in Hong Kong, where the teacher maximises access points for the learner by using multisemiotic resources related to a wide range of subject areas. The data, collected from the KLAs of Science, Information Technology, Art, Music and Physical Education, unambiguously show that different KLA's demand different approaches to the construction of knowledge. These are amply illustrated, as are the hybrid resources used to construct, across the curriculum, knowledge through language. The chapter argues the value of a 'teaching learning cycle' (e.g. Christie and Martin 1997) and a pedagogic model in which the teacher and students take on varying degrees of responsibility in co-constructing meaning in multiple cycles. The ultimate aim of the cycles is to bring the student to the point of independently constructing both matter and meaning through activities whose final goal is knowledge development.

Anne Isaac discusses hybridity as a multidimensional phenomenon (Sarangi this volume), applying the concept to the written stylistic analysis genre – seen as 'a staged, goal-oriented, purposeful activity in which speakers engage as members of [a] culture' (Martin 1984:25) – and considering its pedagogical implications for teaching academic writing to undergraduates for whom English is an L2. Data analysis probes multi-layered hybridity in the discursive organisation of the genre to determine which dimensions of hybridity are most likely to enable students to write more effectively. It reveals four dimensions of hybridity in the stylistic analysis genre which are amply discussed, along with the pedagogical implications of the findings which, among other things, show how innovation may actually enhance the effectiveness of an argument providing three crucial steps are fulfilled.

Srikant Sarangi is the only non-practitioner of SFL to appear in this volume, and we're very happy to have been able to include his different, but not discordant, voice. His chapter offers his current thinking on the interplay of discoursal hybridity, role analysis and professional practice, emphasising how 'hybridity and hybridisation are not simply linguistic ... processes which are signalled through intertextuality and interdiscursivity; they also constitute communicative acts which are mediated by role-relationships in context-sensitive ways'. His playful metaphorical representation of the phenomenon's internal and external dimensions – 'KitKat hybridity' – leads him to argue for the unpacking of the notion to distinguish its simple and complex forms at the interactional level. He contends that the concept of role, and in particular of role-set, can be mapped on to hybrid discourse types by re-examining key discourse analytic studies of professional practice in a range of institutional settings, and focuses especially on the hybrid activity type, genetic counselling. Sarangi ends by urging close attention to this interplay of discourse types and role types, seen as indispensable to analysis – if one would hope to be able to 'account for different forms of hybridity, socio-historically and contingently, as well as ecologically and manifestly'.

Our final grouping is also the largest one: *Registerial – and/or Generic – hybridity*. The title is purposeful; it is meant to mirror the well-known – and essentially incompatible and so also conflictual – theoretical distinction between the 'Hallidayan' take on the relationship between language and social context and what has come to be labelled, rather curiously for some, as the 'Sydney School' position. All our contributors were invited to explicitly declare their own stance *vis-à-vis* these, so that their readers would be able to locate their chapter bias clearly and immediately, as is only right they be able to do.[6] Most have done so, overtly leaning towards one side or the other, while others are more guarded, or perhaps discreet, and still others even openly opt to take a bit from here and another bit from there, according to their purposes. The range of hybrid registers – or genres – that are scrutinised in this section is indeed sizeable and the research questions pursued wonderfully varied.

Geoff Thompson's chapter aims at providing a 'snap-shot' of one stage in the development of particular internet registers: football and newspaper blogs. Thompson explores the hypothesis that informal speech is 'the familiar root stock' onto which features of new discourse types is 'grafted', thus producing hybrid texts that are created by the non-expert writer as s/he comes to grips with the unfamiliar discourse types produced by experts. Using corpus-based methods, he specifically attempts to identify patterns of lexicogrammatical features in such texts. On might say that Thompson's findings are 'hybrid' in themselves. If on one hand variation across the sets of blogs clearly emerges from his analysis of the data, in the sense that 'each set of blogs has generated its own conventions which differ from those of the other sets examined', then, on the other, he also observes 'fundamental similarities in their characteristics; and hybridity is one of the major characteristics which they have in common'. The initial hypothesis that informal speech would be the root stock onto which other types of discourse are grafted is substantiated, but Thompson also finds significant evidence that the process takes place in various ways and to varying degrees, depending on numerous factors influencing how bloggers, through their separate contributions to these ongoing texts, manage, to a greater or lesser extent, to negotiate their computer-mediated participation.

Christian Matthiessen and Kazuhiro Teruya clarify their theoretical and analytical position with their very title – Registerial hybridity: indeterminacy among fields of activity – and continue to do so throughout their chapter. They focus on the mixture of functional varieties of language working in diverse institutional domains, making use of a typology of registers that has been created by Matthiessen and other members of The PolySystemic Research Group at Hong Kong Polytechnic University, and which are, as they put it, 'seen "from above", from the vantage point of context'. Their interpretation of 'hybridity' stems from the idea of indeterminacy that was proposed in Halliday and Matthiessen (1999:547–562) as a way of getting at and teasing out 'fuzziness', 'vagueness', 'ambivalence', etc.. Indeed the authors distinguish, discuss and exemplify a wide range of indeterminacy types: ambiguities, overlaps, blends and neutralisations. In closing, they return to the context-based register typology for the purpose of locating the cases of indeterminacy that have been examined within it, and consider still other kinds of register mixing, including satire as employing 'effective registerial strategies for bringing features of commonly accepted views into critical relief'.

Carol Taylor Torsello asks how we can classify Woolf's *A Room of One's Own* in terms of genre. Her analysis begins with a careful reading of the text to extract all the explicit textual indications of the genre, which, however, point to three different ones – lecture, novel and essay. Her next step is to consider the structure of Woolf's text and compare this structure with ones proposed for the three genres. She finds that it is not impossible to fit the elements of Woolf's text into the structure of each of the three genres, but that important specificities keep the match with each from being completely satisfactory. As a final step she posits a contextual configuration (CC) for Woolf's text and for each of the three genres, and makes comparisons. The best match is with the CC of the essay. Nonetheless, important specificities distance Woolf's text from the typical essay. Taylor Torsello suggests that the metaphor of hybridity fits the generic complexity of this text, because she sees Woolf as making deliberate, selective use of three of the generic 'templates' available to her in her attempt to free herself of the male dominated literary code and create a feminine style and a feminine genre.

Michael Cummings deals with a literary text as well, but a historical text which is a classic reading in introductory anthologies of Old English literature, called the *Sermo Lupi ad Anglos quando Dani maxime persecuti sunt eos*, that is 'the sermon of the Wolf to the English at a time when the Danes were oppressing them severely'. His overall purpose is 'the mutual illumination of this text and SFL register *and* genre theory', especially aiming to show that SFL approaches and categories can also be highly appropriate to examining such a remote historical dialect/text; and then to demonstrate the extent to which Hasan's thoughts on the 'permeability' of register/genre categories (in Halliday and Hasan 1989:107) are invaluable for the task as well. This he effectively does by dissecting this complex persuasive sermon into sequentially distinct sub-texts realising the structural elements and also subgenres which vary and even blend into one another, thus enabling some subtext to carry out multiple functions. Cummings notes how 'the Sermo Lupi is often found to have a difficult and elusive structure'; although his analysis demonstrates the legitimacy of the opinion, it also reveals the intricacy of the text so that it can no longer be said to elude us.

Akila Sellami-Baklouti's chapter addresses the functional significance of hybridity for text analysis, showing that text can be the product of hybrid discursive contexts: genre and discipline, which constitute two interacting cultures. Harnessing the 'activation-construal dialectic' (Hasan 2009b:170) between context, meaning and wording, Baklouti investigates semantic and lexicogrammatical choices realising the interpersonal uses of language in a corpus of 30 Peer Review Reports relevant to two disciplines: Mathematics and Linguistics. A comparative approach shows that the two sub-corpora display some common lexicogrammatical choices, which are explained as being the traces left in the text by the Peer Review Report genre. In addition to these similarities, however, analysis also reveals some substantial differences, which are posited as being motivated by dissimilar disciplinary cultures (Mathematics vs. Linguistics), especially in terms of their research paradigms and community member relationships. Her findings support Baklouti's hypothesis that each sub-corpus is to some degree a hybrid outcome of the interaction of different genres belonging to different cultures. Moreover, she is led to conclude that the dialectical relationship between text and context proves to be essential to showing this kind of hybridity at work.

Like Thompson, Sabrina Fusari investigates register hybridity by combining SFL with Corpus Linguistics. After a brief theoretical overview, her case study of the European sovereign debt crisis as represented in newspaper and institutional discourse is presented. Analysis revolves around two specially prepared corpora comprising: (1) articles from *The Financial Times*, and (2) official documents released by the Council of Europe, all on the debt crisis, published between 9 and 15 December 2011. The keywords investigated ('eurozone', 'debt', 'banks', 'growth') prove to be used differently in the two corpora, both in phraseological and in grammatical terms, and this impacts on how the same crisis and, by extension, the role of European institutions, are represented in the two registers. Findings show that, despite the mutual influence between institutional and newspaper discourse, different views on the debt crisis, and potential ways out of it, are upheld by the City of London (which *The Financial Times* may be considered to represent) and by EU institutions. Finally, the synergy between SFL and Corpus Linguistics proves a valuable instrument for analysing register hybridity (and 'idiosyncrasy', Miller and Johnson 2009), potentially increasing its effectiveness as more sophisticated SFL-aware corpus annotation tools become available.

Ruqaiya Hasan's chapter stands apart, as is fitting. We've dubbed it a 'Closing Statement' as an intertextual bow to the weight of its Jakobsonian predecessor, and thus in tribute to Hasan, an SFL scholar whose work has been inspirational to many of our contributors' own. Hasan would show how permeability '...is a characteristic of certain categories recognised in language on the basis of principled descriptions'. The examples she presents are from both the grammatical and the lexical end of the spectrum but the concept is applicable not only to the stratum of lexicogrammar but also to those of semantics and of context. She firmly holds that '... permeability cannot be taken as a licence for crossing boundaries anywhere, anyhow'. Indeed she suggests that it is perhaps in the nature of language that to function as a communal meaning potential the sign relations will be subject to certain regularities, meaning that permeability has a systematic basis and also that it is grounded in the probabilistic nature of language itself, and perhaps is even, as Zadeh (1997) proposes, a quality of human thought as well. In concluding the chapter, she takes on the myriad issues raised by a juxtaposition of the terms 'permeability' and 'hybridity'; here, as throughout her chapter and indeed as is her wont, posing essential questions and eschewing facile answers.

1.4   In closing

By way of concluding this prologue to the volume, we should say briefly how we see the symbolism of the dice that our colleague, Antonella Luporini, ingeniously designed for the volume's cover. Rather than an interest in the gaming toss of the dice as an age-old symbol of risk-taking and/or fate and/ or irrevocability (as in Caesar's *'iacta alea est'*), we focus on a more subtle and 'scientific' significance: its link with predictability, probability and patterning. It is of course impossible to foretell with certainty the numbers that will turn up; nevertheless, the randomness of a throw is not absolute. Recent applications of chaos theory and mechanics by researchers at the

University of Lodz, Poland,[7] suggest that, with knowledge of initial conditions such as the friction of the table and the acceleration of gravity, outcomes should be to some degree predictable. The connections with what the systemicist does when working 'top-down' in the stratified multiple coding system which is language are evident. Moreover, that any alteration of situational variables that occurs in the ongoing construction of text will alter predictions of meanings/wordings made on the basis of the prior set of contextual parameters is, likewise, obvious; and one probable outcome of such revision, or 'permeable contexts', is 'hybridity'. The knock-on effect of a dice toss is, in short, assured: each roll indeed 'sets the stage for the next step in the pattern revealing itself as one goes along with the game'.[8] We propose that roll then as a metaphor for 'language as a stratified probabilistic system' (Halliday 1991:48).

That a language be probabilistic means that it works with tendencies rather than certainties, which is a characteristic of language akin to another: its indeterminacy, its fuzziness (Halliday 2013[2008]:48). This means a linguistics, and a grammatics, which rightly eschew automatic hook-up hypotheses and water-tight solutions good for any and all seasons. As Halliday assures us, 'systemic grammatics is not uncomfortable with fuzziness. That is, no doubt, one of the main criticisms that have been made of it; but it is an essential property that a grammatics must have...' (2002 [1996]:417). Given his subject matter at this point in his text, Halliday ends his sentence with the qualification 'for intelligent computing'. We take the liberty of presenting the statement minus the proviso, seeing it as valid, tout court, but also with specific reference to SFL, and being so bold as to presume Halliday would agree. Over 30 years ago we wrote, 'the major attraction of Halliday's model for us is its very intricacy, its very courage to be complex' (Miller in Ragazzini, Miller, Bayley 1985:44). Unreservedly, and with no hesitation, we reiterate the judgement today.

Notes

1 Rather than, or in addition to, being simply contingent on the growth of such rhetoric, the judgement could also be a result of it.

2 See e.g., http://rtf.utexas.edu/graduate/courses/fall-2011/rtf-387c-media-cultural-hybridity

3 See e.g., http://schools.walkerart.org/arttoday/index.wac?id=2377. One of these modes is that of political activism, now seen as having a 'hybrid' nature made up of old-fashioned placard-carrying protest, etc. and digital means,

including social networking. We won't broach the much debated question as to whether the latter is a question of 'slacktivism' or not. Cf. http://digital-activism.org/2013/07/the-future-isnt-digital-its-hybrid/

4   See e.g., http://postcolonialstudies.emory.edu/hybrid-postcolonial-music/

5   Of course SFL has often 'hybridised' its own approach with that of CDA (cf. Harrison and Young 2004). Neither is it a stranger to an interest in 'cognition' (cf. Halliday and Matthiessen 1999). But perhaps he would be interested in the description of an integrative model of language and its use, that attends to both the cognitive-interactive aspects and the socio-cultural, working in the framework of the Cardiff Model of SFL, being proposed by Fawcett (forthcoming).

6   Analysts of course are always biased – something that '[...] we can only be aware, and beware, of – and, of course, declare' (Miller 2007:178).

7   In a no longer available blogspot, http://trappedinthe80smoms.blogspot.it/2009/03/icon-of-80s-rubiks-cube.html

8   See http://www.theosophytrust.org/702-dice

References

Bartlett, T. (2012). *Hybrid Voices and Collaborative Change: Contextualising Positive Discourse Analysis*. New York and Abingdon, Oxon: Routledge.

Bawarshi, A.S. and Reiff, M.J. (2010). *Genre: An Introduction to History, Theory, Research, and Pedagogy*. West Lafayette, IN: Parlor Press.

Bhabha, H.K. (1994). *The Location of Culture*. London: Routledge.

Chouliaraki, L., and Fairclough, N. (1999). *Discourse in Late Modernity*. Edinburgh: Edinburgh University Press.

Christie, F. and Martin, J.R. (Eds) (1997). *Genre in Institutions: Social Processes in the Workplace and School*. New York: Continuum.

Fairclough, N. (1995). *Media Discourse*. London: Edward Arnold.

Fawcett, R. (forthcoming). *An Integrative Architecture for Systemic Functional Linguistics and Other Theories of Language*. London. Equinox.

Fetzer, A., and Johansson, M. (2008). Hybridities in political media discourse. *Politics and Culture*, issue 4. http://politicsandculture.org/2010/09/19/hybridities-in-political-media-discourse/

Halliday, M.A.K. (1991). Towards probabilistic interpretations, in E. Ventola (Ed.), *Functional and Systemic Linguistics: Approaches and Uses* (Trends in Linguistics Studies and Monographs 55), 39–62. Berlin and New York: Mouton de Gruyter. http://dx.doi.org/10.1515/9783110883527.39

Halliday, M.A.K. (1994). *An Introduction to Functional Grammar* (2nd ed.). London: Edward Arnold.

Halliday, M.A.K. (2002[1996]). On grammar and grammatics, in R. Hasan, C. Cloran and D. Butt (Eds), *Functional Descriptions: Theory and Practice*, 1–38.

Amsterdam and Philadelphia: John Benjamins. Reprinted in *On Grammar, The Collected Works of M.A.K. Halliday*, J.J. Webster (Ed.), Volume 1, 384–417. London: Continuum.

Halliday, M.A.K. (2013[2008]). Working with meaning: towards an applicable linguistics, in J.J. Webster (Ed.), *Meaning in Context: Implementing Intelligent Applications of Language Studies*, 7–23. London: Continuum. Reprinted in *Halliday in the 21st Century, The collected works of M.A.K. Halliday*, J.J. Webster (Ed.), Volume 11, 35–54. London: Bloomsbury.

Halliday, M.A.K., and Hasan, R. (1989). *Language, Context and Text: Aspects of Language in a Social Semiotic Perspective*. Oxford: Oxford University Press.

Halliday, M.A.K., and Matthiessen, C.M.I.M. (1999). *Construing Experience Through Meaning: A Language-Based Approach to Cognition*. London: Cassell.

Harrison, C. and Young, L. (Eds) (2004). *Systemic Functional Linguistics and Critical Discourse Analysis: Studies in Social Change*. London: Continuum.

Hasan, R. (2000). The uses of talk. In S. Sarangi and M. Coulthard (Eds), *Discourse and Social Life*, 28–47. London: Pearson Education.

Hasan, R. (2009a). *Semantic Variation: Meaning in Society and in Sociolinguistics, The Collected works of Ruqaiya Hasan*, J.J. Webster (Ed.), Volume 2. London: Equinox.

Hasan, R. (2009b). The place of context in a systemic functional model. In M.A.K. Halliday and J.J. Webster (Eds), *Continuum Companion to Systemic Functional Linguistics*, 166–189. London, New York: Continuum.

Kapchan, D., and Turner Strong, P. (Eds) (1999). Theorizing the Hybrid. [Special issue]. *Journal of American Folklore*, 112(445), 239–253. http://dx.doi.org/10.2307/541360

Lauerbach, G., and Fetzer, A. (2007). Introduction. In A. Fetzer and G. Lauerbach (Eds), *Political Discourse in the Media*, 3–30. Amsterdam and Philadelphia: John Benjamins.

Martin, J.R. (1984). Language, register and genre. In F. Christie (Ed.), *Children Course Reader*, 21–30. Geelong: Deakin University Press.

Martin, J.R., and White, P.R.R. (2005). *The Language of Evaluation: Appraisal in English*. Houndmills, Basingstoke: Palgrave Macmillan.

Mesthrie, R., and Blatt, R.M. (2008). *World Englishes: The Study of New Linguistic Varieties (Key Topics in Sociolinguistics)*. Cambridge: Cambridge University Press.

Miller, D.R. (1985). Language, Image, Myth: Preliminary Considerations. In G. Ragazzini, D.R. Miller, and P. Bayley, *Campaign Language: Language, Image, Myth in the US Presidential Election 1984*, 35–73. Bologna: CLUEB.

Miller, D.R. (2007). Towards a typology of evaluation in parliamentary debate: From theory to practice – and back again. In M. Dossena and A.H. Jucker (Eds), *(Re)volutions in Evaluation. Textus* 20(1), 159–180.

Miller, D.R., and Johnson, J.H. (2009). Strict vs. nurturant parents? A corpus-assisted study of congressional positioning on the war in Iraq. In J. Morley and P. Bayley (Eds), *Corpus Assisted Discourse Studies on the Iraq Conflict. Wording the War*, 34–73. London: Routledge.

Threadgold, T. (1989). Talking about genre: Ideologies and incompatible discourses. *Cultural Studies* 3(1), 101–127.

Young, R.J.C. (1995). *Colonial Desire: Hybridity in Theory, Culture, and Race.* London, New York: Routledge.

van Dijk, T.A. (2004). Text and context of parliamentary debates. In P. Bayley (Ed.), *Cross-Cultural Perspectives on Parliamentary Discourse,* 339–372. Amsterdam and Philadelphia: John Benjamins.

Ventola, E. (2012). *Discursive changes – switching genres or mixing them?* Unpublished presentation at the 23rd ESFLCW, 9th–11th July 2012. Italy: Bertinoro.

Zadeh, L.A. (1997). Towards the theory of fuzzy information granulation and its centrality in human reasoning. *Fuzzy Sets and Systems* 90(2), 111–127.

Websites

http://en.wikipedia.org/wiki/Hybridity (last accessed 21 February, 2014).

http://rtf.utexas.edu/graduate/courses/fall-2011/rtf-387c-media-cultural-hybridity (last accessed 18 March, 2014).

http://schools.walkerart.org/arttoday/index.wac?id=2377 (last accessed 14 March, 2014).

http://postcolonialstudies.emory.edu/hybrid-postcolonial-music/ (last accessed 14 March, 2014).

http://digital-activism.org/2013/07/the-future-isnt-digital-its-hybrid/ (last accessed 20 March, 2014).

http://www.everythingismathematical.com/news-throw-dice-predictable (last accessed 10 April, 2014).

http://www.theosophytrust.org/702-dice (last accessed 10 April, 2014).

About the authors

Donna R. Miller holds the Chair of English Linguistics at the Department of Modern Languages, Literatures and Cultures of the University of Bologna, where she coordinates its English Language Studies Programme. Since 2003, she has also directed the Centre for Linguistic-Cultural Studies (CeSLiC). Recent publications include *Language and Verbal Art Revisited: Linguistic approaches to the study of literature* (co-editor M. Turci, Equinox, 2007) and 'Jakobson's place in Hasan's Social Semiotic Stylistics: Further explorations of 'pervasive parallelism' as symbolic articulation of theme', in *Society in Language, Language in Society: Essays in honour of Ruqaiya Hasan* (W. Boucher and J. Liang (eds), Palgrave Macmillan, 2015).

Paul Bayley is Professor of English language and linguistics at the Department of Political and Social Sciences of the University of Bologna. His research interests are directed towards corpus linguistics, with particular attention to domain specific corpora, and discourse analysis within the framework of systemic functional linguistics, focusing in particular on language of the institutions. He has recently co-edited (with John Morley) *Corpus-Assisted Discourse Studies on the Iraq Conflict: Wording the war* (Routledge, 2009) and (with Geoffrey Williams) *Europe Identity: What the media say* (Oxford University Press, 2012).

Part I
Grammatical Hybridity

2

On the (non)necessity of the hybrid category behavioural process

David Banks
Université de Bretagne Occidentale

2.1   Historical introduction

In this article I want to look briefly at the historical development of the notion of behavioural process. I will then look at a number of factors which seem to indicate that behavioural process is not on a par with the other process types. I will finally suggest a way of dealing with the phenomena concerned which avoids the use of a distinct process type such as behavioural process.

Current Systemic Functional theory provides for three semantic metafunctions: Ideational, Interpersonal and Textual. The Ideational metafunction conveys the representational stratum of meaning and this is mainly conveyed through the system of TRANSITIVITY, which is analysed in terms of a number of process types with their related participants and circumstances. The theory provides for three major process types: material, mental and relational; and three minor types: verbal, behavioural and existential.

However, this has not always been the case. Early versions of the theory, as expressed, for example, in Halliday (1968), and Halliday (1970), provide for only three process types: action, mental and relational. A few years later, in Halliday (1973a) (but probably more widely known in the version reprinted as Halliday (1973b)), action process has been renamed material process, and verbal process has been added to the list, giving four process types: material, mental, relational and verbal. These four types are the only ones mentioned in Halliday (1978).

However, by the time we get to Halliday (1985), the model has been extended to the now familiar six process types, of which three are major types: material, mental and relational, and three are said to be subsidiary: behavioural, verbal and existential. Of these subsidiary processes, behavioural processes are said to be 'processes of physiological and psychological behaviour' (Halliday, 1985:128); verbal processes are said to be 'processes of saying' (Halliday, 1985:129), and existential processes 'represent that something exists or happens' (Halliday, 1985:129). While the description of verbal processes clearly marks them as processes of communication, and that of existential processes clearly indicates that they are statements of existence, the description of behavioural process seems much less clear; indeed in the second edition of the same work, Halliday himself acknowledges that this is the 'least distinct' category:

> These [Behavioural processes] are processes of (typically human) physiological and psychological behaviour [...] They are the least distinct of all the six process types because they have no clearly defined characteristics of their own; rather they are partly like the material and partly like the mental. (Halliday, 1994:139).

This quotation is reprinted word for word in the following (third) edition (Halliday and Matthiessen, 2004: 248–250).[1] It would seem reasonable to ask to what extent it is possible to have a category which has 'no clearly defined characteristics'. Surely, in order to be a category, what is included and what is not included in the category must be clear, and this implies clearly defined characteristics.

The system is synthesised in the diagram which is printed on the front cover of Halliday (1994); this has relational process at the top of a circular disposition, with material process at the bottom left, and mental process at the bottom right; it then places verbal process between relational and mental, existential process between material and relational, and behavioural between material and mental. This is all beautifully neat and satisfyingly tidy. But I think it reasonable to ask: since when have natural languages been beautifully neat and tidy? On the contrary, natural languages have the habit of being frustratingly untidy. They very rarely, if ever, fall into neat preprepared boxes. They spread and dangle loose ends in the most unexpected ways and places. But, in my experience, it is precisely this untidiness which makes them of such great interest to the linguist. Linguistic endeavour is largely a question of trying to find some sense in the wilderness of the disorder of linguistic phenomena. Hence, I find the neatness of the diagram suspect. This remains true, even if, as I suspect, the diagram is only intended to have schematic value. Halliday (1994:107) calls it a 'diagrammatic summary'.

Despite having 'no clearly defined characteristics', the following (3rd) edition (Halliday and Matthiessen (2004)) claims that:

> On the borderline between 'material' and 'mental' are the *behavioural* processes: those that represent the outer manifestations of inner workings, the acting out of processes of consciousness [...] and psychological states [...]. (Halliday and Matthiessen, 2004:171)[2]

And later in the same work:

> [...] 'behavioural' process clauses are not so much a distinct type of process, but rather a cluster of small subtypes blending the material and the mental into a continuum [...]. (Halliday and Matthiessen, 2004:255)[3]

Once again, it seems reasonable to ask whether we need a separate category for phenomena which are 'on the borderline', and which are at the point where two categories merge.

2.2   Involuntary or semivoluntary action

I have looked at a range of presentations of the theory; these are necessarily similar, since they are all based on the work of Halliday, and purport to present his work. Of those I consulted, only Lock (1996) does not mention behavioural process, but he does have a mental-action process, which seems to be behavioural process under another name. Among the possible criteria discussed in many of these works is the fact that behavioural process is said to represent involuntary or semivoluntary action. Thus, for example, in their otherwise excellent student textbook, Downing and Locke say:

> A borderline area between mental processes and material processes is represented by **behavioural** processes such as *cough, sneeze, yawn, blink, laugh* and *sigh*, which are usually one-participant. They are considered as typically involuntary; but it may be that there is a slight agency involved. They can be deliberate, too, as in *he coughed discretely, he yawned rudely*, in which the adjunct of manner implies volition. (Downing and Locke, 2006:152)

It seems to me that to say that something is 'typically involuntary', and then to go on to say that 'there may be [...] a slight agency involved', and even that 'they can be deliberate', is, to say the least, bordering on a contradiction, and is certainly not particularly useful. In terms of deliberateness, anything seems to be possible. Moreover, what precisely does 'typically involuntary' mean? Processes such as *laugh* and *sigh* are not usually involuntary. It might be claimed that they indicate mental states, but then so does banging your fist on the table! And I do not think that anyone would claim that that was anything other than material. Ultimately, all material processes that have a conscious actor have some mental component, basically that of intention, but that does not alter their status as material processes. What about the process *cough*? We may sometimes have a very strong urge to cough, but lovers of classical music will tell you that at a classical music concert, where coughing is disapproved of, particularly during a delicate *piano* passage, it is perfectly possible to control that urge.

Bloor and Bloor acknowledge the curious nature of this category:

> As far as clearly defined, discrete classification of Processes is concerned, the bottom of the barrel is *behavioural process*. [...] This is the grey area between material and mental Processes. (Bloor and Bloor, 2004:126)

In their brief discussion they give this extremely odd example:

> (1) The car slid away

They then go on to say that it 'could equally be argued that it is a material Process'. I must admit that I cannot see this example as anything other than material process. But more important for our purposes is the question of the utility of a special category, if can be analysed otherwise anyway.

2.3   Voluntary and involuntary perception

Some use the category of behavioural process to distinguish between mental processes of perception which are voluntary such as *listen to* and *look at* and those which are involuntary, like *hear* and *see*. Thus Thompson says:

> [...] one of the main reasons for setting up this category is that they allow us to distinguish between purely mental processes and the outward physical signs of those processes. For example, many mental perception processes have paired processes which express a conscious physical act involved in perception: 'see' (mental) and 'watch', 'look',

etc. (behavioural); 'hear' (mental) and 'listen' (behavioural) and so on. (Thompson, 2004:103)

Similarly, Eggins states:

> Indicating their close relationship with mental processes, some behaviourals in fact contrast with mental process synonyms: e.g. *look at* is behavioural but *see* is mental; *listen to* is behavioural but *hear* is mental. (Eggins, 1994:250)

Martin, Matthiessen and Painter (1997) give a contrasting table of perception verbs which, on this criterion, are mental and those which are behavioural.

So, we are told that processes on this mental-material border are typically involuntary, like *breathe, faint* and *yawn*, but when we are dealing with perception processes, involuntary process are to be treated as mental process, and it is the voluntary processes that are said to be behavioural. Thus behavioural processes are typically involuntary unless they are perception, in which case they are voluntary. This, does not seem to me to be particularly coherent, and is close, once again, to becoming a contradiction.

2.4   Processes of communication

Some use the category of behavioural process to distinguish between those processes of communication which project and those which do not. Those which accept clauses of projection are said to be verbal process, while those which do not project are said to be behavioural. Thus Matthiessen says:

> The former [verbal processes that do not project] indicate verbal behaviour and can in fact be grouped with behavioural processes. (Matthiessen, 1995:284)

And later in the same work:

> **Processes of verbal behaviour** are on the borderline between **verbal** and **behavioural**; they can alternatively be interpreted as behavioural processes. (Matthiessen, 1995:284)

It will be noted that Matthiessen is fairly permissive on this point. These processes are not necessarily analysed as behavioural; behavioural process is only a possible alternative ('can alternatively be interpreted'). Processes such as *speak, talk, argue* and *converse* are said to be cases of verbal behaviour and are on the borderline between verbal and behavioural process. He distinguishes this from verbal impact, such as *accuse, blame, congratulate*, and *criticise*. These are said to be between verbal and material process, and although these are processes of communication which do not project, he does not suggest an alternative to the analysis of these as verbal process. It can be seen that Matthiessen's position here is fairly nuanced. However the position expressed in Halliday and Matthiessen 1999 is less so:

> Furthermore, behavioural clauses normally do not project, or project only in highly restricted ways. (Halliday and Matthiessen, 1999:136)

This is stated even more categorically in Martin, Matthiessen and Painter (1997):

> Note that there are a number of processes representing verbal behaviour – *talk, chatter, gossip, speak, lie* – that are behavioural rather than verbal; they cannot project. [...] (Note that while behavioural process can, in a written narrative, project by quoting [...] a true verbal process can project both direct and indirect speech in all contexts.)
>
> Included in this behavioural group are processes which concern the creation of a symbolic representation. Verbs such as *characterise, outline* [...] are used here, but again projection is not possible [...] and these are behavioural rather than verbal. (Martin, Matthiessen and Painter, 1997:125–126)

In the case of involuntary or semivoluntary acts, behavioural processes are said to be between material and mental process; in the case of processes of communication which do not project, they are said to be between behavioural and verbal process (though, it seems, analysed as behavioural). If we return to the diagram printed on the front cover of the second edition of Halliday's *Introduction to Functional Grammar*, we see that the position between material and mental is at the bottom centre of the diagram; however the position between behavioural and verbal is actually filled by mental process. behavioural process and verbal process are not adjacent. So, either the diagram has no validity, or the position proposed is erroneous. Thompson (2004), who does not reproduce the diagram, places both behavioural and verbal process between material and mental. Indeed if I were looking for a candidate for the position between material and mental, verbal process would seem to be an excellent candidate. Berry (1975) gives a system network of process types, and in her scheme of things, mental process leads to the choice between internalised and externalised. And, to all intents and purposes, externalised mental process is the same thing as verbal process, or at least, processes of communication.

2.5   Potential behavioural verbs

In an attempt to see the extent of behavioural process, I have produced a list of verbs which can, in an appropriate clause, be analysed as behavioural process. The list was produced by listing all the verbs that were given as examples of behavioural process either as individual verbs or in clauses, in eight books which present the theory. The eight books in question are:

> Eggins (1994)
> Matthiessen (1995)
> Martin, Matthiessen and Painter (1997)
> Halliday and Mathiessen (1999)
> Butler (2003)
> Halliday and Matthiessen (2004)
> Thompson (2004)
> Downing and Locke (2006)

Since these books all present the same theory, and are all based on various editions of Halliday's *Introduction*, it would be reasonable to expect a certain degree of overlap between them. It will also be noted that some authors contributed to more than one of these books. The verbs found are given in Table 2.1. Verbs which are given by at least six of the books are printed in bold; verbs that are given by only one of the books are printed in italics.

Table 2.1: Potential behavioural verbs

Matthiessen 1995	Halliday & Matthiessen 1999	Martin, Matthiessen & Painter 1997	Butler 2003	Eggins 1994	Thompson 2004	Downing & Locke 2006	IFG3 2004
argue		abuse					argue
babble							
						blink	
blubber							
						blush	
box							
breathe	breathe			breathe			breathe
burp							burp
		characterise					
chat		chat					
chatter		chatter					
chuckle							chatter
clean							
collaborate						collapse	
comb							
converse							
cough	cough	cough		cough		cough	cough
cry	cry			cry	cry	cry	cry
dance		dance					dance
		describe					
						die	

Matthiessen 1995	Halliday & Matthiessen 1999	Martin Matthiessen & Painter 1997	Butler 2003	Eggins 1994	Thompson 2004	Downing & Locke 2006	IFG3 2004
discuss							
	dream		dream	dream			dream
dress							
embrace		embrace					
						enjoy	
					examine		
						faint	faint
						fall	
feel		feel				feel	
fight							
flatter		flatter					
frown		frown		frown			frown
gab							
gasp		gasp					
gawk		gawk		gawk			
giggle	giggle						
gossip		gossip					gossip
grimace		grimace		grimace			
grin		grin		grin			
						grow	
							grumble
grunt							
have a row							

Matthiessen 1995	Halliday & Matthiessen 1999	Martin Matthiessen & Painter 1997	Butler 2003	Eggins 1994	Thompson 2004	Downing & Locke 2006	IFG3 2004
							hiccup
hide							
							hiss
hug		hug					
insult		insult					
kiss		kiss					
laugh	**laugh**	**laugh**		laugh	laugh	laugh	**laugh**
							lie down
listen	**listen**	**listen**	**listen**		listen	listen	**listen**
listen to		listen to					
look	**look**		**look**		look	look	**look**
look at		look at					
look over		look over		look over			
		malign					
meditate	meditate	meditate	meditate				
meet							
moan		moan					
							mouth
mumble		mumble					
murmur							murmur
mutter		mutter					
negotiate							
							nod

Matthiessen 1995	Halliday & Matthiessen 1999	Martin Matthiessen & Painter 1997	Butler 2003	Eggins 1994	Thompson 2004	Downing & Locke 2006	IFG3 2004
observe		observe					
		outline					
play		play					
ponder	ponder	ponder	ponder				
		potray					
pout		pout		pout			
praise		praise					
prepare		puzzle					
puzzle	puzzle		puzzle				
			remember				
ruminate		ruminate					
scowl		scowl		scowl			
solve							
shake		shake					
shave							
							shit
shiver		shiver	shiver				
shudder		shudder					
sigh				sigh		sigh	sigh
simper							
sing		sing					sing
							sit down
							sit up

Matthiessen 1995	Halliday & Matthiessen 1999	Martin Matthiessen & Painter 1997	Butler 2003	Eggins 1994	Thompson 2004	Downing & Locke 2006	IFG3 2004
slander		slander					
							sleep
smell		smell				smell	
smile	**smile**	**smile**	**smile**	**smile**		**smile**	**smile**
							snarl
			sneeze			sneeze	sneeze
snicker							
sniff		sniff		sniff			
				snuffle			
snort		snort					
sob					sob		sob
		solve					
speak		speak					
stammer		stammer					
stare		**stare**		**stare**	**stare**	**stare**	**stare**
						stay	
stretch							
stutter		stutter					
sweat		sweat					
talk		talk					talk
tango							
taste		taste		taste		taste	
think		think	think			think	think

Matthiessen 1995	Halliday & Matthiessen 1999	Martin Matthiessen & Painter 1997	Butler 2003	Eggins 1994	Thompson 2004	Downing & Locke 2006	IFG3 2004
				think on			
titter							
	touch						
tremble		tremble				tremble	
twitch		twitch					
undress							
view		view					
						wait	
waltz							
wash							
watch	**watch**	**watch**	**watch**	**watch**	**watch**	**watch**	**watch**
					wave		
weep							
whine		whine					whine
whinge		whinge					
work out		work out		work out			
							worry
						yawn	yawn

The fact that a verb appears in this list does not mean that the author in question claims that this verb is always to be analysed as behavioural, but simply that given an appropriate clause environment it constitutes an example of behavioural process.

The number of potential verbs found in the various authors differs greatly. The greatest number, 95, was found in Matthiessen (1995), while only nine were found in Thompson (2004). Martin, Matthiessen and Painter (1997) has 65, Halliday and Matthiessen (2004), 38, Downing and Locke (2006), 26, Eggins (1994), 21, Halliday and Matthiessen (1999), 13, and Butler (2003), 12. The total number of individual verbs is 133.

Given that a great deal of overlap between these presentations might be expected, it is surprising that there is only one verb that is mentioned by all the authors; this is the verb *watch*. Otherwise, *laugh*, and *listen*, are given by seven of the eight; *cough*, *look* and *stare*, are given by six of the eight. These verbs, as indicated above, are in bold in Table 2.1. Hence only six of the 133 verbs are mentioned by at least six of the eight authors. Even though the authors are obviously not intending to provide exhaustive lists, it is surprising that there is so little overlap between them. This suggests that there is little agreement between the various authors as to what constitutes a potential behavioural verb.

At the other end of the scale, there are a large number of verbs that are mentioned by a single author. These, as indicated above, are printed in italics in Table 2.1. As might be expected, Matthiessen (1995), who gives the largest number of verbs overall, also has the largest number of verbs not mentioned by any other author. In fact, 29 of his 95 verbs (i.e., 31 per cent) fall into this category. But even Thompson (2004), who gives only nine verbs, gives two (22 per cent of his total) that are never mentioned by anyone else. Of the 26 verbs given by Downing and Locke (2006), nine (35 per cent) are never mentioned by anyone else. Even in the case of Halliday and Matthiessen (2004), the third edition of the work on which the others are based, of the 38 verbs found, 11 (29 per cent) are never mentioned by anyone else. In the other books, roughly 10 per cent of the verbs given are mentioned only by a single author. It seems reasonable to conclude from this that there is little consensus on which verbs actually are potential behavioural verbs.

What does this mean? Is behavioural process simply all things to all men? Is it just a rag-bag into which we stuff cases we find difficult to analyse?

2.6   Towards a possible solution

It might have been thought that although behavioural process cannot be granted the same status as the other process types, perhaps it might be useful if one is particularly interested in the area (i.e., where material and mental process blend) it is supposed to cover. However, even this possibility seems to be breaking down, since what behavioural process covers cannot even be said to be an area. It covers a number of phenomena (semivoluntary action, voluntary perception, nonprojecting communication, etc.), but these are dissociated and dispersed. Hence the notion of behavioural process as an area disintegrates. On the other hand the phenomena, and the distinctions that they cover, are real. How can these distinctions be dealt with? I would like to suggest that this can be done at a greater degree of delicacy than that of process types.

If we take a standard presentation of process types, but omitting behavioural process, this would give a system network of the type illustrated in Figure 2.1.

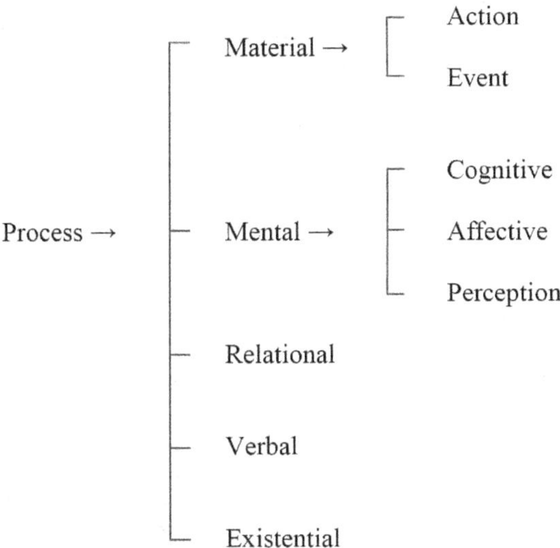

Figure 2.1: Process types

If in the case of perception process, we allow for the further choice between voluntary and involuntary, we would have the system network illustrated in Figure 2.2.

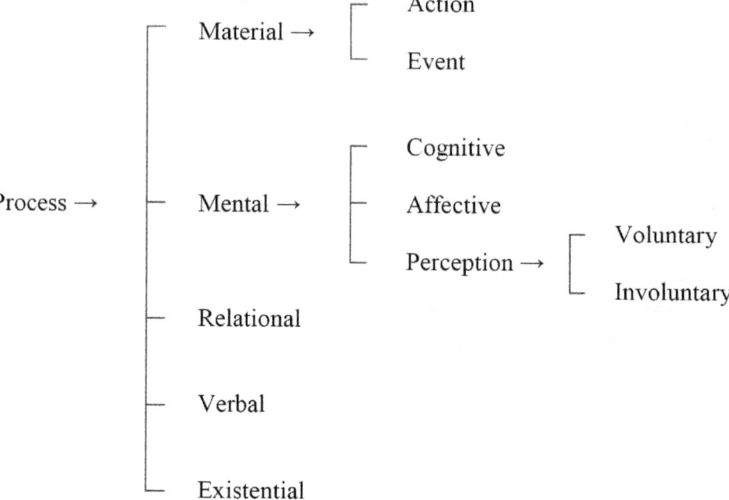

Figure 2.2: Process types, incorporating voluntary and involuntary perception

If we now allow for a choice between projecting and nonprojecting in the case of verbal process, our system network becomes that illustrated in Figure 2.3.

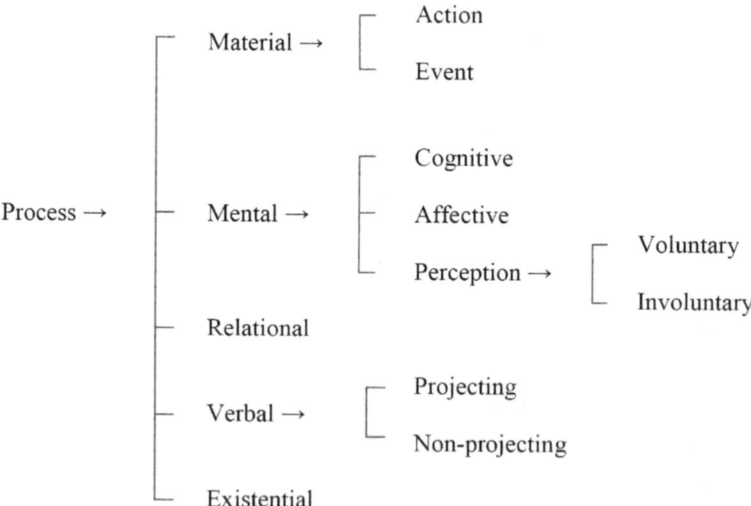

Figure 2.3: Process types, incorporating projecting and nonprojecting verbal process

For those cases not catered for by this system network, which are basically those said to be on the borderline between material and mental process, I feel that they can be analysed either as material or as mental, depending on the particular clause in which they appear; or indeed as both. I think there are a number of cases where more than one process type can be encoded within a single verb. For example, *smile* is basically a verb of material process. It is an action which takes place in the physical world. It is true that it is usually indicative of a particular mental state, but the smiling is not in itself that mental state. However, there are specific contexts where the mental state may be of particular importance, and in such cases one could argue for the addition of mental process as a secondary type to the main material process.

Hence, I am advocating a system with five process types, excluding behavioural process. I have used such a system (Banks 2005) over many years with my students, without it ever causing any serious problems. For example, the following example given as behavioural process in Halliday and Matthiessen 2004, can be treated as mental process:

> (2) He was foolish not to realize that this was happening to him, that he **could** possibly **have dreamt** about it.

Dreaming is a purely cerebral activity, without any corresponding changes in the physical world. On the other hand, the following example, from the same source, can be analysed as material process:

> (3) Sub Inspector Guha too **had fainted** [...]

Here, fainting is definitely something which occurs in the physical world, and thus is an example of material process. However, *Sub Inspector Guha* obviously does not instigate his own fainting, so is not functioning as actor, but rather as affected. Since I suggest distinguishing between voluntary and involuntary perception at a more delicate level, both of the following (from Matthiessen 1995), would be treated as mental process:

> (4) I'**m listening** to them playing.
> (5) I **can hear** them playing.

Similarly, since I distinguish between projecting and nonprojecting communication at a more delicate level, the following example (from Martin *et al.* 1997) would be analysed as verbal process:

> (6) They **described** the new project to the Board.

It is worth noting in passing that the Cardiff variant of the Systemic Functional model finds no place for behavioural process (Fawcett 2008, 2011). Fawcett 2011 gives six process types: action, relational, mental, environmental, influential, and event-relating, but nothing that even approximates to behavioural process.

2.7   Conclusion

Behavioural process, we are told, is a category that has no clearly defined characteristics. It is said to be typically involuntary, though, then again, perhaps not. Moreover, when it occurs as a process of perception, it is the voluntary processes which are behavioural, the involuntary ones being mental. It is said to be placed between material and mental, except when it is nonprojecting communication, in which case it is between behavioural and verbal. There is little consensus on which verbs actually constitute potential behavioural verbs. The phenomena concerned do not even form a cluster, since they are disparate and dispersed. I would suggest that behavioural process is not a useful category, and that the phenomena it is supposed to deal with can be dealt with more satisfactorily at a great level of delicacy.

Notes

1   It appears again word for word in the fourth edition (Halliday and Matthiessen [2013:301]).

2   Repeated word for word in the fourth edition (Halliday and Matthiessen [2013:215])

3   Repeated word for word in the fourth edition (Halliday and Matthiessen [2013:306])

References

Banks, D. (2005). *Introduction à la linguistique systémique fonctionnelle de l'anglais*. Paris: L'Harmattan.

Berry, M. (1975). *Introduction to Systemic Linguistics (Vol. 1). Structures and Systems*. London: B.T. Batsford.

Bloor, T., and Bloor, M. (2004). *The Functional Analysis of English. A Hallidayan Approach* (2nd ed.). London: Arnold.

Butler, C.S. (2003). *Structure and Function. A Guide to Three Major Structural-functional Theories. Part 1, Approaches to the Simplex Clause.* Amsterdam and Philadelphia: John Benjamins.

Downing, A., and Locke, P. (2006). *English Grammar. A University Course* (2nd ed.). London: Routledge.

Eggins, S. (1994). *An Introduction to Systemic Functional Linguistics.* London: Pinter.

Fawcett, R.P. (2008). *Invitation to Systemic Functional Linguistics through the Cardiff Grammar, An Extension and Simplification of Halliday's Systemic Functional Grammar* (3rd ed.). London: Equinox.

Fawcett, R.P. (2011). Problems and solutions in identifying Processes and Participant Roles in discourse analysis. Part 1: Introduction to a systematic procedure for identifying Processes and Participant Roles. *Annual Review of Functional Linguistics*, 3, 34–87.

Halliday, M.A.K. (1968). Notes on transitivity and theme in English, Part 3. *Journal of Linguistics*, 4(2), 179–215. http://dx.doi.org/10.1017/S0022226700001882

Halliday, M.A.K. (1970). Language structure and language function. In J. Lyons (Ed.), *New Horizons in Linguistics*, 140–165. Harmondsworth: Penguin.

Halliday, M.A.K. (1973a). The functional basis of language. In B. Bernstein (Ed.) *Class, Codes and Control, Volume 2. Applied Studies Towards a Sociology of Language*, 343–366. London: Routledge and Kegan Paul.

Halliday, M.A.K. (1973b). *Explorations in the Functions of Language.* London: Edward Arnold.

Halliday, M.A.K. (1978). *Language as Social Semiotic. The Social Interpretation of Language and Meaning.* London: Edward Arnold.

Halliday, M.A.K. (1985). *An Introduction to Functional Grammar.* London: Edward Arnold.

Halliday, M.A.K. (1994). *An Introduction to Functional Grammar* (2nd ed.). London: Edward Arnold.

Halliday, M.A.K. and Christian M.I.M. Matthiessen (1999). *Construing Experience through Meaning. A Language-based Approach to Cognition*, London, Cassell.

Halliday, M.A.K., and Christian, M.I.M. Matthiessen (2004). *An Introduction to Functional Grammar* (3rd ed.). London: Edward Arnold.

Halliday, M.A.K., and Christian, M.I.M. Matthiessen (2013). *Halliday's Introduction to Functional Grammar* (4th ed.). London, Routledge.

Lock, G. (1996). *Functional English Grammar, An Introduction for Second language Teachers.* Cambridge: Cambridge University Press.

Martin, J.R., Matthiessen, C.M.I.M., and Painter, C. (1997). *Working with Functional Grammar.* London: Arnold.

Matthiessen, C. (1995). *Lexicogrammatical Cartography: English Systems.* Tokyo: International Language Sciences.

Thompson, G. (2004). *Introducing Functional Grammar* (2nd ed.). London: Arnold.

About the author

David Banks is Emeritus Professor of English Linguistics at the Université de Bretagne Occidentale, Brest, France. He is chairman of AFLSF (Association Française de la Linguistique Systémique Fonctionnelle). He has published over 80 academic articles, and authored or edited over 20 books. His recent publication, *The Development of Scientific Writing, Linguistic features and historical context,* (Equinox, 2008), won the ESSE (European Society for the Study of English) 2010 Language and Linguistics Book Award. His current research interests include the linguistic analysis of scientific text, and its emergence in English and French in the late seventeenth century, and the application of SFL to English and French.

3

Hybridity in transitivity: Phraseological and metaphorically derived Processes in the system network for TRANSITIVITY

Gordon Tucker

Centre for Language and Communication Research, Cardiff University

3.1   Transitivity and the classification of Processes

3.1.1   Introduction and aims

The analysis of Processes according to PROCESS TYPE in the system of TRANSITIVITY is a central concern for those working within the framework of Systemic Functional Linguistics (SFL).[1] And if the claims made on the basis of such an analysis are to have validity, then the analysis must be robust and reliable. To this end, those who have developed systemic functional theory and descriptions have, to some extent, provided both probes and lexicogrammatical criteria for the classification of Processes. Besides the apparent difficulties encountered in identifying the Process type of what might be considered straightforward cases, for example those based upon a lexical verb, there are those that arise in attempting to capture what is going on when metaphor is involved, often associated with phraseological constructions. In this chapter, I explore the analysis of metaphorically (and metonymically) derived Processes, in terms of their lexicogrammatical behaviour and the Participant Roles inherently associated with them. I suggest that such Processes exhibit hybridity and do so to differing degrees. The exploration is twofold. First, I consider the varying degrees of departure that are found, when metaphor is involved, from the prototypical sense of common lexical verbs such as *give* (cf. Hasan, this volume), and second I take a phraseological expression, *to break someone's heart*, which involves both metaphor and metonymy, and explore how such expressions can be categorised and handled within the existing architecture of a Systemic Functional Grammar, and in particular in the system network representation of the meaning potential available to speakers of a language.

3.1.2   Criteria and tests for Process classification

In a Systemic Functional Grammar (SFG) the system of TRANSITIVITY is set up to account for how language serves to represent perceived situations in human experience.[2] Moreover, language, through transitivity, may be seen to construe situations, enabling us to profile central aspects of situational phenomena and the relevant entities involved. Thus, for example, whilst 'cleaning a floor', as in *I cleaned the floor*, physically involves a complex series of human movements and actions, and a range of entities, what is picked out to represent the situation is encapsulated in the single lexical verb *clean* (the Process) and the participants *I* and *the floor*.

From an SFG perspective, the range of configurations of Processes and Participants found in English, for example, is 'sorted out in the grammar of the clause' (Halliday and Matthiessen 2004:170). What emerges is a 'manageable set of PROCESS TYPES'. And with the concept of 'PROCESS TYPE', we have categorisation/classification.

So rather than simply belonging to a very long list of linguistically construed situations, each situation falls into one 'type' or another, on the basis of similarities and differences between the various situations. And what falls out from observing the linguistic similarities and differences is a primary, broad tri-partite classification into (a) our experience of events and happenings external to us (the material world of experience – material/action Processes), (b) our experience of the inner world of our human consciousness (the mental world of experience – mental Processes) and (c) our generalisations about and classification of our experiences (the world of relations between events and entities – relational Processes).[3]

As it stands, this tri-partite classification seems plausible. We are aware of such differences, even in general terms, as apparently reflected through verbs such as *hit, kiss, build*, etc., versus *think, love, hear*, etc., versus others such as *be, become, have*, etc. And whilst the classification may intuitively appeal, on the basis of the perceived sense of individual verbs such as *hit, think* and *hear*, there may be little to support this classification other than an appeal to notional or conceptual criteria.

This is surely not what Halliday and Matthiessen (2004:170) intend when they write that the system of TRANSITIVITY is 'sorted out in the grammar of the clause'. If the grammar of the clause determines the classification, then there have to be systematic grammatical similarities and differences which underpin the classification. Essentially, then, a material Process is different from a mental or relational Process because it is associated with a different clause grammar. Moreover, it is on the basis of grammatical similarity and difference that a systemic functional grammar models the meaning potential available to speakers in the form of its central formalism, the system network of options; the set of features (options) that are posited in any system in the overall system network are recognised on the basis that the choice of one or another has consequences for lexicogrammatical realisation. If no lexicogrammatical consequence arises from the choice of one or other feature, then the effective difference between them is absent.

Descriptions and accounts of SFG, such as Halliday and Matthiessen (2004), endeavour to spell out some of the lexicogrammatical properties of the clauses associated with the various PROCESS TYPES. For example they set out and discuss the properties of mental clauses, in contrast to material clauses, in Section 5.3.3 (2004:201–207).

Despite the fact that Halliday and Matthiessen's descriptive model, which will be referred henceforth as IFG, is a lexicogrammatical one, particularly in view of their distinguishing the semantic level/stratum of linguistic organisation from the lexicogrammatical level/stratum, in setting out the properties of PROCESS TYPES they appeal to criteria that might be considered semantic in nature (see Butler 2003:368–369 for a discussion of this). Thus, for example, they state that in the case of mental clauses 'there is always one participant, the Senser, who is human' (Halliday and Matthiessen 2004:201). They do, however, make the point that, grammatically, a Senser is realised pronominally as *he* or *she*, for example.

The assignment of distinct sets of participants, such as Actor, Goal, Senser, etc., inherently associated with different PROCESS TYPES is a core feature of the system of TRANSITIVITY. Their importance is more clearly emphasised in a sister SFG model, namely the Cardiff Grammar, henceforth CaG, (Fawcett 2008). In CaG each Participant Role (PR) is identified by a carefully formulated probe called a 're-expression test'.[4] In CaG each of the PROCESS TYPES recognised in the grammar is determined by the set and combination of PRs that are inherently associated with it, by testing the candidate PR(s) in a clause, the PROCESS TYPE selected in the clause may be ascertained.

The CaG approach therefore differs ostensibly from IFG in that, for CaG, the PROCESS TYPES recognised are not identified primarily on the various clause configurations that appear to differentiate them. Fawcett's re-expression tests for PRs are, however, effectively tests of synonymy, based largely on the analyst's ability to identify the relationship between the verb in the clause under investigation and the verb used to test the PR and assign a label to it. Thus, for example, an Agent (Ag) is a role that can be seen as the PR that is 'doing something', since the verb used in the re-expression test for Agent is *do*, as seen below:

> T1 for Agent (Ag) (in many PROCESS TYPES)
> If X is the Agent, the clause can be re-expressed as
> 'What X did was to ....'

Similarly, in the re-expression test for Emoter (Em), a more delicate sub-class of Senser in mental Processes, the comparator verbal expression is 'have a good/bad feeling about/need for'. So the PR in a clause such as (1), *Tara* is identified as the Emoter, since *Tara loved....* is equivalent to *Tara had a good feeling about....*

> (1) Tara loved water which caused some embarrassing moments for Mark. (BNC A65 1563)[5]

But note that the essential criterion for the identification of *Tara* as Emoter is the lexical verb *loved*. If we substitute *loved* in this example with *drank*, as in (2), then *Tara* would not pass the re-expression test for Emoter.

> (2) Tara drank water which caused some embarrassing moments for Mark.

Essentially, Fawcett, in CaG, is establishing PROCESS TYPES by reference to PRs that are themselves established on the basis of PROCESS TYPES. The lexical verbs that Fawcett uses in his re-expression tests tend to be unequivocal, prototypical examples of the PROCESS TYPE in question.

What the two SFG approaches have in common is the overall picture of human experience construed by the grammar of English in terms of the system of TRANSITIVITY. Despite a different approach to PR and PROCESS TYPE analysis, including some additional CaG PROCESS TYPES ('influential' and 'event-relating' PROCESS TYPES), and rejection of others such as IFG's 'verbal processes', both CaG and IFG share a view that the grammar of English sorts out experience into the three overall areas of mental, material and relational Processes.

3.1.3 Prototypicality and hybridity in transitivity

The crux of the problem in identifying PROCESS TYPES, I would argue, is that SFG descriptions are based on prototypical cases, on examples that would appear to fit the identification criteria extremely well. This is true of both the lexicogrammatical properties of the different PROCESS TYPES suggested in IFG and the lexical verbs used in the CaG re-expression tests. One clear reason for potential analytical difficulty is that linguistic categories, like other categories entertained by humans, are fuzzy. As has been argued in the development of Prototype Theory (e.g. Rosch 1978), categories tend to contain good, not so good and poor members. The fuzziness of categories is recognised openly in SFG in respect of PROCESS TYPES, as Halliday and Matthiessen explain (2004:172). They describe the various PROCESS TYPES as continuous regions which, whilst containing prototypical members, shade into adjacent regions at their fuzzy edges.

Already, from the initial tripartite distinction between material, mental and relational Processes, IFG suggests three intermediate types, namely existential, verbal and behavioural, which would seem to possess properties of the two primary PROCESS TYPES either side of them in the continuum. Thus, for example, verbal Processes are intermediate between and exhibit properties of both mental and relational Processes, whilst having at their prototypical core certain properties of their own. The only exception to this are behavioural Processes, which as Halliday and Matthiessen admit 'have no clearly defined characteristics of their own' (2004:248–251). This raises the issue of whether or not there is an identifiable behavioural PROCESS TYPE, an issue fully discussed in Banks (this volume). Banks' conclusion is that the behaviour PROCESS TYPE is not a useful category and that its putative members can be handled elsewhere in the network for TRANSITIVITY.

What the issue of intermediate categories, particularly behavioural Processes, suggests, is that such categories are hybrid in nature; their members share lexicogrammatical properties associated with two or more other categories.

There is another area, hardly discussed (although see Tucker 2001, 2007 and Arús, this volume), where PROCESS TYPE analysis is equally problematic, and indicates hybridity, for a slightly different reason than the fuzzy edged phenomenon discussed above. And that involves linguistic expression that is based on metaphor and metonymy, and often, if not necessarily, phraseological in nature.

The kind of metaphor that is involved is not the freshly created type of metaphor commonly associated with literary texts, but rather the kind discussed by Lakoff and Johnson (1980) in their seminal and aptly entitled work, *Metaphors we live by.* In other words, they are typically expressions that are no longer evidently metaphorical or do not require the addressee to interpret and process the metaphor in order to arrive at the 'target' sense. This kind of metaphor is also different from that typically dealt with under the heading of ideational grammatical metaphor (e.g. Halliday and Matthiessen 2004:636–658). Grammatical metaphor is premised on the idea of congruent realisation versus metaphorical realisation, the prototypical way of representing the world of experience, versus the figurative, metaphorical way of representing it. However, many of the kinds of 'metaphors we live by' are in fact the principal way of representing the experience, and metaphorical though they may be, it is difficult if not impossible to find a 'congruent' representation. I would argue here that most of the examples dealt with are examples of 'lexical metaphor' and that the theory of 'grammatical metaphor' has little to say about them.

It is also important to emphasise the inclusion of metonymy here. The phraseological expression *kicked the bucket* in (3) is better treated involving metonymy, rather than metaphor. Although there are a number of hypotheses about the origin of this expression (e.g. http://en.wiktionary.org/wiki/kick_the_bucket, or http://www.phrases.org.uk/meanings/218800.html), they tend to refer to a manner in which someone died, rather than a description which metaphorically evokes dying, such as *pass away.*

(3) Chatterton and Fagg and a few more like them who've since *kicked the bucket.* (BNC HTG 2121)

The difference between metaphor and metonymy for current purposes here is not, however, central. What is important is that in the case of metaphorically or metonymically derived expressions the source expression and the target sense may be in some kind of conflict. The conflict may be substantial, in cases where the source metaphor/metonym is from one PROCESS TYPE and the target sense is from another. Let us take, for example, the expression *get one's head around* as in (4).

(4) I've never got my head around why they're such a problem (http://www.anythinglefthanded.co.uk/research/school-experiences.html#sthash.HhNOBYwP.dpbs – accessed via Google 02.07.2015)

Here the source expression would clearly seem to be material in IFG terms, whilst the target sense of the expression is equally clearly mental.[6] 'Getting one's head around something' is a cognitive Process of understanding. Yet note that, unlike in prototypical material Processes, the

Complement of the following circumstance of Place, is not a concrete Thing or Location, but an idea expressed through a *why*-clause. Even if circumstances are not inherently associated with PROCESS TYPES, it is clear that the linguistic content in the circumstance in (4) is not congruous with a material Process clause. Neither is the difficulty removed if we consider the verb here to be a 'phrasal verb', *get around*, since we would then have the problem of explaining why a material Process has a clausal Complement, typically associated with mental Processes.

It is not, however, necessarily the case that from metaphorical/metonymical source to target sense there is a radical change in PROCESS TYPE. A material Process, for example, may be used metaphorically to represent another material Process. Nevertheless, even within one PROCESS TYPE the source expression and target sense may exhibit lexicogrammatical differences. The two metonymical expressions, *pop one's clogs* and *kick the bucket*, are both 2-Role Processes (traditionally 'transitive'), yet correspond to the 1-Role Process (traditionally 'intransitive') *die*.

What I wish to suggest here is that the tension that arises when one type of Process is used to express what is semantically a different type of Process, or even a different subtype of the same PROCESS TYPE, is played out in the lexicogrammar of the expression itself. Moreover, it is the intended target sense of the expression that causes, to a lesser or greater degree, a movement away from the prototypical lexicogrammatical behaviour associated with the source. Thus, as we have seen with *get one's head around something*, the expression can become a hybrid.

If indeed this is the case, we have a potential problem in assigning a lexicogrammatical description to the clause, and beyond this, modelling the Process in respect of the system network of options at the heart of the grammar.

3.1.4 The System Network for TRANSITIVITY and the challenge of hybridity

The basis for recognising PROCESS TYPES is the set of lexicogrammatical characteristics that is associated with each type, and the system network of features is organised on this basis. Thus, if a given Process is represented as a mental Process, for example, the selection of features in the mental Process part of the system network will lead to lexicogrammatical realisation at the level of form in terms of the characteristics associated with mental Processes. If there were no distinct sets of options and lexicogrammatical consequences corresponding to each of the PROCESS TYPES in the system network, the network would lack any substantial motivation for its organisation. Moreover, it would lead to unacceptable lexicogrammatical realisation. For example, if in the material Process area of the system network for TRANSITIVITY certain options led to the realisation of the Complement of such a Process by a clause, as in (5), we would have to conclude that the system network was patently wrong.

(5) *He (Subject) washed (Process) that he had more money (Complement)

The choice of Subject and Complement types, in terms of the PRs that they invoke, and the lexicogrammatical units (nominal group, adjectival group, clause, etc.) that are used to realise them are clearly an integral part of the motivated organisation of the system network.

Lexicogrammatical hybridity is consequently a problem for the design and organisation of the system network. If no such hybridity is present, it may well be possible to capture cases where, for example, a material Process is selected metaphorically to represent a mental Process. This would, arguably, work well in a model, such as IFG, where two separate strata are posited, a semantic stratum and a lexicogrammatical stratum. The Process in question would be represented at the semantic stratum as a mental Process, which would then be realised as a material Process at the lexicogrammatical stratum. Naturally some 'rule' or other mechanism would need to be set up, in the relationship between the two strata, in order to capture the metaphoricity involved. Yet, clearly, even here, as far as the lexicogrammatical system network is concerned, the 'mental' Process will be modelled entirely as a material Process.

In CaG there is no similar separation of the semantic and lexicogrammatical strata. The system network of options is semantic in nature, and the lexicogrammar is expressed as a set of structural units (e.g. clause, nominal group, etc.) and corresponding elements of structure of each unit or class of unit (e.g. determiner, modifier, head, qualifier, etc. of a nominal group). It becomes very much more difficult, therefore, in CaG, to model metaphoricity, since the system network would express the 'target' sense of the expression, e.g. mental, and the lexicogrammatical structure would need to correspond to that made available by the subnetwork for mental Processes. Some of the problematicity in this approach might be averted by the introduction of some mechanism that takes a mental Process into the subnetwork for material Processes in order to gather the options that lead to its realisation as a material Process.

In both grammars, even with a potential absence of hybrid structure, it would seem that special mechanisms would need to be set up to provide satisfactory solutions for the use of this kind of metaphor, mechanisms which would be entirely novel in terms of the architecture of models of SFG. If we then bring in hybrid structures, not even such mechanisms would be adequate in providing appropriate descriptions.

In the following sections below, we explore candidate analyses of expressions involving metaphor/metonymy, ultimately with the aim of understanding more clearly how the Processes at the heart of such expressions might be modelled within SFG. This may have consequences for the model's architecture. We will ultimately need to ask ourselves if (a) we can indeed model such expressions, (b) how we can model them, and (c) whether or not we will need to revise the current descriptive framework inherent in the model.

We shall look at the extent to which the Process in a given expression is hybrid or not, on the basis of its use of metaphor/metonymy. Here we consider aspects of the lexicogrammatical analysis that indicate departure away from a prototypical analysis of the Process. Second, we take what appears to be an apparently straightforward phraseological expression that involves metaphor and metonymy and try to provide solutions for its analysis and its location in the system network. The consideration of a single example may seem to eschew the role of any general principles or findings that may emerge from a wider study, although, of course, the validity of candidate solutions to one expression may be further tested on other examples. Furthermore, if we are to be satisfied with the inclusion of any Process in the system network for TRANSITIVITY, any expression using it will need to be individually tested.

3.2   Expressions with the lexical verb *give*

3.2.1   Assessing the degree of hybridity

One way of exploring the lexicogrammatical nature of expressions of this kind is to take a number of expressions that exploit the same prototypical verb but with differing degrees of change in respect of the target sense. We will then be able to ascertain the degree of lexicogrammatical hybridity involved and, at the same time, attempt to assign acceptable descriptions to the expressions in question.

We will also set up the following two-part hypothesis, which will be tested as we proceed:

> (a) As the sense of an expression, as indicated predominantly by the lexical verb, departs from the prototypical sense associated with the verb, its lexicogrammatical behaviour also departs from that associated with the prototype.
> (b) As the sense of the expression moves towards the phraseological or metaphorical, the lexicogrammatical behaviour it exhibits begins to reflect that associated with different transitivity types.

Candidate Processes that are extensively polysemous are those associated with common lexical verbs often found in light verb expressions, verbs such as *have, do, give, take,* etc. Here, specifically, we will consider a range of expressions that use the lexical verb *give.* The clauses under consideration are given in (6) to (12) below.

> (6) The ex-soldier gave him his ticket. (BNC J2G 628) = PROTOTYPE *GIVE*

> (7) the lease [...] gives us the opportunity to do so (BNC JKO 401)

> (8) So I can't give you my view (BNC J9T 852)

> (9) the SSNP gave him the order to kill Bachir (http://www.lebanese-forces.org/forum/showthread.php/52145 – accessed 18/01/2012)

> (10) He gave her a brief hug (BNC JXU 919)

> (11) Greek civilization not only gave rise to philosophy (BNC ASF 415)

> (12) And you don't give a damn (BNC CE5 2722)

One potential point of contention needs to be considered before we proceed further. We are concerned here with the *sense* of the expression in terms of PROCESS TYPE. We can attempt to ascertain the PROCESS TYPE in terms of the PRs and the lexicogrammatical patterns associated with each PROCESS TYPE, but, at the same time, we are making a judgement that the resultant sense of an expression, contrary to appearances, is or is not different from that associated with the source. So, for example, whilst it would appear, lexicogrammatically, that *give,* as in (12) is for IFG a material Process, we would consider the expression *give a damn* as a mental Process. Yet neither the source nor the target analyses would satisfy our criteria for type membership. That is, *give* here is not the prototypical *give* of transferring something from one's own possession to another's. Indeed there can be no participant of Beneficiary with this expression, as shown by the implausibility/impossibility of (13).

(13) *I didn't give her a damn

Arguably, any judgement we make about a PROCESS TYPE classification such as in the examples above is at least partly informed by an awareness of the lexicogrammatical nature of the expression. Such judgements that are made can of course be tested on the degree of departure from the prototype of the lexicogrammar of the expression in question.

3.2.2   The prototype

Let us first establish the nature of prototypical *give*. Again, there is a certain degree of risk in claiming that a given sense of *give* is the prototype. Corpus linguistic research over the years has shown that the most frequently found sense of a lexical item is not necessarily the prototype.

Experimental research on subjects' reactions (in comprehension and production) would appear to indicate that the prototype for *give* involves the physical handing over of something to another person, and Newman (2005) expresses this as 'to pass something by hand to another person so the other person comes to have it' (2005:150). The general sense given at the beginning of the *Online Oxford English Dictionary* (OED 2013) entry for *give* is 'To make another the recipient of (something that is in the possession, or at the disposal, of the subject).' In the examples (6) to (12) above, (6) would correspond most closely to this definition.

Structurally, *give* is a di-transitive verb or three-place predicate. The three arguments correspond to three PRs, informally the GIVER, the THING GIVEN and the RECIPIENT. In SFG, two distinct analyses are found between CaG and IFG. For IFG, *give* is a material Process which is associated with the three participants of Actor, Goal, and Recipient. In contrast the CaG analysis treats *give* as a relational Process, on the grounds that its underlying semantics involves the act of an Agent (Ag) causing a Carrier (Ca) to have a Possessed (Pos) (Fawcett 1987). The 'causing' is also captured by the assignment of the PR of Affected to both the Possessed and the Carrier, making them 'compound' PRs of Affected-Possessed and Affected-Carrier respectively.

Although the IFG and CaG analyses assign the Process *give* to different major PROCESS TYPES, material and relational respectively, there is much less effective difference than might be thought. Through the assignment of compound PRs, the CaG relational Process analysis shares characteristics with the IFG material analysis through the presence of the PRs of Agent and Affected. In the exploration that follows, the CaG analysis will be adopted, but readers may wish to apply the IFG analysis at the same time.

3.2.3 Lexicogrammatical behaviour and probes

In order to test the hypothesis in 3.2.1 above, we need to establish lexicogrammatical criteria which will allow us to compare the various senses that are found in examples (6) to (12). Two of the most salient patterns associated with prototypical *give* in English are the dative alternation and what I will refer to as the dual passive alternation. These two alternations are also typical of other di-transitive (3-Role) verbs, such as *show* and *send*. Using (6) as a base, the alternation potential would produce (14) in respect of the dative alternation, and (15) and (16) in respect of the dual passive alternation.

(14) The ex-soldier gave his ticket to him

(15) He was given his ticket by the ex-soldier

(16) His ticket was given to him by the ex-soldier

In addition to the above alternation criteria, we can probe for the presence of the PRs that have been assigned to the three arguments, by using their respective re-expression tests, namely for Agent, Carrier, Possessed and Affected. All the relevant re-expression tests are given in the Appendix.

3.2.4 Departures from the prototype

More detailed analyses of examples (6) to (12) are provided in Tucker (2014). Here, we shall focus on aspects of the various examples that suggest a movement away from the prototype. The example in (7) represents a situation where the 'giving' involves someone conferring, granting, permitting, enabling, etc. someone to do something or bestowing upon them some quality.

What is given is an abstract entity rather than a physical/concrete entity and the giver is not necessarily the original possessor of that entity, but has the power to give/confer it. This particular example involves metonymy, in respect of the giver, where *the lease* stands in for the person(s) with the power to confer, by means of a linguistic act, *the opportunity*. Again, the PRs associated with prototypical *give* are valid here, passing the re-expression tests, with one exception. In prototypical *give* the Possessed is considered to be an Affected as well, through the act of transfer. However, it is difficult to see *the opportunity* as something that has been 'affected' here, as the re-expression in (17) shows.

(17) ?What happened to the opportunity is that it was given to us

This suggests that, unlike with prototypical *give*, the Possessed does not combine with the Affected to form a compound Affected-Possessed (Af-Pos).

As with prototypical *give*, the various alternation variants are available. Once again, then, with the possible exception of the slight change in PR assignment, the expression conforms to the prototype analysis.

The example in (8) is an act of communication in the sense that the giving is effected through language and, consequently what is given is, to use the IFG term, Verbiage, that is, linguistic expression (Halliday and Matthiessen 2004:255).

Application of the alternation criteria and PR re-expression tests suggests that despite the communicative act nature of this kind of expression, its analysis is consonant with prototypical *give*. On the other hand, it would also pass the re-expression tests for the CaG mental cognition Process PRs of Cognisant (Cog) and Phenomenon (Ph), together with the Agent, which brings about the Process through which the Cognisant 'comes to know' the Phenomenon, here the speaker's *view*. Furthermore, the two kinds of alternation are also characteristic of 3-Role mental Processes, such as *tell*, *show* and *teach*, and hence not necessarily indicators of the prototypical relational Process. Clearly, in this case, our criteria are insufficient to determine the PROCESS TYPE status of communicative act examples such as (8).

A related communicative sense of *give* is found in (9), where *give... order* is equivalent to *order*, as shown in (18).

(18) the SSNP ordered him to kill Bachir

The equivalence alone suggests that *give an order*, like the single verb *order*, is a speech act predicate. Moreover, *give* in this expression is essentially a light verb complemented by a nominalisation, *order*. This pattern is common in English across PROCESS TYPES and with a small range of light verbs, e.g. *give an answer, make a comment, have a wash* etc. At the same time, unlike many of the other light verb constructions, *give + order* is susceptible of analysis according to prototypical *give*. Both sets of alternations are available and re-expression tests would validate the PRs of Agent, Possessed and Affected-Carrier, as shown in (19).

(19) the SSNP (Ag) gave (Pro) him (Af-Ca) the order to kill Bachir (Pos).

Equally, a cognitive mental Process analysis would also be validated by the alternation potential and relevant re-expression tests, as in (20).

(20) the SSNP (Ag) gave (Pro) him (Af-Cog) the order to kill Bachir (Ph)

We can take the mental analysis a step further by treating *give + order* as a Process (Pro) + Process Extension (PrEx), realised by a Main Verb (M) and a Main Verb Extension (MEx), leaving the non-finite clause *to kill Bachir* as the Phenomenon, as in (21). What these 'extension' elements do is to indicate that we are dealing with a 'multi-word' verbal expression, such as phrasal verbs, where the post-verbal part, here *the order*, is not in fact a true Complement of the Process. As in other similar mental Process clauses, the Complement would be the non-finite clause *to kill Bachir.*

(21) the SSNP (Ag) gave (Pro) him (Af-Cog) the order (PrEx) to kill Bachir (Ph)

As was suggested above, *give* participates in various light verb constructions, and this is seen in (9). Again, (9) is roughly equivalent to the single lexical verb alternative in (22).

(22) He hugged her briefly

A prototypical relational Process *give* analysis here begins to fall foul of the alternation criteria and the re-expression tests for Affected-Possessed and Affected-Carrier. In most similar cases, the Process *hug* as *hugged* in (22) is re-expressed as a nominalisation, through a nominal group (as *a brief hug* here). Essentially, expressions such as (9) parallel the PRs in the alternate, (22). The latter is 2-Role material Process with the PRs of Agent and Affected. The nominalisation *a brief hug* is only a PR if we apply a prototypical *give* analysis, according to which this argument would be an Affected-Possessed. In order to reflect the semantic 'lightness' of the support verb and the non-PR status of the nominalised Complement, CaG applies the Process + Process Extension analysis, along with their structural equivalents, Main Verb + Main Verb Extension. This is shown in Figure 3.1.

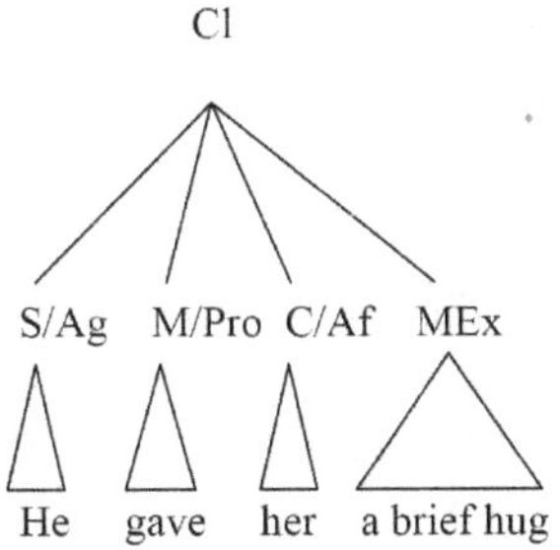

Figure 3.1: *A brief hug* as a Main Verb Extension

Attempts to justify a prototypical *give* analysis in the case of examples such as (11) and (12), repeated below, are seriously thwarted by the results of the alternation criteria and the re-expression tests. Semantically, it is difficult to perceive such expressions as associated with prototypical *give* and the metaphorical relationship itself is extremely weak or absent. On 'feel' alone, (11) would be considered some kind of relational Process clause, there being a potentially causal or sequential relationship between *Greek civilisation* and *philosophy*. Again, on 'feel', (12) appears to be a mental Process clause, partially synonymous with the Process *care*. This view is supported by the existence of examples in which *give a damn* is followed by a clausal Complement expressing the Phenomenon, as in (23).

(23) 'Well, I couldn't give a damn how it looks to you!' (BNC HGT 158)

It is in these latter expressions, such as (10)–(12) that we see arguably the greatest semantic departure from the prototype and the greatest departure from the prototypical lexicogrammatical analysis. The observations above lend some general validity to the original hypotheses expressed in Section 3.2.1. However, as we have seen, there are cases in which the assignment of both a 'source' analysis, reflecting the prototype, or a 'target' analysis, reflecting the contemporary sense, were plausible.

3.3   *Breaking (some) one's heart*: Exploration of a 'straightforward' example

It would be difficult in modern times to interpret *breaking someone's heart* as literally meaning to cause someone's heart to break physically. If we

attempt to define this expression we would use paraphrases that emphasised its membership of the class of mental Processes, such as *'cause deep
emotional pain and grief to somebody'* or as given in the OED, *'Of the heart:
to become overcome with sorrow'.*

The *breaking of someone's heart* may be seen as both metaphorical and
metonymical. From a metonymy perspective *heart* stands in for someone's
emotional state, as in the distinction between 'head' and 'heart', for reason
and emotion respectively. The prototypical material Process *break* is consequently metaphorical or derivative in its use with *heart* as emotion.

The expression *break ... heart* would appear clearly to represent a mental Process whilst being based on the material Process of *breaking*. Indeed,
this is how the Process is classified in IFG, where the participant Senser
– a role uniquely associated with mental Processes – is expressed as a
nominal group denoting a certain body part [...] (cf. English *it breaks my
heart, blows my mind*). (Halliday and Matthiessen 2004:201n). The IFG
view echoes the metonymy approach to *heart* standing in for the person.
Halliday and Matthiessen also go on to add that 'this strategy also includes
figurative expressions that are construed on a material model – *it breaks
my heart that, it blows my mind that'* (2004:203).

This would even almost solve the problem. There remains however the
lexical verb *break*. Whilst the material model as metaphor is unproblematic in respect of the physical *heart* being broken, if we accept that *heart*
in the expression is a metonym for the whole conscious, sentient person
or for the emotional state of the person, then *break* has to be interpreted
metaphorically. Essentially, in order to work, the contribution of *break* and
heart in the expression cannot be considered independently. To achieve
the mental Process (emotion) construal of the expression, both *break* and
heart must be co-selected. This co-selection of items or their underlying
features is at the heart of Sinclair's 'Idiom Principle':

> The principle of idiom is that a language user has available to him or
> her a large number of semi-preconstructed phrases that constitute
> single choices, even though they might be analysable into segments.
> (Sinclair 1987:320)

The single choice involved here is not only the co-selection of the senses
expounded by *break* and *heart* but of all concomitant features, e.g. tense
selections, possessive determiner with *heart*, for example. Many options in
the system network will then be closed off in the process of pre-selection
occasioned by the earlier 'single choice'.

The basic form of Processes with two PRs is common to all PROCESS
TYPES and is therefore not one with which distinctions between PROCESS

Table 3.1 A representative range of clause types associated with break X as a material and mental Process respectively

you broke her jaw	you broke her heart
her jaw was broken (by you)	her heart was broken (by you)
you're breaking her jaw	you're breaking her heart
you broke her jaw in two	you broke her heart in two
her jaw broke	her heart broke
the hammer broke her jaw	*the hammer broke her heart
*the news broke her jaw	the news broke her heart
*it breaks her jaw to leave	it breaks her heart to leave
*it broke her jaw that you had gone	it broke her heart that you had gone

TYPES can be made, irrespective of the different PR labels assigned to the Subject and Complement. In Table 3.1, on the other hand, we have a representative range of clause types comparing a clear material Process, with *jaw* as the Complement of *break*, and the mental Process reading of *break+ heart*.

Despite considerable overlap in construction types, there are significant cases in which one of the two readings appears to be either unacceptable or at best extremely difficult to interpret. First, a physical instrument, such as *the hammer*, as Agent, produces a clause that is difficult to interpret in the mental Process sense. By the same token, when the Affected is a phys- ical object, such as *jaw*, the presence of an Agent such as *the news*, as in *the news broke her jaw* is also difficult if not impossible to interpret. These observations indicate that the respective PROCESS TYPES do not share the same classes of Thing as expressed by the nominal groups at Subject and Complement.

The final two examples are extremely significant in determining the mental Process status of *break … heart*. These are examples of the Enhanced Theme construction (see Fawcett 2003). In this construction, the Process is brought closer to the beginning of the matrix clause by the substitu- tion of the dummy *it* pronoun at Subject for the clause that expresses the Phenomenon, e.g. *that Darlington has only one ambulance after 7pm at night* in (24), which then follows the Process. In mental emotion Processes such as *worry, concern, frighten, please,* etc., the Phenomenon is normally associated with the Subject of the matrix mental clause, but whenever the Phenomenon is itself a situation and thus expressed as a clause, the Enhanced Theme construction is favoured.

> (24) 'It worries me greatly that Darlington has only one ambulance after 7pm at night.' (BNC K55 7121)

Note that this clause would still be acceptable if the clause expressing the Phenomenon were placed initially, as Subject, as in (25), although the degree of acceptability depends, arguably, on the length of the *that*-clause.

(25) That Darlington has only one ambulance after 7pm at night worries me greatly.

An attested example, given in (26), of *break ... heart* with this construction gives sound support to the mental Process analysis.

(26) ...and it broke my heart that I could do little to help her. (BNC JYO 5805)

The clausal or nominal expression of the Phenomenon is consonant with the analysis of mental Process clauses. There remains the issue of the PR of Emoter. As we have seen, possessive + *heart* in this expression stands in, metonymically, for the person whose emotions are affected by the Phenomenon, or for the emotion state of the person. Unlike prototypical mental clauses of emotion, therefore, the Emoter is not directly expressed. A CaG analysis of the expression, with the Phenomenon expressed as a nominal for simplicity here, would be as shown in Figure 3.2.

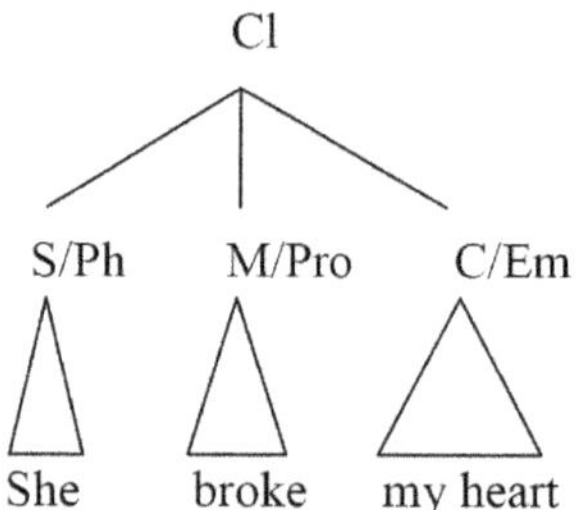

Figure 3.2: *My heart* analysed as Emoter at Complement in the clause

As it stands, this analysis is problematic in two ways. First the application of the Emoter re-expression test would yield something like (27).

(27) ?My heart had a bad feeling about her.

What we want to say, however, is (28).

(28) I had a bad feeling about her.

This would require a mechanism somewhere in the model that handles metonymy, and at present there no such mechanism has been articulated.

The second problem is accounting for the fact that the features that lead to the lexicalisation of *break* and *heart* are obligatorily co-selected, the sense of the Process being dependent on the contribution of both items. Fawcett's solution to this problem is to treat the lexical verb as the Process, realised as a Main Verb (M) and the following nominal expression, e.g. *my heart*, as a Process Extension (PrEx), realised by the element of structure Main Verb Extension (MEx). In adopting this analysis we are able to indicate that *my heart* is not in fact the Complement of *break*, and that *break* is not the sole expression of the overall sense of the Process.

Fawcett then goes on to suggest that the Emoter in such cases is conflated, not directly with the MEx in the clause, but with the 'possessor' element in the genitive cluster, e.g. *Gordon* in *Gordon's heart*, or the determiner, e.g. *my* in *my heart*, as in Figure 3.3 (Fawcett 2009:221).

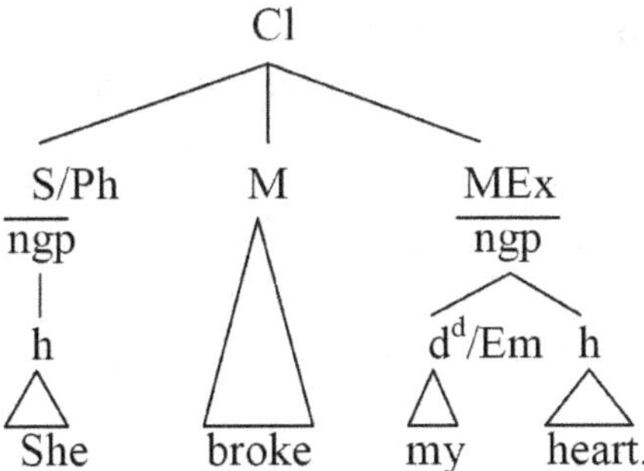

Key: ngp = nominal group, h = head, d^d = deictic determiner

Figure 3.3: Emoter conflated with *my* in *she broke my heart*

Although this solution is more indicative of who the Emoter actually is, it is still only indicated by *my* and again the re-expression test would require the conversion of *my* to an actual reference to the person concerned. Second, the replacement of the Main Verb Extension for a Complement leaves a clear 2-Role Process without a Complement, whilst including the second PR embedded in the Main Verb Extension.

It becomes apparent that none of the proposed analyses above satisfactorily solves the problem in terms of being consistent with the model's architecture. So whilst there are sound reasons to reject the material Process analysis, the preferred mental emotion Process analysis also has its setbacks.

3.4   Conclusions

In discussing such cases as *break someone's heart*, Fawcett himself concludes:

> One solution to such problems is that we should **not** expect to be able to represent every former metaphor that is currently functioning as an idiom in terms of the PRs of the functional syntax (....), and to recognize that the decision to use such an expression is made at an earlier stage of planning. (Fawcett 2009:221)

Note that Fawcett refers to 'an earlier stage of planning' as part of an alternative solution. Yet even if we transfer the responsibility for the production of such expressions to some other component of a wider communicative model, we still have to model the linguistic expression through the system network, associated realisation rules and the functional syntax resource. In this context, a motivated system network representation of the potential for such expressions, together with a valid functional-structural description and a set of PRs, are all requirements of a plausible explanatory model.

It may well be the case that hybridity requires the introduction of new or modified descriptive resources, such as the Main Verb Extension element or some procedure whereby metaphor and metonymy, such as *my heart* standing in for the person, can be captured and explicated. It does appear that descriptions and procedures set up for prototypical cases strain under the weight of hybridity. And, as we observed with substantial semantic departures from the prototypical sense, in the case of common verbs such as *give*, it becomes difficult, if not impossible, to justify analyses based on the prototype. Arguably, wherever little or no doubt remains over the semantic classification of a Process, as in the case of *not give a damn*, for example, we need to fit the linguistic material to the description we set up for a given PROCESS TYPE, however Procrustean this may initially appear. Brushing the problem under the carpet, on the other hand, is surely not the right course of action.

Notes

1   As Fawcett (2008:48) explains, it is a practice in Systemic Functional Linguistics to write the names of all elements of the situation and clause with an initial capital letter, thus 'Process' and 'Participant Role' for example. As the Process in the Cardiff Grammar is associated with the clause element M (Main Verb), I have adopted the initial capital letter convention throughout this chapter.

2   Various terms are used with roughly the same sense as 'Situation' here. Halliday and Matthiessen (2004) prefer 'figure' although previously the term 'process' was used. In other functional theories of language, e.g. Role and Reference Grammar and Functional Discourse Grammar, the term 'State of Affairs' (SoA) is preferred. The term 'situation' is used in the Cardiff Grammar variant of SFG and also by Butler in his comparison of a number of functional approaches (Butler 2003).

3   Fawcett has retained Halliday's original label for material Processes, namely action Processes (see, for example, Halliday 1976:20). Here, in order to avoid possible confusion, I will use Halliday's term 'material'.

4   The use of probes in identifying participants is also found in IFG, although not systematically (see Halliday and Matthiessen 2004:181 for an example).

5   As far as possible, examples are elicited from the British National Corpus (BNC) (Aston and Burnard 1998) or from the Sketch Engine ukWaC web-based corpus (Kilgarriff *et al.* 2004).

6   This source Process would be material for IFG, but Relational/locational for CaG, in the sense that it concerns an Agent that causes his own head, the Carrier, to be in a different Location.

References

Aston, G., and Burnard, L. (1998). *The BNC Handbook: Exploring the British National Corpus with SARA*. Edinburgh: Edinburgh University Press.

Butler, C.S. (2003). *Structure and function: A Guide to Three Major Structural-functional Theories. Part I: Approaches to the Simplex Clause*. Amsterdam and Philadelphia: John Benjamins

Fawcett, R.P. (1987). The semantics of clause and verb for relational processes in English. In M.A.K. Halliday and R.P. Fawcett (Eds) *New Developments in Systemic Linguistics, Vol 1: Theory and Description*, 130–183. London: Frances Pinter.

Fawcett, R.P. (2000). *A Theory of Syntax for Systemic Functional Linguistics. Current Issues in Linguistic Theory 206*. Amsterdam and Philadelphia: John Benjamins. http://dx.doi.org/10.1075/cilt.206

Fawcett, R.P. (2003). The many types of 'theme' in English: their syntax, semantics and discourse functions. Unpublished manuscript. Available at http://www.isfla.org/Systemics/Print/Papers.html (last accessed July 2013).

Fawcett, R.P. (2008). *Invitation to Systemic Functional Linguistics through the Cardiff Grammar: An Extension and Simplification of Halliday's Systemic Functional Grammar* (3rd ed.). London: Equinox.

Fawcett, R.P. (2009). Seven problems to beware of when analyzing Processes and Participant Roles in texts. In S. Slembrouck, M. Taverniers, and M. Van Herreweghe (Eds), *From 'will' to 'well': Studies in Linguistics offered to Anne-Marie Simon-Vandenbergen*, 209–224. Ghent: Academia Press.

Fawcett, R.P. (2011). Problems and solutions in identifying Processes and Participant Roles in discourse analysis. Part 1: Introduction to a systematic procedure for identifying Processes and Participant Roles. *Annual Review of Functional Linguistics*, 3, 34–87.

Halliday, M.A.K., and Matthiessen, C.M.I.M. (2004). *An Introduction to Functional Grammar* (3rd ed.). London: Arnold.

Kilgarriff, A., Rychly, P., Smrz, P., and Tugwell, D. (2004). The Sketch Engine. In Proceedings of EURALEX 2004, Lorient, France; 105–116.

Lakoff, G., and Johnson, M. (1980). *Metaphors We Live By*. Chicago: University of Chicago Press.

Newman, J. (2005). Three-place predicates: A cognitive-linguistic perspective. *Language Sciences*, 27(2), 145–163. http://dx.doi.org/10.1016/j.langsci.2003.12.003

Rosch, E. (1978). Principles of categorization. In E. Rosch and B.B. Lloyd (Eds), *Cognition and Categorization*, 27–48. Hillsdale, NJ: Lawrence Erlbaum Associates.

Sinclair, J. (1987). Collocation: a progress report. In R. Steele and T. Threadgold (Eds), *Language Topics: Essays in Honour of Michael Halliday*, 319–332. Amsterdam and Philadelphia: John Benjamins.

Tucker, G.H. (2001). Getting our heads around it: semantic and syntactic tension in the transitivity analysis of metaphorically derived multi-word verbs. *Studi Italiani di Linguistica Teorica e Applicata*, 30(2), 303–314.

Tucker, G.H. (2007). 'Sorry to muddy the waters': Accounting for speech act formulae and formulaic variation in a systemic functional model of language. In C.S. Butler and J. Lavid (Eds.), *Functional Perspectives on Grammar and Discourse: Papers in Honour of Prof. Angela Downing*, 395–418. Amsterdam, Philadelphia: John Benjamins. http://dx.doi.org/10.1075/slcs.85.21tuc </edb>

Tucker, G.H. (2014). Giving it my best shot: Towards a coherent functional analysis of metaphorically-derived processes including 'light verb' expressions. In M. de los Ángeles Gómez González, F. Ruiz de Mendoza, and F. Gonzálvez García (Eds), *Theory and Practice in Functional-cognitive Space*, 33–52. Amsterdam and Philadelphia: John Benjamins. http://dx.doi.org/10.1075/sfsl.68.02tuc

About the author

Gordon Tucker was formerly senior lecturer in the Centre for Language and Communication Research at Cardiff University. Since his retirement he has retained an affiliation with the University as a Research Associate. He is the co-developer, along with Professor Robin Fawcett, of the Systemic Functional model of language known as the Cardiff Grammar, and has specialised in lexis and phraseology. He is author of *The Lexicogrammar of Adjectives: A systemic functional approach to lexis* (New York: Cassell Academic, 1998) and has published over 40 journal articles and book chapters.

4
Hybridity and process types

Jorge Arús Hita
Universidad Complutense de Madrid

4.1   Introduction

Studies on linguistic hybridity have often focused on the phenomenon arising from languages in contact (e.g. Kraidy 2005; Makoni 2002; Khubchandani 1997), i.e., at the level, in SFL terms, of the context of culture. Within SFL, Hasan's (1996) description of semantic networks is a good example of how hybridity, or permeability, works within the semantic environment. In addition, as attested by the different chapters in this book, it is possible to look at hybridity at different levels across the stratal continuum,[1] including the lexicogrammar, the focus of the present chapter. Specifically, this chapter looks at hybridity at clause level as a way to account for the interpretation of processes such as (1), where the metaphorical use of *run* (versus its literal use in (2)) renders the otherwise material process a hybrid material/relational process.

> (1) The Dorset coast path runs along a spectacular rugged cliffline from Poole Harbour to Lyme Regis

> (2) Screeching MacIans ran for the woods

In what I will here be calling *hybrid processes*,[2] the literal meaning – which we will call A – is transposed to a different area of the lexicogrammar – B – whereby the resulting hybrid meaning – C – is brought about. In this light, an analysis of hybrid processes is proposed in which the literal and the non-literal analyses are combined to yield the intended hybrid meaning.

It will be argued that three levels of hybridity can be distinguished depending on how strongly the metaphor is felt. In a process such as (3), below, the metaphorical load can be said to be quite high; in such cases, the

A meaning is arguably more prominent than the B meaning in the interpretation of the resulting C meaning. In (1) above, on the other hand, the process illustrates a well-established metaphorical use of *run*, where the metaphor is less perceivable and the A and B meanings are quite balanced in their prominence.[3] Finally, (4) illustrates a hybrid process where the A and B meanings have fused to such an extent that they are no longer felt as working in consonance. In this case, we are in front of a new lexicalised meaning, no longer a hybrid but rather, it will be claimed, a highbred (as in 'highbred cattle') resulting from the previous process of hybridity. In order to defend the proposal brought forward and illustrate the different semantic interplays existing within each type of construction, different analyses for the different degrees of hybridity will be proposed.

> (3) Keep up the excellent work – but don't let Flymo eat the money!

> (4) When 'Jacki' came to Glasgow, he grasped quickly what was expected

As seen in examples (1) through (4), the kind of metaphor discussed in this chapter is lexical, rather than grammatical. The discussion will provide an opportunity to question the claim (e.g. Halliday 1998; Simon-Vandenbergen 2003) that whereas in lexical metaphor one signifier has different signifieds, in grammatical metaphor there are different signifiers for one signified.

The chapter is structured as follows: section 4.2 looks at the distinction between Lexical and Grammatical Metaphor in the light of the existing literature; section 4.3 puts forward a proposal for explaining the complex meaning of what, following Simon-Vandenbergen (2003), I will call Lexicogrammatical Metaphor (LGM) from the point of view of hybridity; the different degrees of such hybridity in LGM are explored in section 4.4, before looking, in section 4.5, at the way in which LGM is used in actual texts – journalistic in this case; the final section rounds up the chapter with some concluding remarks and pointers to future research.

4.2   Lexical and Grammatical Metaphors

Before tackling the issue of establishing the different degrees of hybridity within LGM, it will be useful to look at the way in which metaphor is dealt with in the systemic literature. Lexical metaphors such as the use of *fox* in (5) are differentiated from grammatical metaphors, which are epitomised by nominalisations such as *Rapid changes in the rate of evolution* in (6) (from Halliday 1998:193). A third kind of metaphor is that in which the lexical metaphor brings about a reshaping of the transitive configuration, as shown in examples (7) and (8), taken from Halliday (1984[2006]:326) and Simon-Vandenbergen (2003:231), respectively. In (7) the metaphorical use of *see* – motivated by the thematisation of *the fifth day* – brings about a reshaping of the transitive configuration from the congruent material *They reached the summit on the fifth day* to the metaphorical mental realisation. In (8), the transitivity shift happens from material to verbal. This kind of metaphor is called lexicogrammatical metaphor (LGM) by Simon-Vandenbergen, and is the focus of study of the present chapter, as it is precisely within this kind of metaphor that there are grounds to differentiate among degrees of hybridity, as will be argued in due course.

(5) LM: John is a fox

(6) GM: Rapid changes in the rate of evolution are caused by external events

(7) The fifth day saw them at the summit

(8) The journalists attacked the Prime Minister

LM has in general terms been more widely studied than GM, to the point that, as stated by Carretero, 'the literature available on GM cannot be compared with that on LM' (2000:49). The situation, however, is very different in the systemic literature, where GM has received more attention than LM – as attested by the existence of a monographic volume devoted to the former, i.e., Simon-Vandenbergen, Taverniers and Ravelli (2003). LM typically appears in the systemic literature as an element of comparison with GM, so as to better delimit the latter. However, one of the key arguments used to differentiate one type of metaphor from the other is, in my opinion, questionable. Halliday (1998) and Simon-Vandenbergen (2003) claim that LM can be interpreted as 'Same signifier/different signified', whereas GM implies 'Same signified/ different signifier'. This is illustrated by Halliday (1998:190) by means of the Signifier *spoonfeed*, which can have the congruent Signified 'feed baby or invalid with small quantities of easily digested food on a spoon' or the metaphorical Signified 'provide learner with small quantities of carefully chosen instructional materials'. In contrast, GM is illustrated by the Signified 'brake + fail', which can be used congruently, as in, for instance, *the brakes failed* or through a metaphorical signifier, such as the nominalisation *brake failure.*

The distinction between LM and GM as explained in the previous paragraph might seem quite clear-cut. However, it must be pointed out that LM can also be regarded as 'same signified/different signifier'. For instance, if we take the signified 'spend wastefully or extravagantly', it can be realised congruently through the signifier *squander*, as in *don't squander your money*, or metaphorically, through the signifier *eat*, as in *don't eat your money*.[4] It could certainly be argued that *squandering* and *eating* as illustrated here do not necessarily mean exactly the same, but it is a fact that in language there is no such thing as two perfect synonyms – Ravelli (1988:137) points out about metaphorical and congruent realisations that 'each expression thus shares some semantic content but differs in detail' – and, in any case, the same applies to congruent and metaphorical pairs in the context of GM: e.g. *the brakes failed* and *brake failure* do not mean exactly the same thing. Therefore, although LM can be looked at from the point of view of lexis, we can also look at it from the point of view of meaning.

That LM can also be regarded as 'same signified/different signifier' is actually supported by Halliday's (2008:91) own claim that metaphor can be regarded from below or from above, and, as we see in Figures 4.1 and 4.2, the examples used concern LM. Whereas Figure 4.1 offers two different signifieds for the signifier *fruit*, the second one metaphorical, Figure 4.2 shows two possible signifiers for the signified 'outcome of an action; effect', i.e., *results* and *fruit*, the latter metaphorical.[5]

English *fruit* means

>   (i) 'produce of the earth; edible covering on seeds of trees and shrubs'
>   (ii) 'outcome of an action; effect'

Figure 4.1: Metaphor seen from below (after Halliday 2008:91)

English 'outcome of an action; effect' is expressed by

>   (i) *result*
>   (ii) *fruit*

Figure 4.2: Metaphor seen from above (after Halliday 2008:91)

The distinction between GM and LM therefore has to be redefined. If we go back to the examples handled in the previous discussion, i.e., *squandering/eating* for LM and *the brakes failed /brake failure* for GM, a noticeable contrast between both pairs of examples is the fact that in GM the metaphorical realisation, e.g. *brake failure*, will always be metaphorical, never congruent, and the congruent realisation, e.g. *the brakes failed*, will always be congruent, never metaphorical. Conversely, one single realisation, e.g. *eat*, can be either non-metaphorical or an instance of LM depending on the context in which it is used. This, I argue, is the main distinction between LM and GM. In terms of the signifier/signified relationship used by Halliday and by Simon-Vandenbergen, this would be tantamount to saying that, whereas LM can be interpreted as both 'Same signifier/different signified' (view from below) and 'Same signified/different signifier' (view from above), GM can only be looked at from above, i.e., 'Same signified/different signifier'. Or, more elegantly expressed, and less of a tongue-twister: whereas in LM a signifier (e.g. *spoonfeed*) can be congruent (S-d1) or metaphorical (S-d2), in GM a signifier is only congruent (e.g. *the brakes failed*) or only metaphorical (e.g. *brake failure*).

4.3   The complex meaning of metaphors

The previous discussion on the different kinds of metaphor and the difficulty of pinpointing the exact nature of the distinction between LM and GM attests to the complexity of metaphorical meaning. One way of looking at this complexity is to regard metaphorical meaning as a semantic compound. Ravelli (1988:137) illustrates this by means of the representation shown in Figure 4.3, where the single semantic choice (S_1) of congruent

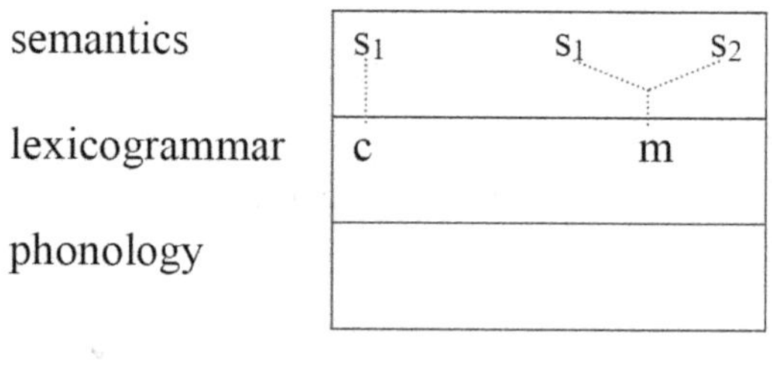

s – semantic choice

c – congruent choice

m – metaphorical form

Figure 4.3: Compound semantics of metaphorical meaning (after Ravelli 1988:137)

lexicogrammatical realisations contrasts with the compound semantic choice (S_1 + S_2) of metaphorical ones.[6] As Taverniers points out, 'what is crucial in this refined model is that the starting point is no longer one single meaning: it is recognised that metaphor also involves a *meaning difference*' (2003:21; original emphasis).

If metaphor involves a meaning difference, the task at hand now is to try to account for it, in spite of Ravelli's claim that explaining the exact nature of that difference is beyond our theoretical reach because 'it would be necessary to represent the level of semantics with system networks as for the lexicogrammar' (1988:138). Yet, even if such representation may be far-fetched, it is the purpose of this chapter to show that a look at the lexicogrammar of metaphorical expressions can offer reliable insights into their nature. We may not be able to bring out the *exact* nature of the difference between the congruent and the metaphorical meanings, but, as will be seen below, the picture obtained makes the journey worthwhile.

To that end I suggest an interpretation of metaphorical meaning in which the literal or congruent meanings (which we will call A) and the intended (B) meanings are hybridised to create the metaphorical (C) meaning, thus trying to capture the synergy of metaphors. This is very much in consonance with Ravelli's account of metaphor as seen in Figure 4.3, above, while additionally providing an arguably more complete view of the rich nature of metaphorical meaning. The A and B meanings would correspond to S_1 and S_2 in Ravelli's representation, and to this we are now adding the C meaning to reflect that metaphors do not simply consist in the mathematical addition of one meaning to another but rather in the creation of a new meaning resulting from the fusion, or hybridisation, of the former two.

Looking at metaphorical meaning as a hybrid helps us to differentiate between more or less metaphorical expressions: we may expect to find different degrees of hybridity depending on how perceivable the metaphor is. Goatly (1997:15) claims that 'The larger the gap between the proposition expressed and the meaning intended, the more metaphorical the utterance will be. The smaller the gap, the more literal the language use'. This is tantamount to saying, from the approach taken here, that the farther apart the A and B meanings, the more metaphorical the resulting C meaning, whereas, conversely, the closer together A and B, the less metaphorical C is. It is, however, necessary to take an additional step in order to explain how the interplay of the A and B meanings is different in highly metaphorical processes and in processes where the metaphor is lighter or easier to process, i.e., what do we mean when we say that two metaphorical processes have different degrees of hybridity.

Giora's graded salience hypothesis refers precisely to the different ways in which the literal and intended meanings in a metaphor interplay, and is therefore a useful way to broach the subject:

> The graded salience hypothesis (Giora, 1997) posits that the factor determining precedence of access is salience. The salient meaning, either figurative or literal, is the one always processed first. The figurative meaning in conventional metaphors is commonly more salient than the literal one, thus in most 'dead' metaphors the figurative meaning is accessed first. Also, context can make either the figurative or the literal meaning more salient, In contrast, when a novel or unfamiliar metaphor is encountered, the salient meaning is the literal one, and the figurative meaning is inferred later by contextual mechanisms. (quoted in Goldstein, Arzouan and Faust 2008:207)

Adapting Giora's proposition to our A + B = C formula, we can say that in conventional metaphors the A (literal) meaning is more salient in novel or unfamiliar metaphors, whereas the B (figurative) meaning is more salient in conventional metaphors. Looking back at the examples seen in the introduction, repeated below for the sake of convenience, this means that in the conventional metaphorical use of *run* in (1) the figurative relational meaning is more salient than the literal material and therefore processed first when working out the C meaning. In the highly novel metaphorical use of *eat* in (3), conversely, the prototypical meaning of *eat* will be the one processed first, i.e., the most salient in the unpacking of the metaphor. These and other examples – including those illustrating metaphors no longer, or not necessarily, perceived as such, e.g. (4) – are revisited in the following section to lay out the main proposal of this chapter, i.e., an account of the different degrees of hybridity in LG metaphor and how they are brought about.

(1) The Dorset coast path runs along a spectacular rugged cliffline from Poole Harbour to Lyme Regis

(3) Keep up the excellent work – but don't let Flymo eat the money!

(4) When 'Jacki' came to Glasgow, he grasped quickly what was expected

4.4   Degrees of hybridity in LGM

Before delving into the internal workings of metaphorical processes, I need to justify why, as said in the introduction, LGM, rather than LM or GM, is the focus of this study. The explanation is quite straightforward: hybridity can in principle not apply to GM since realisations, as seen above, are from this point of view always metaphorical – *brake failure* – or always congruent – *the brakes failed.* Degrees of hybridity can therefore only be found within LM, where, as set forth in section 4.3 and as will be seen again below, the metaphorical meaning is more or less strongly felt. LMs, however, are never purely and exclusively lexical; as Simon-Vandenbergen states: 'These so-called lexical metaphors are better termed lexicogrammatical, as grammatical changes necessarily accompany the lexical transfer' (2003:231). This of course does not apply to metaphorical uses of Nominal Groups, such as *fruit* above, but it does apply to metaphorical uses of Verbal Groups, i.e., Processes, and it is precisely these that we will be looking at. Therefore, dealing with LM in Processes – with a capital *P*, i.e., at group level, such as *run* and *eat* in (1) and (3), above – is tantamount to dealing with LGM affecting whole processes such as (1) and (3) – processes with small *p*, i.e., at clause level. The ensuing discussion of examples will clarify this point. All examples used to support my arguments are taken from the BNC, Mark Davis interface (Davies 2004).

Let us start by going back to the examples commented in the previous sections of this chapter. If we compare the use of *run* in its literal meaning, renumbered now as (9), with the more figurative use of the same verb, renumbered as (10), we may at first feel reluctant to openly call the later *metaphorical*, as it shows a rather trite use of the Process realised by *run*. However, when analysing the process the metaphor is quite obvious, as one struggles with the choice of PROCESS TYPE. In fact, as the suggested analysis shows, both the relational and the material meanings are felt, the former arguably more saliently. Processes (11) and (12 [seen above as 3]), conversely, show a contrast between the literal (11) and metaphorical (12) uses of *eat*, where in the latter the original meaning is highly present, to such an extent that the figurative meaning can hardly be understood without reference to the literal one – unlike in 10, where the original material meaning is less perceptible. The contrast between (10) and (12) in terms of the internal workings of the metaphors they represent is reflected in the fact that in (10) the analysis of the figurative, relational meaning (B) is placed above the literal material (A), whereas in (12) the situation is the reverse, i.e., the analysis of the literal meaning (A) is placed above the figurative meaning (B). This would account for the higher saliency of the figurative meaning in (10) versus the higher saliency of the literal, original meaning in (12). Notice that, although both the A and B meanings in (12) are material: dispositive, the literal A is 'intensive result' whereas the figurative B is 'possessive result' (i.e., if you eat it, you no longer have it, which is not the relevant aspect in the literal use of *eat*).[7]

(9) Literal use of *run*

Screeching MacIans	ran	for the woods
Actor/Medium	Process: material	Circumstance

(10) Metaphorical use of *run*

		The Dorset coast path	runs	along a spectacular rugged cliffline from Poole Harbour to Lyme Regis
C	B	Carrier/Medium	Process: relational and circumstantial	(Circumstantial) Attribute/Range
	A	Actor/Medium	Process: material	Circumstance

(11) Literal use of *eat*

I couldn't believe it when	Bonnie	ate	the money	She loves chewing paper
	Actor/ Agent	Process: material: dispositive: intensive result	Goal/ Medium	

(12) Metaphorical use of *eat*

		Keep up the excellent work – but don't let	Flymo	Eat	the money!
C	A		Actor/ Agent	Process: material: dispositive: intensive result	Goal/ Medium
	B		Actor/ Agent	Process: material: dispositive: possessive result	Goal/ Medium

It often happens, as Simon-Vandenbergen notes, that 'LMs [i.e. LGMs] become conventionalised and reshape the system' (2003:226). This means that when a metaphorical meaning gradually loses its novelty and acquires a new meaning, no longer felt as metaphorical, this new meaning finds its own place within the TRANSITIVITY SYSTEM, now enriched with a new feature. Such is the case with *grasp*, as seen in example (13), where the hybrid meaning C now coincides with a new literal, mental meaning, labelled A' to stress that it is a *new* literal meaning and thus differentiate it from the original literal meaning. The original material meaning A is no longer really felt, hence its analysis in smaller font and detached from the mental meaning in (13). Notice how the system of TRANSITIVITY has been reshaped by the arising of this new meaning, which now occupies its own niche within mental transitivity, and which, as seen in (13), has experienced a major transitivity shift with respect to the original material meaning even affecting the agency of the process: where material *grasp* has an effective Agent . Process . Medium configuration, the mental meaning has a middle one, i.e., Medium . Process . Range. It is worth pointing out that material uses of *grasp*, such as the one illustrated by (14), are nowadays proportionately much less frequent than mental uses: a cursory exploration of hits for verbal *grasp* in the BNC reveals that roughly 70 per cent of uses are mental versus 30 per cent material, and, within the latter, about 60 per cent are figurative, as in *grasp the opportunity, grasp the initiative* and, most notably, *grasp the nettle.*

(13) Literal mental meaning of *grasp* (from an original material meaning)

	When 'Jacki' came to Glasgow	He	grasped	quickly	what was expected
C = A'		Senser/ Medium	Process: mental	Circumstance	Phenomenon/ Range
A		Actor/ Agent	Process: material	Circumstance	Goal/Medium

(14) Literal material meaning of *grasp*

The officer steadied himself by	grasping	the windshield
	Process: material	Goal/Medium

A phenomenon that often comes about with fully systematised new meanings of a process, and which helps to further reshape the system, is their taking on prepositions not existing in the original literal meanings of those processes. Such is the case with the existential use of *flood* in example (15) (from Halliday 1994:341), where the preposition *in* is typical of such existential use, in contrast with the original material *flood* which does not take a preposition. Likewise, the BNC example (16) illustrates a verbal/mental meaning of *frown*, which takes the preposition *upon*, while the original material process takes no preposition. Incidentally, examples (15) and (16) illustrate two processes whose transitive configurations also suffer a shift with respect to the meanings of the same verbs without preposition: existential *flood in*, as in (15), is middle, whereas material *flood* can appear in middle as well as in effective constructions; verbal/mental *frown on*, in turn, is typically the Process in effective constructions, e.g. (16), in contrast with the prototypical effective nature of processes with material *frown*.[8]

(15) Protests flooded *in*

(16) Such a practice was frowned *on* by the church

Comparing verbs with and without preposition in terms of their transitive configurations as well as their place in the TRANSITIVITY SYSTEM opens up a whole array of possibilities for research and discussion. These will be left for a later occasion, as we now need to move on to the application of the theories here presented to the analysis of language in context, to which we turn in the following section.

4.5   LGM in use

In order to see how hybrid meanings and their different degrees of hybridity are used in actual discourse, this section will draw examples from two journalistic texts and discuss the LGMs found therein in the light of the theoretical argumentation put forward in the previous section. The two newspaper articles, chosen randomly for this small survey, are 'New Indications Housing Recovery Is Under Way', from the *New York Times* (1,200 words) and 'Wanted: a manager to run Britain's biggest music festival. Must have Jay-Z on speed-dial and be willing to get their wellies dirty', from the *Independent* (637 words), both of them dated 28 June 2012.

Three LGMs were found in each text. Starting with the *New York Times*, for instance, the first LGM is (17), where *we've hit a bottom* seems to mix the material meaning 'touch the lowest point' with the relational, and more salient in this case, 'be at one's lowest point', the latter being fully exploited in the second part of the clause complex: *and we're starting to come off of that bottom*. The hybridity of *we've hit a bottom* could therefore be represented as B + A = C, with the relational meaning more strongly felt than the material one.

> (17) It feels very much like we've hit a bottom and we're starting to come off of that bottom

The second LGM retrieved is actually very similar in nature to the one just discussed, insomuch as *sales climbed to the highest level* in (18) mixes the material meaning 'ascend' with the more salient relational 'be at the highest point'. Although one may claim that distinguishing between 'ascending' and 'being at the top' is overly splitting hairs in order to consider the latter a metaphorical use, I still think it is necessary to make such distinction, as the sheer action of climbing by no means implies that the participant involved finds itself near the top. Only in certain uses of *climb* – or rather, *climb to*, as in (18) – can the verb be replaced by a relational such as *be*, i.e., *home sales are at their highest level*, which proves its relational nature. This is a relational meaning that has in fact become so conventionalised that it may no longer be perceived as a metaphor, with the added 'complication' – if we compare it to the case of *grasp*, above – that the new meaning of *climb* presupposes the original one, i.e., in order to be at the top, one must have ascended before (whereas no actual material grasping is necessary for understanding something).[9] The most appropriate analysis here would therefore be A' (+A) = C, i.e., the hybrid meaning C coincides with the new literal A', yet, unlike what we saw in the analysis of *grasp* in (13), the original A meaning is still strongly felt, which may lead to problems at the time of differentiating the material (A) and the relational (A') meanings. The discussion on the contrast between the *grasp* and the *climb (to)* types of hybrids is picked up in the concluding section of this chapter.

> (18) And the National Association of Realtors said Wednesday that pending home sales climbed to the highest level since the end of a federal tax credit for first-time buyers in September 2010.

Interestingly, the third and last example from the *New York Times* is very much in the line of the *grasp* type of hybridity. We can see in (19) a very conventional use of *address* in the sense of 'deal with', therefore material, where the original verbal meaning – or its related material in the sense of 'direct' – springs up only when the experiential analysis of the process is undertaken. The fully lexicalised material meaning is overwhelmingly salient, and the formula capturing its hybridity is the same as in the case of *grasp*, i.e., A' (+A) = C, with a smaller A than in the case of *climb to* in (18) to reflect the detachment from the original literal meaning.

(19) politicians in Europe and Washington will fail to address looming problems.

Let us now look at the three cases of LGM found in the *Independent*. The Process realised by *enter* in (20) is congruently used with a material meaning of motion, but here the material meaning, although still felt, is complemented with a relational meaning, in the sense of 'start being in', i.e., circumstantial relational with expression of inceptive phase (see Matthiessen 1995:324 for the notion of *phase* in relational processes). The analysis here would be B + A = C, if we take the relational meaning to be more salient than the material one. Nevertheless, and this is good for many conventional if not yet fully lexicalised metaphors, including (17) above, one cannot but feel tempted to allow for an eye-of-the-beholder position fluctuating between the B + A = C and the A + B = C analyses, depending on the individual's perception of the more salient meaning.

(20) Glastonbury is about to enter a new era

Something similar to what we have just seen can be said of *pick up the reins* in (21). This is a well-established idiomatic expression in English; therefore, its figurative meaning can be retrieved without much processing effort. However, it is arguable which one of the two components of the hybrid meaning is more salient, i.e., the original material meaning or what I see as the figurative relational (possessive, in the sense of 'accepting [therefore starting to have] responsibility'). I would still opt for the B + A = C interpretation, as, although it seems unavoidable to think of the literal meaning of this expression, it is not necessary – unlike in the case of novel metaphors such as *eat* in (12) – to probe it in order to unpack the metaphor.

(21) The split will allow Michael [Eavis] and the Glastonbury team to pick up the reins again

Example (22) provides a nice contrast with (21), as it also includes an idiomatic expression, in this case *earned his stripes*, with the difference that the literal material meaning is here more detached from the metaphorical one – also material, with a hint of relational in the sense of 'gain a position through hard work and accumulated experience' – than in (21), unless, of course, one is in the military. The analysis here is therefore more unquestionably B + A = C, as is the analysis of the other hybrid expression in (22), i.e., *running* in *running the gates*, where the conventionalised effective meaning of *run* as 'control' or 'manage' stands out over the originally congruent middle one.

> (22) 'Melvin definitely earned his stripes running the gates for us during the Eighties [...]'

The discussion of examples (17)–(22) has given us an opportunity to see how the proposed model of hybridity works while at the same time raising some issues that are picked up and further discussed in the final section below.

4.6   Conclusions and pointers to the future

From the discussion in sections 4.4 and 4.5, a number of conclusions can be drawn concerning the degrees of hybridity in LGM. There are, on the one hand, what we could call *truly hybrid* metaphorical processes, such as (10) and (12) in section 4.4, and newspaper examples (17), (20), (21) and (22) in section 4.5. In these processes both the original and the figurative meanings can be felt to a higher or lesser extent. In some cases, e.g. *eat* in (12), there is a high metaphorical load resulting from the strong tensions existing between the original and the added meanings, both of them strongly felt. Since the original literal meaning is in those cases essential to understand the metaphor, I have proposed analysing such novel metaphors as A + B = C, while the analysis for conventionalised metaphors such as *run* in (10), or the four newspaper examples mentioned above, is: B + A = C, some of those examples, notably (20) and (21), allowing for either analysis, although a point has been made for the B + A = C interpretation.

On the other hand, there are those metaphors that have lexicalised and found their own place in the system. These, we could call *highbreds* to reflect the richness of their meaning stemming from the fusion of the original and added meanings.[10] Among these, we find *grasp, climb to* and *address*, as used in (13), (18) and (19), respectively, with the proposed analysis A' (+A) = C or A' (+A) = C, where A' results from the fusion of B + A, with the gradual loss of the original A meaning. The analysis with smaller or larger font '+A' depends on whether the original and highbred meanings are clearly discernible from each other, (13) and (19), or not, (18). In any case, both analyses can be subsumed under a simpler A' = C, which reflects the essential nature of highbreds, i.e., what used to be a figurative meaning has become a new feature in the TRANSITIVITY SYSTEM. The distinction between A' (+A) and A' (+A) hybrids is a potential niche for future research, as it may, for instance, bring a fresh approach to the contrast between homonymy and polysemy: could the different meanings of *grasp* and *address* discussed above be nowadays considered homonyms because the A' (+A) analysis suggests a semantic detachment? Conversely, would material and existential *climb* on account of the A' (+A) hybridity of the latter simply represent two different senses of a polysemous category?

To wrap up, Table 4.1 provides a synoptic view of the different analyses proposed in this chapter, with their corresponding examples and a specification of the kind of hybridity they represent. For the sake of simplicity, I disregard the eye-of-the-beholder possibility for conventional hybrids.

Table 4.1: Summary of hybrid types

Analysis	Hybrid types	Examples
A + B = C	Novel	*don't let Flymo* eat *the money!*
B + A = C	Conventional	*The Dorset coast path* runs *along a spectacular rugged cliffline* *we've* hit *a bottom* *Glastonbury is about to* enter *a new era* *The split will allow Michael [Eavis]...to* pick up the reins *again* *Melvin definitely* earned his stripes running the gates *for us during the Eighties*
A' (+A) = C A' = C	Highbred	he grasped *quickly what was expected* *politicians... will fail to* address *looming problems*
A' (+A) = C		*pending home sales* climbed to *the highest level*

A look at Table 4.1 opens up yet another number of questions that for space constraints have been left out of the discussion here and will be addressed in future research. For instance, it should be noted that, although the proposed analysis of *run* in *running the gates* is the same as that of *run* in *runs along a... cliffline*, the transitivity shift from the original *run* is larger in the former, as it involves effective processes, as contrasted with the typical middle use of motion *run* and existential *run along*. This could arguably imply that effective material *run* is closer to becoming a highbred than existential *run*. Future quantitative analysis will hopefully shed some light on this as well as the other questions raised in this final section.

Notes

1   *Stratal continuum* refers to the different environments in terms of the systemic dimension of *stratification*, i.e. context, semantics, lexicogrammar and phonology (see Caffarel, Martin and Matthiessen 2004:37).

2   This is, as far as I know, the first publication where the notion of *hybridity* is blatantly applied to process types. For a related use of this concept in this volume, see Tucker's chapter, where he speaks of 'lexicogrammatical hybridity'.

3   About the concept of *perceived metaphoricity* and its degrees, see Ortony (1979). I would like to thank Donna Miller for pointing this out to me, as well as for her insightful comments to earlier drafts of this chapter. My thanks also go to Paul Bayley, co-editor of this volume.

4   See the discussion of the BNC example *don't let Flymo eat your money*, in section 4.3.

5   My acknowledgements to Michael Halliday, copyright holder, for letting me reproduce these figures.

6   Reproduced with the publisher's consent. I would also like to thank Louise Ravelli for her cooperation in this matter.

7   *Intensive result* and *possessive result* are based on Matthiessen's (1995:245) classification of material processes according to the type of relational process their result can be considered to belong to.

8   I would like to thank the anonymous reviewer of an earlier draft of this chapter who brought my attention to the contrast between monovalent *frown* and divalent *frown upon*.

9   Being at the top may not in itself presuppose a previous ascension: a macro-corporation resulting from the merger of two companies may be at the top from its very inception. It is the use of *climb* to refer to being at the top that entails that presupposition.

10   I have intentionally resisted the temptation to use the term *dead metaphor* throughout the chapter, as it is hard to draw the dividing line between life and death in the case of metaphors and the hybridity approach here undertaken allows the use of a less macabre terminology, i.e. *highbred*, for fully lexicalised LGMs.

References

Carretero, M. (2000). On lexical and grammatical metaphor, and their teaching in a linguistics curriculum. In J. Bregazzi (Ed.), *Estudios de Filología Inglesa. Homenaje a Jack White*, 49–63. Madrid: Editorial Complutense.

Caffarel, A., Martin, J., and Matthiessen, C.M.I.M. (2004). Introduction. In A. Caffarel, J. Martin, and C. Matthiessen (Eds), *Language Typology: A Functional*

Perspective, 1–76. Amsterdam and Philadelphia: John Benjamins. http://dx.doi. org/10.1075/cilt.253

Davies, M. (2004). *BYU-BNC*, (Based on the British National Corpus from Oxford University Press). Available online at http://corpus.byu.edu/bnc/

Giora, R. (1997). Understanding figurative and literal language: The graded salience hypothesis. *Cognitive Linguistics*, 8(3), 183–206. http://dx.doi.org/10.1515/ cogl.1997.8.3.183

Goatly, A. (1997). *The Language of Metaphors*. London: Routledge. http://dx.doi. org/10.4324/9780203210000

Goldstein, A., Arzouan, Y., and Faust, M. (2008). Timing the metaphoric brain. In Z. Breznitz (Ed.), *Brain Research in Language*, 205–223. New York: Springer. http://dx.doi.org/10.1007/978-0-387-74980-8_8

Halliday, M.A.K. (2008). Day trip boy car theft fury: On the complementarity of system and text. In M.A.K. Halliday (Ed.), *Complementarities in Language*, 77–126. Beijing: Commercial Press.

Halliday, M.A.K. (1998). Things and relations: Regrammaticising experience as technical knowledge. In J. Martin and R. Veel (Eds), *Reading Science: Critical and Functional Perspectives on Discourses of Science*, 185–237. London: Routledge.

Halliday, M.A.K. (1984[2006]). Grammatical metaphor in English and Chinese. In B. Hong (Ed.), *New Papers on Chinese Language Use*, 9–18. Canberra: Contemporary China Centre. Reprinted in M.A.K. Halliday (2006), *Studies in Chinese Language*, Volume 8 of the Collected Works of M.A.K. Halliday, edited by J.J. Webster, 325–333. London and New York: Continuum.

Halliday, M.A.K. (1994). *An Introduction to Functional Grammar* (2nd ed.). London: Arnold.

Khubchandani, L.M. (1997). *Revisualizing Boundaries: A Plurilingual Ethos*. New Delhi: Sage.

Kraidy, M.M. (2005). *Hybridity: Or the Cultural Logic of Globalization*. Philadelphia: Temple University.

Hasan, R. (1996). Semantic networks: A tool for the analysis of meaning. In C. Cloran, D. Butt, and G. Williams (Eds), *Ways of Saying, Ways of Meaning: Selected papers of Ruqaiya Hasan*, 104–131. London: Cassell.

Makoni, S. (2002). From misinvention to disinvention: An approach to multi-lingualism. In G. Smitherman, A. Spear, and A. Ball (Eds), *Black Linguistics: Language, Society and Politics in Africa and the Americas*, 132–153. London: Routledge.

Matthiessen, C.M.I.M. (1995). *Lexicogrammatical Cartography: English Systems*. Tokyo: International Language Sciences Publishers.

Ortony, A. (1979). Beyond literal similarity. *Psychological Review*, 86(3), 161–180. http://dx.doi.org/10.1037/0033-295X.86.3.161

Ravelli, L. (1988). Grammatical metaphor: An initial analysis. In E. Steiner and R. Veltman (Eds), *Pragmatics, Discourse and Text. Some Systemically-Oriented Approaches*, 133–147. London: Frances Pinter.

Simon-Vandenbergen, A.M. (2003). Lexical Metaphor and interpersonal meaning. In A.M. Simon-Vandenbergen, M. Taverniers, and L. Ravelli (Eds), *Grammatical*

Metaphor, 223–256. Amsterdam and Philadelphia: John Benjamins. http://dx. doi.org/10.1075/cilt.236.13sim

Simon-Vandenbergen, A.M., Taverniers, M., and Ravelli, L. (Eds), *Grammatical Metaphor*. Amsterdam, and Philadelphia: John Benjamins. http://dx.doi.org/ 10.1075/cilt.236

Taverniers, M. (2003). Grammatical metaphor in SFL. A historiography of the introduction and initial study of the concept. In A.M. Simon-Vandenbergen, M. Taverniers, and L. Ravelli (Eds), *Grammatical Metaphor*, 5–33. Amsterdam and Philadelphia: John Benjamins. http://dx.doi.org/10.1075/cilt.236.02tav

About the author

Jorge Arús Hita is senior lecturer in English language and linguistics at Universidad Complutense de Madrid. Among his most recent publications within the SFL framework, he is co-author, with Lavid and Zamorano, of *Systemic-Functional Grammar of Spanish: A contrastive study with English* (Continuum, 2010), and of 'Thematic choices in English and Spanish: An SFL analysis of two newspaper genres' (with Lavid and Moratón, in O'Grady, Barlett and Fontaine (eds), *Choice in Language: Applications in Text Analysis*, Equinox 2013).

Part II
Hybridity: Implications for pedagogy and professional practices

5

Re-orienting semantic dispositions: The role of hybrid forms of language use in university learning

Caroline Coffin

The Open University, UK

5.1   Introduction

Let me start this chapter with the voices of two university students:

> OK [...] I'm just going to be honest [...] often I copy it (material in the text book). [laughing] ok. I do, I do, to be honest. I have to because I don't have that knowledge yet. (Nimet)

> I prefer layman's terms. I don't agree with the, you know, using big massive jargon. You walk into someone and speak to them about personalisation they aint got a clue what you're talking about.
> And that was another fear that I had when I came to the course. That you'd go all round and think 'Oh I'm focusing too much on writing about the situation rather than actually doing it hands on' (James)

The quotes above come from university students in their first year of a distance taught undergraduate course in the field of Health and Social Care (henceforth HSC). Like many HSC students they are 'non-traditional' students: both are mature and study part time. Nimet is Turkish and has English as a second language. James comes from a Black ethnic minority group. Both work professionally as carers.

So what do such short quotes reveal and how are they relevant to this chapter? One key point is that they are indicative of how a significant number of HSC students orient to knowledge: Nimet copies from the text book because she does not yet fully grasp its meaning. Her choices in modulation (*I have to*) and negative polarity (*I don't have*) emphasise her relatively weak positioning at this point in her university study. James, on the other hand, appears to have more autonomy and power in relation to how he learns (*I prefer, I don't agree*). Nevertheless he is concerned that the world of abstract knowledge may jeopardise his capacity to act in the world. The wording *and that was another fear that I had* hints at his ambivalent attitude towards academic study. At a later point in the interviews from which these quotes are taken[1] it became clear that both Nimet and James were finding undergraduate study a challenge. It was not clear whether they would complete their qualification.

Such insights are central to this chapter. The fundamental argument is that, for some students, academic study involves orienting to knowledge and meaning making in ways that are fundamentally new and unfamiliar. Of particular relevance to the theme of this edited collection is that hybrid forms of language use occurring in online discussion forums can play a key role in the re-orientation that tertiary study requires, particularly for students such as Nimet and James and in applied contexts such as HSC.

The chapter begins by introducing the research context from which I draw my data and evidence. I also set out the related concepts of semantic disposition and knowledge orientation which have come to inform the research into teaching and learning that colleagues and I have been conducting over the last decade (see Coffin and Donohue, 2014, for a synthesis of this research). In Section 5.3, I then define what I mean by hybrid forms of language use. Section 5.4 provides examples of hybrid forms of language use taken from online discussion forums within a second level HSC undergraduate course. Section 5.5 then develops the argument that such hybrid forms of language use can be exploited by teachers and students for learning purposes. The chapter concludes by arguing that online discussion forums (particularly in applied fields of study) can facilitate the orientations to knowledge needed in tertiary learning environments.

5.2   The research context: Health and social care as a real world problem

Systemic Functional Linguistics (hereafter SFL) is designed to be an applicable linguistics and thus is well placed to conduct 'the theoretical and empirical investigations of real-world problems in which language is a central issue' (Brumfit, 1995:27). In contemporary affluent societies life spans are increasing but that is not necessarily matched by quality of life. As a result, demand on health and social care services is increasing, leading to staff shortages, and/or insufficiently educated professionals.[2] Consequently the education and training of HSC professionals and the contribution that higher education institutions can make is a source of considerable debate (e.g. Council of Deans of Health and Skills for Health 2013). On the ground there are issues of retention and attainment amongst students of HSC with low literacy levels being cited as a key factor (Donohue and Erling 2012).

Against this background, colleagues and I have undertaken a series of research projects set within Health and Social care university study, specifically within a distance learning context. One project (*Health and Social Care: a linguistics and sociology of knowledge based investigation*) focused on variations in first year students' ways of using language and of thinking and how this might impact on their learning (Donohue and Coffin 2012). Another project (*Supporting undergraduate students' acquisition of academic argumentation strategies through computer conferencing*) investigated the role of online discussion forums in the second year of study (Coffin 2013, Coffin, Hewings and North 2012).

HSC is a broad transdisciplinary field of study, drawing on the social sciences (including sociology, politics, history, ethics, geography, psychology and economics) and, in some institutions, the applied sciences (e.g. paramedic science, exercise science, midwifery) as well as on the personal and professional lived experiences of health and social care workers. The data I draw on for this chapter comes from the two studies referred to above, with the primary focus being the data collected from students' study (at second level) of the course, *Perspectives on Complementary and Alternative Medicine* (henceforth CAM). In this course the main disciplinary base is the social sciences, with a major aim being to combine theoretical knowledge with professional dimensions in relation to decision making around health interventions in orthodox and complementary and alternative medicine.

In order to help meet the learning outcomes of the course teachers use online discussion forums. Typically the forums last for approximately 2–3 weeks and are organised around discussion tasks designed to prompt debate relevant to students' prior reading and future written assignment tasks. More broadly, they are designed to encourage students to reflect on, and discuss, various aspects of subject knowledge including the relationship between theoretical knowledge and the real world context of health provision. Below is the task from the opening online discussion forum in the CAM course. This is designed to prompt students' thoughts on the changing context of health care and thus inform the follow up writing task (also set out below):

Online forum task: Outline one reason or factor which you think has led to an increase in the choices available when it comes to making decisions about our health.

Follow on written assignment task: The following description is of an encounter between a Reiki practitioner and a fictional person (Mrs Bannister) who goes to see her. Think carefully about this encounter and write a report on the interactions that took place in the light of your learning throughout Module 1. In particular, your analysis should focus on the context of the interaction: how does the interaction fit into the way that society and health care is changing, along with any ethical considerations for both the provider and the consumer of health care in this situation? (*The case study of the Reiki practitioner and Mrs Bannister follows*).

5.2.1   Data collection

Table 5.1 summarises the total data set that was collected and analysed in relation to two cohorts of students studying the CAM course across two academic years. Sixteen groups (of approximately 15–25 students) participated in five online discussion forums held at different points in the academic year. Their initial and final online discussion data, along with a sample of students' written assignments, were collected and linguistically analysed. Contextualising data was also collected and findings synthesised (as specified in Table 5.1).

Table 5.1 Data summary

Data type	Type of Analysis/ Synthesis
All text data from 16 asynchronous online discussion forums (8 at the start and 8 at the end of the course) (49,223 words)	Linguistic analysis (SFL + corpus)
A sample of 28 individually authored written assignments together with assessment feedback (44,893 words)	Linguistic analysis (SFL + corpus)
4 interviews with teachers recorded and transcribed	Findings synthesised
12 surveys of students conducted and collected	Findings synthesised
7 follow up interviews with students recorded and transcribed	Findings synthesised
Ethnographic style observations and notes arising from meetings with the course leader and a meeting with teachers leading the online discussions	Findings synthesised
Course text books and other teaching-learning resources used	Findings synthesised

For the purposes of this chapter I am selective in the data samples discussed, focusing for the most part on hybrid forms of language use. However, it was through an initial broad brush analysis of patterns of language use in the online forums (using the tools of SFL and supported by corpus searches using concordancing software) that led to a growing awareness of the particular kind of learning potential provided by the hybrid discourse that the forums gave rise to.

5.2.2 Semantic disposition

Using the linguistic lens of SFL across several projects investigating student learning in HSC, it has become clear that different students orient to knowledge in quite distinct ways. Hasan's concept of 'semantic disposition' (e.g. 2009:434) building on work by the sociologist Bernstein (e.g. 1996) is useful in accounting for such variation. In essence, semantic disposition references an individual's predisposition towards making particular kinds of meanings and thus their particular ways of thinking, seeing and being in the world. Hasan makes a strong argument that such dispositions develop as a result of early family and social experiences and the patterns of language interaction that individuals regularly encounter. This is not dissimilar to early theories of socialisation (e.g. Parsons and Bales 1956) which proposed that at an early point in their development a child internalises a cognitive frame of reference that then influences the forms of relations, beliefs and knowledge they go on to develop. Following this line of argument, whilst we might assume a child has agency as to whether and how they appropriate the patterns of language and meaning making which they are recurrently exposed to and engage in, we can also assume that it might be a difficult task to develop patterns to which one has limited access. In other words, whilst from the beginning learning and development is about the unfolding of human capacity, it is a process that happens in interaction with the social environment.

Hasan argues that patterns built up in early childhood may lead to dispositions that do not align well with the patterns of meaning making assumed and required by institutionalised learning, in particular what she refers to as decontextualised meaning making (2009: 403–431). Decontextualised meaning making refers to the abstract representations of the world that are removed from the kind of contextualised 'here and now' meanings referencing the visible, tangible and sensory environment surrounding interactants. This is illustrated in the following short extract in which a father and his daughter, Scarlett (age 3 years), are engaging in dialogue as they water the garden.[3]

> Father: Okay, I think what we should do is water these ones over here. Oh, watch your feet! Go over here. Let's put some more in here. Oh no, there's another earwig in there [...]. Don't know why they're called earwigs but look at him.
> Scarlett: Take him off here. Take him off here.

The contextualised talk around earwigs in the extract above contrasts strikingly with their representation in the following journal article.

> The amount of parental provisioning is thought to reflect the need of offspring. This hypothesis was tested in the case of provisioning food mass to young with controlled clutch size using the maritime earwig, *Anisolabis Maritima* Bonelli (Dermaptera: Anisolabididae). (Suzuki 2011)

Earwigs in the extract above are generalised and taxonomised and an interpretation of their behaviour (*parental provisioning*) is offered in the form of a hypothesis. Rather than the immediate material context of situation prompting the language interaction, it is the longer term goal of scientific study whereby knowledge is generated out of investigating and reflecting on multiple instances and details of material reality over time. As such it is an example of decontextualised meaning making, realised through the kind of abstract nominalised language (e.g. *amount of parental provisioning, provisioning food mass*) that is commonplace in scientific and academic contexts and in many school subjects. It is this kind of language that becomes commonplace as students move into the later years of secondary schooling. (See Christie and Derewianka 2008, Coffin 2006, Schleppegrell 2004 for further discussion.)

Whilst it is unlikely that many young children would be exposed to the degree of abstraction used in scientific journals as exemplified in the extract above, Hasan proposes that children who have engaged frequently in conversations where meanings become decontextualised from their immediate material setting are advantageously positioned when they enter the increasingly abstract world of formal education. An example that Hasan gives of such a conversation is of a mother and child discussion in which a comment on a moth dying leads onto a consideration by the mother and child of the ephemerality of animal life (Hasan 2005:207). Similarly, in the case of Scarlett, her father exploits numerous opportunities arising in the material environment of the garden to begin scaffolding her into the world of taxonomies (i.e., the classification of things or concepts). An example of this follows:

Father: Yeah, this one's got a shell and this one hasn't got a shell [...].
            Yeah, so what's that one called?
Scarlett: A 'nail [snail]. A 'nail.
Father: And?
Scarlett: A [...] what is he? I not know.
Father: It begins with 's'[...] slug.

In this second 'garden' extract, the father uses the creatures he finds to (informally) teach Scarlett how to classify natural phenomena in relation to specific criteria (i.e., creatures with and without shells). Though the father did not actually label the snail as a member of the molluscan class *Gastropoda gastropod molluscs,* he is using the domestic, familiar and sensory world of the garden as a base on which to overlay the beginnings of rudimentary scientific knowledge. In this way, Scarlett, in interaction with her father, is beginning to learn how to sort and classify the natural world. It is this kind of merging of the lived, material world and the increasingly refracted taxonomised and conceptual world that I will return to in Section 5.3.2. A key point here is that, although the material context of an interaction may permit and, at times, serve as a catalyst for, more abstract concepts and meanings built up through academic study, not all interactions are amenable to this kind of 'inter-permeation'. Neither do all children have equal exposure to such permeable contexts. Nor is the potential for permeability necessarily taken advantage of, even where the opportunity exists.

5.2.3   Semantic disposition, knowledge orientation and learning

As commented above, the specialised knowledge domains of secondary school subjects and university disciplines (see Coffin and Donohue 2014 for an extended discussion of the latter) are built through different kinds of linguistic resources to those of everyday reality, cultivating, as Maton (2011: 75) puts it, specialised 'gazes'. In order to help learners relate to these new ways of seeing and understanding the world, schools and universities could benefit from recognising and engaging with learners' existing semantic dispositions. As this chapter will now attempt to demonstrate, skilful scaffolding by teachers can enable students to bridge from more familiar contextualised meaning making to more decontextualised unfamiliar meaning making. Sustained exposure and practice can establish orientations to knowledge whereby students are more in tune with the educational enterprise they find themselves in. As Hasan underlines:

> In mastering an academic register [...] the pupil is not just mastering so many words and syntactic structures; s/he is also learning at the same time a new mode of thinking, a new approach to ways of meaning (Hasan 2011:95).

In the sections that follow, I will propose that making the transition into new ways of meaning and establishing new knowledge orientations can be facilitated, in particular, by hybrid forms of language which bring into close proximity the world of lived experience and the world of concepts. My research into online forums has shown that hybrid language use is particularly common in these environments and that they therefore have a rich pedagogic potential. The next section elaborates on what I mean by hybrid forms of language.

5.3   Hybrid forms of language

Compare the following extracts.

Extract 1
There is now a wide range of CAM healthcare on offer, i.e. an increase in pluralism. People have many different needs and priorities and the importance they give to health will change as their circumstances change. Maslow's model of 'hierarchy of needs' demonstrates this. This wide choice in a plural health market can give consumers more opportunities for becoming healthy.

Extract 2
Totally with you on course material i too know nil about the subject however i am enjoying the course it's nice to have your views challenged now and again isn't it?

Whilst the first extract would most likely be identified as written language the second has features that suggest it is spoken interaction written down. In fact, both extracts come from an online forum in HSC. Thus they both use a writing system and the written medium. However, online forums are designed to be interactive – hence the dialogic features of extract 2 such as the use of the tag question, *isn't it* and the *I* and *you* pronouns. (Note though that, as illustrated by extract 1, not all participants in online forums take advantage of their interactive features.) The process of categorising extracts 1 and 2 suggests that, as users of language, we have a sense that some forms of language use are more common in writing (e.g. greater degrees of impersonality and abstraction as exemplified in extract 1) and some are more typical in speech (e.g. more dialogism with a sense of a 'listener'/respondent and less abstraction).

It is the fact that, at this point in our language history, we are still conscious of distinctions between speech and writing and the kind of language patterns that go with each that I can formulate my argument that online discussion forums provide the material conditions for written and spoken patterns of language use to work alongside each other and at times be integrated into a compressed hybrid form – what I will refer to as 'written dialogue'. Sections 5.3.1 and 5.3.2, drawing on Halliday (1996), explore further what I mean by spoken and written patterns of language use.

5.3.1   Speech and patterns of spoken language

In speech we use the sound system by means of our vocal apparatus to express wording in order to make meaning. Clearly, the lexicogrammatical and discourse semantic choices we make through our wording vary enormously in relation to their contexts of situation. The contextual variables of field, tenor and mode (comprising the register construct within SFL) help to account for this variation. That is, speech may be more or less spontaneous and more or less dialogic with the channel often playing a particularly influential role (e.g. telephone, TV, computer based voice conferencing, etc.). However, characteristically and prototypically, speech is fluid and spontaneous (such as in face to face conversation between family or friends). As a generalisation we can say that spoken rather than written language tends to have many of the following features (see Halliday 1996: 339–354):

(a) backtracking
(b) rewording
(c) an 'I and you' system of person in grammar to create dialogue and a constant exchange of roles between speaker and listener
(d) attitudes are often explicit
(e) less lexically dense and more grammatically intricate
(f) organised around the clause and thus construing reality as processes – a world of movement and flux, continuous, elastic and indeterminate

(g) experience interpreted dynamically rather than synoptically
(h) typically communicative, only becoming archival under certain
     conditions.

In many ways, as Halliday (1996) has observed, the medium of speaking
is similar to spoken language: language is 'in flux', realised as 'movement
and continuous flow, of our bodily organs and of sound waves travelling
through air' (Halliday 1996:352).

5.3.2   Writing, writing systems and patterns of written language

Historically, writing did not begin as language written down, as a new way
of doing old things through the duplication of the functions of speech.
Rather it emerged as a result of the impact between talking and drawing
whereby language was mapped on to another semiotic system of images
to form abstract symbols and graphic patterns relating to elements of
language.

Initially a primary purpose for writing was the tabulation of goods.
Thus, from the beginning, it was associated with non-clausal registers.
Over time, writing systems have developed features that are prosodic (e.g.
punctuation) and paralinguistic (e.g. typeface, indentation, line spacing).

Writing requires an engagement of the body with its material environment whereby a person makes and records marks on paper or a screen.
The medium of writing is thus similar to written language: it represents
language 'in fix' i.e., realised as text in material form, stable and bounded
on paper or screen (Halliday 1996:352).

Like spoken language, written language is not homogeneous – patterns
of language vary in relation to specific contexts of use. Nevertheless, as
a generalisation, the following syndromes of lexicogrammatical features
tend to be associated with written language, particularly in formal textual
products (where writing as activity and the process of drafting is erased
from view) (see Halliday 1996:339–354):

(a) declarative mood dominant
(b) judgement often depersonalised
(c) high lexical density, more nominalisations
(d) organised around the nominal group and thus construing reality as
     entities – a world of things and structures, discontinuous, rigid and
     determinate

(e) experience interpreted synoptically rather than dynamically

(f) typically archival, a form of recording and building information

(g) typically objectifies the world as a basis for systematic knowledge (often abstract and taxonomised)

5.3.3 Fusing speech and writing: Written dialogue, hybridity and articulacy

The sections above distinguished speech and writing, showing how each are associated with different patterns of grammar and hence meaning making. For how long we will continue to have a sense of someone 'talking like a book' or 'writing like they speak' is a matter of debate (see Crystal 2001[2006]; Herring 2012). This is particularly the case in an era when new technologies are offering the material conditions for greater and more intense (compressed) interaction between the two media. Online discussion forums, for example, provide an interactive and relatively spontaneous context for writing ('speaking' through writing or 'written dialogue') and this context, I would propose, provides a friction point at which new 'hybrid' ways of meaning making can occur.

As I will show in the examples that follow in Section 5.4, in online discussion contexts the once sharp distinctions between speech and writing in academic contexts are increasingly softening and blurring. In this way, online discussions bring into closer interaction the clausal/personal representation of the world with a more abstract nominal interpretation thus orienting (and in some cases reorienting) learners to quite different ways of constructing relations and realities.

Furthermore, such contexts bring reading and writing practices closer together with listening and speaking practices. In the written dialogue of online discussions, as thoughts unfold dynamically across the screen and through time, and these thoughts enter into dialogue, writing becomes more like speech and reading becomes more like listening. Through its written form dialogue is not quite so unselfconscious and intuitive as it would be in face to face interaction. Equally, in its dialogic form, writing is not always quite so self-conscious and 'designed' as it would be in a formal academic writing context.

At this point in the evolution of language form and use, it may be timely and more accurate, therefore, to reconsider concepts of literacy and oracy and to take seriously the notion of articulacy – the making of meaning in language in whatever medium (Halliday 1996:367).

5.4 Hybrid forms of language use: Online discussion forums in the context of health and social care

As Kress *et al.* (2001) and others have pointed out, educational knowledge has always been multimodal and teaching and learning a 'multimodal accomplishment', with teachers and learners drawing on the complementary nature of spoken and written media as an integral part of the overall process (classroom discussion and written assignments being examples of traditional pedagogic activities working alongside and complementing each other). One could argue, therefore, that online written dialogue simply provides another context for the dialectic between the spoken and the written. What I am proposing here, however, is that the use of one semiotic resource – writing – has the inbuilt potential for a more intensive fusion, a greater coming together and, consequently, greater permeability of the spoken and the written, the clausal and the nominal.

The first question to ask is to what degree the potential is currently being exploited. What can we learn by looking at an online discussion as a form of dialogue? What can we learn by looking at it as a form of writing? Using the data collected from HSC (as detailed in Section 5.2), I explore this question by considering three features to have emerged from the language data – interactivity, spontaneity and clausal/nominal construals of the world.

5.4.1 Interactivity

An analysis of the data showed that online debate macrogenres (as classified by Coffin 2013) are collaboratively constructed through teacher and student contributions of a wide range of genre stages and phases, including prompts, challenges and agreements. The identification of these stages showed that participants were anticipating and responding to alternative views and voices (in a way similar to face to face conversation). For example, messages served to endorse (through agreement) prior claims, but also pushed for further interaction by asking for clarification, probing for additional information and perspectives or challenging what had been proposed. Below, an extract (extract 3) from one of the online forums illustrates a sequence of Agree, Challenge, Claim + Evidence, Agree, Recommendation:

Extract 3

Maureen: I agree Kathy, (*Agree*) but don't you think that if a person is desperate they will find the money from somewhere hoping it will work? (*Challenge*)

Tanya: Yes CAM can be expensive, especially as one treatment is never enough. Some health authorities are changing though and now pay for patients to have treatments like acupuncture, relaxation techniques and aromatherapy. I work for my local PCT and we even offer tai chi as an aid to relaxation and improving balance. (*Claim + Evidence*)

Kath: No doubt about it, Maureen. Some people will be desperate enough to try anything, even if they can't really afford it. (*Agree*) Possibly, the remedy is – more effective CAM on the NHS (Hi Tanya) and more research into CAM so that people can choose well and don't waste money and time. (*Recommendation*).

In the data collected, there was one unexpected finding: across all CAM forums just over half of the claims that were made were not responded to. This underlines a feature of asynchronous online interactivity which is somewhat different to face to face interactivity. In a face to face situation it would be unusual if students were to offer ideas and perspectives and the majority of these were simply ignored and/or were followed by completely unrelated claims. In the online environment, however, the absence of a response or the lack of cohesion across messages is relatively commonplace. There seem to be two main reasons for this:

(a)   the asynchronous feature of conferences; and

(b)   students often responding directly to the initial pedagogic task rather than to prior responses to it.

5.4.2   Spontaneity

Text in online forums is transmitted in a way that enables both instantaneous responses and delayed ones (i.e., from minutes to hours or even several days). Significantly, because contributions are produced in written form it is possible both to plan and edit messages or respond rapidly and compose them 'on the fly' (though these are never as instant as in a face-to-face conversation or instant messaging). In the data collected I found examples of both. The following message (extract 4), for instance, has typos (*mind mind*) and there is the absence of written conventions (i.e., a lack of capitalisation for *i* at the start of the second sentence). There is also the use of textese (2) and minor or abbreviated clauses (*thank goodness, and re CAM*). Arguably these are analogous to the 'errors' of false starts, repetition and mid utterance changes characterising face-to-face spontaneous chat.

Extract 4

Thank goodness!!! i also share your views on the issues of black mailing children 2 sleep in own bed *and re CAM*. It has cross *mind mind* a few times from reading people's message as 2 whether anyone else has any exp. of CAM other than as a patient.

In contrast, extract 5 provides evidence of a student taking time to compose their contribution as indicated by the frequency of nominal groups (in italics) and the overall lexical density:

Extract 5

A post modernity era featuring an increase in consumer culture provides Mrs B with *an increase of information of alternative approaches to her health*. Following on from *the counter-culture changes in the 1960's promoting questioning of authority in health provision* this led to *an increase in and acceptance of CAM.* So Mrs B was able to form *the opinion that her GP was busy and that her current problem did not warrant medical intervention*. She chose her own health care in light of accepted practice and *the information now freely available*. I think I have said much the same as others, maybe just a little differently?? Abbie.

Aside from the final two clauses and sign off the message above (extract 5) is characterised by the patterns of written language outlined in Section 5.3.2. Other data I analysed provided a different kind of evidence of the amount of crafting and editing work that may go into the composition of a message. In the following extract (extract 6) Karalena accidentally posted a message followed by an edited version (extract 7):

Extract 6

First version

Mrs Bannister. There may be many factors why she did not *bother her doctor* and went to a Reiki practitioner instead for instance, *did she feel her complaint was serious enough at the time*, or may be lacked confidence in her doctor due to previous meetings or even found it difficult to arrange a consultation due to a stroppy receptionist.

Extract 7
Second (edited) version
There may be many factors why she did not *choose to see her doctor* and visit a Reiki practitioner instead. *Maybe she felt her condition was not serious enough at the time,* she may have lost confidence in her doctor due to previous meetings or even found it difficult to arrange a consultation due to a stroppy receptionist. *Factors we all may have experienced at times or know of someone who has.*

It is significant to note that in her second message Karalena makes more prominent (through her selection of lexis) the concept of choice – *she did not choose to see her doctor* as opposed to *she did not bother to see her doctor.* She also changes an interrogative structure – *did she feel her complaint,* etc. to a declarative one – *maybe she felt her condition.* Finally, in the second, edited version she moves to a high level generalising clause and thematises reasoning – *Factors we all may have experienced.* These changes are significant because they suggest that students such as Karalena are exploiting the slowed down pace of forum interaction to practise the editing and shaping skills of academic writing. In this way, the opportunities and motivation to hone a piece of writing place the composition process of online interaction much closer to that of writing than to spontaneous speech. At the same time, the dialogic context comprising a responsive audience of peers and a teacher may have provided the motivation (or pressure) to do this.

In sum, the data showed that in its written form dialogue is not quite so unselfconscious and intuitive as it would be in face-to-face interaction. Equally, in its dialogic form, writing is not always quite so self-conscious and 'designed' as it would be in a formal academic writing context.

5.4.3   Clausal and nominal construals of the world: Interweaving the academic and the professional

The topic of the first CAM online discussion forum, as set out in Section 5.2, was healthcare choice, with the task itself providing a further narrowing of the subject matter to 'the factors leading to choice'. This was a topic covered in the first few chapters of the students' course book. I was interested to see to what extent the students discussed the issue (a) through the lens of abstract concepts developed through the decontextualising and taxonomising processes of academic knowledge building (i.e., theorised knowledge) and/or (b) by reference to lived experience using the narrative details of the case study of Mrs Bannister or their own professional and personal experience. An analysis of the data revealed two points of particular pedagogic significance. The first is concerned with the complementarity of more clausal and more nominal construals of HSC knowledge.

Below are two extracts (extracts 8 and 9) from the forum discussion. At this point in the discussion, the focus was on the limiting effect of money on choice. In the first message (extract 8), Chloe uses both technical terms (*post modernity, later modernity*) and abstract nominal groups (e.g. *spirituality, a move towards science and technology*) to represent the high level generalised position that fewer people attend formal religious services and may be seeking alternatives. She then argues that choice has always been limited by money and at this point moves to a specific example whereby there is a gear shift in the language used and a specific human participant becomes thematised (*she*). Thus, within the same response we see the movement of general (and abstract) to specific (and concrete). The 'specific' however is Louise (who is part of a case study in the course text book) and as such is thus part of the academic domain set up in the course.

Chloe's text matches the desired movement in HSC from general concepts to specific lived experience in the form of case study material. At the same time, it should also be noted that these are part of an interactive dialogue, hence the use of *you* and *I*. The movement between more decontextualised and more contextualised meanings contrasts with the meanings that Amy makes (in a follow up message to Chloe, extract 9 – discussed below) and how these re-orient the discussion.

> **Extract 8**
>
> Chloe: *In the post Modernity or late modernity period* (as named by giddens) there has been *a move towards science and technology* but also *a reduction in formal religious attendance.* As *you* say, perhaps people are missing *this need for spirituality* but instead of heading back to *formalised religious* are looking for alternatives that are not being dictated to them. *I* also believe, however, that choice is only really available if you have money to spend and *I* think this has always been the case even *in the pre modernity period.* If you take the example of Louise in the course book, *she* has lots of choice in theory but little money and this actually equates to no choice.

In Amy's response to Chloe (extract 9) there is a further gear shift from a professional case study to a personal experience and a corresponding change to language use which has no technicality and little abstraction. The Participants (in italics) tend to be concrete and/or human and overall the language is more informal and conversation like: e.g. (a) the use of explicit attitude (in APPRAISAL terms, JUDGEMENT and AFFECT) (*Good point Chloe, choice is great, moaned*), (ii) vocatives (*Chloe*), (iii) contraction (*it's out there*), (iv) lack of capitals (*it*) and (v) the use of an emoticon (*:o*).

Extract 9
Amy: Good point Chloe, *more money* usually equals *more choice. I* also believe that *choice* is *only available* if *you* know *it's* out there. When *I* was in *a lot of pain with my back* I simply took *painkillers* and awaited *my physio appointment. It* never even occurred to me to I had *a choice* and could try *a CAM therapy* because *I* didn't know *what* was out there. *I* talked/moaned to *various friends and colleagues* and *not one of them* mentioned *CAM therapies* either. *Choice* is *great* but only if *you* realise *you* have *it.:o*)

What is particularly significant about extracts 8 and 9 above is that the complementary models of a more clausal and a more nominally construed world exist seamlessly side by side. In other words, a more theorised account of social phenomena gains power through lived experience being brought in as evidence. More importantly, in an online forum these two interpretations can be interactively built. Furthermore, should students only contribute one or other model, the slowed down pace of the online dialogue opens up space for pedagogic 'interventions' whereby the teacher (or indeed peer) can ratchet up or down the level of abstraction and thus explicitly model for other participants the inherently hybrid nature of HSC knowledge.

The second finding of particular pedagogical significance revealed through data analysis was systematic variation in individual students' responses. Compare for example the following two messages (extracts 10 and 11) posted in quick succession by Laura and Karalena, noting in particular their use of field specific terms and concepts (in italics) and the degree to which their construal of health choice is oriented to the clausal or the nominal.

Extract 10
Laura: I feel that the rise in *consumerism, depersonalisation* and *paternalism* within *orthodox* (*biomedical model*) *medicine* has resulted in the *disempowerment of patients*. In the current climate this is no longer acceptable. People have come to distrust and in my opinion, feel dissatisfaction with what was once *the dominant model of health*. (??? chapter 3 political and historical perspectives 3.4 resurgence of CAM).

Extract 11

Karelena: Mrs Bannister. There may be many factors why she did not bother her doctor and went to a Reiki practitioner instead for instance, did she feel her complaint was serious enough at the time, or may be lacked confidence in her doctor due to previous meetings or even found it difficult to arrange a consultation due to a stroppy receptionist.

From the perspective of field, Laura's response shows a more nominal abstract construal of events – she uses numerous field specific, abstract concepts (*biomedical model, disempowerment of patients,* etc.) to present a response to the question. Karelena's message in contrast hones in on the more concrete case study and lived experience of Mrs Bannister where the factors are restricted to an individual case and cannot be generalised beyond this. Her construal is more clausal in orientation. (It is significant to note that, as discussed in Section 5.4.2, Karalena's edited version did move towards generalisation. Nevertheless it did not reach the level of abstraction of Laura's contribution.)

Laura and Karelina's responses demonstrate the two complementary means of construing HSC knowledge as illustrated in my initial examples – on the one hand, the use of general and abstract social science concepts, and on the other hand, the use of concrete and specific examples of lived experience (usually in the form of case studies). What is pedagogically significant here is that each of the two students has chosen to orient to one or other of these strands of knowledge building. That is, either the decontextualised (Laura) or the contextualised (Karalena).

Given that for both students this is a consistent pattern throughout the online discussion it would seem that their contrasting linguistic construals of the field reveal something important about their overall semantic disposition, and thus their knowledge orientation to HSC and, more broadly, to their modelling of the world. Indeed, if we take into account an analysis of their assignments and assignment marks for the year, alongside assessment feedback as indicators of their overall academic orientation and their take up of the academic values of HSC, then Laura is more closely aligned and Karalena less so. That is, Karalena received an average mark of 57 across the year and her teacher's comments on her assignments suggested that her analytical skills required further development (also confirmed by SFL analysis of her essays):

You obviously feel strongly about the ethical issues around CAM – it is great to have your own opinion, but in an assignment like this it is important to back up your statements with published evidence and also put forward both sides of the argument before drawing your conclusions. (*comment on Karalena's first assignment*)

In your essay, rather than simply listing the models, use them to analyse the information you got from Mrs X. This shows that you have read them and understood them to such an extent that you can apply them yourself. (*comment on Karalena's third assignment*)

Laura, on the other hand, received an average of 68 marks and the feedback on her assignments suggested that she was orienting to academic knowledge making (through her conceptual framing) in ways that were recognised and rewarded by her teacher.

Arising out of the examples discussed in this section comes a key pedagogic question – how can students be guided (in an online forum) to reclassify and conceptually reframe their personal and professional lived experience (or indeed vice versa)? Section 5.5 addresses this question.

5.5   The pedagogic potential of online discussion forums: Re-orienting semantic dispositions

Analysis of the survey and interview data revealed that many students and teachers were unsure about how online forums could facilitate the teaching-learning process. I found that, even though teachers might have received technical training in the use of forums, their experience in the pedagogic aspects of these was generally limited. Time and workload was an issue as well as the feeling that online discussions did not provide a satisfying learning experience for many of their students. A number of both teachers and students felt anxious or even hostile towards the use of online discussion. Their response is likely to represent university teachers and learners beyond the research context, particularly in an era where online teaching and debate are becoming common features of all university study (and not just within distance education; see for example, Landers (2013)). The two comments below reveal typical concerns.

You are trying to focus on the issues, but actually in a conversation kind of way – hard. (*Interview data, Naomi, teacher*)

> It has its down sides [...] because you know it could be a few days before anybody looks at your messages and you look at other people's messages, so you do lose the instant sort of answer and discussion really. (*Interview data, Eve, student*)

Based on the teacher and student interview and questionnaire data (alongside the linguistic analysis), it would seem that there is an important role for professional development which focuses on the pedagogic and linguistic dimensions of online discussion, rather than just the technical. With input from linguistic experts, such professional development could raise university teachers' awareness of the unique way language functions in the online discussion environment and use this as a basis for designing strategies to exploit the teaching-learning potential of the medium.

In particular, in view of the hybrid nature of online language use, somewhere between informal, spontaneous speech and formal, academic writing, teachers and students could develop strategies for taking advantage of what each has to offer – on the one hand, the informal dialogic exchange of opinions and co-construction of knowledge, and on the other, the opportunity for consolidation and abstraction. Furthermore, in applied subjects such as HSC they could exploit the potential of being able to bring together in close proximity more written/nominal and more spoken/clausal interpretations of social phenomena. In the data collected there are some examples of such strategies being put to use.

In the example below, for instance, the teacher first endorses students' prior contributions. She then moves up the ladder of abstraction by bringing together in nominal form other key aspects of the issue (*awareness, evidence, knowledge, choice issues*).

> the points about spiritual searching are very valid I think. So is the point about money [...] *Awareness*, and *evidence* and *knowledge* are of course also crucial to *choice issues* [...]. What things do you think might affect people's ability to find out about CAM therapies?

In the following extract a different teacher uses a summary genre to move up the ladder of abstraction and bring into interaction key concepts.

> To summarise what I see as the 'story so far' drawn from preceding emails [...] I suggest the following:
> (a) Increased information available to 'all'
>   (i) media – TV, radio etc.
>   (ii) internet
> (b) Unpleasant 'side-effects' of orthodox medicine

> (c) Dissatisfaction with the NHS – economic/political strands
>   – MRSA
>   – long waiting lists
>   – impersonal approach (of orthodox medicine)
> (d) more autonomy/independent thought
> (e) orthodox medicine's inability to solve certain conditions.

The potential of online forums to provide a summary or synoptic view of a debate such as illustrated above is immense. This is because all interactions are recorded and thus provide a searchable archive. In other words, the archived nature of written dialogue makes it possible to view the flux and flow synoptically and to impose retrospectively, if not prospectively, a hierarchical structure in which the more general significance of the discussion can be abstracted out and made prominent. However, in the data collected, it should be emphasised that only one summary was identified across the 16 forums.

The illustrations above provide concrete examples of how forums can provide permeable contexts – a kind of 'third space' (cf. Bhabha (1990)) – allowing different worlds to combine. I would argue that such a space provides a transition point for students (such as Nimet and James – see chapter introduction) to learn to navigate between a more familiar everyday world and a less familiar conceptual world. More importantly, both the archival and dialogic aspects of the pedagogic space can be exploited and made an object of students' attention in order to develop metaawareness of the nature of HSC knowledge building. In this way students can be guided to reclassify and conceptually reframe their personal and professional lived experience and so develop new knowledge orientations.

5.6   Conclusion

In conclusion it would seem that online written dialogue provides the material conditions for hybrid forms of language use and meaning making to occur. As such, and particularly in applied fields of study (such as HSC), online discussion forums can facilitate the new orientations to knowledge necessary in tertiary learning environments. As Halliday (1996) predicted nearly two decades ago, the two worlds of spoken and written language, having been pushed about as far apart as they could go (from about 1450 to 1950 in modern Europe), are now moving together again (Halliday 1996:355–356). I have argued that the type of meaning making that occurs when the different grammatical patterns associated with speech and writing come together in a single communicative space construes experience in ways that are complementary. Moreover, as I have illustrated, skilful scaffolding by teachers can exploit these spaces to support students in shifting from more familiar contextualised meaning making to more decontextualised unfamiliar meaning making, an academic shift that remains elusive for some students. By helping to re-orient a student's semantic disposition and thus their orientation to HSC knowledge building, teachers build their capacity to articulate meaning.

SFL analysis and the examples discussed in this chapter have illustrated some of the scaffolding strategies that can be used to develop students' articulacy. Nevertheless, as I have already suggested, how effectively teachers and students do this may depend on their experience and attitudes. I have therefore proposed that professional development could serve to develop metalinguistic awareness in this relatively new pedagogic environment, providing teachers with the means to take full advantage of the hybrid nature of online written dialogue.

Notes

1   The interviews were conducted as one of the research projects outlined in Section 5.2.
2   In the UK for example, by 2035 it is projected that those aged 65 and over will account for 23 per cent of the total population (Office of National Statistics (2012). Trends suggest that people are living a greater proportion of their lives in ill health. Centre for Workforce Intelligence (2013).
3   This data was collected for the Open University, UK.

References

Bernstein, B., (1996). *Pedagogy, Symbolic Control and Identity: Theory, Research, Critique*. London: Taylor and Francis.

Bhabha, H.K. (1990). The Third Space – an interview with Homi Bhabha. In J. Rutherford (Ed.), *Identity: Community, Culture, Difference*, 207–221. London: Lawrence and Wishart.

Brumfit, C.J. (1995). Teacher professionalism and research. In G. Cook and B. Seidlhofer (Eds), *Principle and Practice in Applied Linguistics*, 27–42. Oxford: Oxford University Press.

Centre for Workforce Intelligence (2013). *Big picture challenges for health and social care: implications for workforce planning, education, training and development*, Horizon Scanning, Consultative version, www.cfwi.org.uk (accessed online 14 September 2013).

Christie, F., and Derewianka, B. (2008). *School Discourse: Learning to Write Across the Years of Schooling*. London: Continuum.

Coffin, C. (2006). *Historical Discourse: The language of Time, Cause and Evaluation*. London: Continuum.

Coffin, C., and Donohue, J. (2014). *A Language as Social Semiotic Approach to Teaching and Learning in Higher Education* (Language Learning Monograph Series). Chichester: Wiley-Blackwell.

Coffin, C. (2013). Using systemic functional linguistics to explore digital technologies in educational contexts. *Text & Talk*, 33(4/5), 497–522.

Coffin, C., Hewings, A., and North, S. (2012). Arguing as an academic purpose: The role of asynchronous conferencing in supporting argumentative dialogue in school and university. *Journal of English for Academic Purposes*, 11(1), 38–51. http://dx.doi.org/10.1016/j.jeap.2011.11.005

Council of Deans of Health and Skills for Health (2013). *The higher education contribution to education and training for healthcare support worker roles* (accessed online 4 November, 2015) http://www.councilofdeans.org.uk/2013/07/research-study-the-higher-education-contribution-to-education-and-training-for-healthcare-support-worker-roles/

Crystal, D. (2001[2006]). *Language and the Internet*. Cambridge: Cambridge University Press. http://dx.doi.org/10.1017/CBO9780511487002

Donohue, J., and Coffin, C. (2012). Health and social care professionals in the academy: A systemic functional linguistics perspective. *Journal of Applied Linguistics and Professional Practice*, 9(1), 37–60.

Donohue, J.P., and Erling, E.J. (2012). Investigating the relationship between English for academic purposes and academic attainment. *Journal of English for Academic Purposes*, 11(3), 210–219. http://dx.doi.org/10.1016/j.jeap.2012.04.003

Halliday, M.A.K. (1996). Literacy and Linguistics. In R. Hasan and G. Williams (Eds), *Literacy in Society*, 339–376. London: Longman.

Hasan, R. (2005). *Language, Society and Consciousness*. London: Equinox.

Hasan, R. (2009). *Semantic Variation: Meaning in Society and in Sociolinguistics*. London: Equinox.

Hasan, R. (2011). *Language and Education. The Collected Works of Ruquaiya Hasan* (Vol. 3). London: Equinox.

Herring, S.C. (2012). Grammar and electronic communication. In C. Chapelle (Ed.), *Encyclopedia of Applied Linguistics*, 2338–2346. Hoboken, NJ: Wiley-Blackwell. http://dx.doi.org/10.1002/9781405198431.wbeal0466

Kress, G., Jewitt, C., Ogborn, J., and Tsatsaliset, C. (2001). *Multimodal Teaching and Learning: The Rhetorics of the Science Classroom*. London: Continuum.

Landers, J. (2013). *Negotiating community and knowledge in asynchronous online discussions in higher education*, unpublished Educational Doctorate, the University of Technology Sydney, Australia.

Maton, K. (2011). Theories and Things: The Semantics of Disciplinarity. In F. Christie and K. Maton (Eds), *Disciplinarity: Functional Linguistic and Sociological Perspectives*, 62–84. London: Continuum.

Office of National Statistics (2012). *Population Ageing in the United Kingdom, its Constituent Countries and the European Union*. Accessed online 1 October 2012: http://www.ons.gov.uk/ons/dcp171776_258607.pdf

Parsons, T., and Bales, R. (1956). *Family, Socialization and Interaction Process*. London: Routledge and Kegan Paul.

Schleppegrell, M.J. (2004). *The Language of Schooling: A Functional Linguistics Perspective*. London, New York: Routledge.

Suzuki, S. (2011). Provisioning mass by females of the maritime earwig, Anisolabis maritima, is not adjusted based on the number of young, *Journal of Insect Science*, accessed online 1 October 2012 http://www.ncbi.nlm.nih.gov/pubmed/22239204. http://dx.doi.org/10.1673/031.011.16001

About the author

Caroline Coffin is Professor in English Language and Applied Linguistics at the Open University, UK. Since the early 1990s she has been interested in exploring language use from a social semiotic perspective. In particular she has used the tools of SFL to investigate digitally mediated language use, argumentation and disciplinary knowledge making. Published books include *A language as social semiotic approach to teaching and learning in higher education* (Wiley-Blackwell, 2014, with Donohue), *Exploring Grammar: From formal to functional* (Routledge, 2009, with Donohue and North) and *Historical Discourse:The language of time, cause and evaluation* (Continuum, 2006).

6

Teaching through English: Maximal Input in Meaning Making

John Polias and Gail Forey

Lexis Education and Hong Kong Polytechnic University

6.1   Introduction

In this chapter, we focus on language education and pedagogy, and propose a pedagogic model in which the teacher uses a tremendous variation of hybrid modes. In a review of the pedagogy used, we discuss the value of Systemic Functional Linguistics (SFL) and in teaching through English in different key learning areas (KLA) in Hong Kong. In these KLA, the material and the semiotic are construed by the teacher through the teacher maximising the access points for the learner by using multisemiotic resources related to the subject matter and the goals of learning. The chapter focuses on a wide range of subject areas taught in English, which reflects the diversity of the learning that takes place in secondary schools in Hong Kong. The data presented in this chapter have been collected from the Physical Education KLA, Information Technology and Music; data from different subject areas will be the topic of discussion of additional papers. The data show that different KLA demand different approaches to the construction of knowledge. In Hong Kong, teaching through English, which is referred to in Europe as Content Language Integrated Learning (CLIL, see Dalton-Puffer 2011), is a key issue as English is not the mother tongue for the majority of the teachers and learners.

Within the context of teaching through English and with a focus on pedagogy and the hybrid resources used to construct knowledge through language across the curriculum, we outline the value of a 'teaching and learning cycle' (TLC). The TLC was first developed during the 1980s as a curriculum cycle under the umbrella of the Metropolitan East Disadvantaged School's Programme (Callaghan and Rothery 1988, Rothery 1996, Christie and Martin 1997, Martin 1999) and combines SFL, a neo-Vygotskyan

(1978) model of psycholinguistics and Bernstein's (1971) insights into society and education. It has undergone various iterations since the 1980s; the version in this article has extended that developed by Polias (2010a,b) and Custance, Dare and Polias (2011). We outline the pedagogic model, and demonstrate the application of this model, using Hong Kong data. In this chapter, we propose a more complex TLC, where permeability, hybridity and reiteration are common features. This permeability and hybridity is realised by the teacher providing multiple ways of making meaning regardless of the KLA in order to scaffold (Wood *et al.* 1976, Hammond 2001) the development of knowledge. We model how the TLC has been adopted by teachers in Hong Kong who draw from a wide range of registerial typologies (see Matthiessen and Teruya this volume). These typologies include a range of genres across the local secondary school curriculum (for details related to educational genres, see Martin and Rose 2008, Knapp and Watkins 2005). The seminal work identifying educational genres by Martin (1999), Rothery (1996), and Christie and Derewianka (2008) among others has provided valuable insights for applied linguistics and pedagogic development. We adopt the concept of genre as defined by Martin (1985) as a staged, goal-oriented social process and incorporate later work on educational genres in the professional development (PD) workshops. We view Matthiessen's registerial typologies as complementary to the work on educational genres. These typologies of 'socio-semiotic processes' have the contextual variable of field as the entry point, where the social semiotics provides a framework affording the identification of activities that are happening within a given context. Matthiessen (see Matthiessen, Teruya and Lam 2010) outlines eight types of socio-semiotic processes – expounding, reporting, recreating, sharing, doing, enabling, recommending, and exploring. In terms of the genres, there are a varied range of key educational genres that have been presented in recent publications; see, for example, Coffin, Donohue and North (2008), Martin and Rose (2008), Knapp and Watkins (2005), Macken-Horarik (2002). Each of these outlines a slightly different range of genres, all feasible and all with pedagogic value. Matthiessen's socio-semiotic process typologies allow us to group genres under eight macro sociosemiotic-activities.

In this chapter, we do not intend to present a theoretical comparison between Matthiessen's socio-semiotic processes and Martin's genres. Rather, our focus is to discuss how, in a series of workshops, we provide opportunities for in-service teachers to understand patterns of socio-semiotic meaning and the range of genres used in specific key learning areas. We are concerned with raising awareness in teachers for the need to understand how matter and meaning are construed through language and other semiotic resources within their specific discipline.

Developing an understanding of matter and meaning for secondary school learners in a wide range of subjects across the curriculum involves a range of genres and activities, written and spoken word, images, movement, gesture, sound, colour and other semiotic resources in order to provide the maximum exposure needed to scaffold the learner to construe both matter and meaning. In different KLA's, the teacher shunts between matter (congruent) and meaning (abstraction), and so Halliday's (2005) discussion of 'meaning' (in an extended sense: semiotic and social) and 'matter' (biological and physical) is useful in helping us understand what is happening in the classroom. In subjects such as Physical Education (PE), the teacher uses congruent language patterns accompanying action. The action and language patterns will naturally depend on the age and ability of the learner. In other subjects, such as in science, the teacher uses abstract meaning to construe knowledge. To use PE and Science as examples, the teacher in a gymnastics lesson may physically support and manipulate a student to help them do certain movements, such as a forward roll. The semiotics involves the physical movement of the body through certain key poses, and the meaning is congruent. The learner physically experiences the movement, the talk of the teacher accompanies the action as the teacher supports this kinesthetic experience, and the social and semiotic are symbiotically realised. However, in a Physics lesson, the learner may develop knowledge about the performance of a forward roll in abstract ways, through a construal of the forces and vectors involved. The language used in both subject areas will have permeable resources of abstract and congruent meaning for the learner, with a dependency on abstract meanings through linguistic and symbolic (mathematical) resources in the Physics class and congruent linguistic and embodied meanings in the PE class. In either subject area, the language and action together develop the knowledge of the subject.

In our work with teachers of PE, Information Technology (IT) and Arts in Hong Kong teaching their subject in English, our focus is on pedagogy. A pedagogic model, as outlined in Figures 6.1, 6.2 and 6.3, is introduced in the workshops and the teachers are asked to apply this model in their classrooms. An integral feature of the workshops is having the teachers of the same subject area working together to plan a lesson, 10 minutes of which they will micro-teach to the other teachers attending the PD workshop. Our discussion here focuses on how the teachers of subjects in which actions play a crucial role scaffold students in their learning. For example, we consider how the physical and aesthetic in relation to the matter of movement in a PE lesson are accompanied by language in order to make

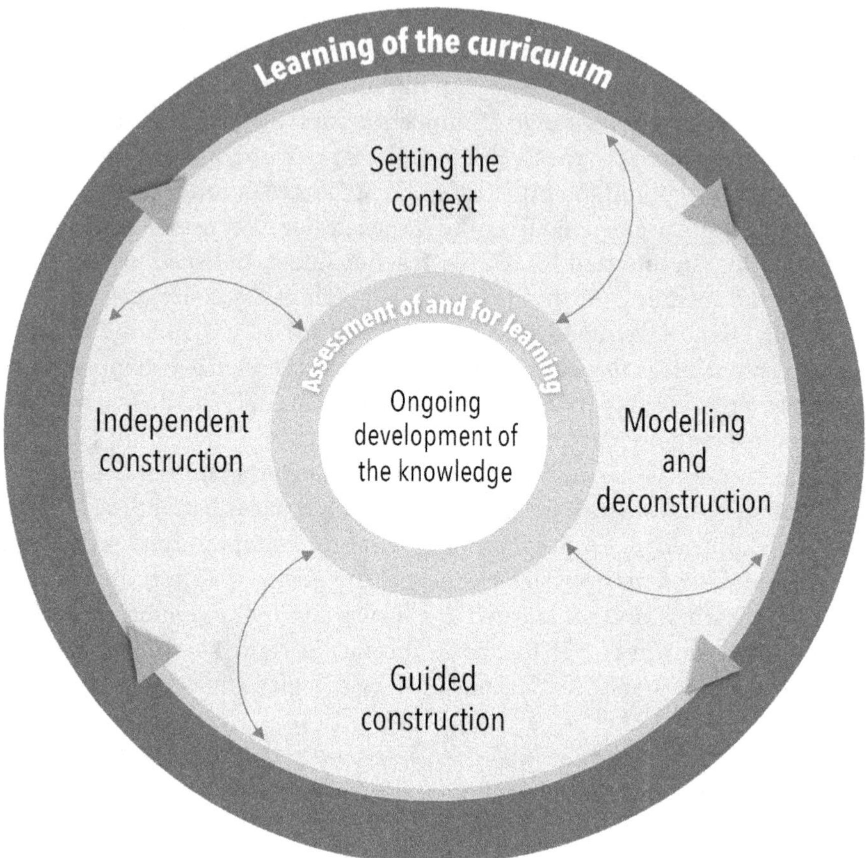

Figure 6.1: A Teaching and Learning Cycle (adapted from Callaghan and Rothery [1988] and Custance, Dare and Polias [2011])

meaning. Following the TLC, we propose that the teacher and the learner are involved in setting the context, the teacher takes on the responsibility of modelling and deconstructing the meanings for the students and through a process of gradual handing over to the student though Guided Construction, the student, when ready, is then given the opportunity to independently construct both matter and meaning. This process is outlined in Figure 6.1. The meaning at a macro-level is controlled by the curriculum, while at the heart of all activities in the teaching is the scaffolding of the student to an ongoing development of knowledge.

The teacher, throughout the lesson, the unit of work and the subject as a whole, is continually engaging in this cyclical teaching and learning. Figure 6.2 shows how this might look over several lessons. As the class moves through the larger TLC, there are opportunities to engage in smaller cycles of teaching and learning. These mini-cycles ought to be planned but some can also be viewed as contingent cycles, taken up when the immediate situation demands it. The time needed for the mini-cycles can vary greatly, depending on what is determined as necessary in any situation. However, it would typically transpire that the more planned the TLC is, the more likely that the mini-cycles are planned, too.

The mini-cycles give the opportunity for greater, ongoing student engagement in the lesson and ensure that there is both macro-scaffolding (Hammond and Gibbons 2005) and micro- or contingent scaffolding (Michell and Sharpe 2005). This is exemplified in Figure 6.4, where we see in the Modelling and Deconstruction stage of the TLC in a PE class that the teacher interacts with the students at an early stage of their learning in such a way that the apparently small incremental steps provide the contingent micro-scaffold that the teacher deems necessary.

The tools for making the meanings that construct the discipline knowledge and the manner in which those resources are applied are crucial to the success of the scaffolding affordance inherent in the TLC model. Using Deacon's (2012) claim that language processing involves complex synergies

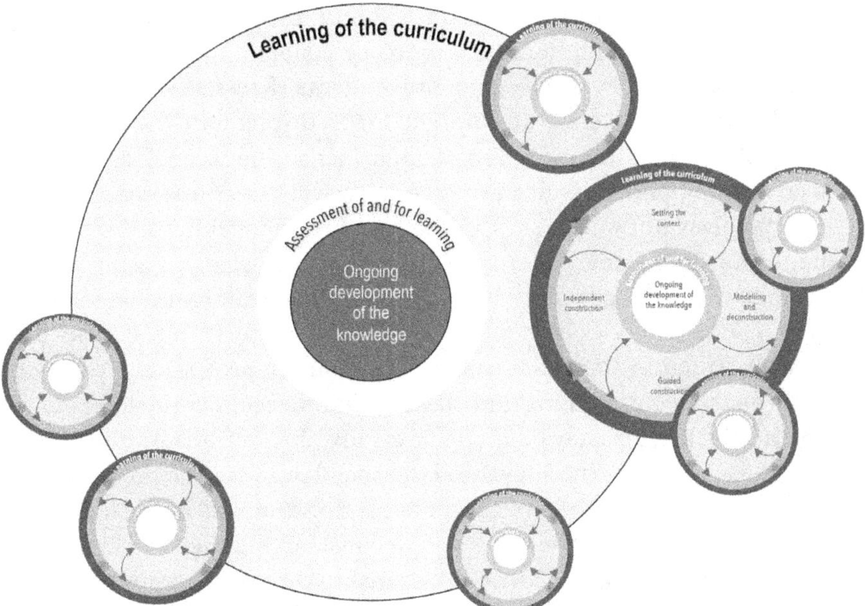

Figure 6.2: Mini-cycles within a larger Teaching and Learning Cycle (adapted from Custance, Dare and Polias [2011])

between multiple brain systems and Hebbian theory (Hebb 1949, Doidge 2007), which suggests that simultaneous activation of brain cells leads to significant increases in synaptic strength between those cells, we can consider that students learn more effectively (in other words, the system of the neural networks are stronger) if they are simultaneously given multiple ways of accessing meaning. Multiple ways of making meaning involve the teacher providing maximal opportunities for input but also the students engaging with those meaning-making resources in different ways. In any lesson, this may involve, for example, verbal texts which are comprised of various combinations of spoken and written language; visual images of varying degrees of animation and dimensionality; manipulation of and variation of artefacts; and group work and discussion in which the size and make-up of the groups and the purpose of the group work can vary markedly. However, using multiple meaning-making resources may not necessarily result in effective and efficient learning if the teaching is not informed by them. What is impressed on the teachers in the PD workshop is that the teacher needs to consider the ways the various meaning-making resources are used and ensure they resonate with the patterns of knowledge to be learned in order to ensure a pedagogical resonance (Polias 2010a,b). The 'what' that is intended to be taught and learned resonates or works constructively with 'how' the teaching is done. In this way, the challenge of the task need not be reduced. The task should maintain a high challenge (Mariani 1997); achieving success is more a consideration of the manner of the support afforded by the teacher and students (Kress *et al.* 2001).

In addition, the teacher, at different times throughout the lesson, has the capability to shift, in a Bernsteinian sense, between stronger and weaker framing and classification (see Martin 1999). Such multiple patterning involves not only a shift in the framing and classification but also in the responsibility shared for the construal of knowledge. As outlined in Figure 6.3, the TLC generally involves the teacher and student typically sharing responsibility during the setting of the context. In the Modelling and Deconstruction stage, the teacher takes on the professional responsibility through strong framing and classification to scaffold the learners. At this point, the teacher may be modelling a text, by focusing on the generic structure, i.e., the goal, the stages and the social purpose of a text. This may involve breaking down the key components, for example, of the long jump in an athletics class, or modelling and deconstructing the key elements of perspectives in an art lesson, or the relationship between the number of pixels and the quality of an image in an IT class. Within Guided Construction, the teacher is shifting responsibility to the students, scaffolding learning until the teacher is confident that success can be achieved independently.

The timing of handing the responsibility over to the student, so the student is independently constructing the meanings, may vary from one learner to another. At this point, the teacher moves into the role of observing and, if necessary, making a professional decision to intervene and offer deeper or critical support. Ideally, the need to provide guidance to the learner in a structured manner, similar to the previous stages in the TLC, is no longer necessary because the whole process has provided the macro-scaffold for success. If there is a need for this kind of support, then one would question whether the previous activities have prepared the student for the expected degree of success when working independently.

As Figures 6.2 and 6.3 illustrate, we suggest that the TLC is a repeated pattern that occurs through the lesson and unit of work. The teacher offers maximal input and develops a 'stronger brain' through activities that are patterned, repeated and carried out with moderate challenge. Where the challenge and support equate to the zone of proximal development (Vygotsky 1978; Gibbons 2002, 2006, 2008; Hammond 2001), the learner is successfully scaffolded into the appropriate development of knowledge.

During the PD workshops, the complex TLC is introduced, as is the notion of patterned language, patterned visuals, and patterned actions, which are repeated and recycled within time periods that may vary from very short time frames to macro time scales, such as a unit of work. Teachers are introduced to the importance of language and they are asked

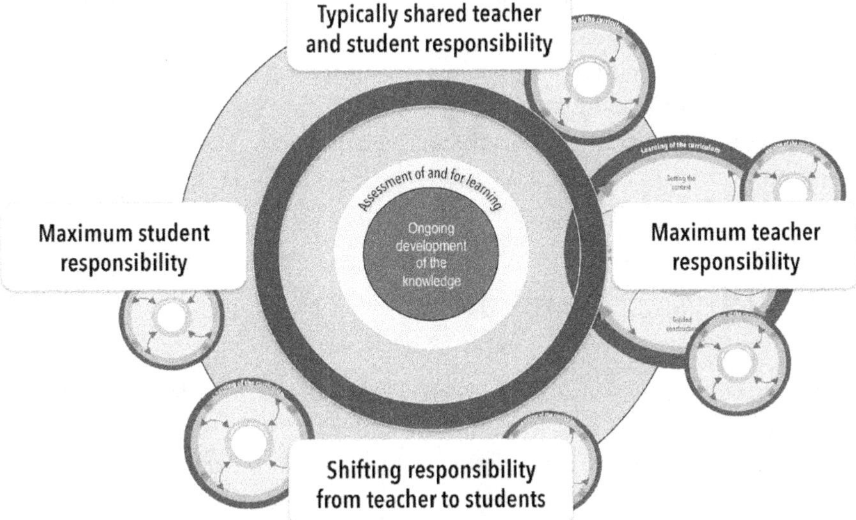

Figure 6.3: Scaffolding the responsibility of teaching and learning

to deconstruct the meaning-making potential of language and, to some extent, other semiotic systems within their own KLA. Applying this knowledge to their teaching, the teachers work through the TLC by identifying what it is the class will set out to learn and the optimal sequence of that learning. They continue through the cycle by presenting and deconstructing for the students model examples of that knowledge. However, it is not sufficient to simply provide good models; it is necessary to deconstruct for the students the patterns in that knowledge and the decision-making processes a 'knower' takes so that these typically invisible and silent processes are made explicit to the students. As a result, the teacher would need to be explicit about what, how and why they are doing or thinking what it is they are thinking and doing. As the teacher provides the model text verbally and visually (both animated and static), the students are included more actively and the teachers shift in their control from the foreground to the middle ground and, in the final Independent Construction stage, to the background. In this process, the teacher gradually moves further and further away from being responsible for the construction of knowledge in the class and we can see this as transferring responsibility through Guided Construction within their KLA. By the time the teachers and students have reached the point of independent construction, the transfer is complete for that TLC.

During the Guided Construction stage of the workshops, teachers from the same KLA are given the opportunity to co-plan material that they could incorporate into their subject area curriculum. The teachers are asked to zoom out to the level of a unit of work and then zoom in to planning a 10-minute micro-teaching session, where they focus on Setting the Context, Modelling and Deconstructing, or Guided Construction. The co-planning provides the teachers with the opportunity to apply in a supportive context what they have been introduced to in the previous workshops.

6.2   Physical Education

To begin our discussion of the role of the TLC as a pedagogic resource across the curriculum and teaching through English in an EFL context, we will use illustrations from PE. Figure 6.4 is an example from two PE teachers whose objective was for their learners to understand and be able to perform the standard long jump using the sail technique. The two teachers developed the plan to introduce the long jump in their lesson. Their lesson

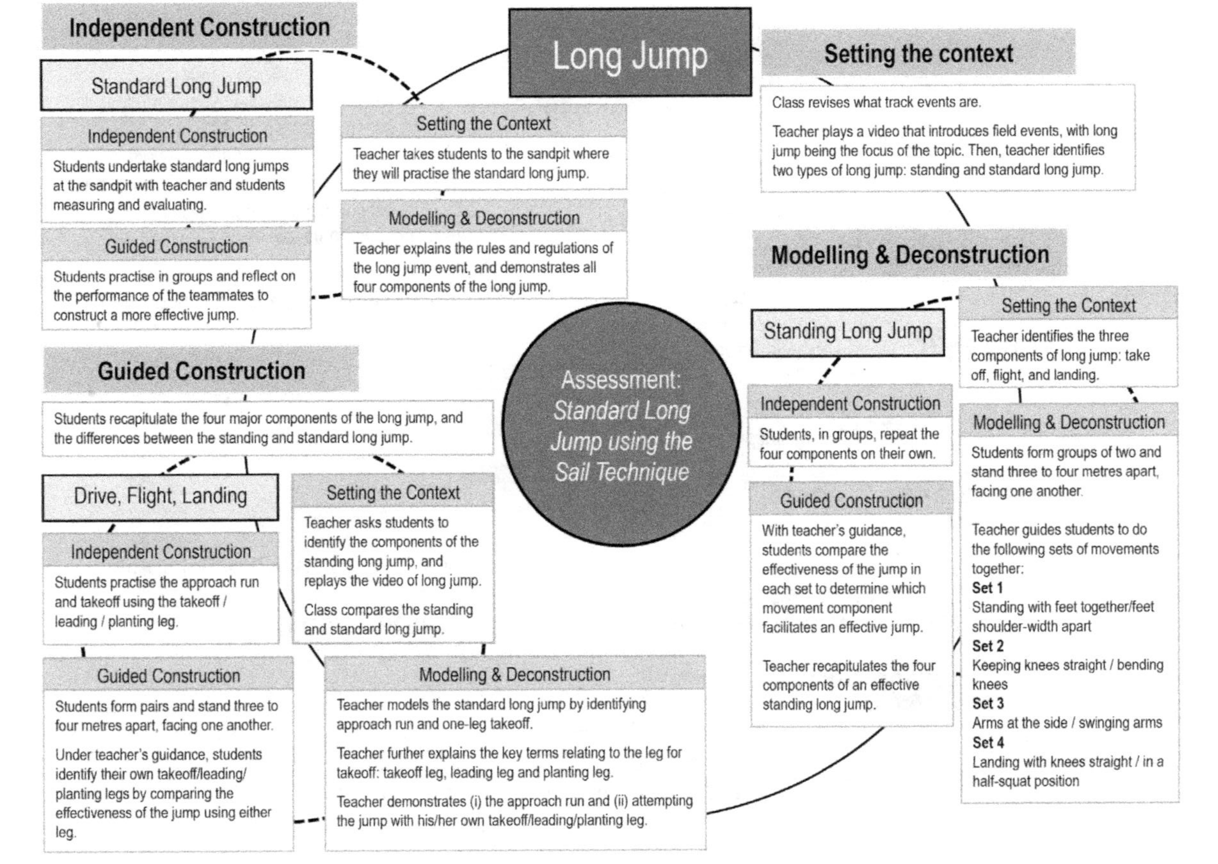

Figure 6.4: Example of planning the TLC in a long jump lesson

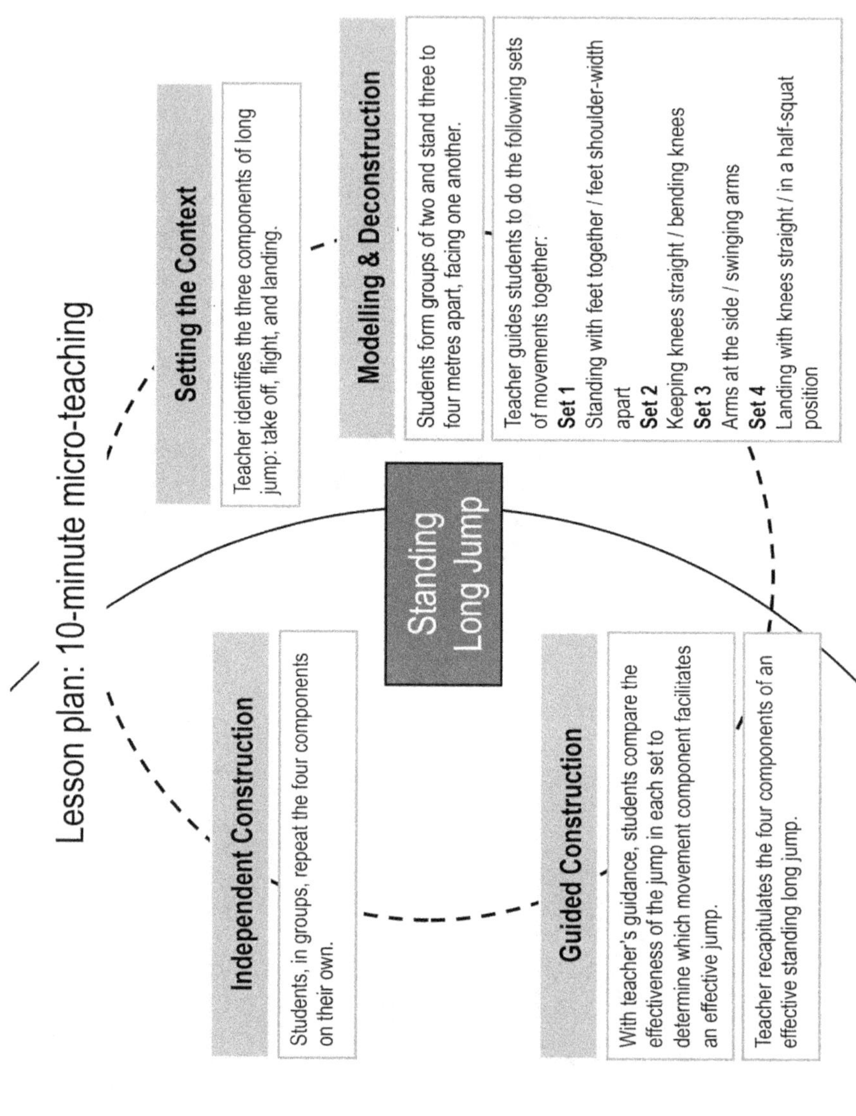

Figure 6.5: Example of a 10-minute phase, itself acting as the Modelling and Deconstruction stage of a TLC of a long jump lesson

plan focuses on the standing and standard long jump, which is part of a larger unit of work on jumping events within athletics.

Figure 6.5 focuses on a particular phase within the TLC, and we are able to see that an approximately10-minute phase in a lesson represents a complete mini-cycle within the broader TLC. The two PE teachers took the class (their PE, IT and Art peers) through this 10-minute cycle in the PD workshop as a micro-teaching session.

As shown in Figure 6.5, the PE teachers can easily adapt the TLC as a pedagogic model in their micro-teaching. The aim of the deconstruction stage here is to allow the students to both understand the language and the physical movement of jumping and to compare and contrast which movements are the most effective to incorporate into a standing long jump. We focus now on how the teacher combines the verbal explanation and the kinesthetic experience outlined in Step 1, Figure 6.5; that is, performing a standing jump with feet together and then with feet apart.

(1) T   okay so err so first of all we're going to do the standing long jump, standing long jump. OK so. First of all let's try to jump with both legs put it together and just simply jump forward […] just feel it first put your legs together, okay, go

     Ss {students jump forward with both legs together]

     T   okay and then the second stage, try this time not put your legs together, but try to open your legs separate your legs like the shoulder width okay like shoulder width and then jump forward {Teacher demonstrates} to feel it which one you think is better […]

     T   okay so so which one do you think you feel more comfortable with put your legs together or put your legs apart?

     Ss {all students call out at the same time} together, together, apart, apart, the same, try again

     Ss {chatter}

     T   together {the class jump with their legs together, they move back to their starting place} apart {the class jumps with their feet apart}, the same so actually, you can see the distance from my observation I think, if you put your legs apart like shoulder width I think you can jump better, okay. So this is the first key point Guys remember that you have to put your legs apart, like shoulder width okay

At this point in the lesson, we can see the modelling and deconstructing stage, where the teacher is breaking down the elements involved in performing a standard long jump compared with a standing long jump. The teacher is using an enquiry model to allow the students to experience the action, as well as to test the more efficient kinesthetic movement of whether to jump with their feet together or apart. The teacher introduces the necessary key language features: standing long jump, shoulder width apart, legs together. The students are supported strongly during this process to understand the specialised terms used since the language is accompanied by concrete action. The teacher is continually reminding the students to build up some muscle memory, *just feel it,* enabling the students to relate the movement to the command of jumping forward. The students test the prediction of which one will be more effective, legs apart or legs together. If the students are undecided or a little confused, the teacher steps in to take control and scaffold the students' learning. She states *from my observation, I think, if you put your legs apart, like shoulder width, I think you can jump better, okay.* As pointed out by Christie (2005), the teacher needs to assess when to guide and when to consolidate learning so that misconceptions can be dealt with at an early stage. The teacher signals the importance of this key concept by making an explicit reference, *so this is the first key point.* The teacher, thus, deconstructs the key components of performing a standing long jump and provides all learners with the opportunity for success.

In the remainder of this chapter, we use two examples from IT and Music to illustrate further our focus on the role of the TLC as a pedagogic resource.

6.3   Information Technology

As for the PE lesson, we will use an example of micro-teaching in IT to illustrate what might happen in the Modelling and Deconstruction stage versus the Guided Construction stage. The topic of the lesson is on how to calculate the capacity or the file size of an image. This example of micro-teaching was repeated by the teacher, after feedback was provided, and the transcript comes from the second attempt. The feedback from the class of teachers after the first attempt suggested that the process for calculating the file capacity during the Modelling and Deconstruction needed to be written down alongside the calculations so that the students could follow what the teacher was saying and showing by having a static visual representation of the process (see Figure 6.6). The difficulty for students when a process is simply spoken and not written down by the teacher is that it cannot be recalled easily by the students when it comes to them doing the calculation. Here is the transcript from the second attempt for both the Modelling and Deconstruction stage and Guided Construction stage.

Figure 6.6: Teacher writes the process for calculating file size alongside the calculations so the visual representation of the steps can serve as a scaffold for the students.

(2a) T I will try another approach to teach the same topic to see if you have a better understanding of what capacity is. Okay students, today I'm going to teach you about capacity. Capacity is the file size of an image. We can easily calculate the file size of an image if we know the size of one pixel. So what we're going to do is, if you have the size of one pixel, you need to multiply the size of one pixel by the total number of pixels of the image and what you will have is the total size of the image. That is the basic idea of capacity. Is that okay? I'm going to show you an example of how to do the calculation.

S Can I ask you a question? When you talk about the size of the pixel, you're not talking about area.

T No, I'm not talking about area because a picture uses many dots composed together.

S So when you say size of a pixel what do you mean by size?

T The file size of a pixel [...] How big it is [...] how much space that is used to store the pixels.

(2b) T Okay, let's see the example.
A photo has the resolution of 2048 multiplied by 1536 with a colour depth of 24 bits. What is the file size of this photo?

To do this, I have some steps for you to follow and written down on the right-hand side screen.

First of all, you need to write down the formula to calculate the capacity. What is this (formula)? It is 'Capacity equals resolution multiplied by colour depth'.

So what we have to do next is find information from the question.

From the equation, what information do we need? We need to find the data. The first one is the resolution; that is, 2048 multiplied by 1536.

And the other data we need is the colour depth, which is 24 bits. Okay?

The third thing we need to do is check whether the unit of colour depth is correct or not. It is very important as I said a moment ago. We can calculate the size of files very easily if we can have the size of one pixel, so we have to check carefully to see whether the question has the right units of the colour depth. So I can give you a hint – the unit should be bits, so we check it in the question [...] It is in bits, so everything is ready so we can use it for the final (calculation).

Next we are going to substitute those values directly into the formula. And we will have the equation like this. And finally we get the answer.

There are three things when tackling this question that you have to do...

You have to do the substitutions in the equation so that I know that you can do it.

Secondly, you calculate your answer and don't forget to write the unit. It is very important. Okay?

(2c) T   We will do another example and I want you to do it with me. Let's see this example. 'A photo has the resolution of 800 multiplied by 600 with a colour depth of 8 bits. What is the file size of this photo?' Okay, so the first thing is to write down the formula. Can anyone tell me what the formula is?

Ss   Capacity equals resolution times colour depth.

T   Okay. Secondly, we have to find the information from the question. So can any of you do me a favour? Mary?

S   (writes on the board)

T   Okay, thank you. Anything you want to add?

Ss   Yes, I want to add the equals sign.

T   Okay. Can we calculate the answer right now?

Ss   No.

T   No. What should I add?

Ss   Colour depth.

T Colour depth. How many bits?

Ss 8.

T 8.

S So am I allowed to change the units of the colour depth?

T If you change the units it will change the final result.

S That's right. So what do we have to think about? What was the third point you made in your previous slide? The third point was…

T Oh yes you have to check the units of the colour depth. Okay. Can you tell me whether we have the correct unit now?

Ss Yes.

T Yes, that's fine. So I'll put the small letter 'b' there. So, what should I do next?

Ss Calculate.

T I'll use the calculator.

From the above transcript, we can see how the teacher moves from one phase to the next, how the teacher ensures that all the students have multiple access to learning resources. In Example 2(a), the teacher outlines that he has restructured this lesson, *I will try another approach to teach the same topic to see if you have a better understanding of what capacity is.* As noted previously, the teacher gave the same lesson before, but the feedback from the students (his colleagues) was that they were still not able to fully comprehend how to calculate the size of an image. The results were quite different this time, as the whole class was able to follow the ideas presented, and could successfully apply the calculations independently. In Example 2, we have divided the transcript into the organisation as planned by the teacher, where he sets the context of the lesson (Example 2a), models and deconstructs the knowledge through strong scaffolding (Example 2b), and then constructs with the students the calculation of the picture size with the students (Example 2c). The three sections of the lesson are clearly scaffolded for the student. The teacher provides explicit signals of the shift from one stage to the next, e.g. *Okay students, today I'm going to teach you about capacity. Capacity is the file size of an image (2a); Okay, let's see the example (2b);* and *we will do another example and I want you to do it with me (2c).*

Throughout this part of the lesson, the students are actively involved and, in the Guided Construction, the teacher invites a student to the front of the class to write the calculation on the board. He states, *so can any of you do me a favour? Mary?* and the student comes to the front and writes on the board. At this point, the teacher is in control but jointly developing and assessing the success of the students' knowledge and still ensuring that the knowledge being developed is accurate. Rather than correcting the calculation, the teacher thanks the student saying, *okay, thank you,* and allows the student to revise their calculation by raising the question, *anything you want to add?* However, the latter question and other similar questions, such as 'are you sure?' or 'is she right?', rather than set up a dialogue, can create insecurity in the students, especially if the answer given is correct. In these situations, the student assumes, because the teacher is questioning their answer, that they are wrong. If the answer given is incorrect, the teacher knows the answer is incorrect and where the problem lies. Dialogic enquiry guided by the teacher involving the student and the rest of the class to enquire and review the calculation presented is to be encouraged. Requesting that the student review the calculation on the board is a good shift away from simply chalk-and-talk. However, it also affords instances where the student remains baffled and can be humiliated. Therefore, it may be more helpful if the teacher could be more explicit and, in this way, be more supportive. The teacher could identify for the student exactly where the problem is so that the student is not guessing what the teacher is getting at. Such contingent scaffolding, where the student has the opportunity to self-correct the exact point of the error, will result in a greater feeling of achievement by the learner.

An important point to note is that during the Modelling and Deconstruction stage of the lesson, the teacher presents the students with the tools for doing the calculation by themselves and together with him. For example, he states initially, *First of all, you need to write down the formula to calculate the capacity. What is this (formula)? It is 'Capacity equals resolution times colour depth'.* As the process unfolds, he uses rhetorical devices to focus the students' attention on the salient points. For example, he uses *What is this (formula)?* to present to the students the formula, which they write down in their books. Then, later, during the Guided Construction stage, when he asks the students for the formula, *Can anyone tell me what the formula is?* this is not a question that can be answered only by one or two students but by all the students, *Capacity equals resolution times colour depth.* This is visible in Figure 6.6, where the instruction on the right side is 'Write down the formula' and then on the left side, where the calculations are written, 'Capacity = resolution × color depth'. As noted above, having the steps in the calculation consistently available acts as a scaffold for the students' learning throughout the activity. It is available on the whiteboard regardless of whether the student turns a page in their book. In addition, if the teacher finds that students are struggling, the teacher can use this semiotic resource as a reference point to support the students' knowledge development. The teacher builds the field and provides the context for what is going to follow, provides a clear example, works through the example and finally hands over to the students for them to consolidate their knowledge through practice with the teacher. With each example they practice on, the teacher hands over more and more responsibility to the students.

6.4   Music

In a completely different subject, we can see how the music teacher is setting the context, and modelling and deconstructing the target knowledge. This time, the teacher draws on a wider range of semiotic resources, combining language (spoken and written), visuals (static and animated, including photos, videos and diagrams) and sound (music and sound effects), to teach the students about an African drum, the djembe, and how to play this instrument. As we can see from Figure 6.7 and from Example 3a, the teacher is introducing, probably for the first time for many students,

Figure 6.7: Slide 1 used in the music lesson, showing the drum and its name

details about the djembe and a well-known African exponent of this drum, Mamady Keïta. These two key pieces of information are represented both verbally, through the introduction of the words, and visually, through the first two slides in the lesson. In this micro-teaching, the teacher closely interacts with the PowerPoint slides to scaffold the students' learning (in the actual classroom, the teacher uses a real djembe), both in focusing on the lexical meanings being introduced and in helping the students pronounce unfamiliar words. She also uses body language to cover the 'D' in djembe to scaffold the correct pronunciation.

> (3a) T   {shows Slide 1 (Fig. 6.7)} Today we're going to teach African drum and the name is Djembe…what you need to do is {the teacher puts her hand over 'D' on Slide 1} think about it…so
> SS Djembe
> T   …{d}jembe. And it actually comes from the saying {points to "Anke djé" on Slide 2} something like that. It means everyone gathers together in peace. OK? One of the famous African drummers is Mamady Keïta and he came to Hong Kong a few years ago and {Slide 3 shows a photo of her with Mamady Keïta}
> SS {positive reaction from the students}
> S   Which one is Mamady?
> SS {general laughter}
> [...]

The lesson continues for a few more minutes before the teacher moves in to the Modelling and Deconstruction stage, which is quite short and is promptly followed, almost seamlessly, by the Guided Construction stage. The aim of the micro-lesson is for the students to understand what this African drum looks like and how to play the basic sounds, culminating with all of the students in the class playing a well-known song. The introduction provides all the class with the necessary knowledge. During Guided Construction, the students also have a handout, a clock-face on a sheet of A4, which is exactly the same as the PowerPoint, Slide 5.

> (3b) [...]
> T   So, may I know the name of this instrument?
> SS Djembe
> T   Yes, djembe. And anyone of you know how to play djembe?
> SS No.
> T   No. Actually, if you know how to…anyone of you know how to play basketball? If you know how to play basketball, you know how to play the drum.

SS {general laughter of disbelief}
T   {shows Slide 4 (Fig.6.8)} So the basic sound produced by the instrument, there are three: first one is the bass, and the second one is open and third one is slap.

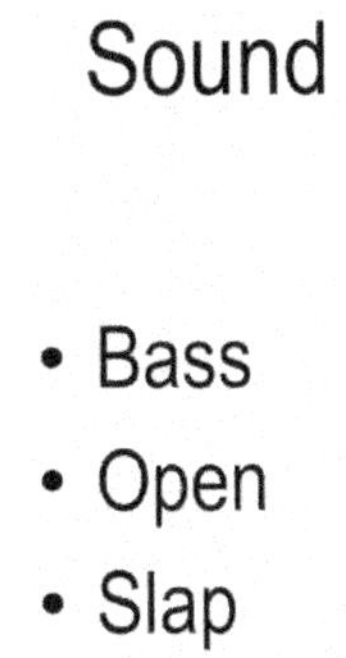

Sound

- Bass
- Open
- Slap

Figure 6.8: Slide 4 used in the music lesson, showing the three major sounds produced

(3c) T   So before we learn how to play [...] actually you've got this clock with you, right? So the first one is the bass. Bass is, we need to use our hand {holds up left hand} [...] Which part of our hand? The palm, OK? We need the palm and the contact point will be from the centre {places hand over the clock image on Slide 5 (Fig. 6.9)} half-way to the 12 so it's around here {starts patting the place on the clock face}.
SS {mimic what the teacher is doing}
T   OK, so, OK, thank you. As you already learned the tempo yourself, which is adagio, which means very slow, I will give you the tempo first, so 4-3-2-1 [...] use your left hand so 1-2-3-4 [...] left hand, OK.
SS {hit the beat on their clock faces and continue}

In comparison with the PE lesson, in which the student's body is the tool to be manipulated in achieving the objective of the lesson, a long jump, and in contrast to the IT lesson, in which the actions are more to do with carrying out calculations, this music lesson is concerned with acting on an instrument to achieve the goal of the lesson. In this lesson and in all music lessons, the teacher cannot rely on language to do a lot of the work. That is why, for example, there is musical notation. In this lesson, we find a clear example of the limitations of language. To identify on a circular drum surface the points where it should be struck, the teacher uses a clock because it is easier to say the hour marks and, in that way, visualise the places to strike the drum. This parallels what pilots, for example, do in using the clock to identify the location of other planes. Making use of a range of

Clock

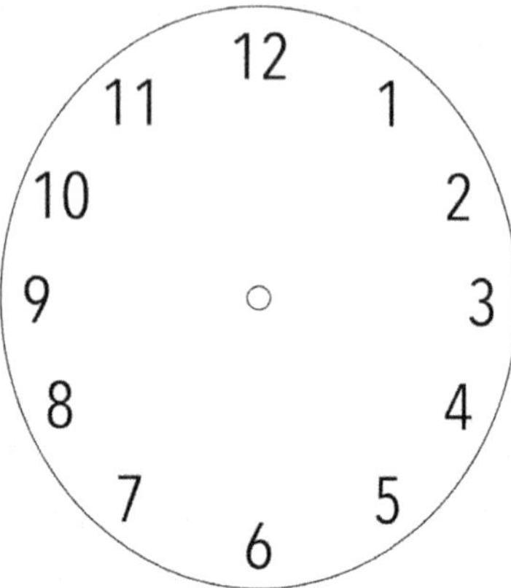

Figure 6.9: Slide 5 used in the music lesson, showing the clock face used to represent the drum

semiotic resources – the face of a clock, hand movements, the isolation of parts of the hand, and the verbal scaffold of the teacher – allows the students to be guided by the teacher in jointly constructing the playing of the djembe and for everyone in the class to be participating confidently and achieving success. The teacher's choices of semiotic resources at the appropriate time and manner affords the teacher and students the potential to have a successful lesson because the pedagogy resonates with the knowledge to be taught in the lesson.

6.5   Conclusion

Within the overview of the pedagogy provided in the present chapter, we have shown that the TLC is a model that allows for the flexible and repeated patterning of meaning and matter in KLA across the curriculum. We have demonstrated the adaptability and hybridity of the TLC in a range of subject areas We have also demonstrated how the teacher macro-scaffolds students through planning large cycles and mini-cycles of modelling and deconstructing of the learning, Guided Construction and, finally, handing over of the learning to the student in the independent construction. Importantly, the teachers of PE, IT and music micro-scaffold their students through both the repeated patterning of the meanings and in the use of multiple ways of making meaning. Teachers in these subject areas draw, to a greater or lesser extent, on a variety of semiotic resources: through spoken and written language, and through static and animated visuals, including the various parts of students' and teachers' bodies. In PE and music lessons, especially, the role of language accompanying action is integral to successful learning. However, as we have seen, even in the IT lesson the teacher draws from a range of maximal input to scaffold the students' learning. The TLC has proven itself to be adaptable, resourceful and an exemplary pedagogic tool for teachers to use to support learning in the classroom, whether the teaching is happening in L1 or L2 contexts.

References

Bernstein, B. (1971). *Class, Codes and Control, Volume 1: Theoretical Studies Towards a Sociology of Language.* London: Routledge and Kegan Paul. http://dx.doi.org/10.4324/9780203014035

Callaghan, M., and Rothery, J. (1988). *Teaching Factual Writing: A Genre-Based Approach.* Sydney: Metropolitan East Disadvantaged Schools Program.

Christie, F. (2005). *Classroom Discourse Analysis: A Functional Perspective.* London: Continuum.

Christie, F. and Martin, J.R. (Eds) (1997). *Genre in Institutions: Social Processes in the Workplace and School.* New York: Continuum.

Christie, F., and Derewianka, B. (2008). *School Discourse: Learning to Write across the Years of Schooling.* London: Continuum.

Coffin, C., Donohue, J., and North, S. (2009). *Exploring English Grammar: From Formal to Functional.* London: Routledge.

Custance, B., Dare, B., and Polias, J. (2011). *How Language Works: Success in Literacy and Learning.* Adelaide: Department of Education and Child Development (DECD) Publishing.

Dalton-Puffer, C. (2011). Content-and-Language Integrated learning: From practice to principles? *Annual Review of Applied Linguistics,* 31, 182–204. http://dx.doi.org/10.1017/S0267190511000092

Deacon, T. (2007). *Language and complexity: Evolution inside out. Plenary Paper,* 37th International Systemic Functional Congress, Vancouver.

Deacon, T. (2012). Beyond the symbolic species. In T. Schilhab, F. Stjernfelt, and T. Deacon (Eds), *Symbolic Species Evolved.* 81–96. New York: Springer. http://dx.doi.org/10.1007/978-94-007-2336-8_2

Doidge, N. (2007). *The Brain that Changes Itself: Stories of Personal Triumph from the Frontiers of Brain Science*. New York: Penguin Books.

Education Bureau (2009). *Fine-tuning the Medium of Instruction (MOI) – Frequently Asked Questions*. Retrieved 13 February 2013 from http://www.edb.gov.hk/index.aspx?nodeID=7339andlangno=1#Q14

Firkins, A., Forey, G., and Sengupta, S. (2007). Teaching writing to low proficiency EFL students. *English Language Teaching Journal*, 61(4), 341–352. http://dx.doi.org/10.1093/elt/ccm052

Gibbons, P. (2002). *Scaffolding Language, Scaffolding Learning: Teaching Second Language learners in the mainstream classroom*. Portsmouth, NH: Heinemann.

Gibbons, P. (2003). Mediating language learning: Teacher interactions with ESL students in a content-based classroom. *TESOL Quarterly*, 37(2), 247–273. http://dx.doi.org/10.2307/3588504

Gibbons, P. (2006). *Bridging Discourses in the ESL Classroom: Teachers, Students and Researchers*. London: Continuum.

Gibbons, P. (2008). 'It was taught good and I learned a lot': Intellectual practices and ESL learners in the middle years. *Australian Journal of Language and Literacy.*, 31(2), 155–173.

Gibbons, P. (2009). *English Learners, Academic Literacy, and Thinking: Learning in the Challenge Zone*. Portsmouth, NH: Heinemann.

Halliday, M.A.K. (2005). On matter and meaning: The two realms of human experience. *Linguistics and the Human Sciences*, 1(1).

Hammond, J. (Ed.) (2001). *Scaffolding: Teaching and Learning in Language and Literacy Education*. Newtown, NSW: Primary English Teaching Association.

Hammond, J., and Gibbons, P. (2005). Putting scaffolding to work: The contribution of scaffolding in articulating ESL education. *Prospect*, 20(1), 6–30.

Hebb, D.O. (1949). *The Organization of Behavior*. New York: Wiley and Sons.

Hong Kong Department of Education. (2002). English Language Curriculum Document. Hong Kong: Hong Kong Government Printer.

Knapp, P. and M. Watkins (2005). *Genre, Text, Grammar: Technologies for Teaching and Assessing Writing*. Sydney: University of New South Wales Press.

Kress, G., Jewitt, C., Ogborn, J., and Tsatsarelis, C. (2001). *Multimodal Teaching and Learning: The Rhetorics of the Science Classroom*. London: Continuum.

Macken-Horarik, M. (2002). Something to shoot for: a systemic functional approach to teaching genre in secondary school science. In A.M. Johns (Ed.), *Genre in the Classroom: Multiple Perspectives*, 17–42. Mahwah, NJ: Lawrence Erlbaum Associates.

Mariani, L. (1997). Teacher support and teacher challenge in promoting learner autonomy. *Perspectives: A Journal of TESOL-Italy.* 23(2). Accessed 30 Aug 2013 from http://www.learningpaths.org/papers/papersupport.htm

Martin, J.R. (1985). *Factual Writing: Exploring and Challenging Social Reality*. Geelong: Deakin University Press.

Martin, J.R. (1992). *English Text: System and Structure*. Amsterdam and Philadelphia: John Benjamins. http://dx.doi.org/10.1075/z.59

Martin, J.R. (1997). Analysis genre: functional parameters. In F. Christie and J.R. Martin (Eds), *Genre and Institutions, Social Processes in the Workplace and School*, 3–39. New York: Continuum.

Martin, J.R. (1999). Mentoring semogenesis: 'genre-based' literacy pedagogy. In F. Christie (Ed.), *Pedagogy and the Shaping of Consciousness: Linguistic and Social Processes*, 123–155. London: Cassell.

Martin, J.R. (2006). Metadiscourse: designing interaction in genre-based literacy programs. In R. Whittaker, M. O'Donnell, and A. McCabe (Eds), *Language and Literacy: Functional Approaches*, 95–122. London: Continuum.

Martin, J.R. (2009). Genre and language learning: a social semiotic perspective. *Linguistics and Education*, 20(1), 10–21. http://dx.doi.org/10.1016/j.linged.2009.01.003

Martin, J.R., Christie, F., and Rothery, J. (1987). Social processes in education: A reply to Sawyer and Watson (and others). In I. Reid (Ed.), *The Place of Genre in Learning: Current Debates*, 35–45. Geelong, Australia: Deakin University, Centre for Studies in Literacy Education.

Martin, J.R., and Rose, D. (2008). *Genre Relations: Mapping Culture*. London: Equinox.

Matthiessen C.M.I.M. and Teruya K. (this volume). Registerial hybridity: indeterminacy among fields of activity.

Matthiessen, C., K. Teruya and M. Lam (2010). *Key Terms in Systemic Functional Linguistics*. London: Continuum.

Michell, M., and Sharpe, T. (2005). Collective instructional scaffolding in English as a second language classrooms. *Prospect*, 20(1), 31–58.

Polias, J. (2010a). Improving schooling through understanding the role of language in learning. Plenary: *Association of China and Mongolia International Schools EAL/ESL Conference 2010*, The British International School, Shanghai.

Polias, J. (2010b). Pedagogical resonance: improving teaching and learning. In C. Coffin (Ed.), *Grammar and the Curriculum*, 42–49. London: National Association for Language Development in the Curriculum. NALDIC.

Rothery, J. (1996). Making changes: developing an educational linguistics. In R. Hasan and G. Williams (Eds), *Literacy in Society*, 86–123. London: Longman.

Sheridan, J.G., and Mueller, F.F. (2010). Fostering kinesthetic literacy through exertion in whole body interaction. *Proceedings of the Workshop on Whole Body Interaction at the Conference on Human Factors in Computing Systems*, SIGCHI, United States.

Vygotsky, L.S. (1978). *Interaction Between Learning and Development. Mind in Society: Development of Higher Psychological Processes*. Cambridge, MA: Harvard University Press.

Wood, D., Bruner, J.S., and Ross, G. (1976). The role of tutoring in problem solving. *Journal of Child Psychology and Psychiatry, and Allied Disciplines*, 17(2), 89–100. http://dx.doi.org/10.1111/j.1469-7610.1976.tb00381.x

About the authors

John Polias is a Director of Lexis Education, an international consultancy in teaching and learning, which has written a series of professional development courses, such as *Teaching ESL Students in Mainstream Classrooms: Language in Learning across the Curriculum* and *How Language Works: Success in literacy and learning.* John's other principal interests lie in developing cross-curriculum pedagogies that are underpinned by the role of language and this has led to the forthcoming publication *Apprenticing Students into Science: Doing, talking, writing and drawing scientifically.*

Gail Forey is an Associate Professor and Associate Director for The Research Centre for Professional Communication in the English Department at the Hong Kong Polytechnic University (PolyU). She has carried out research and published in the areas of written and spoken workplace discourse, Systemic Functional Linguistics, discourse analysis, language education and teaching development. Her publications are focused on two distinct areas – language education and communication in the workplace. She has recently co-edited two books: *Text Type and Texture* (2009) with Geoff Thompson, and *Globalisation, Communication and the Workplace* (2010) with Jane Lockwood.

7

The multilayeredness of hybridity in the written stylistic analysis argument

Anne Isaac

University of New South Wales (Canberra)

7.1   Introduction

Genres have formed the cornerstone of academic literacy instruction over the past three decades. Yet, while genre still tends to be taught as a distinctive set of stable rhetorical conventions used by a discourse community to achieve its communicative purposes, it is more likely to be described as complex, dynamic and hybrid in current genre theories. From a poststructuralist perspective, it is 'impossible to not mix genres' (Derrida and Ronell 1980:57), since they are neither 'pure', nor static. Hence, rather than 'belonging to' a genre, a text represents a performance that 'participates' in several genres and continuously 'reconstitutes' them (Threadgold 1989).

Beliefs about the nature of genres and their teachability vary within the three dominant genre schools. New Rhetoric theorists (e.g. Miller 1984 [1994]) tend to treat genres as 'slippery and evolving – and [...] thoroughly contextualised' (Johns 2002:4), and therefore as too unstable and complex to teach and learn in a classroom. By comparison, approaches to genre in Systemic Functional Linguistics (SFL) (especially Martin 1984) and English for Specific Purposes (ESP) (Swales 1990) are more pedagogically oriented and have traditionally emphasised the prototypical schematic structure and linguistic features of genres. More recently, however, less monolithic descriptions of the discourse community and writing context have evolved in ESP, while Hasan has expanded SFL theory by proposing that contexts and texts are not only mutually constitutive, but also mutually permeable (2000). Hasan's proposal forces us to acknowledge that beyond encoding hybrid and fluid dimensions of the social contexts in which texts are performed, textual hybridity reciprocally and cumulatively alters those contexts, and potentially, subsequent performances of the genre(s) involved.

Addressing the mutual permeability of texts and contexts challenges English for Academic Purposes (EAP) instructors to balance both simplicity and authenticity, as well as conformity and individuality, when teaching genres and assessing students' writing: 'Genres must be taught as both constraint and choice so that individual awareness can lead to individual creativity' (Devitt 2004:191). However, such classroom practices are only possible if they are informed by knowledge about the multilayeredness of hybridity (Sarangi this volume) in specific genres, and about the relative importance of hybrid features in students' texts.

7.2   Aim and objectives

This chapter describes a study that explores multiple dimensions of hybridity in the stylistic analysis genre, which is often employed in developing second language (L2) undergraduates' writing skills. The stylistic analysis is quintessentially hybrid, given its function of reconstruing the meanings of the text under analysis. Bakhtin aptly called it 'a double-voiced narration of another's words' (1981:341). The study aims to raise the awareness of teachers of stylistics-based EAP subjects to the presence and implications of hybrid elements in the stylistic analysis. Specific objectives are to relate these features to permeable dimensions in the social context and to distinguish between hybridity that enhances a text and that which detracts from its effectiveness.

7.3   Theoretical framework

The study draws mainly on SFL theory, which treats texts and the social environments in which they function as stratified semiotic systems linked by a principled and dialectical relationship (Halliday 1978), such that language use can typically be predicted by the context and the context typically deduced from the text (Eggins 2004:8). Accordingly, context and text are viewed as operating at two levels. At a more abstract level, *the context of culture* represents a 'reservoir' (Bernstein 2000:158) of a community's institutions (or situation types), goals, values and practices. At a less abstract level, the *context of situation* represents one situation type (or *instance*) of a community's characteristic practices. For the purposes of this chapter, the influence of the cultural and situational contexts on language use can be encapsulated in the notions of *genre* and *register* respectively. Genre explains how a discourse community's social purposes in using language are institutionalised in a text's typical schematic structure. (Martin 1984:25). Halliday's notion of *register* explains how a text's patterns of interpersonal, experiential and textual meanings and wordings are determined by the three key situational variables of *field, tenor* and *mode*, that is, '[...] the underlying social activity, the persons or "voices" involved in that activity, and the particular functions accorded to the text within it' (2007:277).

Within this overarching framework, the tools of genre and register make it possible to analyse texts in all their 'messiness' (Chouliaraki and Fairclough 1999:144) and relate their organisation, patterns of meanings (semantics) and wordings (lexicogrammar) to the presence of typical and hybrid variables in the cultural and situational contexts in which the texts were performed. Nevertheless, some aspects of the model require fleshing out to better accommodate Hasan's (2000) conceptualisation of the mutual permeability of texts and contexts. First, it needs to be stressed that the distinction between the two contextual layers is an analytical one, with each layer representing a different lens for looking at the same phenomenon. For instance, we 'participate in many simultaneous cultures' and their genres, each a part of the 'mental life' (Halliday 2007:284) that comes with us to any context of situation. This acknowledgement is especially relevant for L2 students, whose interpretations and enactment of texts in L2 situational contexts are also influenced by values and knowledge of practices from their first language (L1) sociocultural and disciplinary contexts.

Second, following ethnographic approaches to the discourse context (e.g. Adam and Artemeva 2002), I distinguish between a global layer of the cultural context (e.g. the knowledge and meaning making practices of the community of Anglophone stylisticians worldwide) and a local layer (i.e., the version of these practices taught in a specific stylistics course and classroom). This elaboration helps to explain how students, like those in this study, may be asked to follow a hybrid genre structure for the purpose of apprenticing them into more complex genres.

Third, the most permeable dimension of the context of situation is the individual writer. Further articulation of the tenor variable is needed to account for the relationship between textual hybridity and the sociocultural, psychological and individual factors that shape the writer's voice, which can be simply defined as the linguistic means that portray her/his textual identities.[1] The beginnings of such an account can be found in contemporary SFL (e.g. Martin 2010) and sociolinguistic approaches to linguistic individuality, particularly Johnstone's view that each person has a unique linguistic *repertoire*, as no two people are identical or have identical experiences with language (1996). More broadly, adopting agentive and emergent theories of language use makes it possible to see every linguistic act as a hybrid construction of conscious and unconscious choices, shared conventions and idiosyncratic and sometimes inventive strategies in response to ongoing situations and the communicative problems they pose (see Johnstone 1996).

7.4   The context, data and participants

The context of the study is *Exploring style and meaning in language* (ESML), a one-semester stylistics-based EAP subject offered to L2 international undergraduates at an Australian university. The primary data consists of:

(a)   a model of the schematic structure of the stylistic analysis presented to the ESML students;

(b)   10 students' preliminary drafts of their first stylistic analysis argument; and

(c)   an extract from 'The Letter', by Sally Morgan (1988), the literary text under analysis. The narrative critiques the history of the 'stolen generations', namely, children of mixed racial origins removed from their Aboriginal families by the Australian government over a period of 100 years. Not only is hybridity and its treatment within society a central theme of the story; 'The Letter' also has a hybrid form that brings together two genres, an internal monologue narrated by Bessie, an elderly Aboriginal woman, and a letter written by her sister, Nellie, to her 'stolen' daughter, Elaine. Each narration construes a different context of situation and 'message': Bessie's monologue, set in the present, describes her thwarted attempts to deliver the letter to Elaine following Nellie's death, and conveys the story's universal teaching about the power of hope and perseverance. The letter, set in the past, describes Elaine's removal and Nellie's lifelong efforts to be reunited with her, evoking the narrative's local political meanings.

Secondary data includes transcripts of post semester ESML student interviews.

In this chapter, I focus principally on the A grade text of Aliénor, from France, as compared to the less successful texts of her peers, particularly the B grade argument of Susanne, from Germany, and C grade text of Johanna, from Sweden. The three Arts students' scores on the university's diagnostic language test indicated that Susanne's reading and writing skills (100 per cent, 89 per cent) were more advanced than those of both Aliénor (75 per cent, 68 per cent) and Johanna (78 per cent, 44 per cent). Susanne and Aliénor also had a stronger literature background than Johanna, and more experience of stylistic analysis. However, these contextual variables did not effectively predict the calibre of each student's first stylistic argument, as discussed below.

In light of the small sample size, the results of the analysis of the ESML drafts were strengthened through comparison with trends reported in qualitative studies of similar texts (e.g. Macken-Horarik 1996, 2006, Rothery and Stenglin 2000), and in interdisciplinary and/or intercultural studies of novice and expert academic writing more generally (e.g. Fløttum, Dahl and Kinn 2006, Siepmann 2006).

7.5   Analysis

The data examination used the tools of genre and register analysis to:

(a) explore hybridity in the purposes, staging and register patterns of the stylistic analysis genre, particularly the version modelled for the ESML participants; and

(b) compare hybrid organisational, semantic and lexicogrammatical features in the more and less successful participants' drafts against such hybridity in the ESML model.

However, owing to the scope of this chapter, only trends revealed by the genre analyses of the stylistic argument and the ESML data are discussed below.

7.6   Results

7.6.1 Dimensions of hybridity in the purposes and staging of the stylistic analysis genre

Exploration of the stylistic argument indicates that hybridity in its functionality and staging can be related to permeable dimensions in the cultural context of stylistics, 'a middle ground between linguistics and literature' (Carter 1982a:7). In other words, hybrid textual features of the stylistic analysis detailed below can be seen as activated by and, at the same time, construing the hybrid expectations and rhetorical conventions of the disciplinary context, and more specifically, the ESML interpretation of these conventions.

In particular, examination of the ESML version of the stylistic analysis reveals that it incorporates elements of the literary *response* (Rothery 1995) and *expository argument* genres. Within the field of literary criticism, the social purpose of response genres is to discuss and interpret literature. Three response genres that feature in school and university language and literature curricula and in L2 teaching are the *personal response* and the Leavisite and New Critical *interpretations*.[2] Each response genre typically elicits different reading practices, reflecting its distinctive purposes. The personal response, which encourages students to discuss their own reactions to literary texts, is likely to evoke a 'partial and often idiosyncratic' reading of literature that Macken-Horarik classifies as *tactical* (2006:11). Interpretations ask students to identify the text's higher order psychological and cultural, especially moral, significance, either by exploring characters' behaviours (Leavisite interpretations), or by deconstructing the literary work's semiosis or meaning making process (New Critical interpretations). Although both interpretive tasks require a *symbolic* reading that connects 'concrete details of events and characters to their abstract significance' (Macken-Horarik 2006:20), Leavisite interpretations tend to mislead weaker students to perform a *mimetic* reading, with literature treated as imitating life (Macken-Horarik 1996).

In terms of its social purposes, the ESML stylistic analysis task bears similarities with each of the above response genres: it also requires the reader/analyst to recognise ethical and affective meanings evoked by the narrative, and like the New Critical interpretation, to relate these meanings to salient patterns of semiotic features, and to evaluate the rhetorical effects of these features. Like interpretive approaches, stylistic analysis privileges a symbolic reading of the narrative. However, whereas New

Critical practices appeal to general intuitions about language to support interpretations, stylistic approaches refer to 'systematic and explicit knowledge of communicative and linguistic norms' with the aim of making an interpretation 'replicable' (Carter 1982a:6, 9).

Functional similarities between the response and stylistic analysis genres are realised in the staging of each genre. Viewed typologically, that is, in terms of their distinctive characteristics, all response genres share the following stages:

TEXT EVALUATION ^ TEXT SYNOPSIS ^ REAFFIRMATION OF
TEXT EVALUATION

However, viewed topologically, i.e., in terms of their closeness to and distance from related genres, the interpretation and stylistic analysis genres fulfil a basic argumentative function, with students required to argue the merits of their interpretation of the literary text, and to conclude by reiterating this interpretation. The function of the analytical argument is to 'prove or make plausible a controversial standpoint' (Kienpointner 2012:115) through analysis. The staging of the analytical argument differs depending on whether it presents one side of an issue (exposition), or two sides, with one evaluated as more valid (discussion).

In light of the importance of arguments in undergraduate curricula, and the EAP orientation of ESML, the stylistic analysis task was presented to the participants as an analytical expository argument that required them, first, to state a position or Thesis (about the literary extract's key meanings and the linguistic/stylistic patterns that construe them); and second, to support their Thesis through a process of reasoning and the providing of evidence from the narrative. The recommended staging of the first ESML stylistic analysis shown below was modelled in a detailed guide with prompts and questions relating to stages (CAPITALS) and embedded sections (curly braces {}) of the text. The square bracketed Arguments and Evidence stage and the recursion symbol (П) indicate that more than one argument may be used to support the Thesis.

EVALUATION ^ {Synopsis • Personal Reaction • Interpretation}
THESIS {+ Outline} ^ [ARGUMENT/S and EVIDENCE] П ^
REAFFIRMATION OF THESIS and EVALUATION

The first and final stages echo elements of response genres, while the final three stages feature in analytical arguments. The inclusion of a brief Personal Reaction section in the first ESML stylistic argument task followed an approach to stylistic analysis that encourages students to reflect on aspects of the text that have affected them most powerfully, and to use these responses as a basis for their analyses (Carter 1982b). Although reminiscent of the personal response genre, the Personal Reaction in the ESML model invited students to take up a personalised voice in one discrete phase of their writing only.

To sum up, the first stage of the hybridity analysis emphasises how commonalities in the social purposes and schematic structure of response and stylistic analysis genres realise the permeability of stylistics both as a discipline and as it was practised in ESML. At the same time, the overview identifies distinctive functions of each genre that elicit different qualities of readings of the literary text. As will be seen in Section 7.6.2, the type of reading realised by a student's performance of the stylistic argument can be used as a gauge of the extent to which her/his text, or any of its stages, achieves the genre's specific social purposes.

7.6.2 Key dimensions of hybridity in the purposes and staging of the ESML stylistic analyses

The results of the genre analysis of the higher and lower graded ESML participants' stylistic arguments are described below. Typical and hybrid organisational features in the texts are related to the findings reported in Section 7.6.1, particularly those concerning the influence of the local cultural context – in the form of the modelled ESML genre structure – and factors that permeate this context, namely, the individual analyst's unique disposition, and the L1 and L2 linguistic and cultural repertoires and literary experiences s/he brings to the act of writing. In addition, I evaluate the impact of hybrid elements on the participants' voices, the portrayal of their identities and the effectiveness of their writing.

7.6.2.1 Hybridity in the successful stylistic analyses

The comparative genre analysis revealed that the more proficient ESML students tended to innovate on and individualise the staging of the modelled argument genre to a greater extent than their less proficient peers. I focus here on Aliénor's A grade text, which is coherent, cogent and insightful, and includes ample supporting linguistic evidence from the narrative. Example (1) illustrates her ability to relate patterns of language choices in the narrative to its central and implicit problematic, Bessie's journey from despair to hope on re-reading Nellie's letter:

(1) The difference between Nellie's positive attitude towards life and
the pessimism of Bettie [sic] is striking. At the beginning of the passage, Bettie's feelings are very negative. The sentence '... it looked like
it would be the last', and the adjectives 'faded and worn' [describing the
letter] suggest despair and lack of faith in the future. But the verb '(I)
read it again' launches the action forward. It is a first step.

The example highlights how Aliénor infers Bessie's state of mind from
her thoughts and actions, and, symbolically, from descriptions of the state
of the letter.

Table 7.1 summarises the comparison of the modelled ESML genre
structure and that in Aliénor's draft. The table shows that the organisation of her argument generally conforms to that of the model, but that she
embroiders on and/or departs from it through the inclusion of hybrid features, four of which are examined below.

First, in her Evaluation, Aliénor completes a comprehensive and con-
densed Synopsis of the events, characters, social context and universal
themes construed by the narrative. Unusually, she also overviews and evaluates its composition and aesthetic effects, e.g.:

(2) The absence of characters in the passage is striking.

In fact, paragraph 2 shifts between the Synopsis and a succinct
Personal Reaction section in which she evaluates her responses to the
story's meanings and style, in a manner that constructs her voice as sensitive but analytical, e.g.:

(3) [...] the first adjective to qualify the text [...] is moving.

In spite of its somewhat fluid organisation, the hybrid Synopsis/Personal
Reaction does not detract from Aliénor's writing. Instead, it emphasises
her ability to read and deconstruct 'The Letter' as a symbolic artefact
rather than as a 'window' on life (cf. Macken-Horarik 2006), qualities that
in turn portray her as an experienced reader of literature and an able, albeit
apprentice, stylistician.

A second set of hybrid features revealed by the genre analysis concerns
aspects of the staging of Aliénor's draft that are not fully articulated. In
particular, the connection between her stages of Interpretation (the importance of blood ties) and Thesis (the pivotal role of the letter in highlighting
this theme) is incomplete. There is also some slippage in the articulation of
Argument 1, which initially posits that one aspect of the letter's role is *the
transmission of a particular message* and only later (paragraphs 5 and 9)

Table 7.1 Comparative staging of the ESML model stylistic analysis and Aliénor's text

Model	Aliénor's draft	Para.	Focus
EVALUATION	EVALUATION		
Synopsis	Synopsis	1	The narrative & the extract
	Synopsis &	2	Key stylistic features (*specified*)
Personal Reaction	Personal Reaction 1		Aesthetic & affective reactions to rhetorical devices &
		3	meanings
Interpretation	Interpretation		The importance of blood ties
THESIS	THESIS	4	Goal: to analyse the central role of the letter
Outline	Outline		Foci: how the letter i) transmits 'a particular message' ii) 'leads to the revival of hope'
ARGUMENT/S & EVIDENCE	ARGUMENT 1 & EVIDENCE		
	Preview	5	The purpose of the letter: to reaffirm blood ties (*not fully explicit*)
		6	To inform Elaine
	Micro-Argument 1.1		i) about the circumstances of their separation
	Micro-Argument 1.2	7	ii) about Nellie's inability to prevent her removal (*implied*)
	Micro-Argument 1.3	8	iii) that she was loved & not abandoned
	Micro-Argument 1.4	9	iv) about her identity
	TRANSITION: Review Synopsis Preview Argument 2	10	The presence of two narrators
	ARGUMENT 2 & EVIDENCE		The letter's role in bringing about the revival of hope
		11	The 2 narrators' contrasting dispositions:
	Micro-Argument 2.1	12	i) Nellie
		13	ii) Bessie
	Micro-Argument 2.2		The role of the letter in Bessie's change of heart
	Personal Reaction 2		Aesthetic & affective reactions to rhetorical devices
REAFFIRMATION OF THESIS & EVALUATION	REAFFIRMATION OF THESIS & EVALUATION	14	The pivotal role of the letter Nellie's restraint makes the narrative original

specifies that the letter's purpose is to reunite Elaine with her mother and her Aboriginality. Furthermore, the Thesis of Micro-Argument 1.2 in paragraph 7 is merely implied. These features are activated by and portray her L2 status and developing academic writing proficiency in English. Potential explanations for less explicit sections of Aliénor's draft are:

- cognitive overload involved in L2 writing (cf. Clyne 1987);
- the tendency for L2 writers to model their ideal reader on their actual reader and so assume the latter's understanding of unarticulated information (Hedeboe 2007); and
- the conceivably more *reader responsible* writing pattern she brings to the context of situation from French, placing the primary responsibility for effective communication on the reader, rather than on the writer, as in English (cf. Hinds 2001). This explanation is supported by the findings of a comprehensive interdisciplinary and intercultural study of academic discourse (Fløttum *et al.* 2006).[3]

Importantly, however, while these hybrid features of Aliénor's draft require higher processing effort by the reader, they do not prevent her/him from following her argument.

Third, the elaborate structure of Aliénor's two Arguments and Evidence stages, with four micro-arguments in the first, and two in the second, is a further indicator of her skill and confidence in performing the argument genre in English and, undoubtedly more so, in French. The intricacy of her draft distinguishes her stylistic analysis from those of her peers, and appears to have been influenced by her training in the French *dissertation littéraire*, which stipulates the need for 'ordered precision and academic rigour' (Siepmann 2006:134) in the development of a two or three part argument, each featuring a Thesis and several sub-parts (e.g. http://www. etudes-litteraires.com/dissertation.php). Likewise, her incorporation of a Transition stage (paragraph 10) echoes instructions for writing French literary essays, which require the inclusion of a stage to review the previous argument and its findings, and to preview the following one (e.g. http:// www.etudes-litteraires.com/bac-francais/technique-dissertation.php). Aliénor's Transition stage tightens the structure of her essay, reinforces her second argument, and extends and reconstrues the modelled genre structure (i.e., the L2 context of culture). Moreover, the analysis suggests the value of including a Transition stage within the ESML model, highlighting the ongoing, reciprocal effects of the mutual permeability of context and text.

Fourth, there are two digressions from Aliénor's discussion of Micro-Argument 1.4 (paragraph 9). The first relates 'The Letter' to Sally Morgan's own life, while the second is an analysis of the daughter's reaction to the news of her Aboriginal origins. Each instance could be interpreted as a brief assimilation of the Leavisite interpretation genre, as well as a momentary shift by Aliénor towards seeing the narrative as mirroring reality. Furthermore, the digressions evoke theories that posit cultural differences in argument styles, with German and French thought to be more tolerant of digressive writing than English.[4] However, although these departures are not directly relevant to her arguments, I would maintain that they do not reduce the effectiveness of her writing: unlike digressions in the less successful ESML arguments, both are concise (3 and 4 sentences long), analytical and depersonalised. In the second case, Aliénor's insights into Elaine's predicament underscore her attunement to the narrative's meanings, her emotionally mature and contemplative disposition and L2 proficiency, e.g.:

(4) And it is interesting to analyse the daughter's reaction, which is the denying of her aboriginality. Elaine is like the prisoner in Plato's cave. She prefers to stick to the shadows, because [the] truth is painful.

Indeed, Aliénor's figurative language indexes an advanced level of vocabulary knowledge (Littlemore, Krennmayr, Turner and Turner 2014) and projects her identity as that of a native speaker or, at least, someone with a high degree of intercultural competence. Yet, the scholarly allusion to Plato's cave portrays her as being from somewhere else: her expression bears the hallmark of the elegant style valued in formal French writing (see Siepmann 2006:145–146), and her knowledge of the Classics, while integral to Philosophy studies at the *Baccalauréat* level, is atypical of first year Australian undergraduates.

In short, the discussion of the comparative genre analysis results has focused on hybrid dimensions in Aliénor's text and their potential relationships to factors that permeate the context of culture (as represented by the modelled stylistic analysis structure), namely, her L2 linguistic and cultural proficiency, patterns that she brings to the context of situation from her experience of argumentation in French, and her individual disposition. These qualitative insights not only demonstrate how Aliénor's draft 'repeats, mixes, stretches, and potentially reconstitutes' the modelled genre (Bawarshi and Reiff 2010:21), but also how her performance in turn extends, elaborates and redefines the context, and reciprocally, the model (as with the Transition stage, for instance). At the same time, most hybrid qualities in Aliénor's stylistic argument are shown to enhance her writing and depict her as a sensitive, symbolic reader of literature who recognises the ESML task requirements, and is a sufficiently skilled academic writer to fulfil them competently.

7.6.2.2 Hybridity in the less successful stylistic analyses

The genre analysis revealed that by comparison to Aliénor's draft, the other nine participants' arguments are generally less complex and less well controlled. Apart from the texts of the three German students who had studied stylistic analysis in high school, the staging of the lower graded drafts was also less innovative and closer to the modelled genre structure. Below, I discuss three trends in the less successful drafts, with special attention to Susanne's (B grade) text and, to a lesser extent, Johanna's (C grade) argument.

One hybrid characteristic shared by several lower graded analyses is a lengthy Evaluation stage, especially the Synopsis and Personal Reaction sections. For instance, Aliénor's Synopsis totals 250 words, Susanne's, 780, and Johanna's, 349. Typically, longer Synopses retell the narrative's events in detail, often identifying similarities with the author's life, and present the writers' impressions of the protagonists, sometimes supported by citations from the narrative. Extended Synopses indicate that writers have conflated the stylistic analysis and Leavisite interpretation or personal response genres. Hybridity of this kind detracts from the quality of the text, because it signals a misreading of the stylistic analysis task requirements, and a focus on the narrative's mimetic qualities – i.e., those that enable the reader to identify with the world it construes – rather than its semiotic ones. In the majority of less successful drafts, these hybrid dimensions appear to stem from the writers' lesser language proficiency, their greater familiarity with writing Leavisite interpretations and, more fundamentally, a lack of technical tools and experience with text deconstruction in their L1 and/or L2 secondary and/or tertiary literature courses (cf. Rothery and Stenglin 2000).

However, the reasons for Susanne's extended Synopsis lie elsewhere, given her advanced L2 proficiency and prior experience of doing stylistic analysis in German. As shown in Table 7.2, there are in fact two Synopses in Susanne's draft, the first contextualising the narrative and the extract (paragraph 2), the second, the content and characters (paragraphs 5–12). One possible explanation is that her second Synopsis may be a kind of backgrounding digression, or *Exkurs*, identified by Clyne as characteristic of German argumentation (1987). A simpler or additional explanation may be that she spent little time planning her draft because she preferred writing interpretations over stylistic analyses, as she asserted in her feedback interview.

Similarly, wordy and recurring Personal Reaction sections in several lower graded arguments go beyond the passing commentary invited by the modelled ESML task. Rather, this conflation of the personal response and stylistic argument genres, like the extended Synopsis, reflects the permeation of the L2 cultural context by the L1 and L2 literature background and English language proficiency that the individual writer brings to the context of situation. Long Personal Reaction sections in the lower scored drafts realise their writers' mimetic conception of the narrative and, at times, a tactical reading (Macken-Horarik 2006). For example, in her third Personal Reaction section, Johanna expresses her affective response to the narrative, her identification with Nellie, and her belief that the text is biographical:

> (5) I liked the text and I felt I could relate to Nellie and her struggle.[...] This extract makes me want to know what happened to these ladies [the protagonists] further on and triggers me to learn more about the Aborigines.

Johanna's involved reaction, accentuated by the presence of personal pronouns, underscores her interpolation within the stylistic analysis of a different genre (the personal response or informal oral discussion) from a different cultural context (e.g. a bookclub or school classroom). However, such hybridity 'mis-recognises' the requirements of the academic cultural context (Macken-Horarik 2006:11) and so weakens her writing.

A third hybrid quality that reduces the effectiveness of the less successful ESML arguments is the writers' tendency to delay or omit articulation of the Thesis and its connections to the Interpretation and Arguments. For instance, Susanne's Thesis is not articulated until the final paragraph of her text (i.e., the Reaffirmation stage):

> (7) Nellie is so non-judgemental, even indifferent against the people who caused her so much pain, the reader feels asked to be furious for her. [...] In that way the text gets its political dimension and becomes a powerful accusation against the racistic so called Aboriginies Protection Board [sic].

Her observation – that Nellie's restraint is a compelling rhetorical device used in 'The Letter' to construe the text's political message and to engage, and enrage, readers – is a perceptive one, as are her Micro-Arguments. Together they attest Susanne's background in stylistic and interpretive approaches to literature. However, her argumentation lacks a detailed linguistic analysis, and with one exception, evidence from the literary extract to support her claims. Had she articulated her Thesis statement earlier,

Table 7.2 Comparative staging of the ESML model stylistic analysis and Susanne's text

Model	Susanne's draft	Para.	Focus
EVALUATION Synopsis	EVALUATION Personal Reaction	1	The separation of mother and child is an 'inhumane cruelty'
Personal Reaction Interpretation	Synopsis 1 & Interpretations 1 & 2	2	The narrative & the extract The 'strengths of love and family bonds' The 'harm' done to Aborigines
THESIS Outline	Outline &	3	Goal: to understand the story's impact on the reader Foci: i) the structure of the text ii) other stylistic means (*unspecified*)
	Interpretation 2 (*reprise*)		An 'accusation' against the stolen generations policy
ARGUMENT/S & EVIDENCE	ARGUMENT & EVIDENCE Micro-Argument 1	4	The narrative structure
	EVALUATION Synopsis 2 or *EXKURS*	5 → 12	Content and characters
	TRANSITION: Review Outline	13	Goal: to find out i) 'what makes this story so impressive' ii) 'by what means'
	ARGUMENT & EVIDENCE Micro-Argument 2 Micro-Argument 1 (*reprise*)	13	Emotional intimacy is created by language choices & the narrative structure
	Micro-Argument 3.1	14	The omission of information
	Micro-Argument 3.2	15	The omission of explicit judgement
REAFFIRMATION OF THESIS & EVALUATION	REAFFIRMATION OF THESIS & EVALUATION	16	Nellie's restraint causes the reader to condemn the Australian government

she might have analysed linguistic features that construct Nellie's ostensibly non-judgemental voice. Like Aliénor, Susanne includes a Transition stage that reviews her Outline (paragraph 12). But unlike the Transition in Aliénor's essay, Susanne's emphasises that the core requirement of the stylistic analysis task has barely been tackled. In her feedback interview, she attributed this result to inadequate time spent planning her draft. However, the organisation of her draft may equally have been shaped by her L1 experience of argument writing. For example, both the 'point-late' articulation of her Thesis and the spiral staging of her draft shown in Table 7.2 have been found to be reminiscent of German text structures (see Siepmann 2006:142).

Delaying the Thesis stage clearly weakens the effectiveness of Susanne's writing. However, in other lower graded drafts, the absence of a Thesis or Outline statement is even more undermining because the Reaffirmation stage is reduced to a repetition of the essay's contents, or of preceding Personal Reaction sections, as in Example (6) above. Moreover, because of their inability to connect the Interpretation and Thesis, most writers of the less successful drafts are confined to arguing that certain linguistic or rhetorical devices make it easier to understand the narrative's meanings and so involve readers. Each semiotic feature is noted, often fleetingly, in a series of sub-points, and usually with little substantiating evidence.

The hybrid organisational elements in the lower graded drafts detailed above reconstitute the stylistic analysis and reconstrue the local (ESML) context of culture but in ways that are likely to jar with an academic reader's expectations. In particular the failure to connect – and in some cases, to articulate – the Interpretation, Thesis and Arguments, impacts negatively on the quality and coherence of these drafts. In addition, Synopses and Personal Reactions that realign the purposes and structure of the stylistic analysis genre with those of personal and/or interpretation responses were shown to realise mimetic or tactical readings of the narrative. Each of these traits weakens the writers' voices, projecting their identities as more novice and subjective readers and analysts of literature, and less competent L2 writers by comparison to Aliénor.

7.7 Pedagogical implications

For teachers of stylistics-based approaches to EAP, there are three outstanding implications of the results of the analysis reported in Sections 7.6.2.1 and 7.6.2.2. First, to return to the question raised by the introduction to this chapter about how best to teach genres: the analysis of the ESML drafts affirms the relevance of using a basic model to apprentice L2 students into the writing of the stylistic argument. The preceding discussion indicates that *all* novice stylisticians, particularly those with lower proficiency levels, would benefit from more explicit modelling of the structure of texts. Most importantly, the discussion makes it clear that a pedagogy for inducting students into the stylistic analysis genre should focus on enabling them to:

(a) articulate their Interpretation of the literary text's key meanings;
(b) link the Interpretation to their Thesis, which should specify the linguistic/stylistic patterns that construe these meanings; and
(c) connect the Interpretation and Thesis to the Outline of their argument.

Most hybrid versions of these organisational elements were shown to detract from the quality of the ESML arguments, underlining the need for further measures to build the text deconstruction skills of weaker students like Johanna. Such 'scaffolding' (Wood, Bruner and Ross 1976) might involve providing targeted instruction and practice in drafting Interpretation, Thesis and Outline statements, and additional practice in analysing specific linguistic/stylistic patterns. Honing these argumentation skills would better equip students to recognise and realise the organisational requirements of argument writing in other disciplines. The analysis of Aliénor's text suggests that once they have mastered these crucial steps, more advanced writers can be encouraged to show greater flexibility and individuality in staging other aspects of their writing.

Second, lessons learned from the lengthy Synopses and Personal Reactions in the less successful drafts indicate that their writers did not understand the distinctive functions of the stylistic analysis genre, as opposed to those of the personal and interpretation response genres. This finding has two implications, the first, more obvious, one being the need to devise teaching activities that foreground functional and organisational differences between these genres, and activities that enable students to recognise why certain features that cross genre lines may be successful and others not. For instance, we can show students how digressions that analyse characters can be powerful, providing they are succinct, depersonalised and highlight the analyst's attunement to the narrative's implicit meanings rather than her/his identification with characters or themes. The second, underlying, but more fundamental implication precedes even the modelling of the stylistic analysis task: it concerns the need to provide students with opportunities to explore and discuss differences in the ways they approach literary texts, and by extension, to sensitise them to the principal 'mechanisms by which narratives 'go to work' on readers' (Macken-Horarik 2003:285), namely, by engaging their empathy, but simultaneously inviting them to pass moral judgements on characters and the values they stand for.

7.8   Conclusion

The study reported here sheds new light on the concept of hybridity in texts and contexts, and its implications for genre-based teaching, in EAP settings especially. From an analytical perspective, the study is innovative in its use of SFL theory to identify multiple layers of hybridity in the stylistic analysis genre and by its attempts to relate these elements to specific contextual variables.

From a pedagogical perspective, the study provokes teachers to think about hybridity in students' texts that is integral to the genre models with which we provide them and that we *expect* to find in their writing, for example a blend of the response and argument genres, such as that in the modelled ESML stylistic analysis task. Equally, the study raises teachers' awareness about *unexpected* hybrid organisational dimensions in students' texts, such as digressions, and additional, missing, delayed, extended or redundant stages or sections.

Finally, linking such hybrid textual elements to the calibre of students' readings of the literary text can help us rationalise our intuitions about instances of hybridity that enhance students' writing and those that do not. These insights have the potential to give teachers greater confidence in assessing students' texts and ultimately in developing more balanced and effective ways of teaching genres.

Notes

1   For a more detailed analysis of the concept of voice, see Isaac (2012).
2   See Belsey (2002) and Carter (1982a) for further discussion of F.R. Leavis' traditional approach to literary criticism and New Critical approaches.
3   Other studies have, however, characterised French as *writer responsible* (see Siepmann 2006).

4   While these theories remain controversial, cultural variations in rhetorical patterns across languages have been identified in a growing body of intercultural studies (see Fløttum *et al.* 2006, Siepmann 2006).

References

Adam, C., and Artemeva, N. (2002). Writing instruction in English for Academic Purposes (EAP) classes: introducing second language learners into the academic community. In A.M. Johns (Ed.), *Genre in the Classroom: Multiple Perspectives*, 179–196. Mahwah, NJ: Lawrence Erlbaum.

Bakhtin, M.M. (1981). Discourse in the novel (1934–5). In M. Holquist (Ed.), *The Dialogic Imagination: Four Essays by M.M. Bakhtin*, 259–422 (Translated by C. Emerson & M. Holquist). Austin, TX: University of Texas Press.

Bawarshi, A.S., and Reiff, M.J. (2010). *Genre: An Introduction to History, Theory, Research, and Pedagogy*. West Lafayette, IN: Parlor Press LLC.

Belsey, C. (2002). *Critical Practice* (Rev. ed.). London: Routledge.

Bernstein, B. (2000). *Pedagogy, Symbolic Control and Identity Theory: Theory, Research, Critique* (Rev. ed.). Lanham, MD: Rowman and Littlefield.

Carter, R. (1982a). Introduction. In R. Carter (Ed.), *Language and Literature: An Introductory Reader in Stylistics*, 1–17. London: Unwin Hyman.

Carter, R. (1982b). Style and interpretation in Hemingway's 'Cat in the rain. In R. Carter (Ed.), *Language and Literature: An Introductory Reader in Stylistics*, 65–80. London: Unwin Hyman.

Chouliaraki, L., and Fairclough, N. (1999). *Discourse in Late Modernity: Rethinking Critical Discourse Analysis*. Edinburgh: Edinburgh University Press.

Clyne, M. (1987). Cultural differences in the organization of academic texts. *Journal of Pragmatics*, 11(2), 211–241. http://dx.doi.org/10.1016/0378-2166(87)90196-2

Derrida, J. (1980). The law of genre. (Translated by A. Ronell). *Critical Inquiry*, 7(1), 55–81. http://dx.doi.org/10.1086/448088

Devitt, A.J. (2004). *Writing Genres*. Carbondale, IL: Southern Illinois University Press.

Eggins, S. (2004). *An Introduction to Systemic Functional Linguistics* (2nd ed.). London, New York: Continuum.

Fløttum, K., Dahl, T., and Kinn, T. (2006). *Academic Voices: Across Languages and Disciplines*. Amsterdam and Philadelphia: John Benjamins. http://dx.doi.org/10.1075/pbns.148

Halliday, M.A.K. (1978). *Language as Social Semiotic*. London: Edward Arnold.

Halliday, M.A.K. (2007). The notion of 'context' in language education (1991). In M.A.K. Halliday (2007). *Language in Education*, Volume 9 of the Collected Works of M.A.K. Halliday, edited by J.J. Webster, 269–290. London and New York: Continuum.

Hasan, R. (2000). The uses of talk. In S. Sarangi and M. Coulthard (Eds), *Discourse and Social Life*, 28–47. London: Longman.

Hedeboe, B. (2007). On the 'internal dialogue' between an examination task and pre-university students' responses. In A. McCabe, M. O'Donnell, and R. Whittaker (Eds), *Advances in Language and Education*, 201–216. London: Continuum.

Hinds, J. (2001). Reader versus writer responsibility: A new typology (1987). In T.J. Silva and P.K. Matsuda (Eds), *Landmark Essays on ESL Writing*, 63–73. Mahwah, NJ: Lawrence Erlbaum.

Isaac, A. (2012). Modelling voice as appraisal and involvement resources: The portrayal of textual identities and interpersonal relationships in the written stylistic analyses of non-native speaker, international undergraduates. Unpublished PhD thesis, University of Canberra, Canberra.

Johns, A.M. (2002). Introduction: genre in the classroom. In A.M. Johns (Ed.), *Genre in the Classroom: Multiple Perspectives*, 3–13. Mahwah, NJ: Lawrence Erlbaum. http://dx.doi.org/10.1017/CBO9780511550386.004

Johnstone, B. (1996). *The Linguistic Individual: Self-expression in Language and Linguistics*. New York: Oxford University Press.

Kienpointner, M. (2012). When figurative analogies fail: fallacious uses of arguments from analogy. In F.H. van Eemeren and B. Garssen (Eds), *Topical Themes in Argumentation Theory: Twenty Exploratory Studies*, 111–126. Heidelberg, London, New York: Springer Dordrecht. http://dx.doi.org/10.1007/978-94-007-4041-9_8

La dissertation littéraire. Accessed on 29 March 2013 from http://www.etudes-litteraires.com/dissertation.php

La technique de la dissertation. Accessed on 29 March 2013 from http://www.etudes-litteraires.com/bac-francais/technique-dissertation.php

Littlemore, J., Krennmayr, T., Turner, J., and Turner, S. (2014). An investigation into metaphor use at different levels of second language writing. *Applied Linguistics*, 35(2), 117–144. http://dx.doi.org/10.1093/applin/aml004

Macken-Horarik, M. (1996). Construing the invisible: specialized literacy practices in junior secondary English. Unpublished PhD thesis, The University of Sydney, Sydney.

Macken-Horarik, M. (2003). Appraisal and the special instructiveness of narrative. *Text*, 23(2), 285–312. http://dx.doi.org/10.1515/text.2003.012

Macken-Horarik, M. (2006). Recognizing and realizing 'what counts' in examination English: perspectives from systemic functional linguistics and code theory. *Functions of Language*, 13(1), 1–35. http://dx.doi.org/10.1075/fol.13.1.02mac

Martin, J.R. (1984). Language, register and genre. In F. Christie (Ed.), *Children Writing: Reader*, 21–30. Geelong: Deakin University Press.

Martin, J. (2010). Semantic variation: modelling realisation, instantiation and individuation in social semiosis. In M. Bednarek and J. Martin (Eds), *New Discourse on Language: Functional Perspectives on Multimodality, Identity and Affiliation*, 1–34. London, New York: Continuum.

Miller, C.R. (1984 [1994]). Genre as social action. *Quarterly Journal of Speech* 70(2), 151–167. Reprinted in A. Freedman and P. Medway (Eds), *Genre and the New Rhetoric*, 23–42. London: Taylor and Francis.

Rothery, J. (1995). *Exploring Literacy in School English: Write it Right: Resources for Literacy and Learning*. Sydney: Disadvantaged Schools Program Metropolitan East Region, NSW Department of School Education.

Rothery, J., and Stenglin, M. (2000). Interpreting literature: the role of APPRAISAL. In L. Unsworth (Ed.), *Researching Language in Schools and Communities: Functional Linguistic Perspectives*, 222–244. London, New York: Cassell.

Sarangi, S. (this volume). Activity types, discourse types and role types: interactional hybridity in professional-client encounters.

Siepmann, D. (2006). Academic writing and culture: an overview of differences between English, French and German. *Meta*, 51(1), 131–150. Accessed on 29 March 2013 from http://www.erudit.org/revue/meta/2006/v/n1/012998ar.html. http://dx.doi.org/10.7202/012998ar

Swales, J.M. (1990). *Genre Analysis: English in Academic and Research Settings*. Cambridge: Cambridge University Press.

Threadgold, T. (1989). Talking about genre: ideologies and incompatible discourses. *Cultural Studies*, 3(1), 101–127. http://dx.doi.org/10.1080/09502388900490071

Wood, D., Bruner, J.S. and Ross, G. (1976). The role of tutoring in problem solving. *Journal of Child Psychology and Psychiatry* 17(2), 89–100.

About the author

Anne Isaac is a lecturer in Academic Language and Learning at the University of New South Wales (Canberra). She has researched and published in the areas of stylistics-based approaches to language teaching, L2 vocabulary development and testing, and prosody and fluency in spoken interaction. Her recent work includes 'Appraising Appraisal', a co-authored chapter that assesses the viability of Appraisal theory in analyzing narratives and students' responses to them; and a PhD that proposes a model for describing the writer's voice (or self-portrayal) and its development in academic writing.

8

Activity types, discourse types and role types: interactional hybridity in professional-client encounters

Srikant Sarangi

Danish Institute of Humanities and Medicine/Health (DIHMH), Aalborg University, Denmark

8.1 Introduction

This paper is an extension of my earlier work on interactional hybridity in professional practice (Sarangi 2000, 2010a, 2011), as manifest through the configurations of discourse types and role types within a given activity type. The main thesis is as follows: hybridity and hybridisation are not simply linguistic (textual, semiotic, multimodal) processes which are signalled through intertextuality and interdiscursivity; they also constitute communicative acts which are mediated by role-relationships in context-sensitive ways. Context here is conceptualised as the figure-ground relations, i.e., 'a fundamental juxtaposition of two entities: (1) a focal event; and (2) a field of action within which that event is embedded' (Duranti and Goodwin 1992:3):

> Describing what is being contextualised as the focal event implies that it is in some sense more salient and noticeable than its context ... there does seem to be a fundamental figure-ground relationship implicated in the organisation of context, with the figure, what we are calling the focal event, standing out from a more amorphous ground as the official focus of attention. (Duranti and Goodwin 1992:32)

The notion of context can be expanded to encompass, following Malinowski (1935), 'context of situation' and 'context of culture'. As regards context of situation, for a long time sociological studies have focused on orderliness of interaction. The notion of orderliness also underscores pragmatic studies of action and interaction, enshrined in Grice's (1975) principle of cooperation and its attendant maxims. However, if we delve deeper, hybridity emerges as an inherent feature of orderliness.

The interaction order as conceptualised by Goffman (1983) implies hybridity, routinely manifest in the production and reception roles *vis-à-vis* the participation framework. Within the tradition of conversation analysis, Sacks (1992) stresses the notion of orderliness in the so-called grammar of interaction, which can be extended to include hybridity as an orderly phenomenon. The notion of activity type (Levinson 1979 [1992]), which is premised upon prototypes characterised by fuzziness along the more-or-less continuum, rather than an either-or categorisation, embodies hybridity at structural, sequential and stylistic levels. This hybridity at the interactional level is manifest through discourse types and role types (see below), which are characteristic of the participation framework in a given encounter.

8.2   KitKat hybridity

I am proposing a notion of 'KitKat hybridity' based on an everyday phenomenon. Phil Hammond, a physician by training, is well known as a TV Doctor for his BBC television and radio programmes. In his 2007 book, *Medicine Balls*, he writes: 'the KitKat is three layers of cream-filled wafer covered in an outer layer of chocolate. This qualifies it to appear on both biscuit and chocolate shelves of the supermarket, thus doubling its exposure and sales' (Hammond 2007:ix). So, hybridiity encompasses internal and external dimensions: internally, it is the compositional constituents of an entity such as KitKat; and externally, the entity is categorised based on criteriality, that KitKat can legitimately appear on both biscuit and chocolate shelves in a supermarket. In a comical vein, Hammond then applies the KitKat analogy to his own book: '*Medicine Balls* is a semi-autobiographical medico-political self-help comedy novel with poems. Please let me know in which section of the store you found it – biscuits or chocolate' (Hammond 2007:ix)

In introducing the notion of hybridity, I first draw attention to the ontological and epistemological difficulties associated with interactional hybridity, which no doubt serves utilitarian ends as does the KitKat. This leads me to suggest a need for unpacking hybridity in order to recognise simple and complex forms of hybridity at the interactional level. I then offer illustrative examples from professional practice in genetic counselling, which has been characterised as a hybrid activity type (Sarangi 2000).

Genetic counselling reconfigures several aspects of: the medical consultation; therapy/counselling; the service encounter, as well as the gatekeeping encounter, thus underscoring the interrelationship between role types and discourse types, resulting in interactional hybridity.

8.3 Hybridity as an interdisciplinary project: Ontological and epistemological considerations

In the domain of life sciences, the notion of hybridity can be traced back to Gregor Mendel (1822–1884) – himself part monk and part scientist. In his ground-breaking 'Experiments in Plant Hybridisation', he conducted experiments on ornamental plants to breed new colour variants by artificial insemination (see Bowler 1989). Then he crossed varieties of peas (e.g., yellow or green as well as round, angular, wrinkled) and counted all the alternative types of offspring in the first and later generations. This led him to formulate the concept of the gene which accounts for hereditary transmission. Genes are described as 'dominant' or 'recessive' and the distinction between these can be defined as follows: 'Those characters which are transmitted entire, or almost unchanged by hybridisation, and therefore in themselves constitute the characters of a hybrid, are termed dominant, and those which become latent in the process, recessive' (cited in Weatherall 1995:233).

Mendel's experiments with plants were followed by breeding experiments with the fruit fly by Thomas Hunt Morgan and his colleagues, who explained the phenomenon of 'crossing over' or 'recombination' involving the transmission of more than one gene. Hybridity implies intervention to alter the existing order – in simple and complex formats. This thinking, in later years, set the stage for hereditary explanations about human beings (see Francis Galton's [1979] *Hereditary Genius*) and diseases (see Joseph Adams' [1814] *A Treatise on the Supposed Hereditary Properties of Diseases*).

In the humanities and social sciences, many alternative terms to hybridity have been proposed – intertextuality, heterglossia, polyphony, blending/mixing, lamination, appropriation, etc. Central and common to this cluster of notions is that the notion of hybridity retains the meaning of crossover or recombination, but gains a different connotation. In the post-modern era, hybridity has a positive edge (as opposed to hybrid as a negative attribute – see Brah and Coombes (2000) on the inter-racial dimension of hybridity in biology, with overtones of impurity and stereotyping). When hybridity is viewed positively, the focus shifts to hybridisers – their agency, actions and roles on the one hand and the critical influence of social/institutional factors underpinning any form of hybridity, on the other. In other scholarly traditions, hybridity implies in-betweenness, i.e., ambiguity, which can be linked to prototype theory more generally.

In the 1970s, Eleanor Rosch (1973, 1977, 1978) proposed 'prototype theory' to capture how people generally categorise phenomena by matching them against the prototype or ideal exemplar (see also Berlin and Kay 1969). In terms of representationality, the key question is not whether an entity belongs to a category but whether it retains a prototypical status. Rosch argues that prototypes represent a basic level of categorisation, e.g. 'chair', as opposed to a superordinate level, e.g. 'furniture', and a subordinate level, e.g. 'dentist's chair'. Prototypes are also about graded categorisation encompassing attribute-value, which echoes Wittgenstein's approach to categories, in terms not of commonality, but of similarities and correspondences, say, between different kinds of games (board games, ball games, card games, etc.). The notion of 'family resemblance' thus becomes salient, which amounts to a calibration of conceptual distance. In prototype theory, how attribution is made – i.e., how one determines which of the constituent categories will contribute which feature – remains problematic. This is also true of interactional hybridity, as we will see below.

Given the multiple meaning trajectories associated with hybridity, a key analytic challenge emerges: which exclusion/inclusion criteria do we adopt in order to identify what constitutes interactional hybridity? In terms of identifying hybridity, is it a feature of the setting or a feature of language use, although both are mediated through role performance? How durable and systematic do the constituents have to be to qualify as a hybrid phenomenon? Following the analogy of genetic inheritance, are there dominant and recessive forms of hybridity at the interactional level? More generally, how do we go about explaining the conditions and consequences of interactional hybridity?

8.4   The conditions and consequences of interactional hybridity: Two activity type scenarios

Following Wittgenstein's (1958) notion of language games, activity types can be characterised as goal-oriented events with constraints on participants and inferences (Levinson 1979 [1992]). In language/communication research it is usual practice to audio- and/or video-record naturally occurring activity types before undertaking micro-level analysis of the data. We can regard these researcher-mediated recording sessions as a special kind of activity type. In addition to the much discussed 'observer's paradox' or 'Hawthorne's effect', there also prevails what I have called the 'participant's paradox' (Sarangi 2007a), which straddles, following Goffman, between 'the sphere of participation' and 'the sphere of interaction'.

Let us consider two such settings to tease out the analytic difficulties in labelling an activity as hybrid or not. The first one concerns a problem-based learning (PBL) tutorial in the context of medical education in Hong Kong (Storey 2012). The researcher is co-present in the tutorial to manage the recording equipment, which gives her very little participation status as far as the main tutorial activity is concerned. However, we learn that the researcher, in her role as a language instructor outside of this tutorial activity, has had a professional relationship with the tutor and the students. It transpires, however, that none of the participants orients to the researcher in terms of this past relationship. It is therefore safe to assume that although this tutorial as an activity type includes the co-presence of an outsider-researcher, the activity retains its integrity as a prototypical tutorial activity and does not become hybrid in terms of the researcher's participant status. Hybridity can, however, be located at the levels of talk and interaction types concerning the ratified participants – the tutor and the students – as the PBL session combines elements of tutor-led explanations/elicitations and student-led presentations.

The second setting concerns ultrasound scan encounters involving midwives and pregnant women in South Africa (Gilstad 2012). As in the PBL setting above, the researcher is co-present to manage the recording equipment. But she has an additional participant status, as she is part of the evaluation team responsible for assessing the effect of an educational training programme targeted at the midwives, by focusing on how they communicate with the pregnant women in real-life clinic encounters marked by linguistic and ethnic diversity.

Let us consider a brief example from the hybrid activity type reported in Gilstad (2012). Nobuntu is the advanced midwife and Jabulile is the pregnant woman. The extract begins with Nobuntu detecting a twin pregnancy during the ultrasound examination (the English translation of Zulu is provided in brackets). The researcher is co-present.

Data Example 1

01 Nobuntu: *Nansi inhliziyo yengane, nansi intamo yakhe bese kuba ikhanda.*
(Here's the baby's heart and here is the neck and then the head)
Kunelinye ikhanda la, uyalibo?
(There's another head in there, can you see it?)

02 Jabulile: *Uyaguquka ....*
(Is the baby turning?)

03 Nobuntu: *Nangu la ....* (Here it is ...) ------ ((Pointing at the screen)) -----

04 Jabulile: *Owesibili? ... Hhayi, angifune ma-twins ...*
(Is it the second one? No I don't want any twins ...)

05 Nobuntu: *Ehhe ..* (Yes.)

06 Jabulile: *Hhayi bo, ngeke kuphume ama-twins la, ngiyawesaba, ngiwes-aba* kabi.
(No way! I cannot give birth to twins, I'm scared of them, and I'm really scared ...)

07 Nobuntu: ((Looking at Jabulile)) ------ ((Laughing)) --- ((Looking at the researcher)) I am just saying to her --- ((Adding gel on the abdomen)) --- I am not sure...there is something I have seen...I thought it was a single baby...But when I see it properly, I see two fetal hearts. --- ((Indicating two with two fingers)) ---

08 Researcher: Two foetuses?

09 Nobuntu: ((Looking at the screen)) --- This is the first. --- ((Indicating on the screen. Moves the transducer from the left side to the right side to get the image of the other foetus. The head appears)) --- Maybe look at the head. --- ((Pointing at the screen)) ----- -- That's the head. And we move here, and there is another __ ((Short glimpse at the researcher before turning back to look at the screen)) __ There is another one.

10 Researcher: ((Laughing)) another

11 Nobuntu: ((Looking at Jabulile)) _______ They are both facing down.
Awuthi ngibone ukuthi zingaki lezingane zakho ezisesiswini
(Let me see how many babies you have in your belly ...)

With regard to the participation structure, both the researcher and the midwife orient to the researcher's evaluator role explicitly, as is evident in the code-switching between Zulu and English, in the initiation of laughter and in the display-type question-answer sequences, all of which are aimed primarily at each other. Through code-switching, among other things, we notice a shift in the participation structure. In turn 07, in terms of gesture and body positioning there is also evidence of the researcher's status as an active interactant rather than as a mere onlooker participant. It is worth noting the use of metacommentary ('I am saying to her...') and the use of third person reference for Jabulile, as a way of relegating the pregnant woman to a third party overhearer status, who only re-enters the conversation as a ratified participant in turn 11.

Thus interactional hybridity in terms of participation structure is achieved through a combination of interactional and linguistic devices. In Goffman's terms, the researcher here enters the 'sphere of interaction' and influences the encounter being observed, unlike the researcher in the PBL setting above, who retains her status only in the 'sphere of participation', i.e., is 'someone within range who is treated and treats himself [herself] as being out of frame, a mere bystander to be disattended' (Goffman 1974:224).

In the example above, the shift in talk, especially the code-switching, indexes a shift in participatory context. The researcher and the midwife in this ultrasound encounter did not participate in a predetermined manner. This reminds us of Hasan's critical stance on hybridity as a mere combination/fusion of already existent entities:

> [...] the metaphor of genre combination as also that of hybridity appears less than desirable, since both imply an unfortunate reification of the process of register, as if what is happening is simply a co-location or a fusion of two (or more) already existing recognisable objects. Registers/genres are not peaches and plums that can be hybridised into nectarines. (Hasan 2000:43)

However, in the sphere of interaction/participation, there is always an element of pre-existence of discourse features; but when incorporated into a given encounter, these features assume a character of contingency and create new meanings along the lines of language/semiotic tokens or discourse types deriving their meanings from context of use or the activity type (Sarangi 2000, see below). This is the dynamics which Hasan (2000) captures as inter-relationality between shift in talk and shift in context.

Let us revisit a brief example from her study (mother-child interaction in the home setting, where the mother is getting Kirsty ready for school):

Data Example 2

01 Kirsty:	mummy I think I'm going to get cold today	
02 Mother:	I have no idea what the weather is going to be like today I'll send your sweatshirt or your cardigan or your jumper or whatever you'd like over too	
03 Kirsty:	I want — I want a short-sleeved cardigan — a long-sleeved one if it goes hot I'll have to wear a short-sleeved one so** —	
04 Mother:	**yep well see yesterday I thought it was going to be cold and you were really hot by the end of the day so I think the best thing is to put a short-sleeved tee-shirt on you and a cardigan	

05 Kirsty:		yeah I think we don't know what day its going to be
06 Mother:		no it's a bit [?] in spring and autumn, isn't it? Stand up straight so I can get your duds on – in winter it is cold and in the summer it's hot and in the spring and the autumn it's funny (RUTH IS HEARD CRYING) oh Ruth! (to Kirsty) she's jammed her fingers in the sewing box [? put] her hand on top of the [? lid] .. silly monkey!
07 Kirsty:		silly monkey!
08 Mother:		she had her hand in [? the box]
09 Kirsty:		yeah
10 Mother:		and she had the other hand on top pushing it down squashing her hand (Kirsty laughs) oh you're a goose Ruth!
11 Kirsty:		oh you're a goose! Do goosies do that?
12 Mother:		no no but you often call people a goose if they're silly
13 Kirsty:		hmm
14 Mother:		you know <<if you eat too much >> I say you're a little pig – you're a little piggy-wig
15 Kirsty:		yeah (laughing)
16 Mother:		well <<if people are silly>> you say 'silly goose!' and sometimes you can say they're a donkey 'you silly donkey!'
17 Kirsty:		silly donkey! (laughs)
18 Mother:		and <<if they're fussy>> what do you say?** I think you'd say they're a hen .. or a mother hen

(source: Hasan 2000:32)

Shifts in talk, as Hasan demonstrates, also involve shifts in role. We have here evidence of mother-daughter talk, inclusive of an affective stance in attending to Kirsty's dress needs in light of variable weather conditions, as well as an authoritative tone ('stand up straight so I can put the duds on', turn 06). As a mother, she also attends to the other child, Ruth, while engaging with Kirsty. Throughout the episode, the mother also takes on the role of a teacher which is evidenced by shifts in talk – notice especially the longer stretches of explanation about coordinating dress with weather (turns 04 and 06), the use of analogies (e.g., goose, pig, donkey) to explain silly behaviour (turns 10 and 14) and the use of a rhetorical question in turn 18. While performing a teacher role, the mother, however, refrains from explicitly correcting Kirsty's linguistic error such as 'goosies' in turn 11. Kirsty, reciprocally, occupies the pupil role, which is marked by topical statements, question formulations, minimal responses and the repetition of utterances (turns 03, 05, 11, 13 and 17).

8.5 Activity types, discourse types and role types

In my previous work (Sarangi 2000, 2010a, 2011), I have argued that activity types are constituted in discourse types and it is the latter that account for 'interactional hybridity'. While activity type is a means of characterising settings (e.g., a medical consultation, a service encounter, a university seminar), discourse type is a way of characterising forms of talk/text (e.g., explanation, promotional talk, interrogation, troubles telling, formulaic speech, reported speech, online commentary, repetition, etc.) as well as forms of interaction (e.g., question, question-answer sequence, hyper-questioning, overlap, interruption, laughter, pause, silence, touch, nodding). The same discourse types can feature in different activity types and may serve different functions. The interactional hybridity within a given activity type is further exacerbated by the corresponding role types that are available to participants, as in the case of the mother shifting to a teacher role in the illustrated example above.

As Goffman (1974:269) puts it:

> [...] whenever an individual participates in an episode of activity, a distinction will be drawn between what is called the person, individual, or player, namely, he who participates, and the particular role, capacity, or function he realises during that participation. And a connection between these two elements will be understood. In short, there will be a *person-role formula*. (original emphasis)

8.6 Role, role-set and hybridity

Let us consider the notion of role in some detail. Rather than treating role as a rigid social category, many scholars, Goffman (1959) in particular, have argued in favour of an interactional, situational basis for role performance in social interaction – with 'role embracement' and 'role distancing' constituting the two ends of the spectrum (for a detailed discussion, see Sarangi 2010a, 2011). Shifts in role, or what Goffman (1981) sees as shifts in footing, are an integral feature of participation framework.

The concept of role – theorised on the intersection of psychology and sociology – is intimately connected with status. Merton (1968) develops the concept of 'role-set' (as distinct from 'multiple roles') in relation to status, and by extension, to the social system. Merton variously glosses 'role-set' as 'the complement of role-relationships' and as a 'complex of roles' associated with status-set. An example of a role-set would be mother, daughter, wife, daughter-in-law, sister-in-law, etc. This may be seen as a common and simple role-set, but can potentially take on a complex character, e.g., in the context of genetic counselling, when a decision to undergo a predictive genetic test for oneself or for a child is made, because of unintended consequences associated with the risks of knowing, and disclosing, genetic test results. Likewise, a genetics health professional's role-set will include those of medical expert, counsellor, educator, advocate, gatekeeper, etc.

According to Merton (1968:422–434), the key features of role-set can be listed as follows:

- Role expectations will frequently conflict, but there are social mechanisms for coping;
- differences of power among members of the role-set will set priorities;
- a person may not be seen in action by members of the role-set (e.g., absent parents in classroom);
- any member of the role-set may not know that his demand conflicts with that of another member;
- occupants of similar statuses may support each other against threats from members of the role-set (e.g., teachers united against parents);
- a person may abridge his role-set so as to make the remaining set more workable;
- the composition of a role-set is ordinarily not a matter of individual choice; although the composition of a role-set is determined by the social structure, shifts between roles within a role-set is a matter of individual choice.

Generally speaking, Merton sees role-set as a potential source of conflict even when significant members of the role-set are visibly absent. He, however, argues that such conflicts are not noticeable in everyday practice due to 'social regularity'. Coser (1975) expands Merton's theoretical framework and suggests a distinction between simple and complex role-sets in order to emphasise the fact that the ability to take the role of others enhances empathetic understanding, tolerance and even individual autonomy:

> Complex role-sets and differentiated roles are not alienating restrictions on individuality; they are its basic structural precondition. (1975:259)

Ecologically speaking, role-sets can be seen as role-hybridity, not always in conflict, but often in a complimentary relation. As we will see, in the context of genetic counselling, The relevance of Coser's remark becomes apparent as empathetic understanding of the client's situation becomes manifest.

There are, however, limitations to Merton's characterisation of role-set for discourse analytic purposes. When he exemplifies the role-set of a medical student *vis-à-vis* other students, teachers, physicians, nurses, social workers, etc., Merton is not thinking of the interaction order which can trigger role shifts *vis-à-vis* talk-context interrelationship. For Merton, the role-set becomes an external attribute rather than an internal attribute. Consider a physician who in a clinic encounter with patients will enact different role types from within an available role-set, e.g., shifting constantly between therapeutic and pedagogic roles. The notion of role-set, as conceptualised by Merton and Coser, does not anticipate interactional hybridity as such. In what follows I would argue that interactional hybridity – in simple and complex forms – is integral to the enactment of role-set in a given activity type.

Rommetveit (1955) suggests a distinction between prescribed role, subjective role and enacted role and sees these three categories as inter-linked. More precisely, the enacted role is underpinned by prescribed and subjective roles and typically there is alignment across the three perspectives. From a discourse analytic perspective, the enacted role (or what Goffman [1959] regards as 'role performance') is of intrinsic interest. In pragmatics and discourse analytic literature, the linkage between language and role is well established (Mehan 1983). Elsewhere (Sarangi 2010a, 2011), I have developed this role-language-context linkage by mainly focusing on professional role performance. Here I extend it to both professional and client role-sets in situated professional-client encounters in genetic counselling.

8.7 Role hybridity in professional-client encounters in genetic counselling

As an activity type, genetic counselling has similarities and differences with other counselling and therapy activity types – e.g., psychotherapy, marital counselling, HIV/AIDS counselling – and is recognisable as a hybrid activity type (Sarangi 2000). In addition, it incorporates features of many other activity types: mainstream medical consultation, gatekeeping and service encounters, etc. In line with this hybridity, the counsellor takes on certain roles, e.g., expert, gatekeeper, service provider. By a similar token, given the clients' genetic status as carriers, affected or unaffected, and, given the familial basis of genetic conditions, their positioning in the counselling setting can be discerned as parents, partners, sibling, children, etc. As we will see in the data examples, hybridity – both from the perspectives of counsellors and clients – can be identified at the levels of 'discourse types' and 'role types'.

The discourse types can range as follows: problem formulation (including gist, upshot); offer of 'response' vs. 'reply' (Goffman 1981); use of reflective questions (Sarangi *et al.* 2004, Sarangi 2010b); hypothetical questions (Peräkylä 1995); framing of information as advice (Silverman 1997); use of backchannelling cues and repetition (echoing and mirroring), interpretive summary (Ferrara, 1994); use of reported speech to endorse a given state of affair (Hall, Slembrouck and Sarangi 2006), etc. (See Sarangi 2013 for an extended discussion.)

Genetic counsellors (GC) articulate their role *vis-à-vis* clients in both research interviews and in actual genetic counselling encounters. This can be seen from the following account in an interview setting.[1]

Data Example 3a

GC: My role is to check that they've thought about all the various facets because, yes, they're experts in their experience of it, they've lived in their families but some people are focused on having that test for one particular reason, now I don't think that's a reason not to have the test but I'd see my role as checking that they've thought about all the other possible outcomes in order to prepare them for the test result. Sometimes you get a feeling that there's some conflict or uncertainty or whatever, it just seems to be something that's more fraught or difficult or tense or something that's a feeling in the room, and in those situations I wouldn't say to people, I don't think you should have the test, because I don't really think that, what I do think, usually is they just need some more time to process it and I'll say that.

In the above extract, the role-positioning of the counsellor is justified in relation to typical client profiles. The gatekeeper role becomes an integral part of the counsellor role, constituting a recognisable role-set. The counsellor role is foregrounded in preparing the clients through self-reflection for the test result – akin to a teacher checking pupils' understanding. Clients are, however, accorded the role of 'experts of experience', but may not be engaging adequately with issues at hand. The process-orientation of genetic counselling which emphasises the reflective aspect of clients' decision making against the backdrop of psychosocial issues becomes evident in genetic counselling sessions via the hybrid role-taking of the genetic counsellor.

Consider the following short extracts from genetic counselling encounters.

Data Example 3b-3e (N3 = Genetic Nurse; GC3 and GC7 = Genetic Counsellors)

(3b) N3:   I just wondered if it was something that you talked about between you before you came here if you'd (.) talked about it between yourselves

(3c) GC7:   It's about giving you options again you're in control but it's not forcing anything on anybody and (.) you know if you want the information of the test (.) then we'll we'll give you it (.) I'd rather not go through the testing (.) if you didn't want to know at the end

(3d) GC7:   you've got to think about you as well and that's what today's about a little bit just thinking about you (.) and as a couple (.) and what works for you two (.) 'cause parents spend a lot of time thinking about what's right for the children and forgetting what's right for them (..) (you've) just got to balance it up so we just need to spend (.) ten minutes or so thinking about that

(3e) GC3:   we talked a (.) a bit about last time (.) um (.) was (.) having children ((coughs)) your feelings or both of your feelings about that has (.) has that still been something that you sort of been (.) talking about something that you've been (.) thinking about

In 3b, the hypothetical if-constructions are aimed at enabling clients for self-reflection within the ethos of nondirectiveness of genetic counselling. In 3c, the hypothetical constructions are accompanied by a contrast structure – testing will be offered on the condition that the client is prepared for and is willing to absorb the test result even if it shows uncertain significance. In 3d, we detect a coercing of the client to think about herself as a person and as a partner rather than merely to adopt a parental role (cf. the person-role formula discussed earlier). A role-tension is alluded to, with the imperative of a balancing act. In other words, we notice here an available role-set for clients to consider in the decision-making process. There is the suggestion that the best interests of self are not always served by upholding the best interests of the children. In 3e, the role-set extends to include the role of partner and that of future parent.

The examples above point to the importance of clients' self-reflection regarding various consequences of their actions and decisions, including unintended ones. Adoption of such roles indexes interactional hybridity, which is evident in reflective talk. The complexity in the available role-set can be mapped on to the multi-faceted self-other dynamics (Sarangi 2007b).

8.8 An extended example from the genetic counselling activity type

In this section I will consider a single genetic counselling encounter in more detail, retaining the focus on role-talk-context dynamics. The client, a woman in her mid-40s, has had several relatives dying of breast cancer at a young age. Because of this family history, the client has been receiving regular mammograms for the last few years. The extract starts with the female genetic counsellor (GC) explaining to the client (CL) that the faulty gene is unlikely to have been passed down through her side of the family, as her mother, a first order relative, has reached her 70s without having developed any cancers.

In my analysis, I consider the participant structure in this activity type, with a particular focus on the interplay between discourse types and role types (affordable within the role-set). To begin with, we can expect the role-set of the genetic counsellor to include the following constituent roles: biomedical expert; psychosocial counsellor; therapist; service provider; gatekeeper; mediator; advocate, etc.

Data Example 4a
01 GC: women who have the faulty gene, by her age we'd say at least
       two thirds of them would have had cancer by now
02 CL: yes
03 GC: yeah. (pause) I'm not sure whether you're going to be pleased
       about this or not, but I- I think you're in the group of women
       that we'd think are low risk. ((pause))
04 CL: oh right
05 GC: mm. and therefore I think you're in the group of women for
       whom we'd say- probably additional screening is not necessary
06 CL: ri::::::ght

```
07 GC:  now- (.) you've just had a mammogram
08 CL:  mm
09 GC:  and when you're fifty you qualify for the ((region)) breast
        screening programme anyway
10 CL:  =oh right
11 GC:  =in which case you would start having them three-yearly from
        that point anyway.
12 CL:  oh right
```

The episode opens with GC adopting the role of the medical expert by using the information giving format (here, inheritance patterns in cancer) which includes delivery of good/bad news. She draws upon epidemiological trends (see turns 01 and 03) and categorises CL as 'low risk' and this is intended as reassurance. The risk assessment in turn 03 is based on biomedical expertise, but it has an element of psychosocial counselling ('I'm not sure whether you're going to be pleased about this or not'). Beginning with turn 05 (see also 07, 09, 11), GC shifts her role to being a service provider as well as a gatekeeper in outlining what the normal practice is and how eligibility for the breast screening programme in the region is determined for different kinds of at-risk cohorts, including the 'low risk' cohort that CL now belongs to. The notion of 'low risk' is itself a biomedical/epidemiological category, partly influenced by resources available to healthcare providers. In swiftly moving to future screening provision, GC is not allowing CL to contest her 'low risk' status and what it means to her. The gatekeeper role is accompanied by the language of eligibility (note 'additional screening is not necessary' in turn 07; 'when you're fifty you qualify' in turn 09) which is foregrounded by stressing the causal link ('therefore' in turn 05) between population trends, individual 'at risk' status and the current service provision. In her service provider role, she outlines how CL's screening programme will be managed in the future (turn 11). GC's role as an institutional gatekeeper is implicit but it informs the decision about CL's ineligibility for breast screening until she is 50. In formulating CL's current and future 'at risk' status, it is to be noted that GC orients to CL's primary role as an individual, a middle-aged woman *vis-à-vis* other women in the general population in her category.

GC's adoption of the discourse type of information giving format during the delivery of good/bad news is complemented by CL's adoption of the discourse type of minimal responses such as 'yes' (turn 02) and 'mm' (turn 08). However, what is striking about CL's minimal responses is that on three occasions (turns 04, 10 and 12) an element of surprise/newsworthiness is shown (with the 'oh' prefix in 'oh right') and on one occasion (turn 06) the elongated 'ri:::::ght' signals a dispreference, almost bordering on disbelief.

In prioritising the information provider and service provider roles, at this point GC perhaps fails to respond to these surprise/dispreference tokens in her role as psychosocial counsellor.

GC, however, embraces the psychosocial counsellor role as the interaction unfolds.

Data Example 4b (continues from 4a)
13 GC: em (.) I mean having (.) said that, what's going through your mind <u>now</u>, is it sort of like- ((pause))
14 CL: ehm ((pause)) ((exhales, sighs)) *pf::::::* (.) I- I (don't feel) very comfortable with it, I almost felt like >>uh I wish I hadn't come then<<
15 GC: <u>mm</u>
16 CL: because I had my mammogram <u>every year</u>
17 GC: yeah
18 CL: but ehm ((pause))
19 CL: obviously I do appreciate what you've said about- about the risk and that. (.) ehm but I still got- (.) ehm an irrational emotional sort of thing because of ((cousin who died from breast cancer at 30))
20 GC: I understand that and-
21 CL: =and
22 GC: =and the experience you go through in your family is more powerful than anything I can say to you
23 CL: ((emphatically)) <u>mm</u> what you're saying to me makes sense (.) em ((pause))
24 CL: ((tats)) but I can understand what you're saying and I also understand about ehm resources and one figure or another (.) I mean in the ideal world every woman would have one (.) ehm every year (.) and obviously I do appreciate that. (.) but ehm
25 GC: I mean it's not only resources in terms of pure cost-cutting, but it is ehm little bits of additional x-ray you're getting, and also the fact that you're- you know (.) before the menopause- (.) you know, it's not as reliable- you know (.) mammograms aren't as reliable as after the menopause and
26 CL: no
27 GC: ehm
28 CL: so what you're actually sort of suggesting perhaps is that I wouldn't need any screening now until I'm fifty, that's what you're sort of putting to me (.) isn't it?
29 GC: yea::::h (.) but I'm not- I don't think that we ever should <u>discount</u> the emotional <u>side</u> of things
30 CL: mm

31 GC: because we're (.) I think we're here to give health care and
       health care isn't just about (.) fears
32 CL: mm
33 GC: it's about people feeling confident and comfortable, too
34 CL: mm
35 GC: about their own health. and (.) I mean I think it would be- I
       need to get the confirmation for the diagnosis (.) I need to talk
       to someone else about what I've said (.)
36 CL: mm

In turn 13, we notice a role shift on GC's part – now orienting to the psychosocial issues as a counsellor. This role-shift is marked by a shift at the level of discourse type – from information giving format to an open question format ('what's going through your mind') followed by minimal responses indicative of active listening (turns 15, 17, 20). GC's minimal responses allow CL to express her feelings/emotions/anxieties. CL's response in turn 14 is marked by hesitation and halted speech culminating in 'I don't feel very comfortable with it, I almost felt like uh I wish hadn't come then'. This shows that GC's assessment of CL's at-risk status so far has been far from reassuring. With the help of minimal responses as a discourse type, GC encourages CL to tell her side of the story, which CL frames as 'an irrational emotional sort of thing' (turn 19) at a psychosocial level, in juxtaposition to the epidemiological stance adopted by GC earlier. By bringing up the topic of the 'cousin who died from breast cancer at 30', CL underscores, in a manner of justification, her own increased risk status based on her belief in patterns of inheritance. CL thus orients herself to not just being a woman in the general population, but as someone who has a history of breast cancer in the extended family. This information is disregarded by GC as a cousin counts as a second-order relative when calculating familial risk, which does not therefore alter the risk status of CL. We notice GC generally empathising with CL in turn 20.

In turn 22, GC maintains her counsellor role in highlighting the familial aspect of genetic inheritance by issuing what Ferrara (1994) calls an interpretive summary. In what follows (turns 23 and 24), CL acknowledges GC's overall gatekeeping stance in rationing resources such as breast screening, although such a stance was not explicitly marked by GC, as we have seen earlier. As far as CL is concerned, she continues to shift her role from being an ordinary middle aged woman to being a member of a family with the history of breast cancer, to being an advocate for all women who should have the right to breast screening ('in the ideal world every woman would have one [mammogram] every year', turn 24). Here CL also picks up on GC's gatekeeping role aimed at safeguarding limited resources. This challenge from CL prompts GC to return to her medical expert role by explicitly distancing herself from her gatekeeping role, the latter amounting to monitoring 'resources in terms of pure cost-cutting'. We see a justification of GC's decision about not recommending CL for additional screening under the current circumstances as one which is informed by biomedical evidence instead: 'mammograms aren't as reliable as after the menopause'. In turn 28, CL formulates an interpretive summary – a discourse type usually associated with professionals – as a way of clarifying where she stands with regard to future screening. This framing, with its metapragmatic overtones, is confrontational as it is intended to exert force on GC to reconsider her position (note especially the tag question 'isn't it' in turn 28). For a moment, it seems the various roles within the role-set seem incommensurable. GC, in turn 29, attests her counsellor role (as opposed to a gatekeeper role characterised by rationing and rationality) as she reinforces the significance of 'the emotional side of things' and frames this with the use of collective pronoun 'we' to underscore the professional psychosocial ethos of genetic counselling and then extends it to healthcare delivery in general (turns 31, 33, 35), thus embracing her health provider role.

The interaction continues as follows (turns 35 and 36 are repeated from the previous extract).

Data Example 4c
35 GC: about their own health. and (.) I mean I think it would be- I
         need to get the confirmation for the diagnosis (.) I need to talk
         to someone else about what I've said (.)
36 CL: mm
37 GC: but I'm just wondering if at this point (.) I might write to the
         breast clinic and say how about we kind of- go fifty fifty and
         say that you've got another <u>one</u> mammogram before you're
         fifty (.) so maybe not next year but in two years time
38 CL: mm
39 GC: and then when you're fifty- and that- would that? [give you
         some more reassurance]
40 CL: [well, that- that would give me more] confidence and reassur-
         ance, yes it would do
41 GC: yeah, yeah
42 CL: and I know- I mean it is an emotional thing (.) it's not- but
         then a lot of these things are (.) or <u>even</u> psychological some of
         these eh-
43 GC: mm. (.) and know I completely understand that when you've
         lost a cousin of similar age at such a young age (.) that is very
         powerful and scary (.) really?
44 CL: and I had to fight quite hard to get any breast screening <u>at all</u>

45 GC: yeah
46 CL: eh a lot of people thought I was just being sort of paranoid or-
47 GC: yeah
48 CL: but it wasn't actually just paranoia (.) there- >>I suppose there
        is a certain amount<< when you've got somebody close in
        the family like that (.) and also at the time my children were
        small and I thought oh- fancy having to leave them without a
        mother
49 GC: yeah (.) yeah
50 CL: and also, <u>now that I'm on my own</u>, so I'm a <u>single</u> mother,
        even though my children are older, ((daughter)) is only fifteen,
        she's coming up to fifteen, so she's ((whispering)) *she-s still
        my baby*
51 GC: mm
52 CL: so there's that sort of additional uh what would happen if (...)
53 GC: yeah, [yeah I understand]
54 CL: [and in just another-] another year or two (.) when they're sort
        of (..) <u>sufficient</u>
55 GC: yeah
56 CL: then it-
57 GC: I completely (.) take on board-
58 CL: =that's all I'm saying
59 GC: =on board completely [...]

In turns 35 and 37 we notice an interesting role shift as far as GC is concerned, continuing in the spirit of collective responsibility. Adopting a mediator role, she is now willing to negotiate with colleagues and possibly revisit the previously pronounced decision about CL's ineligibility for additional screening at the present time. She uses constructed dialogue with the breast cancer clinic ('how about we kind of go fifty fifty [...]') to strike a bargain on behalf of CL by adopting an advocacy role, despite her explicit statement earlier about the reduced medical benefits of mammogram before menopause. In the following turn, GC foregrounds her counsellor role to provide 'more reassurance' as part of the counselling process as well as counselling outcomes. This prioritising of reassurance aligns with CL's emotional and psychosocial concerns (turn 42). In turn 43, GC recycles CL's earlier concern about the cousin's death at a young age, framed as 'very powerful and scary'. This is indicative not only of active listening but also of counselling more generally, which remains primarily oriented to psychosocial issues, even though the risk status of CL does not alter because of the cousin's premature death. From this point onwards, CL adopts the role of someone who has had to fight a moral battle against all odds to procure breast screening on the grounds of familial inheritance. To this role, she adds her role-responsibility as a single mother of small children, one of whom she still regards as 'my baby'. The whispering tone signals how both GC and CL orient to motherhood in acknowledging that grown-up children always remain babies in their mothers' eyes. Here we can identify a conflation of roles – responsible parenting and affective mothering. A hypothetical scenario follows in turn 52, which underscores CL's continuing responsibility to care for her young children without having to remain anxious about her own at-risk status. Throughout this episode (turns 44–59), GC not only displays her counsellor role through minimal responses, she also positively aligns with CL as a fellow woman.

8.9   Conclusion

The key argument of this paper is that activity types, in themselves fuzzy and mappable along a cline of corresponding prototypes, are made up of discourse types and role types and that it is the interplay between discourse types and role types that renders activity types interactionally hybrid – some in more complex form than others. Analytically, it is possible to map the various role types available to both professionals and clients onto discourse types within the activity type of genetic counselling. The analysis above points to a complex, rather than simple, form of hybridity, to use Coser's (1975) useful distinction. Its complexity is manifest not only in terms of the number of roles from within the role-set of genetic counsellor that have been activated (e.g. biomedical expert; psychosocial counsellor; therapist; service provider; gatekeeper; mediator; advocate) but also in the extent to which the professional role-set aligns with the shifting roles of the client from within her role-set (a woman; a single mother; a spokesperson for women). Although constituents within a role-set such as parent, mother, partner can be embraced effortlessly in everyday settings, in the context of genetic counselling this role-set assumes complexity, especially if it concerns screening as part of risk management. The role-set for genetic counsellors, however, is likely to be more routinised and durable, although variations are probable, depending on specific genetic conditions and client profiles. The interrelationship between role-sets and discourse types is marked by dynamism, which mediates the activity type and contributes to interactional hybridity in simple or complex configurations.

There are occasions where one can notice 'relative incompatibility' between a counsellor role and a gatekeeper role. Equally striking would be a sense of incompatibility when the counsellor takes on the role of an advocate/mediator on behalf of absent or co-present family members who may be affected by the decisions made by an individual client regarding genetic testing and (non)disclosure of genetic test results to significant others. The incompatibility may be manifest in terms of a professional nondirective ethos of counselling in general vs. family-oriented counselling, which privileges articulation of different family members' potential concerns – because of the familial basis of genetic conditions. Indeed, the subtle incompatibilities, or even the manifest conflictual characteristics, which are associated with role types within a role-set can be circumvented through strategic use of discourse types in a given activity type. Activity analysis must pay attention to the interplay of discourse types and role types in order to account for different forms of hybridity, socio-historically and contingently, as well as ecologically and manifestly.

Transcription Conventions

(.): micropause
(..): pauses up to one second
(...): pause exceeding one second
((gap)): indicates an interval of longer length between speaker turns and an approximation of length in seconds
.hhh: inhalation
CAPITAL LETTERS: indicate increased volume
<u>Underlining</u>: spoken with emphasis
> > .... < < : spoken with speed
word: indicates decreased volume
question mark [?]: rising intonation
[text in square brackets]: overlapping speech
((text in double round brackets)): description or anonymised information
(text in round brackets): transcriber's guess
^^^^: untranscribable
= a continuous utterance

Notes

1   The data extracts are drawn from three funded research projects: 'Risk Communication in Genetics Counselling', The Leverhulme Trust (1998–1999); 'Communicative Frames in Counselling for Predictive Genetic Testing',

The Wellcome Trust (2001–2004); and 'Genetics, Health and Identity' as part of the Centre for the Study of the Economic and Social Aspects of Genomics, Economic and Social Research Council (ESRC, 2003–2008).

References

Adams, J. (1814). *A Treatise on the Supposed Hereditary Properties of Diseases.* London: J. Callow.

Berlin, B., and Kay, P. (1969). *Basic Color Terms: Their Universality and Evolution.* Berkeley: The California University Press.

Bowler, P.J. (1989). *The Mendelian Revolution.* Baltimore: Johns Hopkins University Press.

Brah, A. and Coombes, A.E. (Eds) (2000). *Hybridity and Its Discontents: Politics, Science, Culture.* London: Routledge.

Coser, R.L. (1975). The complexity of roles as a seedbed of individual autonomy. In L.A. Coser (Ed.), *The Idea of Social Structure: Papers in Honour of Robert K. Merton,* 237–263. New York: Harcourt Brace.

Duranti, A. and Goodwin, C. (Eds) (1992). *Rethinking Context: Language as an Interactive Phenomenon.* Cambridge: Cambridge University Press.

Ferrara, K.W. (1994). *Therapeutic Ways with Words.* New York: Oxford University Press.

Galton, F. (1979). *Hereditary Genius.* London: Julian Freidman.

Gilstad, H. (2012). *Obstetric Ultrasound Expertise as Manifest in Encounters between Midwives and Pregnant Women: A Case Study from KwaZulu-Natal in South Africa,* Unpublished Doctoral Thesis, NTNU, Trondheim, Norway.

Goffman, E. (1959). *The Presentation of Self in Everyday Life.* Garden City, NY: Doubleday Anchor Books.

Goffman, E. (1974). *Frame Analysis: An Essay on the Organisation of Experience.* New York: Harper and Row.

Goffman, E. (1981). *Forms of Talk.* Oxford: Basil Blackwell.

Goffman, E. (1983). The interaction order. *American Sociological Review,* 48(1), 1–17. http://dx.doi.org/10.2307/2095141

Grice, H.P. (1975). Logic and conversation. In P. Cole and J.L. Morgan (Eds), *Syntax and Semantics* (Vol. 3). *Speech Acts,* 41–59. New York: Academic Press.

Hall, C., Slembrouck, S., and Sarangi, S. (2006). *Language Practices in Social Work: Categorisation and Accountability in Child Welfare.* London: Routledge.

Hammond, P. (2007). *Medicine Balls.* Edinburgh: Black and White Publishing.

Hasan, R. (2000). The uses of talk. In S. Sarangi and M. Coulthard (Eds), *Discourse and Social Life,* 28–47. London: Longman.

Levinson, S. (1979 [1992]). Activity types and language. *Linguistics* 17, 365–399. (Reprinted in Drew and Heritage Eds [1992] *Talk at Work: Interaction in Institutional Settings,* 66–100. Cambridge: Cambridge University Press).

Malinowski, B. (1935). *Coral Gardens and their Magic*. London: Allen and Unwin.

Mehan, H. (1983). The role of language and the language of role in institutional decision making. *Language in Society*, 12(2), 187–211. http://dx.doi.org/10.1017/S0047404500009805

Merton, R.K. (1968). *Social Theory and Social Structure* (enlarged edition). New York: Free Press.

Peräkylä, A. (1995). *AIDS Counselling: Institutional Interaction and Clinical Practice*. Cambridge: Cambridge University Press. http://dx.doi.org/10.1017/CBO9780511597879

Rommetveit, R. (1955). *Social Norms and Roles: Explorations in the Psychology of Enduring Social Pressures*. Minneapolis: University of Minnesota Press.

Rosch, E.H. (1973). Natural categories. *Cognitive Psychology*, 4(3), 328–350. http://dx.doi.org/10.1016/0010-0285(73)90017-0

Rosch, E.H. (1977). Classification of real-world objects: Origins and representations in cognition. In P.N. Johnson-Laird and P.C. Wason (Eds), *Thinking: Readings in Cognitive Science*, 212–222. Cambridge: Cambridge University Press.

Rosch, E.H. (1978). Principles of categorization. In E.H. Rosch and B.B. Lloyd (Eds), *Cognition and Categorization*, 27–48. Hillsdale: Lawrence Erlbaum Associates.

Sacks, H. (1992). *Lectures on Conversation*, 2 vols. Edited by G. Jefferson and introduction by E.Schegloff. Oxford: Blackwell.

Sarangi, S. (2000). Activity types, discourse types and interactional hybridity: the case of genetic counselling. In S. Sarangi and M. Coulthard (Eds), *Discourse and Social Life*, 1–27. London: Pearson.

Sarangi, S. (2007a). The anatomy of interpretation: Coming to terms with the analyst's paradox in professional discourse studies. *Text & Talk*, 27(5–6), 567–584. http://dx.doi.org/10.1515/TEXT.2007.025

Sarangi, S. (2007b). Other-orientation in patient-centred healthcare communication: unveiled ideology or discoursal ecology? In G. Garzone and S. Sarangi (Eds), *Discourse, Ideology and Ethics in Specialised Communication*, 39–71. Berne: Peter Lang.

Sarangi, S. (2010a). Reconfiguring self/identity/status/role: The case of professional role performance in healthcare encounters. *Journal of Applied Linguistics and Professional Practice* 7(1): 75–95. Also published in G. Garzone and J. Archibald (Eds) (2010) *Discourse, Identities and Roles in Specialized Communication*, 33–57. Bern: Peter Lang.

Sarangi, S. (2010b). The spatial and temporal dimensions of reflective questions in genetic counselling. In A. Freed and S. Ehrlich (Eds), *Why Do You Ask?": The Function of Questions in Institutional Discourse*, 235–255. Oxford: Oxford University Press.

Sarangi, S. (2011). Role hybridity in professional practice. In S. Sarangi, V. Polese and G. Caliendo (Eds), *Genre(s) on the Move: Hybridisation and Discourse Change in Specialised Communication*, 271–296. Napoli: Edizioni Scientifiche Italiane (ESI).

Sarangi, S. (2013). Genetic counselling communication: A discourse-analytical approach. In *Encyclopaedia of Life Sciences*. Chichester: John Wiley and Sons; http://dx.doi.org/10.1002/9780470015902.a0005630.pub2

Sarangi, S. (forthcoming). Owning responsible actions/selves: Parental accounts in the context of childhood genetic testing. In J.-O. Östman and A. Solin (Eds), *Discourse and Responsibility in Professional Settings*. London: Equinox.

Sarangi, S., Bennert, K., Howell, L., Clarke, A., Harper, P., and Gray, J. (2004). Initiation of reflective frames in counselling for Huntington's Disease predictive testing. *Journal of Genetic Counseling*, 13(2), 135–155. http://dx.doi.org/10.1023/B:JOGC.0000018823.60761.e0

Silverman, D. (1997). *Discourses of Counselling: HIV Counselling as Social Interaction*. London: Sage.

Storey, A.M. (2012). *The Display and Negotiation of Expertise and Uncertainty in Problem-Based Tutorials in Medicine: A discourse analytic approach*. Unpublished Doctoral Thesis, Cardiff University, UK.

Weatherall, D. (1995). *Science and the Quiet Art: Medical Research and Patient Care*. Oxford: Oxford University Press.

Wittgenstein, L. (1958). *Philosophical Investigations*. Oxford: Blackwell.

About the author

Srikant Sarangi is professor at Aalborg University, where he directs the Danish Institute of Humanities and Medicine/Health. Since 1998 he has been Editor of *TEXT & TALK, An Interdisciplinary Journal of Language, Discourse and Communication Studies* (Formerly TEXT, Mouton de Gruyter). His research interests include: discourse analysis and applied linguistics; language and identity in public life; institutional and professional discourse; quality of life and risk communication in diverse domains; intercultural pragmatics; racism and ethnicity in multicultural societies. Among his publications are *Sociolinguistics and Social Theory* (with Coupland and Candlin (eds), Pearson Education, 2001), and *Language Practice in Social Work: Categorisation and accountability in child welfare* (with Hall and Slembrouck, Routledge, 2006).

Part III
Registerial and generic hybridity

9

Hybridisation: How language users graft new discourses on old root stock

Geoff Thompson

University of Liverpool

9.1   Introduction

At times, language users are likely to find themselves coping with the production of types of discourse which are to a greater or lesser extent unfamiliar to them. Some of these text types (e.g. in the academic sphere) are well established, with more or less explicitly formulated conventions and with expert users who may monitor and guide novices. Others involve social roles which are recurrent in the culture but which any individual may occupy relatively infrequently and will typically learn to handle at least partially on their own (e.g. in many asymmetric dyads, such as solicitor-client consultations, only one of the participants is trained to carry out their role). While there has been much research on how novices are helped to become more proficient in handling unfamiliar discourses, there has been somewhat less attention paid to the personal linguistic resources that they bring to the task (though see, for example, Ivanič 1998).

An extra dimension has been added in recent years by the rapid spread of the internet: this has made available opportunities for any user to produce for public consumption text types such as film and restaurant reviews which were previously likely to be produced only by experts. In this chapter, I focus on an exploration of the lexico-grammatical features of texts which result when non-expert writers go about mastering unfamiliar discourse types. The initial hypothesis is that the result will be a hybrid between the discourse types with which they are already familiar (their individual repertoires, in Martin's 2006 terms) and features of the target register as produced by experts, and that the parts played by these two main sources will in principle be identifiable.

Preliminary studies of discourse produced by non-experts, in blogs and in asymmetric dyads (e.g. Thompson 2009), suggested that informal speech is, unsurprisingly, the default register that is drawn on. This is the familiar root stock, as it were, onto which features from new discourse types – with experts' texts as models which the non-experts can draw on to a greater or lesser extent – may be grafted to produce hybrid texts. In the study reported on here, I set out to explore this possibility in greater depth. I use internet texts produced in various contexts to investigate the linguistic characteristics of some of the hybrids, and to illustrate corpus-based methods by which these characteristics may be probed. The data come from two kinds of online blogs, each with expert and novice contributors. One set comprises football match reports written by experts, and blog entries in which fans (and occasionally opponents) of the football team in question respond to the match report and/or each other; and the other, consisting of two sub-corpora, brings together leader articles from two newspapers, one 'quality' and the other 'popular', followed by blog entries on the topic of the leader article written by readers of the newspaper. All the data is from 2012. A reference corpus of informal conversation is also used, to allow a comparison between the blogs and, on the one hand, the experts' texts and, on the other, unplanned spoken discourse.

9.2   Starting points

My first encounter with the phenomenon explored in this study came a number of years ago, when one of my MA students decided to look at an example of an online football fanzine (Bietsch 2002). At the time, these were a relatively new venture for UK football supporters, and one incidental question that arose was what models the writers might have drawn on in deciding how to produce this unfamiliar register.

The most obvious potential model was cyclostyled football fanzines of the kind investigated by McCarthy (1993). However, those were also written by ordinary fans and appeared not to go through a process of editing by 'expert' writers; so they raised exactly the same question. A more likely source seemed to be match reports in newspapers, particularly the local newspapers. However, even a cursory comparison indicated that the aims of the two types of text were very different: the newspaper reports of the same match typically set out to give a roughly chronological and relatively impartial account of the match, while the online fanzine text focused on the writer's overtly partisan evaluation of different reactions in the press to the match and of the individual players. The differences also showed up, naturally enough, in the language choices. For example, the newspaper reports exhibited a clear content-oriented method of development (Fries 1981[1983]) in the thematic choices, suggesting careful planning of the discourse. On the other hand, Themes in the online fanzine were far less clearly patterned, switching abruptly between different kinds of topics and between an orientation towards content and towards interpersonal negotiation in a way that was reminiscent of, or perhaps even imitating, the spontaneous nature of conversation (Thompson and Thompson 2009). Not only other readers but players were addressed directly. Example (1) illustrates both of these features.

> (1) Finally, a word to Robbie. Keep plugging away, son. A striker's game is about sharpness and confidence. He has neither at the moment, and that is understandable. But don't assume he's finished. He's had these spells before. They don't last long, do they?

An alternative model which appeared more promising, particularly because of this possible link with spontaneous speech, was post-match commentaries on television. These are produced by people who have training (or at least public practice) in commenting on matches. The following transcript of an extract of this kind of commentary (from BBC 'Match of the Day' 27 June 2010) shows a number of the features which are found in the online fanzine:

> (2) You can look at every single goal we've conceded today and you're scratching your head as if to say goodness me how poor was our defending. I mean that ball travelled from their 6-yard line to ten yards from our goal and no-one has touched it. And defensively, I mean it's just so so poor, you can't defend – you just – they're so bad you don't even – you're lost for words, it's that bad. You wouldn't see that on a Sunday morning under-10 game.

Shared features include: the orientation towards evaluation (e.g. *so so poor, so bad*) rather than simple recounting of the match; the identification with the team (e.g. *our defending*); the use of *you* ambiguous between generic and direct address (in this case to the other members of the group discussing the match); markers of spoken discourse such as *I mean*. There is also a feature not present in the fanzine: uncompleted clauses (*you can't defend – you just – they're so bad you don't even – you're lost for words*) – this is a point I will come back to below.

Bietsch's study raised the issue of possible models for the production of unfamiliar discourse, but this was not the main focus and was therefore not followed up in a systematic way. In a later study, I took a more quantitative, though much narrower, approach: the data there was a small corpus of doctor-patient consultations (Thompson 2009). The link with the theme of the present article is that, whereas doctors are trained to fill the role of doctor and receive plenty of exposure and practice – both explicit guidance and practical apprenticeship – patients generally have to make it up as they go along: they have to work out how to 'be a patient' (linguistically) for themselves (within the framework provided by the doctor, of course). The study focused on the ways in which the two interactants asked yes/no questions. The following examples illustrate the four main possible forms of realisation of this speech function: full yes/no interrogative in (3); question tag in (4); interrogative with ellipsis of part or all of the Mood element (i.e., Finite and Subject – see Halliday and Matthiessen 2004:152) in (5); and queclarative (a declarative clause with the function of eliciting a yes/ no response) in (6).

(3) Patient: is it like a thing I've got with my spine

(4) Patient: you wouldn't think it was so painful would you

(5) Doctor: waterworks ok
    Patient: yeh fine

(6) Doctor: so it got worse overnight
    Patient: yeh

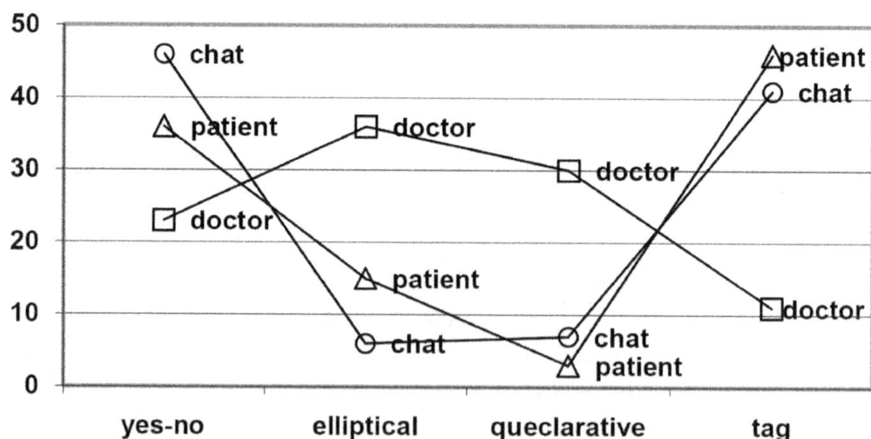

Figure 9.1: Yes/no question forms
(Totals: doctor 229 instances; patient 66 instances; chat 224 instances)

The main purpose of the analysis was to check whether doctors exhibited systematically different patterns of yes/no questions from patients; but I also compared the results against a corpus of casual chat of similar size. Figure 9.1 shows the distribution of the four realisation options in the three sub-corpora in percentages.

In terms of my present interests, the salient point to emerge is the similarity between the profile for the patient and the casual chat, particularly in the low relative frequency of queclaratives and the high frequency of tags, and particularly when viewed against the very different profile for the doctor. Whereas the differences between the profiles for the doctor and patient and for the doctor and chat are statistically significant at the 0.0005 level of probability (df = 3, χ^2 = 134.812 and 58.791 respectively), those between the profiles for the patient and chat are at best marginally significant (df = 3, χ^2 = 7.632, p > 0.05). This suggests that, in this small area of linguistic use at least, the patients were to a certain extent drawing on the familiar resources of conversational patterns to cope with a relatively specialised communicative situation for which they had no specialised preparation.

However, while both of these earlier studies thus supported to some extent the intuition that casual conversation is the default register that language users fall back on in unfamiliar contexts, neither provided direct evidence of possible hybridity of the kind that is of interest here. Patients have no obvious 'model' which might interact with their conversational resources; and they are also not performing a role that is open to public scrutiny. The online fanzine is a public document but of a text type that, at the time, did not yet have agreed conventions of its own; and the analysis remained at an informal level. The stimulus for undertaking the study reported in the rest of this paper was therefore the goal of investigating the issue of how untrained users coped with producing unfamiliar public registers in more systematic detail.

In embarking on an analysis of the possible hybrid nature of the blogs, I assumed that in terms of register (Halliday and Hasan 1985[1989]) the nature of the data meant that the field (the kind of social activity being carried out) would be more or less held constant at the least delicate level, but the tenor (the relations between interactants) and mode (the medium through which the discourse is realised) would be the aspects of the context in which variation might show up; so I focused especially on choices in interpersonal systems, which construe the tenor of the context, with textual systems, construing the mode, included where it seemed relevant. My assumption about constant field in fact turned out to be mistaken to some extent, but the analyses I undertook did nevertheless prove revealing. However, it should be emphasised that, as Tables 9.1 and 9.5 show, the samples are small and any conclusions can only be tentative.

9.3   Football blogs

The first set of data that I examined consisted of entries in a regular blog on the website of Arsenal Football Club in London. There is a section of the website in which an 'expert' posts a report on each match, and fans have the opportunity to respond to the report in various ways. The experts' texts thus provide a potential model which the bloggers may or may not draw on in writing their contributions to the blog. I also used a comparator corpus of casual conversation, on the basis of the starting hypothesis that the blogs would be hybrid texts showing a combination of features from expert models on the one hand and chat on the other (see Biber 1988 and Crystal 2001 for differing but largely compatible accounts of features which are typical of unplanned, informal speech). Table 9.1 gives a basic description of the data. Note that a 'message unit' (MU), as the term is used here, may be made up of a traditional T-unit – an independent clause with its own mood choice, and any clauses dependent on it – or of a stretch of text such as a minor clause (e.g. *Morning* in Example (19) below) orthographically marked off as a separate sentence.

Table 9.1: The football data

Conversation	Football-bloggers	Football-experts
7,217 words	6,504 words	2,990 words
714 message units	534 message units	185 message units

Analysing interpersonal choices at the level of the clause can start with the patterns of selections in the system of SPEECH FUNCTIONS for independent clauses (Halliday and Matthiessen 2004:134).[1] Table 9.2 shows quantitative results. Not too much can be concluded from the figures in Table 9.2, since the differences between each pair of registers, including conversation and blogs, are statistically highly significant. Certainly, the blogs share with

Table 9.2: Speech functions in the football data

Speech function	Conversation		Football-bloggers		Football-experts	
statement	535	75%	437	82%	180	97%
question	72	10%	26	5%	5	3%
command	23	3%	39	7%	0	
offer	5	1%	2	0%	0	
exclamation	0		8	2%	0	
minor clause	79	11%	22	4%	0	

conversation the use of more varied speech functions (18 per cent and 25 per cent of non-statement choices respectively), whereas the experts' texts are almost completely made up of statements. However, within that greater variation, it is noticeable that minor clauses such as *Thanks* form a markedly larger proportion in conversation than in the blogs: in other words, while the blogs are more similar than the experts' texts to conversation in some ways, it is not the case that patterns of conversational features are straightforwardly transferred into the blogs.[2]

Staying at the level of the clause as a whole, but looking from a textual perspective, Table 9.3 shows the proportion of clauses in each corpus which are incomplete in some way. The rationale for examining this aspect here is that formal planned discourse is typically explicit, using grammatically complete clauses, as a reflex of the fact that the interaction is not face-to-face and the writer is therefore less able to assume cooperation on the part of the addressees; casual conversation between intimates, on the other hand, is typically characterised by implicitness, which Hasan (1984[1996]:215) hypothesises is 'a symbolic means of construing closeness of relationship'. Thus, although it is a choice from the textual component of the lexico-grammar, it can be seen as directly related to interpersonal concerns.

Table 9.3: Incomplete MUs in the football data

MU form	Conversation		Football-bloggers		Football-experts	
elliptical	150	21%	116	22%	10	3%
uncompleted	52	7%	0		0	

'Elliptical' in Table 9.3 means that the 'missing' elements come at the start of the clause – thus typically comprising the Subject and sometimes the Finite and/or the Predicator. In the following example from a blog, possible versions of the ellipted elements are indicated in square brackets (in all the following examples, the text is given as it appears on the websites, with no corrections or amendments):

> (7) Andy, [that is a] nice post I'm happy, [It] Always amazes me to see other teams supporters on here (with the exception of Ice who is a regular) [they have] obviously nothing better to do.

'Uncompleted' indicates that the speaker did not finish the MU for whatever reason. The unfinished MU is marked with [...] in Example (8) taken from the conversation corpus:

> (8) But he's not [...] he's very into magical realism and all that sort of crap you know

As with speech function choices, the picture is mixed. While both written text types differ from conversation in avoiding uncompleted MUs, the blogs are clearly very close to conversation in frequency of elliptical MUs. Both elliptical and uncompleted MUs are typical of casual conversation, but they occur in different contexts. Elliptical elements, as defined here, can be fairly straightforwardly 'filled out' on the basis of grammatical structure, and project an expectation of collaborative work on the part of the addressee: they are, in a sense, other-oriented (cf. Hasan (1996 [1984]). Uncompleted MUs, on the other hand, are often self-oriented: the speaker is reformulating his/her utterance for some reason. One possible reason why there might be this skewed pattern of occurrence in blogs (and the same pattern is found in another blog corpus that I have analysed – Thompson forthcoming) is that, while writers utilise the greater planning time available in even rapid writing to avoid uncompleted MUs, they are at some level aware of, and wish to exploit, the collaborative conversational tone projected by elliptical MUs.

Table 9.4 narrows the focus to interpersonally significant features within the clause, the linguistic resources used to refer to interactants. Interactant reference is a typical marker of more 'involved' registers (in Biber's terms – e.g. 1988), of which the most involved are informal spoken registers.

Once again, the picture that emerges is slightly mixed, but with generally much closer affinities between conversation and the blogs. The only point where the blogs and the experts' texts are more similar is in the use of *we/us/our* to refer to the team, which is a feature that is specific to this group of text types (and perhaps more generally to partisan discourse about sports teams). It is thus related to the field of the discourse.

Overall, therefore, in terms of certain potentially significant features the blogs appear to be more similar to conversation than to the experts' texts.

Table 9.4: Interactant reference in the football data

Interactant reference	Conversation		Football-bloggers		Football-experts	
	no.	*	no.	*	no.	*
I/me/my	268	34	215	33	5	2
you/your (specific)	130	17	170	26	0	0
you/your (generic)	15	2	11	2	4	1
we/us/our (joint)	44	6	2	0	9	3
we/us/our (team)	0	0	86	13	90	30
we/us/our (exclusive)	23	3	26	4	0	0

* per 1,000 words

Apart from the use of *we/us/our* (which anyway seems to belong to the broader register of partisan sports talk), there is little to suggest that the experts' texts have much in common with those of the bloggers, let alone being drawn on by them. However, with the kind of study being conducted here, such quantitative overviews serve primarily as a way into exploring the data from more qualitative perspectives, indicating possible lines of enquiry. They can be seen as a means of sketching the broad semiotic habitat of individual choices in texts (see Thompson 2001[2007]). At this point, therefore, it is useful to turn to the texts themselves.

Example (9) is a typical extract from an expert's text which had the potential to serve as a model for the bloggers.

> (9) The aftermath of our victory over City saw Spurs lose to Norwich and Chelsea fail to beat Fulham. Wins over Wolves and Wigan, our next two opponent, would almost guarantee a top-three finish and automatic Champions League qualification, not to mention an improvement over last season's finish. It would be a remarkable result after the start to the season we had. On a related note, with Newcastle in the best form of the team's below us it's looking more and more likely that Spurs could miss out on the Champions League altogether. Wouldn't that be sweet?

This shows some similarities to the blog and TV commentary illustrated in Examples (1) and (2): there is overt evaluation (e.g. *sweet*), identification with the team (e.g. *our victory*), interactive mood choices (the interrogative in the final sentence), and a general favouritism towards the home team. There are also slips which one would expect to be edited out in more carefully prepared texts (e.g. the missing plural marker on *opponent*, the intrusive apostrophe in the plural *team's*). At the same time, the text is clearly a written text: for example, apart from the slips, the punctuation and the grammar are standard; complex nominal groups are relatively frequent, most notably functioning as Subject Themes (e.g. *The aftermath of our victory over City* – see Berry 2013 on typical thematic choices in formal and informal texts); and experiential grammatical metaphor is deployed (e.g. *the aftermath … saw …*).

Some of the blogs appear to aim at least partially at a similar register, as in Example (10):

> (10) Thanks for the fresness Andy.
> 'It shows we're not a one man team' My favorite line by far. It good to see the team winning as the team. Not that I minded the incredible Van Persie show any more than I minded the Henry years but in order

for us to progress more guys have got to step up more often and the last month (QPR the glaring exception) the TEAM has done just that.

This focuses on evaluating the team's performance and assessing future possibilities, the main topics of the experts' texts; and there are some structures and lexical choices that seem more associated with relatively formal registers (e.g. *in order for us to progress*). However, there is even less evidence of (self-)editing (*fresness; It good*), and there are features which are associated with more informal registers, such as elliptical MUs (*My favourite line by far; Not that I minded*) – cf. Table 9.3. It is also noticeable that the blog is overtly dialogic: the blogger directly addresses *Andy*, the expert who wrote the text to which this blog is responding, and comments on his text.

A number of the blogs exhibit this mixture of certain features which are similar to those in the experts' texts together with features associated with informal spoken discourse, as was predicted. However, more frequently the blogs display interactive features of a kind that I had not predicted. As just now remarked of the opening of Example (10), one recurrent characteristic is that the blogs are overtly dialogic, with the writers engaging supportively with other bloggers – Example (11) – or combatively, even aggressively, especially with supporters of other teams who submit blogs – Example (12).

> (11) @LeftCoast – Well said, my friend. You know we're doing something right when we attract the vitriol and bile of opponent supporters on an Arsenal blog.

> (12) [from a Manchester City fan] haha pathetic..if beating us when we have been poor for weeks is massive progress then i must congratulate you for your optimism..what is it 7 years without a trophy now. [response 25 minutes later from an Arsenal fan] since when did man $ity twats show up on here? seriously, after a loss you have nothing better to do than find an arsenal blog to comment on? your comments only make the victory all the sweeter.[3]

It seems likely that the dialogic nature of the blogs encourages the use of other features associated with conversation: direct address and more generally interactant reference, elliptical MUs and interactive mood choices, as well as informal lexis (*pathetic; twats*). As a rough indication of the frequency, over half the blogs (about 57 per cent) are primarily supportive or dismissive responses to other blogs, compared with only about 15 per cent which primarily comment on the team's performance. Around a quarter of the blogs combine both – in the case of Example (13) the blogger explicitly signals the switch:

(13) Thanks to the Mancs [*Manchester City fans*] for visiting our site –
now sod off. You can sort out your own mess up there. ...
Back to the post. Steady on there Andrew about 3rd being nailed on.
Six games to go and still too close to call.

In the blogs which are wholly or partly response-oriented, the close relationship with conversation seems salient. However, given the present-day context, it seems highly plausible that the relationship is in fact at one remove: rather than drawing directly on conversation, the bloggers may well be drawing on their previous experience of computer-mediated communication in general (see Herring 1996 on features of CMC), particularly of more intimate and inherently dialogic forms of CMC, such as other types of blogs, instant messaging, etc. – and these in turn will exhibit strongly the kinds of features of informal conversation explored above. In general, conversation seems to be the rootstock in the background: in many respects the blogs essentially represent the oral medium in the graphic channel (see Hasan 1999 on this distinction), rather than drawing in any direct way on possible written models. It is true that the bloggers will also tend on some occasions to draw to some extent and more or less expertly on more formal registers, when they focus on the kind of analysis that they meet in the prompt text; but this does not appear to be a major element. It is also worth bearing in mind that they almost certainly read other blog entries on the site and will probably use those consciously or unconsciously as 'models': they are not reinventing the text type each time they contribute.

Thus my original hypothesis is not fully borne out here: the bloggers are mainly not aiming to imitate 'expert' writers except rather sporadically. The hybridity is more generic, in the sense that it seems to belong to a wider set of online text types; and the blogs are more strongly oriented than I hypothesised towards dialogue and informal linguistic choices.

9.4   Newspaper blogs

In order to test the hypothesis further, I chose data which seemed likely to exhibit different characteristics while maintaining the variable of blogs responding to or prompted by an expert text. These were taken from the website of the *Guardian*, a UK 'quality' newspaper whose stated main market is AB/C1 social groups (managerial and professional/supervisory and clerical).[4] The experts' texts are produced by professional political commentators, often updated during the day; the blogs are produced by readers of the newspaper. I would certainly not claim that no *Guardian* readers will contribute to the Arsenal football blog; but the two groups of bloggers are likely not to overlap greatly, and any who do contribute to both are likely to approach them in different ways.

Starting again with a brief quantitative overview, Table 9.5 shows the basic details of the data. As can be seen, unlike the football blogs, the word count of the experts' texts is higher than that of the blogs, reflecting the longer, more complex texts produced by the experts.

Table 9.5: The *Guardian* data

Conversation	*Guardian*-bloggers	*Guardian*-experts
7,217 words	5,153 words	9,874 words
714 message units	380 message units	558 message units

It is worth noting that commands may be realised not only by imperative clauses but also by declarative or, occasionally, interrogative clauses (cf note 1). This is particularly relevant here because many of the experts' texts, like the editorials which appear in the newspaper itself, may be characterised as macro-commands: their overall purpose is to recommend a course of action to be taken by the government or other bodies and individuals; but in the *Guardian* there is a strong tendency to realise commands not by imperatives but by modalised declaratives (see Thompson 2012 on editorials in the newspaper). Table 9.6 shows the frequencies in the three sets of data. As with the football blogs, the blogs here show slightly more similarity to the conversation data, especially in the higher frequency of questions. However, it is noticeable that the blogs and experts' texts share a higher proportion of commands. This may be an indication that the blogs are following the example of the experts' texts in this respect.

Table 9.7 shows the proportion of incomplete MUs. The pattern is very similar to the football data, with the blogs relatively close to conversation

Table 9.6: Speech functions in the *Guardian* data

Speech function	Conversation		*Guardian*-bloggers		*Guardian*-experts	
Statement	535	75%	277	73%	508	91%
Question	72	10%	64	17%	16	3%
Command	23	3%	26	7%	34	6%
Offer	5	1%	0		0	
Exclamation	0		2	1%	0	
minor clause	79	11%	11	3%	0	

in terms of elliptical MUs, but with uncompleted MUs occurring only in the conversation data. Elliptical MUs do occur slightly more often in the experts' texts than would perhaps be expected, indicating that there is some degree of interactivity even in these relatively formal written texts. However, this feature is markedly rarer than in the blogs and the conversation data.

Table 9.7: Incomplete MUs in the *Guardian* data

MU form	Conversation		*Guardian*-bloggers		*Guardian*-experts	
Elliptical	150	21%	72	19%	23	4%
Uncompleted	52	7%	0		0	

The final set of findings relate to interactant reference – see Table 9.8. Here the differences between the three sets of data are greater than any similarities. In terms of the whole profile, the blogs appear to be broadly speaking intermediate between the conversation and the experts' texts. The main exception is the occurrence of reference to *we* as society in general in the blogs and experts' texts but not in conversation. This seems roughly equivalent to *we* as the team in the football data in that it reflects the particular field of discourse, in this case analysing the state of society.

Overall, therefore, the quantitative results suggest that the *Guardian* political blogs, while displaying more similarities to conversation than do the experts' texts, are less strongly oriented towards conversation, and may be more truly hybrid, mixing features of the two potential discoursal sources.

This is largely borne out when we turn to the qualitative analysis of the blogs. There are certainly features which are overtly dialogic. Although *you*

Table 9.8: Interactant reference in the *Guardian* data

Interactant reference	Conversation		*Guardian*-bloggers		*Guardian*-experts	
	no.	*	no.	*	no.	*
I/me/my	268	34	53	10	0	0
you/your (specific)	130	17	16	3	3	0.3
you/your (generic)	15	2	5	1	5	0.5
we/us/our (joint)	44	6	0	0	0	0
we/us/our ('society')	0	0	23	4	12	1
we/us/our (exclusive)	23	3	14	3	0	0

* per 1,000 words

is relatively infrequently used, the bloggers sometimes, as with the football blogs, address the expert writer of the prompt text. Some of these are metatextual comments on the management of the blogs, as in (14) – the use of *please* here is indicative of the mainly more courteous tone of these blogs (although *would you care to … please* is certainly still fairly coercive):

> (14) Andrew, would you care to comment on the new 'proactive' moderation on this page, please?

Very occasionally (only six times in the data), the blogger directly addresses a politician or other person involved in the current events being discussed – (15) is an example:

> (15) I was appalled at the unctuous Cameron's performance on AM on Sunday morning. There has to be an intervention of sorts. Prime Minister, answer the damned question!

More frequently there are responses to other bloggers. These are sometimes addressed to the other blogger, such as (16):

> (16) Good points, Spongebob!

However, (17) is a more typical instance of a blog responding to another blogger:

> (17) Response to zapzo13, 30 April 2012 9:32AM
> 'Why are we paying tv licensing when the BBC is the worst TV channel, the way they coverage the real issue and the cameron affair, do we need to be treated like idiots or is the way in UK to pay and get ripped off as BBC and the conservative party and doing it.'
> Many of the staunchest supporters and defenders of the BBC will not be there for them next time their role is questioned. Their news coverage is laughable when levels of journalistic integrity seem higher on Sky.
> What's the point of independent broadcasting when it patently isn't independent?

It is worth noting in (17) that not only is the other blogger not explicitly addressed (let alone abused, as frequently occurs in the football blogs), but this response is much less overtly interactive in general than those in the football blogs. The blogger's focus is on the topic of discussion, engaging with the quoted opinion; and a number of the lexical choices are from a more formal register (*staunchest supporters*; *levels of journalistic integrity,* etc.). There is an interrogative functioning as a rhetorical question (i.e., a statement in persuasive form), which might seem to indicate that the blogs are more interactive; but this is a relatively frequent linguistic strategy in the experts' texts: 16 per cent (10 of 64) of interrogatives in the blogs and 18 per cent (6 of 34) in the experts' texts are rhetorical compared with just 1 per cent (1 of 72) in the conversation data. It is also worth noting the explicit metalinguistic labelling of the entry as a *response* and the careful punctuating of the quotes, which also occurs in other response blogs – the usual convention in these blogs is clearly to show that one is literate!

This focus on the topic of the discussion is also demonstrated in the relatively frequent blogs which respond to the content of the expert text, as in (18), where the first part (set off by being left-indented in the original) is a quote from that text followed by the blogger's comment:

> (18) Of course, George Osborne will not be worrying about Cable nabbing his office. It's not going to happen. But he might be mildly concerned about the fact that at the weekend the Daily Mail was speculating about him being sent to the Foreign Office, with William Hague taking his job in a reshuffle.
> (Sigh)
> Even if it were to happen, it wouldn't make any difference to policy. They have written a story about the economy (bankrupt/credit card/ interest rates and all) and they are going to stick to it. The only thing that would knock them off course is a serious lurch into recession (ie. –2% or more in the next quarter) or a downgrade.

Example (18) shows the blogger consciously playing on the hybrid nature of the blog, inserting a written realisation of his physiological reaction to the quote, *(Sigh)*; and he does not feel it necessary to make his text as explicit as an editorial would be – e.g. presumably *they* refers to the whole government rather than the specific politicians mentioned in the quote; and the list of aspects of the economy in brackets is allusive rather than fully articulated. However, apart from this relative vagueness, which is characteristic of casual conversation (see e.g. Jucker *et al.* 2003), the linguistic choices in the text are almost indistinguishable from those that could be found in an editorial. The main part of the response addresses the point raised in the expert text in a way designed to project the writer as knowledgeable on the topic of economic policy.

Even when the language is markedly more informal (with features such as elliptical MUs and self-reference) and the content more personal opinion, as in Examples (19) and (20), it is noticeable that the contributors comment on the topic rather than interacting directly with other bloggers:

> (19) Morning. Vince Cable as chancellor. I don't think Osborne would be too pleased. Interesting thought though, would stir things up even more!

> (20) Fingers crossed Labour don't let this go until Cameron refers Hunt to Alex Allan.
>
> Something I saw pop up on the news yesterday was the tantalising prospect of Rebekah Brooks releasing texts and emails between her and Cameron. If anyone has dirt that'll wipe the smug smile off his face, it's her.

In these cases, the impression of hybridity seems to be largely produced by the combination of topic-oriented content and conversation-like wording.

It is difficult to quantify the number of blogs at each point on a continuum from those like (18), which are most similar to the experts' texts, to those like (19) and (20), which are closest to informal conversation in their wording, not least because a number show a mixture, often in different sections of the same blog. For instance, the opening of Example (21) is towards the 'expert' end of the cline, but as it progresses the blogger becomes more irate and the language becomes markedly less formal in grammatical structure:

> (21) Cameron has made a statement, along with several tory Ministers and MP's. Perhaps Cameron should demand a statement from Miliband as to why the then PM Brown didn't resign when Spads [Special Advisors – GT] at No.10 were disgracefully smearing, lying, and spinning against the then oppositions front bench and their family members!
>
> Typical hypocritical Labour. Loss of data no Ministerial resignation. Baby P mess, no Ministerial resignation. Labour showed no integrity at all when in office.

However, working with a very broad characterisation, roughly a quarter of the blogs fall at the 'expert voice' end, another quarter at the 'conversation' end, and another quarter are somewhere in the middle of the cline. All of these focus on the topic being discussed in the related editorial. The remaining quarter comprise those which comment on the blog procedure (e.g. (14)).

The results above suggest that, taken as a group (while of course allowing for individual variation), the *Guardian* bloggers handle the new register confidently, moving between, on the one hand, dialogic entries which are close in characteristics to blogs in other areas (while still largely keeping the topic of discussion in mind), and, on the other, entries which seem to draw on their familiarity with editorials and other similar texts (while usually incorporating some more conversational lexico-grammatical choices, presumably construing their awareness of the less formal, and less formalised, context of blogging). What emerges is then a more balanced hybridity than that found in the football blogs: a relatively new register, political blogging, which is intermediate between the two types of discourse on which they appear to be drawing.

As noted in reference to some of the examples above (e.g. (18)), the *Guardian* bloggers tend to display a reasonable level of expert knowledge of the political topics being discussed. One factor which may have an influence is the nature of the readership mentioned at the start of this section: on the *Guardian* website, the typical readers are described as 'young and affluent ... arts lovers ... engaged, influential and well-connected' – and, one might add, often educated to tertiary level. It seems plausible that it is part of the self-image that the bloggers are aiming to construct that they wish to appear literate and familiar with both the topics and the register of political commentary. In order to check this, I carried out a parallel analysis of a corpus of experts' texts and blogs from the website of the *Daily Mail*, which I will report more briefly here for comparison. The *Mail* is another UK newspaper, which is usually labelled a 'middle-market' publication. There is debate over the characteristics of its target audience, but it is generally agreed that the readership is on the whole more politically and socially conservative than that of the *Guardian*.[5]

The findings from the quantitative analyses of the *Mail* blogs are actually broadly similar to those of the *Guardian* in many respects. The main points where they differ are that there are fewer questions and more commands (7 per cent questions and 13 per cent commands, compared with 17 per cent and 7 per cent in the *Guardian* blogs), and more frequent use of *you* referring to specific addressees and *we* referring to society (10 and 13 occurrences per thousand words respectively, compared with three and four per thousand words in the *Guardian* blogs). These apparently simple quantitative differences point towards the features of the blogs which cause them to exhibit very different characteristics from those of the *Guardian*.

In discussing these features, it is worth starting with an extract from one of the experts' texts, since these appear to influence the tone of the blogs. Example (22) is typical:

> (22) There is one other compelling reason to vote for Mr Johnson: Ken Livingstone.

> During his time in office (2000–2008), 'Red Ken' – a hard-line socialist throwback whose views have offended large sections of society – was spendthrift and divisive.
>
> Now we discover he is also a stinking hypocrite – attacking tax avoidance while refusing to come clean about his own murky affairs.

What is immediately noticeable here is the overt, even virulent, evaluation directed towards a particular politician (e.g. *stinking hypocrite*). There is no careful weighing of the options, as is characteristic of *Guardian* editorials (Thompson 2012) and no attempt to be moderate in the criticism: this is in its way even more openly partisan than the texts of the football experts.

The blogs, almost without exception, exhibit similarly extravagant *ad hominem* evaluation:

> (23) Cameron does not like to read the truth you can see what he is with his rants they say when you shout you know you have lost and he will loose he is aroggant and should not be a leader remeber when he wanted our votes mr nice guy

The uncertain control of graphological conventions in Example (23) fits with the features associated with unplanned spoken discourse, such as run-on sentences with loose, or no, connectivity, an imperative command to the reader (*remeber*), an unattached nominal group (*mr nice guy*), etc. An extreme example of this informally-worded abuse is (24) – this is the whole of the blog entry:

> (24) Cant stand the two clowns Maude and Field.

The two examples above are also representative in that they are strongly negative: of the 126 blogs in the corpus, only four are positive, with a further five which combine praise for one politician with criticism of another. The *Mail* bloggers are in general very unhappy with the state of the country as they see it, and frequently set up an opposition between the politicians and the mainstream society represented as *we*:

> (25) If Cameron listened to anyone (apart from the voices in his head) we wouldn't be in the situation in which we now find ourselves.

In roughly two-thirds of the blogs, the conversational tone is allied with a dialogic orientation. However, the dialogue is not with other bloggers or the moderator: there are no instances in the data of responses of this kind.

Instead, the specific *you* who is addressed is one of the politicians involved in the events (as noted above, this also occurs, but very infrequently, in the *Guardian* blogs). Both (26) and (27) are addressed to Frank Field, a Member of Parliament who had been asked in 1997 by the then Prime Minister to prepare a report on possible welfare reforms. Like many of the blogs with a named addressee, these examples include commands directed at the addressee. Example (27) in fact takes this interactive orientation to unusual lengths, enacting a complete dialogue with imagined 'replies' from Field to the questions and commands.

> (26) Mr. Fields how naive can you get? You were only there as window dressing so Cameron could say, see how serious I am about the poor, plus he could rub Labour's nose in it by getting your backing. You were played, so get used to it.

> (27) It's par for the course, Frank, but then you probably don't remember in 1997 being asked by Tony Blair, all those years ago, to 'think the unthinkable' on welfare reform? Ah, so you do recall this? Well, write an article for the DM explaining all of the reforms (increasing welfare to make it better than working doesn't count!) made by Labour as a result of your efforts! What's that you say: Blair side-lined you and eventually you were elbowed out of government? Oh, dear. So, after 13 years of 'investment' by Labour in welfare it's now all the fault of Cameron for the lack of progress? How can that be?

This all suggests that the *Mail* bloggers are perhaps taking the largely censorious, and certainly evaluative, tone of the editorials, but hybridising that with informal conversational resources to a greater extent than the *Guardian* bloggers. It is worth noting that none of the experts' texts in the *Mail* corpus includes direct address to a politician: this kind of one-sided admonitory dialogue appears to be something that the bloggers themselves have introduced. This convention is perhaps derived from the inherent feature that the kinds of blogs examined here are intended to be dialogic – they are contributions to an ongoing exchange (which in itself encourages an orientation towards conversational discourse); but simulating an exchange with addressees who are highly unlikely to read, let alone respond to, the blog may be related to the bloggers' greater familiarity with face-to-face interaction, and thus a further reflex of the hybrid nature of this register.

9.5   Conclusion

One factor that needs to be borne in mind in assessing the findings of this study is that, unlike, for instance, the discourse of doctors' patients, the football and newspaper blogs are not individual hybrids reinvented more or less each time they occur: they are, after all, public and available as models for subsequent bloggers. It has emerged from the analysis that each set of blogs has generated its own conventions which differ from those of the other sets examined. Within one set of blogs, individual bloggers may make slightly different patterns of choices along a broad cline from those which are more like the 'model' texts to those which are more conversational or dialogic; but they generally do this within the conventions built up by previous bloggers (and to a large extent not only in blogs on that website but in related types of blogs in general).

Thus my original assumption that the field variable – the area of social activity in which the blog is located – could be taken as held constant has turned out to be slightly misleading. This is in fact predictable: as Hasan (1999:272) has argued, the three contextual variables 'permeate each other'. The social activity of discussing football is different, in ways which impact on the language produced in blogs, from that of discussing politics. This affects not only fairly obvious features such as who *we* refers to in different areas of experience, but also more far-reaching aspects such as the kind of persona that is likely to be adopted by bloggers. That is, field and tenor are intertwined. It is by no means impossible that, for example, football blogs might comprise serious analysis of matches by bloggers aiming to project themselves as informed, sophisticated and literate. However, it appears that in our culture this is not an option that is often taken up. It seems likely that this may be influenced by (and reinforce) connections between the place of football in our society and stereotypical notions of 'blokeishness'; but exploring that line of enquiry is beyond the scope of this chapter. At the same time, the differences between the *Guardian* and *Mail* blogs, which can be taken as being broadly within the 'same' social activity, indicate that the ways in which bloggers position themselves interpersonally may vary markedly: political discussion may be seen in terms of presenting one's considered views on the issues of the day or as taking a personal stance in support of or (more often) in opposition to individual politicians.

Nevertheless, despite the clear variation across the sets of blogs, there are fundamental similarities in their characteristics; and hybridity is one of the major characteristics which they have in common. In these blogs, casual conversation remains the root stock onto which other types of discourse are grafted; but it does so in different ways and to different extents. It shows up in lexico-grammatical features at clause level and/or dialogic exchange structures at discourse semantic level; but how exactly it shows up depends on a range of factors. One factor is the extent to which blogs are influenced by the experts' texts which offer a possible model for bloggers in producing possibly unfamiliar text types (as was hypothesised); but their influence may be greater (as with many of the *Guardian* blogs) or much less (as with most of the football blogs). Bloggers may also generate their own conventions, as with the use of direct address to politicians in the *Mail* blogs.

Internet resources offer fertile ground for the emergence of new registers, as, amongst other opportunities, they have made it possible for language users to produce for public consumption types of text which typically were previously written only by specialists in the field. Registers do not spring Minerva-like from some single originator: they evolve by combining, building on and extending existing registers. It is predictable that casual conversation will play an important role in the evolution of registers within the broad domain of blogging, because of the conditions under which they are formed – in particular, the salience of the function of individual blog entries as turns in an ongoing exchange, and the fact that bloggers may in some cases be less accustomed to handling written channels of expression than oral ones. At the same time, awareness of the more specialised texts which accompany and prompt the blogs is likely to influence how bloggers construct their participation in the exchange. Thus hybridity is a natural consequence. Happily for the discourse analyst, the evolution of these hybrid registers is often both unusually rapid and observable, and allows insights into the process by which the registers come into being before they become relatively fixed and conventionalised. The aim of the present chapter (written within one of those registers which have become fixed and conventionalised) has been to present a snap-shot of one phase in the evolution.

Notes

1   It may be worth stressing that speech functions are not always realised straightforwardly by mood choices (Halliday and Matthiessen 2004). For example, some of the statements in the data are realised by interrogative clauses (i.e. rhetorical questions in traditional terms).
2   Crystal (2001) actually argues that blogs show more similarities with written text than with spoken. However, this does not seem to be borne out by the

analyses I have conducted – admittedly with a rather different focus from those on which Crystal's conclusions are based.

3   In the 2011–2012 season, Manchester City aroused a great deal of envy because the owners had gone on a lavish spending spree, paying very large sums to buy new players – hence jibes like *man $ity* here, or in another blog *Man$hity*. The envy was not lessened when Manchester City did in fact win the League title that season.

4   The definition of the letter grades used by the *Guardian* is maintained by the Market Research Society. Their website notes: 'Social Grade is the "common currency" social classification (the "ABC1" system) used by the advertising industry and employed throughout marketing, advertising and market research.' (https://www.mrs.org.uk/cgg/social_grade) .

5   On the target audience of the *Mail*, see e.g. the report commissioned by the newspaper's publishers at http://www.prweek.com/article/656160/media-analysis-just-does-read-daily-mail).

References

Berry, M. (2013). Contentful and contentlight Subject Themes in informal spoken English and formal written English. In G. O'Grady, T. Bartlett, and L. Fontaine (Eds), *Choice in Language: Applications in Text Analysis*, 243–268. London: Equinox.

Biber, D. (1988). *Variation across Speech and Writing*. Cambridge: Cambridge University Press. http://dx.doi.org/10.1017/CBO9780511621024

Bietsch, W. (2002). *Liverpool FC Fan Match Reports: Genre Analysis of an Emerging Microgenre*. Liverpool: University of Liverpool MA dissertation.

Crystal, D. (2001). *Language and the Internet*. Cambridge: Cambridge University Press. http://dx.doi.org/10.1017/CBO9781139164771

Fries, P.H. (1981). On the status of theme in English: arguments from discourse. *Forum Linguisticum* 6, 1–38. Reprinted, 1983, in revised form, in J.S. Petöfi and E. Sözer (Eds), *Micro and Macro Connexity of Texts*, 116–152. Hamburg: Helmut Buske.

Halliday, M.A.K., and Hasan, R. (1985[1989]). *Language, Context and Text: Aspects of Language in a Social-semiotic Perspective*. Geelong, Vic.: Deakin University Press. Republished by Oxford University Press.

Halliday, M.A.K., and Matthiessen, C.M.I.M. (2004). *An Introduction to Functional Grammar* (3rd ed.). London: Arnold.

Hasan, R. (1984[1996]). Ways of saying: ways of meaning. In R. Fawcett, M.A.K. Halliday, S. Lamb and A. Makkai (Eds), *The Semiotics of Culture and Language Volume 1: Language as Social Semiotic*, 105–162. London: Frances Pinter. Reprinted in C. Cloran, D. Butt and G. Williams (Eds) (1996). *Ways of Saying: Ways of Meaning: Selected Papers of Ruqaiya Hasan*, 191–242. London: Cassell.

Hasan, R. (1999). Speaking with reference to context. In M. Ghadessy (Ed.), *Text and Context in Functional Linguistics*, 219–328. Amsterdam and Philadelphia: John Benjamins. http://dx.doi.org/10.1075/cilt.169.11has

Herring, S.C. (Ed.) (1996). *Computer Mediated Communication: Linguistic, Social and Cross-Cultural Perspectives*. Amsterdam and Philadelphia: John Benjamins. http://dx.doi.org/10.1075/pbns.39

Ivanič, R. (1998). *Writing and Identity: The Discoursal Construction of Identity in Academic Writing*. Amsterdam and Philadelphia: John Benjamins. http://dx.doi.org/10.1075/swll.5

Jucker, A.H., Smith, S.W., and Lüdge, T. (2003). Interactive aspects of vagueness in conversation. *Journal of Pragmatics*, 35(12), 1737–1769. http://dx.doi.org/10.1016/S0378-2166(02)00188-1

Martin, J.R. (2006). Genre, ideology and intertextuality: a systemic functional perspective. *Linguistics and the Human Sciences*, 2(2), 275–298.

McCarthy, M. (1993). Grammar, discourse and the fanzine. In Y. Ikegami and M. Toyota (Eds), *Aspects of English as a World Language*, 147–161. Tokyo: Maruzen.

Thompson, G. (2001[2007]). Corpus, comparison, culture: doing the same things differently in different languages. In M. Ghadessy, A. Henry and R. Roseberry (Eds), *Small Corpus Studies and ELT*, 311–334. Amsterdam and Philadelphia: John Benjamins. Reprinted in W. Teubert and R. Krishnamurthy (Eds) (2007) *Corpus Linguistics: Critical Concepts in Linguistics*, Volume 5, 68–87. London and New York: Routledge. http://dx.doi.org/10.1075/scl.5.18tho

Thompson, G. (2009). Just checking: questions and social roles. In M. Shiro, P. Bentivoglio, and F. Ehrlich (Eds), *Haciendo Discurso. Homenaje a Adriana Bolívar (Talking Discourse: In Honour of Adriana Bolívar)*, 141–156. Caracas: Universidad Central de Venezuela.

Thompson, G. (2012). Intersubjectivity in newspaper editorials: construing the reader-in-the-text. *English Text Construction*, 5(1), 77–100. http://dx.doi.org/10.1075/etc.5.1.05tho

Thompson, G. (forthcoming). *Conjunctive Relations in Discourse: A Tri-functional Study of Six English Registers*. London: Equinox.

Thompson, G., and Thompson, S. (2009). Theme, Subject and the unfolding of text. In G. Forey and G. Thompson (Eds), *Text-Type and Texture*, 45–69. London: Equinox.

About the author

The sad news of the passing of yet another highly regarded SFL scholar, **Geoff Thompson**, reached us as we were proofing this book. Geoff was an Honorary Senior Fellow in the School of English at the University of Liverpool and received an honorary doctorate from Linnaeus University in Sweden. He was also Guest Professor at Sun Yat-sen University in

Guangzhou, and the University of Science and Technology in Beijing. One of the Editors of the journal *Functions of Language*, his many valued publications include *Introducing Functional Grammar* (Routledge, 3rd edition, 2014), and numerous edited volumes and articles on various areas in Applied Linguistics, including SFL, Language Teaching and Learning, and Grammar and Society. Geoff will be sorely missed.

10

Registerial hybridity: Indeterminacy among fields of activity

Christian M.I.M. Matthiessen and Kazuhiro Teruya
The Hong Kong Polytechnic University

10.1 Introduction

In this chapter, we are concerned with the 'hybridity' of registers – the mixture of functional varieties of language operating in different institutional domains[1] (with 'register' being used in the original sense of the term in Systemic Functional Linguistics, e.g. Halliday, McIntosh and Strevens 1964; Hasan 1973; Halliday 1978; Matthiessen 1993; 2015; Lukin *et al.* 2008).

For example, registers involving some kind of event line include both (1) recounts of events that have actually taken place as one prominent way of chronicling or recording the past and (2) narratives of events that are imagined to have taken place in a fictitious world. These two registers are clearly distinct prototypes, operating in different institutions such as the institution of academic history and the institution of entertainment-and-recreation, and involving different professional writers such as historians and fiction writers. However, factual recounts and fictional narratives shade into one another in biographical narratives that are based in part on the lives of real people. This blurring between the two is what Halliday (2011:Section 5.3) characterises as the current 'fashion for fake histories', relating it to 'the reaction against the dominance of ideational meaning in some highly technologised cultures':

> In literature, there is now a fashion for fake histories – fictional stories woven around real people and events, blurring the distinction between chronicle and fantasy and weaving a web of interpersonal tensions and emotions. [...] The reaction **against** the perceived tyranny of information is a flight into the interpersonal regions of meaning (original emphasis).

In order to explore such registerial hybridity further, we will draw on a context-based typology of registers – that is, a typology of functional variation in language seen 'from above', from the vantage point of context (see Matthiessen 2006; Teruya 2007; Matthiessen, Teruya and Lam 2010; Matthiessen 2013; 2015). We introduce this typology in the following section.

Having introduced it, we will present an interpretation of 'hybridity' based on the notion of indeterminacy that was put forward in Halliday and Matthiessen (1999:547–562) as a way of getting at 'fuzziness', 'vagueness', 'ambivalence' and the like (cf. Halliday 1995; Matthiessen 1995). We will introduce the following types of indeterminacy in Section 10.3: ambiguities, overlaps, blends, neutralisations and complementarities.

In the remainder of the chapter, we will discuss the first four of these types of indeterminacy (leaving complementarities for another occasion) – ambiguities in Section 10.4, overlaps in Section 10.5, blends in Section 10.6, and neutralisations in Section 10.7. In the Conclusion (Section 10.8), we return to the context-based register typology and locate the cases of indeterminacy we have discussed within it. We round off the chapter with a brief consideration of other kinds of register mixing.

10.2 Register typology based on field of activity

Since registers are functional varieties of language operating in different contexts – the variation being variation according to the context of use – it makes sense to start developing register typologies based on **context**, more specifically on the contextual parameters of **field, tenor** and **mode** (see e.g. Halliday 1978).[2] Different settings of field, tenor and mode values correspond to different registers.

In using the context-based register typology, we will focus on field to begin with – more specifically on the **field of activity** in the context, distinguishing eight primary fields of activity, each of which can be further differentiated:[3] see Figure 10.1. We can group these eight fields of activity into three superordinate categories depending on whether the field of activity is primarily a process of meaning (semiotic), a process of behaving (or 'doing'; social) or a transition between the two – i.e., semiotic processes, semiotic processes potentially leading to social processes and social processes:

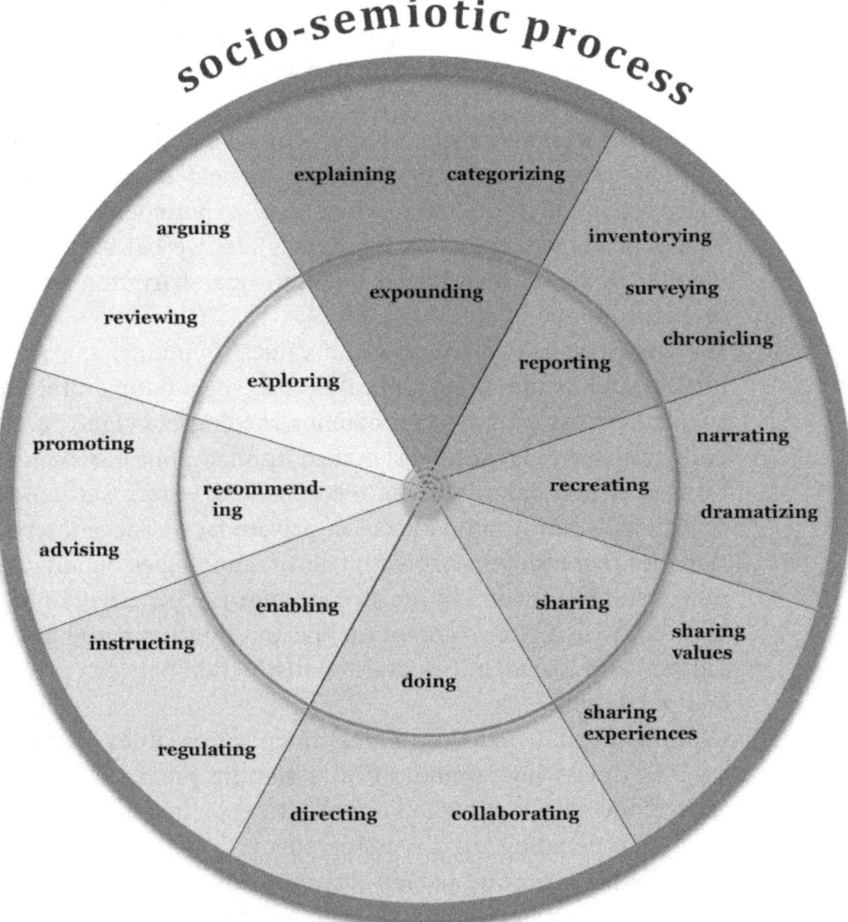

Figure 10.1 The eight primary fields of activity and their subtypes

- **semiotic processes** (i.e., 'meaning' processes – semiotic processes constitutive of context, manifested through social processes):
  - **expounding** knowledge about general classes of phenomena (rather than particular phenomena), theorising our experience of the world in terms of a commonsense (folk) or uncommonsense (scientific) model by explaining why general classes of events take place or by categorising general classes of entities (in terms of taxonomies, hyponymic and/ or meronymic, and/ or characterisation);

- **reporting** on particular phenomena (rather than general classes of phenomena), by recording or chronicling (the flow of) particular events, inventorying particular entities, or surveying particular places;
- **recreating** various aspects of life – involving any of the eight different types of context according to field of activity, typically imagined (fictional) rather than experienced (factual: experienced personally or vicariously), as verbal art with a 'theme' (in the sense of Hasan 1985), through narration and/ or dramatisation;
- **sharing** personal experiences and values (opinions) as part of establishing, maintaining and calibrating, negotiating interpersonal relationships – in terms of tenor, ranging from (and potentially transforming) strangerhood to intimacy, but in sustained form involving fairly intimate relationships; in terms of mode, traditionally and prototypically in private face-to-face interaction, but increasingly enabled by new technologies opening up new channels of sharing (epistolary, telegraphic, telephonic – and now with an explosion of mobile and Internet based possibilities, with a tendency to blur the distinction between private and public spheres);
- **exploring** public values (opinions) and positions (ideas, hypotheses) by reviewing commodities (assigning them values on a scale from very positive to very negative) or by arguing about positions, debating or discussing them – in terms of tenor, typically between one person (a professional or a member of the general public) and some segment of the general public, so between strangers; in terms of mode, typically using media channels, either 'old' media channels (print, radio, TV) or 'new' media channels (mobile and/ or Internet-based);

- **semiotic processes** potentially leading to **social processes** (i.e., 'meaning' leading to 'doing'):
  - **recommending** some course of action (typically some kind of social process – exhortation in the strong form), either for the sake of the addressees by advising them to undertake it for their own good or for the sake of the speaker by promoting some type of goods-and-services;
  - **enabling** some course of action (typically some kind of social process), either literally enabling (empowering) them by instructing them in some type of procedure or constraining them by regulating their behaviour;

- **social processes** (i.e., 'doing' processes – social processes constitutive of context, semiotic processes facilitating [i.e., 'meaning' facilitating 'doing']):
  - **doing** – performing some form of social behaviour, on one's own or as part of a team, with semiotic processes ('meaning') coming in to facilitate this social behaviour through direction or collaboration.

These fields of activity are ***permeable*** in relation to one another. Once we have set them up as 'prototypes', we can begin to explore indeterminacy between two or more of them.

10.3 Indeterminacy and hybridity

The notion of 'hybridity' has a long history, of course; it has been taken over from the study of biological systems[4] and applied to the study of social and semiotic systems – most recently in the last two decades or so as part of postcolonial studies, associated with Homi Bhabha and other prominent scholars in this area – in discourses that bristle with grammatical metaphors such as *cultural criticism, cultural ambivalence, estrangement, representations, mimicry, dominance, identity, ephemerality, subversion, (cultural) imperialism, colonialism, neo-colonialism, post-colonialism, control, homogenisation, globalisation.* And the term is now fairly wide-spread; here is a little sample from the 208 occurrences in COCA:[5]

> To the degree, as well, that Johnny Appleseed in Philip Seymour fuses behaviors coded both masculine and feminine, he incarnates a much more radical cultural and gendered **hybridity** finally than Natty Bumppo. D.H. Lawrence, thinking in part about Natty, memorably described the 'essential American soul' as 'hard, isolate, stoic, and a killer' (63).

> Current research on **hybridity** in the visual arts helps to tease out Euro-Christian and Mesoamerican forms and meanings in the ritual objects that nuns wore on their bodies.

> In 'Bridging the Divide in Contemporary US Catholic Social Ethics', *Theological Studies* 66 (2005) 401–40, I analyze such **hybridity** in terms of the mutual clarification of 'radicalist' and 'public' approaches to Christian social responsibility.

> Bhabha's characterization has been rightly criticized and could be read as overemphasizing the subversive and insurgent potential of **hybridity**. However, his formulation also gestures towards, but perhaps does not fully develop the threat inherent within **hybridity** itself; an 'almost the same but not quite' that unsettled normalized knowledges and disciplinary powers. Conceptualizing **hybridity** as potentially resistive and oppressive, as both generative of invisibility and additional optics of surveillance, this article examines the territoriality of mixed-race identities. The problem, as I see it, is not with postcolonial languages of **hybridity**, ambivalence, or mimicry, but with their metaphorical deployments and ...

> What I conceived as a particularly striking case of postcolonial **hybridity** (most) people in Osogbo found perfectly normal – by now.

In this highly metaphorical type of discourse, people are rare as participants in the transitivity structures of clauses, as illustrated by in the extracts above; but they do sometimes figure as participants, as e.g. *the coloniser, the colonised* and *the Other*.

In order to explore registerial hybridity, we will draw on linguistic work exploring **indeterminacy.** Indeterminacy is an inherent central feature of language – not an optional extra or a fringe phenomenon; it is embodied in all metafunctional modes of meaning – indeterminacy in the construal of our experience of the world as meaning (ideational indeterminacy), indeterminacy in the enactment of our roles and relations as meaning (interpersonal indeterminacy), and indeterminacy in the transformation of these two modes of meaning into a flow of discourse (textual indeterminacy). Halliday and Matthiessen (1999:547–562) proposed a typology of kinds of indeterminacy, which we can characterise as follows in terms of texts:

(a) **ambiguities** ('either a or x'): one text can be interpreted as an instance of either of two distinct registers;

(b) **blends** ('both b and y'): one text can be interpreted as a fusion of two different registers;

(c) **overlaps** ('partly c, partly z'): two registers overlap so that certain texts display features of each: they are borderline cases;

(d) **neutralisations**: in certain contexts, the difference between two registers disappears;

(e) **complementarities**: certain texts can be interpreted in contradictory ways in the assignment to registers.

We will discuss registerial ambiguities, blends, overlaps and neutralisations here, leaving registerial complementarities for another occasion;

but among these, registerial ambiguities may not be seen by all scholars as being included under the heading of 'hybridity' – although one of the nominalisations that occurs in the environment of 'hybridity' in texts where it is used is 'ambivalence', which would appear to be (a kind of) ambiguity.

In our discussion in this chapter, we will explore to what extent we can find examples of these different forms of indeterminacy when we try to assign texts to the different categories in our context-based typology of registers. We have set out examples of registerial indeterminacy in Table 10.1, based on the fields of activity shown in Figure 10.1.

The examples in Table 10.1 are, of course, not exhaustive; and they are based on the field of activity – the nature of the socio-semiotic process – rather than on any of the variables within the contextual parameters of tenor and mode.[6] But tenor and mode are also sources of mixture. For example, Skype and similar applications allow users to combine speaking

Table 10.1: Examples of registerial indeterminacy between pairs of fields of activity (field of activity 1 and field of activity 2)

Type of indeterminacy	Field of activity 1	Field of activity 2	Hybrid register	Examples
Ambiguity	reporting	recreating	fictional recreations of news reports or of historical chronicles	Fictional accounts mistakenly thought to be factual, e.g. Daniel Defoe's *Journal of the plague year*; Orson Wells' *The War of the Worlds*
Overlap	reporting	expounding	recounting shading into explaining sequentially	
	recommending	exploring	evaluation shading into promotion	review of product with characteristics of advertisement; extracts of reviews quoted in promotional material
Blend	reporting	recreating	imaginative recreations of actual events	fake histories; biopics
	reporting	recommending	advertisements dressed up as news reports	advertorials; infomercials
neutralisation	sharing	exploring	personal opinions in public domain	user reviews provided by websites

and typing, i.e., to operate with – and switch between – two channels at one and the same time; and even typing is like speaking in terms of medium. In general, new technologies involving the Internet and also mobile devices invite registerial mixtures.

As we noted above, registerial indeterminacy is inherent in language – an essential property of language as a complex adaptive system; and this is very evident in the evolution of languages: while languages tend to be meta-stable – i.e., achieve stability because they are constantly changing, constantly adapting to their environments – registers may come and go and old registers morph into new ones; for example, news stories morphed into news reports around the 1860s (see e.g. Nanri 1993; Iedema, Feez and White 1994), and correspondence among scholars morphed into research articles (see Swales 1990). New registers do not emerge out of a vacuum; they evolve out of existing resources as new adaptations.

Register mixing is thus pervasive and part of the potential for adaptation inherent in languages. It makes sense to distinguish the mixing of registers from the faking or forgery of texts as instances of particular registers. **Textual forgery** is, of course, a fairly common phenomenon – one that forensic linguists have turned their attention to, as have other scholars interested in establishing authorship. A famous case is the 'Hitler Diaries' that were 'discovered' three decades ago, in 1983. Such 'forgery' is of course central to texts produced in 'recreating' contexts: novelists and short story writers routinely recreate all sorts of texts, but the process of recreating all sorts of aspects of life is inherent in recreating contexts (but this may of course lead to ambiguity: see Section 10.4 below). For example, writers routinely make up and include conversations in their stories.

This feature of texts operating in 'recreating' contexts is related to another kind of phenomenon that we find in texts operating in other contexts – perhaps in particular in 'reporting', 'expounding' and 'exploring' contexts. In these contexts, texts may project (quote or report from) parts of texts from other contexts. For example, news reports may quote parts of speeches from 'exploring' contexts; book reviews in 'exploring' contexts may quote passages from books under review. While such examples can be interpreted as instances of **intertextuality** and **heteroglossia** (for relevant interpretation, see Lemke, 1995), they do not represent the kind of registerial indeterminacy that we are concerned with here.

To round off this brief discussion of what may or may not be interpreted as registerial indeterminacy, let us note another pervasive phenomenon that we would not consider to be registerial mixing in the sense we are using the term here. In particular on occasions where people interact face-to-face in spoken languages, contexts of situation may unfold in parallel within the same 'material situational setting', or they may overlap, with interactants weaving in and out of different contexts of situation: see Figure 10.2. For example, if the members of a family are seated around a dinner table (the material situational setting; see e.g. Hasan 1985), they are likely to interact in a number of different contexts of situation, at the same time or in succession: they may be reminiscing about personal experiences in a 'sharing' context, they may be facilitating the eating of the meal in a 'doing' context, and parents may be regulating their children's behaviour in an 'enabling' context. We would not interpret this as register mixing: the texts instantiating the different registers operate within their own clearly defined contextual boundaries although as shown by Hasan (2000) such boundaries may of course be permeable.

Let us now discuss the different kinds of registerial indeterminacy that we will explore here, starting with ambiguities (Section 10.4) and then proceeding to overlaps (Section 10.5), blends (Section 10.6) and neutralisations (Section 10.7).

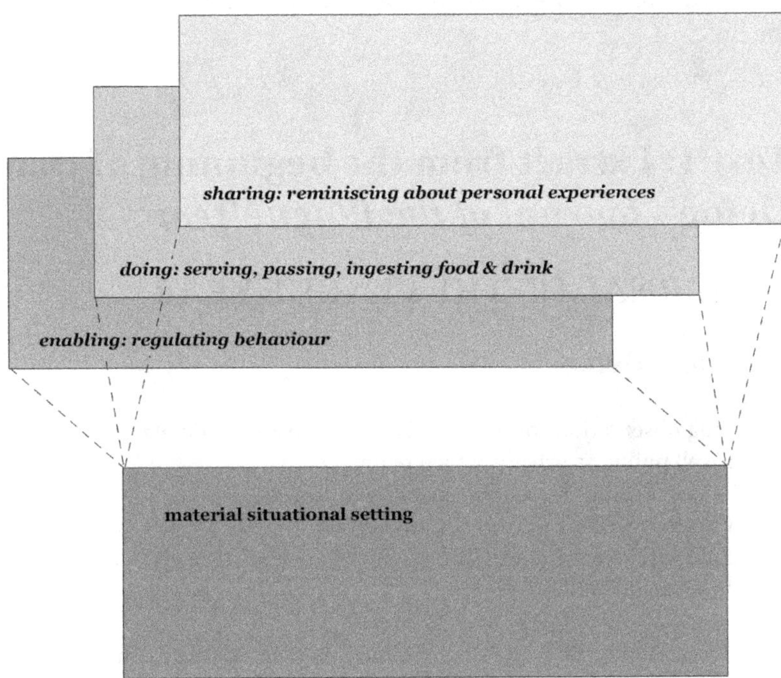

Figure 10.2: Simultaneous contexts of situation unfolding within the same material situational setting

10.4 Ambiguous texts

The most likely area of ambiguity is perhaps the distinction in fields of activity between 'recreating' and 'reporting' – represented as adjacent to one another in Figure 10.1. This is basically the ambiguity between fictional narratives ('recreating') and factual recounts ('reporting'). One well-known example is the unforeseen and unfortunate success that Orson Wells and his team had early in his career in the late 1930s with *The War of the Worlds* when they recreated radio news reports of an alien invasion of our planet; this recreated radio coverage so realistically that they created mass panic.

Another classic example is Daniel Defoe's *Journal of the Plague Year*, which appears to be a chronicle, supposedly written by H. F. (later identified as Defoe's uncle Henry Foe), within the reporting field of activity but which is actually an imaginative narrative recreation of events during the plague year – a text with features of both reporting and recreating contexts. Defoe, who was born around 1660, wrote the journal as if he had been an eyewitness, as can be seen from the extract from the beginning of the journal in Text 1 – he would have been around four to five years old at the time.

Text 1: Extract from the beginning of Daniel Defoe's *Journal of the Plague Year*[7]

A JOURNAL OF THE PLAGUE YEAR

By Daniel Defoe

> being observations or memorials of the most remarkable occurrences,
> as well public as private, which happened in
> London during the last great visitation in 1665.
> Written by a Citizen who continued
> all the while in London.
> Never made public before

> It was about the beginning of September, 1664, that I, among the rest of my neighbours, heard in ordinary discourse that the plague was returned again in Holland; for it had been very violent there, and particularly at Amsterdam and Rotterdam, in the year 1663, whither,

they say, it was brought, some said from Italy, others from the Levant, among some goods which were brought home by their Turkey fleet; others said it was brought from Candia; others from Cyprus. It mattered not from whence it came; but all agreed it was come into Holland again.

We had no such thing as printed newspapers in those days to spread rumours and reports of things, and to improve them by the invention of men, as I have lived to see practised since. But such things as these were gathered from the letters of merchants and others who corresponded abroad, and from them was handed about by word of mouth only; so that things did not spread instantly over the whole nation, as they do now. But it seems that the Government had a true account of it, and several councils were held about ways to prevent its coming over; but all was kept very private. Hence it was that this rumour died off again, and people began to forget it as a thing we were very little concerned in, and that we hoped was not true; till the latter end of November or the beginning of December 1664 when two men, said to be Frenchmen, died of the plague in Long Acre, or rather at the upper end of Drury Lane. The family they were in endeavoured to conceal it as much as possible, but as it had gotten some vent in the discourse of the neighbourhood, the Secretaries of State got knowledge of it; and concerning themselves to inquire about it, in order to be certain of the truth, two physicians and a surgeon were ordered to go to the house and make inspection. This they did; and finding evident tokens of the sickness upon both the bodies that were dead, they gave their opinions publicly that they died of the plague. Whereupon it was given in to the parish clerk, and he also returned them to the Hall; and it was printed in the weekly bill of mortality in the usual manner, thus –

Plague, 2. Parishes infected, 1.

The people showed a great concern at this, and began to be alarmed all over the town, and the more, because in the last week in December 1664 another man died in the same house, and of the same distemper. And then we were easy again for about six weeks, when none having died with any marks of infection, it was said the distemper was gone; but after that, I think it was about the 12th of February, another died in another house, but in the same parish and in the same manner.

This turned the people's eyes pretty much towards that end of the town, and the weekly bills showing an increase of burials in St Giles's parish more than usual, it began to be suspected that the plague was among the people at that end of the town, and that many had died of it, though they had taken care to keep it as much from the knowledge of the public as possible. This possessed the heads of the people very much, and few cared to go through Drury Lane, or the other streets suspected, unless they had extraordinary business that obliged them to it.

This increase of the bills stood thus: the usual number of burials in a week, in the parishes of St Giles-in-the-Fields and St Andrew's, Holborn, were from 12 to 17 or 19 each, few more or less; but from the time that the plague first began in St Giles's parish, it was observed that the ordinary burials increased in number considerably. For example:

From December 27 to January 3	*{ St Giles's*	*16*
	{ St Andrew's	*17*
January 3 to January 10	*{ St Giles's*	*12*
	{ St Andrew's	*25*
January 10 to January 17	*{ St Giles's*	*18*
	{ St Andrew's	*28*
January 17 to January 24	*{ St Giles's*	*23*
	{ St Andrew's	*16*
January 24 to January 31	*{ St Giles's*	*24*
	{ St Andrew's	*15*
January 30 to February 7	*{ St Giles's*	*21*
	{ St Andrew's	*23*
February 7 to February 14	*{ St Giles's*	*24*

Whereof one of the plague.

Defoe's work has the linguistic features of a journal rather than of a novel, including factual displays such as the tables of deaths. Originally, in the eighteenth century, it was thought to be a factual journal, but, by the end of the century, this view had been revised. Since then, there has been considerable debate about what kind of work it is, ranging from views that it is a 'historical novel' to views that it is a 'sham history'. Baker (2009) summarises the reception of the *Journal* and views of it as follows:

When Defoe published it, he, as usual, left himself off the title page, ascribing the story to H. F. 'Written by a Citizen,' the title page falsely, sales-boostingly claimed, 'Who Continued All the While in London.' People believed that for a while; but by 1780, at least, it was generally known that Defoe was the book's author. Then someone did some arithmetic and realized that Defoe had been a young child when the plague struck London – whereupon they began calling the book a historical novel, unequalled in vividness and circumstantiality. Walter Raleigh, in his late nineteenth-century history of the English novel, called the book 'sham history.' In a study of 'pseudofactual' fiction, Barbara Foley says the *Plague Year* 'creates the majority of its particulars.' And John Hollowell, investigating the literary origins of the New Journalism, writes that Defoe's book is 'fiction masquerading as fact.' Is it?

In a detailed scholarly study, Bastian (1965) reviews the different claims about Defoe's journal, ranging from claims that it is pure fiction to claims that it can be treated as a factually accurate account. Having navigated through this minefield of views, he identifies the most likely sources that he thinks Defoe relied on. Of course, both historians and novelists use sources in the way that Defoe is likely to have done, based on Bastian's (1965) careful account.

While we have presented *Journal of the Plague Year* as a case of registerial ambiguity – and a good deal of the debate around it since it first appeared **treats** the classification of it as a matter of 'either-or', it is of course also possible to view it in terms of another form of registerial indeterminacy: as a blend of what would come to be considered prototypical histories and prototypical novels.

Defoe developed a very extensive registerial repertoire during his life; he is, among other things, known as a pamphleteer, poet, journalist (in his originally weekly newspaper *The Review*, started in 1704) and novelist. Indeed, Mueller (2005) calls him a 'master of genres', tracing part of his engagement with, and development of, genres over time. And Watt (1957[1987]:34) focuses on Defoe, Fielding and Richardson in his study of the 'rise of the novel' crediting Defoe and Richardson with realism:

> Of no fiction before Defoe's could Lamb have written, in terms very similar to those which Hazlitt used of Richardson, 'It is like reading evidence in a court of Justice'. Whether that is in itself a good thing is open to question; Defoe and Richardson would hardly deserve their reputation unless they had other and better claims on our attention. Nevertheless there can be little doubt that the development of a narrative method capable of creating such an impression is the most conspicuous manifestation of that mutation of prose fiction which we call the novel; the historical importance of Defoe and Richardson therefore primarily depends on the suddenness and completeness with which they brought into being what may be regarded as the lowest common denominator of the novel genre as a whole, its formal realism. (1957 [1987]:34)

In view of his pioneering contributions to a range of emerging registers, Defoe would be an appropriate focus in a separate study of permeable contexts and registerial hybridity.

10.5 Overlaps

In overlaps, two registers intersect so that certain texts display features of each. For example, 'exploring' and 'recommending' intersect: overlaps occur between texts operating in the 'exploring' and 'recommending' sector. One example is reviews. They are located within the 'exploring' sector; they explore a commodity – a product or a service – by evaluating it. The bandwidth of the channel for reviews has expanded considerably in the last decade and a half: nowadays, reviews appear not only in newspapers and magazines (whether in print or online), but also as part of websites concerned with certain commodities such as films, books and music.

For example, the website Goodreads provides user reviews of books, and it has now become something like a social networking site as well as for book lovers. Like user reviews in general, the reviews vary considerable in length, expertise and orientation (ranging from more subjective to more objective). Another element of variation is whether they include an **_explicit_** recommendation or not.[8] For example, the review in Text 2 contains no explicit recommendation to readers of the review. However, many reviews contain an explicit recommendation – semantically, a form of 'command', which is often realised by an 'imperative' clause or a 'modulated declarative' one; for instance:

(1) Now, fetch this book. Sit! Read. Good job!

(2) All dog lovers should read this book.

(3) A must-read for every dog lover.

(4) A must read!!

(5) If you love text books, this is for you. If you were hoping for fun stories about how smart dogs are, skip this!

Text 2: Example of a user review of *The Genius of Dogs: How Dogs are Smarter than You Think,* by Brian Hare and Vanessa Woods[9]

ASHLEY'S REVIEW

4 of 5 stars

> This is a book filled with charts and graphs. Don't let that fool you, this book is actually really interesting. It starts off slow, but then it gets interesting as the author gives personal examples and gets more into detail about his research.

In contrast with Text 2, the review in Text 3 contains an explicit recommendation. This recommendation takes the form of reading advice, the nuclear segment being the modulated declarative clause *All dog lovers should read this book*; and it is placed as the macro-New of the whole review (for the notion of macro-New, see Martin 1993). The recommendation is organised around the reading advice, as is shown by the rhetorical-relational (RST, Rhetorical Structure Theory) analysis in Figure 10.3 (for rhetorical-relational analysis, see e.g. Mann, Matthiessen and Thompson 1992 [2001]; Matthiessen 2015). The other parts of this text segment can be interpreted as providing motivations for readers who are dog lovers to follow the advice. The rhetorical complex in Figure 10.3 is similar to the kinds of complex we find in many texts operating in 'recommending' contexts. Such texts recommend a course of action to the addressee through a proposal or set of proposals, and they support this proposal segment with propositional segments linked to it through the rhetorical relation of 'motivation'.

Text 3: Example of a user review with an explicit recommendation10

THE GENIUS OF DOGS: HOW DOGS ARE SMARTER THAN YOU THINK BY BRIAN HARE, VANESSA WOODS (GOODREADS AUTHOR)

Peggy Tibbetts's review

Mar 27, 13
5 of 5 stars

Read in March, 2013

Anyone who has ever shared true companionship with a dog has wondered: Does my dog think? 'The Genius of Dogs' not only asks, but answers the question. Co-written by husband and wife research team Brian Hare and Vanessa Woods, this book focuses primarily on Hare's lifetime evolution into anthropology and his research into animal cognition. In order to distinguish how dogs think, Hare researched how other animals think including humans, bonobos, chimpanzees, wolves, foxes and cats. Then he compared domesticated dogs to wild dogs, dingoes, and New Guinea Singing Dogs. In some cases the outcomes were surprising. In others, the results were what I would have expected based on my own interactions with dogs, as well as other animals. No matter what, the accounts of Hare's travels to animal research centers all over the world and his discoveries along the way are certainly fascinating as well as entertaining. Hare's scientific analysis is based on decades of research into animal cognition and reveals the unique 'genius' of dogs that sets them apart from all other species. But this is no dull treatise. Woods' engaging narrative is peppered with amusing anecdotes, plus glimpses into Hare's childhood and personal life which bring to light his deep affection and devotion not only to dogs, but the entire animal kingdom.

'The Genius of Dogs' presents ample evidence to support the subtitle, 'How Dogs are Smarter than You Think.' Some readers will never look at their dogs the same way. Others will look at their dogs and say, 'I knew it,' with the assurance their dogs understand exactly what they mean. All dog lovers should read this book. If you understand your dogs better, you can help them live longer, happier lives.

The kind of overlap illustrated here makes good sense in view of the **persuasive** nature of the activities of both exploring and recommending. If readers give positive value to books in reviews, these books will seem more attractive to potential buyers, and they therefore will be more likely to buy these books. It is not surprising that Amazon has just acquired Goodreads for around one billion US dollars (announced at the end of March, 2013), an acquisition that has been met with very mixed reactions.

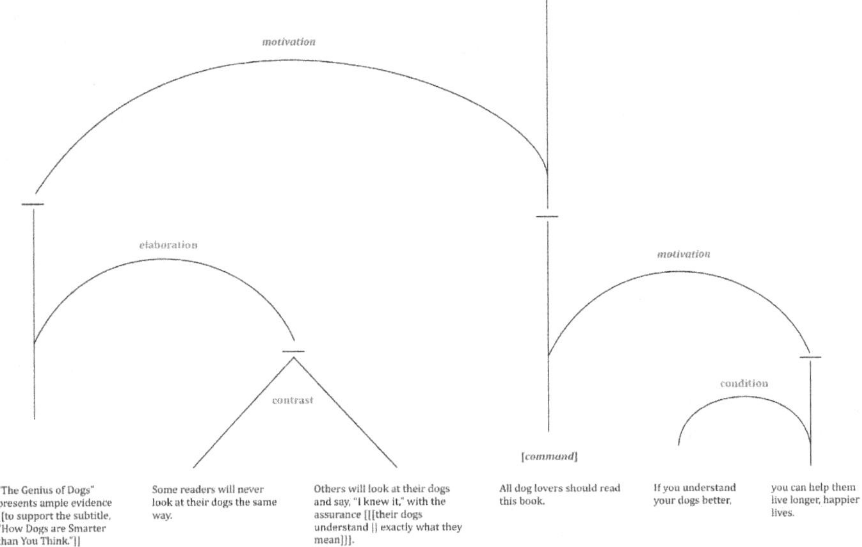

Figure 10.3: Rhetorical-relational analysis of the last paragraph of Text 2

10.6 Blends

Overlaps shade into blends, but whereas overlaps are borderline cases – partly like one register, partly like another, and thus **intermediate** between the two, blends are more like **fusions** of two (or potentially more) registers. In Halliday and Matthiessen (1999:550–551), an example of an overlap the 'behavioural' type (see Banks, this volume) within the grammatical system of PROCESS TYPE is given: they are partly like 'material' processes, and partly like 'mental' ones. And we give as an example of a blend the combination of 'probability' and 'ability' in instances such as *they might win* *tomorrow*, which means both 'they may be able to win' and 'it is possible that they will win'.

Registerial blends include what have been called 'hybrid genres' or 'cross-genres'. In discussions of such mixed genres, the focus is usually on fiction and film, and examples given are combinations of folk genres, e.g. action-comedy, romantic comedy, and tragicomedy. These all fall within the 'recreating' sector of Figure 10.1, and they seem to blend ways of engaging readers and viewers, e.g. by at the same time amusing and scaring them (comedy horror). However, other forms of registerial mixing have of course also been recognised. One well-known example is that of the advertorial.

The term 'advertorial' is a combination of 'editorial' and 'advertisement'; but actual examples are more like combinations of news reports and advertisements – i.e., blends of reporting and recommending.[11] Many seem to be fairly transparent examples of advertisements that are simply represented on a fairly low level of layout as news reports, or as media interviews. These are probably all hard-sell advertisements, pushing a particular product or service, with obvious details about how to purchase or subscribe to it. However, soft-sell advertisements promoting an image and/or agenda may be more like news features, and in a sense harder to detect and thus more like true blends.

An example of such a blend of 'recommending' and 'reporting' is given as Text 4. This is a 'feature' that appeared in the *South China Morning Post*, Hong Kong's main daily English newspaper, in 2009: *Express Rail Link to Put Hong Kong on Fast Track to Greater Prosperity*. Starting with the wordplay in the headline based on the concrete and abstract senses of *track*, this text certainly has the properties of a feature article, including the scene-setting beginning with Alex Cheung on his way from Hong Kong to Guangzhou. However, there are clearly properties that suggest that it is not an objective or unbiased feature article. The benefits of the Express Rail Link are expressed throughout the text like a positive prosody; but there is no mention of the cost of the project, of who will pay for it – nor is there any mention of the environmental impact or any other potentially negative side effects. And the macro-New of the text distils the benefits in the most positive terms, echoing the headline's *fast track to greater prosperity* with *the fast track to an exciting new era in communications for the city*, just as one would expect in a promotional text. Further, the attentive reader will find 'Sponsored Feature' in the upper right-hand corner of the article. However, the sponsor or sponsors are not identified.

Figure 10.4 Example of a 'sponsored feature'

Text 4: Example of a 'sponsored feature'[12]

EXPRESS RAIL LINK TO PUT HONG KONG ON FAST TRACK TO GREATER PROSPERITY

It's 6.30 a.m. on the morning of October 15, 2015. Hong Kong businessman Alex Cheung folds up his newspaper, settles back into his seat in the air-conditioned comfort of the train carriage, flips open his laptop and starts his working day.

The high-speed train eases out of West Kowloon precisely on time. As he downloads his emails, football fan Mr Cheung reflects on the fact that the will arrive in Guangzhou in just 48 minutes – just three minutes more than it takes his beloved Arsenal to play one half of a match.

After being carried at speeds of up to 200 km per hour, reaching Shenzhen in an astonishing 14 minutes, Mr Cheung just has time to examine his briefing papers and finish his gourmet coffee before the train pulls into the imposing station in Guangzhou's buzzing business district of Shibi.

As he steps off the train, Mr Cheung waves across to a group of accountant friends from his company's Guangzhou office on the opposite platform, preparing to board a train for one of their twice-weekly Hong Kong meetings.

The time is still only 7.18 a.m. Back in Central, a city is slowly waking – and yet here at the New Guangzhou Station, one of the largest passenger station in Asia, the heart of an extraordinary nationwide network connecting all major mainland cities of China is beating fast.

This scenario is no futuristic fantasy. It is a nearby time of fast, convenient travel and seamless links to all corners of the country that is only years away for Hong Kong if work begins end of this year on the city's 26 km stretch of the 140-kilometre Guangzhou-Shenzhen-Hong Kong Express Rail Link.

[…]

For Mr Cheung and for millions of other Hong Kong people, the Express Rail Link is the fast track to an exciting new era in communications for the city – a future full of convenience, connectivity and opportunity.

10.7 Neutralisations

Unlike blends and overlaps, neutralisations are based on the disappearance of differences between two fields of activity. This may happen because of the nature of the tenor or the mode of the context. The last example in the list in Table 10.1 above, user reviews, can be interpreted as an instance of registerial neutralisation through mode, more specifically channel: because of the technologies first of broadcasting and then of the Internet, the latter with applications like Facebook, Twitter, Goodreads, and other social networking websites, the boundary between the private and public spheres have become blurred (see Macnamara 2010; cf. also Shirky 2010).

Traditionally, personal experiences and values would be exchanged in face-to-face casual conversation – located within the 'sharing' sector of Figure 10.1. Sharing personal experiences and values in this way helps people form, calibrate and negotiate interpersonal relations within different groups such as those of family, friends and work mates. Conversation, more specifically gossip, is interpreted by Dunbar (1996) as a substitute for grooming within a group – verbal grooming. Traditionally, casual conversation involved a small group and was typically private, although there may always have been eavesdroppers. However, with modern technology, there are now new channels (within mode) making it possible for such sharing to be completely public (with eavesdroppers transforming into lurkers).

This already became possible with twentieth century mass media – radio and TV – and was exploited in talk shows where conversations about highly personal issues such as infidelity involving two or more people were transformed into public entertainment, as a way of 'exploring' communal values. And now, in the early twenty-first century, new channels have opened up based on the Internet and mobile technology further blurring the distinction between the private and public spheres, and thus between 'sharing' and 'exploring'. The founder of Facebook, Mark Zuckerberg, has famously said that privacy is no longer a social norm.[13] This has, not surprisingly, generated a great deal of debate; but Macnamara (2010) suggests that privacy has in a sense been a fairly short interlude in human history – the difference now of course being that personal experiences and values can potentially be accessible to anyone around the world linked into social media, not just other members of one's tribe.

To explore the blurring – or even neutralisation – of 'sharing' and 'exploring', let us focus on examples of evaluating a commodity, more specifically a particular film, *The Shawshank Redemption*. We will start with prototypical sharing in a face-to-face conversation among close friends and family around a dinner table: see Text 5.[14] This passage is an extract from a long dinner table conversation; it is characteristic of casual conversations (see e.g. Eggins 1990; Eggins and Slade 2005) – the interactants drift into sharing evaluations of *The Shawshank Redemption*, and then drift into sharing views about prisons. It starts with Mother reminding everyone that they've all seen the film, and this is followed immediately by positive evaluations – Craig: *Yeah that was wonderful*, and Jane: *Oh tremendous*. Then they share some memories of the film, and Father offers an explicitly subjective evaluation: *Well that was the part of the film I liked the best*. These comments are characteristic of evaluations in 'sharing' contexts – there is often not much in the way of analysis of what is being evaluated, and the evaluations are subjective (on the model of 'I like' / 'I don't like'). Thus personal opinions offered in private are, in principle, quite different from what professional critics offer in public as they contribute reviews in 'exploring' contexts. However, as already indicated, the situation has changed.

Text 5: Evaluations of the "Shawshank Redemption" in a casual conversation unfolding in a 'sharing' context; [= beginning of overlapping turn

CRAIG: [when you think the more people
FATHER: [What do they what do they see when they look and see no cash on these premises and they think oh what's the world coming to.
MOTHER: But we've all seen the Shawshank Redemption.
CRAIG: Yeah that was wonderful.
JANE: [Oh tremendous.
MOTHER: And that was and that that's sort of you've seen that, haven't you?
KATE: Mmm.
MOTHER: And that's the um you know when the guy gets out after being keeping the library in the prison for ever.
JANE: [And just kills himself.
CRAIG: Hangs himself.
MOTHER: [Kills himself because he just doesn't know what to do.
FATHER: But then the other side of it was
JANE: [He didn't want to get out.

MOTHER: No.
FATHER: [When the when the when the other bloke had been in
there for ever joined ah.
CRAIG: [Went to the San Rouge
FATHER: [Down on the south on to Cuba or whatever it was, and
lived a happy life.
MOTHER: Yeah.
KATE: Yeah. As if. [*laughs*]
FATHER: Well that was the part of the film I liked best.
JANE: You like a happy ending.
FATHER: I like a happy ending.
CRAIG: The point is the more sentencing.
KATE: [I like the idea of Tom Robbins waiting for me Tim Tim
Robbins waiting for me on a beach somewhere.
CRAIG: [we're going to have to change our opinions so we've got
institutions that can cater. We're going to need nursing
homes
[overlapping inaudible 2 secs]
MOTHER: It's unbelievable.
CRAIG: And I mean we're the
JANE: [Well it just the they're such they're the pits prisons. I mean
there there's
FATHER: [Prisons.
JANE: When I when I went to the ombudsman's office we used to
do I we used to go and visit the prisons or you know we'd
we'd in fact actually had carte blanche in prisons we could
wander around we could go into the cells and do all that
sort of stuff. So I've seen more of of prisons and children's
institutions than most people because you
KATE: [Or than you would care to.
JANE: Or you would care to. And they really are horrendous. I
mean they're they're they're … ugly scary places, {CRAIG:
Mmm.} which um you just … you you wouldn't put you
wouldn't put anybody. I mean, they they really are just such
awful places you know you read these sort of various things
about
MOTHER: [But they're supposed to be
JANE: Motels and God knows what
MOTHER: [Oh no that's that's ridiculous.
JANE: And it's just – I mean, it's just horrible. They're violent and
they're …
CRAIG: Well to give you an idea
JANE: [Dreadful.

The situation has changed in that people can now publicise their personal opinions. Thus the Internet Movie Database (IMBD) enables users to post their own reviews of films. These user reviews vary greatly – and one area of variation is precisely the region between 'sharing' and 'exploring'. The example in Text 6 seems fairly close to what we could expect to find in a casual conversation among friends sharing views about a film; the frame of reference is the writer (*I have ever seen*; *I saw the movie*; *never happened to me before*) and the evaluations tend to be explicitly subjective, drawing on the resources of 'emotive mental' clauses with the reviewer ('I') as Senser: (*I first read the book*) *and I didn't like it that much*; *I like the end more than in the book.* (And like the user reviews discussed above, this one also includes a recommendation – of the kind one would give a friend: *Watch the movie, it is great.*)

Text 6: User review from IMDB towards 'sharing' end of the cline between 'sharing' and 'exploring'[15]

ONE OF THE BEST MOVIES I HAVE EVER SEEN, 23 APRIL 1999

Author: Anna Schönhütte from Brühl, Germany

This movie is one of the best I have ever seen. I first read the book, and I didn't liked it that much, but then I saw the movie. And that's a things that's never happened to me before, the movie was better than the book. It's the other way normally. But in this case, the movie is so much better, I like the end more than in the book. Watch the movie, it is great.

User reviews such as Text 6 thus illustrate the blurring of 'sharing' and 'exploring' contexts: a user can express personal opinions in an explicitly subjective way in a public venue, and thus kontribute to the calibration and negotiation of communal values. At the same time, within the envelope of variation, we also find many examples of user reviews that are closer to the kind of analytical reviews we would expect from professional reviewers working within the 'exploring' sector – for example, Text 7.

Text 7: Extract from user review from IMDB towards 'exploring' end of the cline between 'sharing' and 'exploring'[16]

EMOTIONALLY FULFILLING, 19 FEBRUARY 2008

Author: gcd70 from Melbourne, Australia
*** This review may contain spoilers ***

From the director of 1990s 'Buried Alive' comes perhaps the strongest drama of 1994. 'The Shawshank Redemption' is emotionally fulfilling in every way, uplifting its audience again and again. Darabont's screenplay, adapted from (and expanded upon) Stephen King's short novella 'Rita Hayworth and the Shawshank Redemption,' is at once soul stirring, heart-rending and disarmingly funny. As director, Frank Darabont brings this poignant and oft times surprising (largely unpredictable thank goodness) script to the screen with the kind of loving care that only a writer/director can, ensuring that all the right elements are brought to the surface.

Startling performances from Tim Robbins, Morgan Freeman and the entire support cast help make this picture a powerful production. As convicted double murderer Andy Du Fresne, Robbins portrays innocence and determination superbly. He's a man who not only strongly believes he has a future, but that it's a good one. Freeman is spot on as the world weary 'Red,' the lifer who specialises in the supply of merchandise ('whatever you want') to other inmates. He is gradually transformed, and always surprised, by Andy's optimism, geniality and brilliance. In support of these two leads are some very strong turns which provide an over all feast of superlative acting talents.

The cinematography is superb, capturing some spectacular images of the foreboding Shawshank prison, while Thomas Newman's music is awe inspiring and must be duly recognised as a truly moving composition.

'The Shawshank Redemption' is a long movie, though it would seem that to shorten it would mean to miss out on some powerful, if not crucial scenes. In this light, the editing team have done a marvellous job.

What makes this film so effective is Darabont's brilliant script and astute direction, coupled with the strong acting and great support production. Darabont achieves all his objectives, making us laugh, cry, listen and think, he both surprises and inspires us many times. We're left in the end with an uplifting and wholly satisfying movie, which is unexpectedly memorable and magnificently rewarding. A definite triumph of the human spirit.

Perhaps the conclusion could be called simplistic, but certainly not expected, and that's what makes this story so great. 'The Shawshank Redemption' comes from nowhere to really hit you with its well written characters and even its carefully researched history. Wonderfully emotionally telling and thankfully intellectually sharp, its a pleasure that you must treat yourself to! Look for two brilliantly played characters in the form of the menacingly sinister Warden (Bob Gunton) and the despicable, ruthlessly violent Captain of the Guards (Clancy Brown).

This user review (Text 7) is much more analytical; the reviewer refers to various technical aspects of the film – the source, the screenplay, the direction, the cinematography, the editing, the acting. And the evaluations tend to be objective rather than subjective; the reviewer draws on the resources for evaluation provided by 'relational' clauses and nominal groups, as in

[clause: relational]
'The Shawshank Redemption' is **emotionally fulfilling** in every way
Startling performances from Tim Robbins, Morgan Freeman and the entire support cast help make this picture **a powerful production**.
The cinematography is **superb**
[nominal group]
this **poignant and oft times surprising (largely unpredictable thank goodness)** movie
a **startling** performances
a **marvellous** job
Darabont's **brilliant** script and **astute** direction
well written characters and even its **carefully researched** history
two **brilliantly played** characters

There is thus a continuum from 'sharing' to 'exploring' fields of activity – with blurring or neutralisation in the middle range of this continuum, as illustrated by Text 6. Ontogenetically, there is of course a move from 'sharing' to 'exploring'; as learners go through the school system, they learn how to transform sharing strategies into exploring ones – how to morph subjective views into views that appear to be objective (cf. Christie and Derewianka 2008). However, new technologies are creating new possibilities – possibilities that we can interpret as a neutralisation of private sharing and public exploring.

10.8 Conclusion

In this chapter, we have explored registerial hybridity – the mixing of registers – in terms of one of the three contextual parameters, viz. field, more specifically (within field), field of activity (or socio-semiotic process). In other words, we have explored registerial hybridity in terms of 'what's going on' within context, pointing to and illustrating different kinds of indeterminacy (ambiguity, overlap, blend and neutralisation). The examples we have discussed are summarised diagrammatically in Figure 10.5.

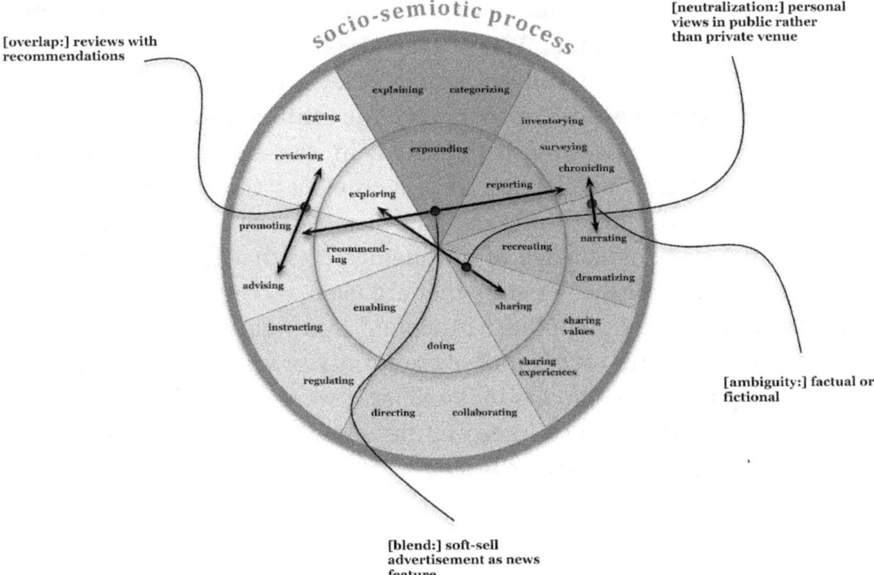

Figure 10.5: Examples of indeterminacy – ambiguities, overlaps, blends and neutralisations

Figure 10.5 is based on Figure 10.1, which is a **topological** representation of our differentiation of fields of activity. Topological representations are designed to bring out indeterminacy: see Martin and Matthiessen (1991[2010]). Thus the fields of activity in Figure 10.1 are arranged to bring out areas of potential indeterminacy – e.g. between 'exploring' (exposition) and 'expounding' (factorial explanation); but as our discussion has shown, indeterminacy is not restricted to adjacent sectors in the display such as 'recommending' and 'exploring: non-adjacent sectors of activity also shade into one another – e.g. 'recommending' into 'reporting' and 'sharing' into 'exploring', as we have illustrated in the previous sections.

As we have noted at the beginning, we based our exploration of registerial hybridity on the field of activity within the contextual parameter of field. There are of course many other examples of registerial hybridity, an interesting type being what Halliday (1996 [2007]:118–119) calls the **Disneyland register** occurring in the context of the Disneyfication of Western man (I say 'man' advisedly), whereby the off-duty executive reverts semiotically to childhood while retaining the material make-up of an adult.

Everyday folk labels for examples of registerial hybridity include **satire, irony, spoof** and **pastiche**. These can be very effective registerial strategies for bringing features of commonly accepted views into critical relief. There are innumerable examples, but perhaps two particularly striking and well-known ones are Jonathan Swift's 'A Modest Proposal' (1729) [extract in Text 8] and Mark Twain's 'War Prayer' (1905) [extract in Text 9]. While they are almost two hundred years apart, they are strategically similar in their use of satire to expose, respectively, the attitude towards the poor in Ireland and the attitude towards the enemy in war – towards fellow members of the human family that are treated cruelly as 'the Other'.

Such satires are interesting examples of registerial mixing. Their writers have the double challenge of producing texts that can be interpreted as being instances of the registers that are used as 'vehicles' – like Swift's creation of a political pamphlet of the kind that was very popular during his time, and Twain's creation of a traditional prayer, while at the same time making linguistic choices that will, as it were, tip the balance for the addressees so that they also interpret the texts as polemical explorations. Twain's ingenious strategies are brought out by Martin (2006) in his analysis of the *War Prayer*.

Text 8: Extract from Jonathan Swift's (1729) satirical 'A Modest Proposal or Preventing the Children of Poor People From Being a Burden to Their Parents or Country, and for Making Them Beneficial to the Public'.[17]

It is a melancholy object to those who walk through this great town or travel in the country, when they see the streets, the roads, and cabin doors, crowded with beggars of the female sex, followed by three, four, or six children, all in rags and importuning every passenger for an alms.

[...]

I have been assured by a very knowing American of my acquaintance in London, that a young healthy child well nursed is at a year old a most delicious, nourishing, and wholesome food, whether stewed, roasted, baked, or boiled; and I make no doubt that it will equally serve in a fricassee or a ragout.

I do therefore humbly offer it to public consideration that of the hundred and 20 thousand children already computed, 20 thousand may be reserved for breed, whereof only one-fourth part to be males; which is more than we allow to sheep, black cattle or swine; and my reason is, that these children are seldom the fruits of marriage, a circumstance not much regarded by our savages, therefore one male will be sufficient to serve four females. That the remaining hundred thousand may, at a year old, be offered in the sale to the persons of quality and fortune through the kingdom; always advising the mother to let them suck plentifully in the last month, so as to render them plump and fat for a good table. A child will make two dishes at an entertainment for friends; and when the family dines alone, the fore or hind quarter will make a reasonable dish, and seasoned with a little pepper or salt will be very good boiled on the fourth day, especially in winter.

I have reckoned upon a medium that a child just born will weigh 12 pounds, and in a solar year, if tolerably nursed, increaseth to 28 pounds.

I grant this food will be somewhat dear, and therefore very proper for landlords, who, as they have already devoured most of the parents, seem to have the best title to the children.

[...]

Text 9: Extract from Mark Twain's (1905) 'War Prayer'[18]

It was a time of great and exalting excitement. The country was up in arms, the war was on, in every breast burned the holy fire of patriotism; the drums were beating, the bands playing, the toy pistols popping, the bunched firecrackers hissing and spluttering; on every hand and far down the receding and fading spread of roofs and balconies a fluttering wilderness of flags flashed in the sun; daily the young volunteers marched down the wide avenue gay and fine in their new uniforms, the proud fathers and mothers and sisters and sweethearts cheering them with voices choked with happy emotion as they swung by; nightly the packed mass meetings listened, panting, to patriot oratory with stirred the deepest deeps of their hearts, and which they interrupted at briefest intervals with cyclones of applause, the tears running down their cheeks the while; in the churches the pastors preached devotion to flag and country, and invoked the God of Battles beseeching His aid in our good cause in outpourings of fervid eloquence which moved every listener.

[...]

An aged stranger entered and moved with slow and noiseless step up the main aisle, his eyes fixed upon the minister, his long body clothed in a robe that reached to his feet, his head bare, his white hair descending in a frothy cataract to his shoulders, his seamy face unnaturally pale, pale even to ghastliness.

[...]

'Lord our Father, our young patriots, idols of our hearts, go forth into battle – be Thou near them! With them – in spirit – we also go forth from the sweet peace of our beloved firesides to smite the foe. O Lord our God, help us tear their soldiers to bloody shreds with our shells; help us to cover their smiling fields with the pale forms of their patriot dead; help us to drown the thunder of the guns with the shrieks of their wounded, writhing in pain; help us to lay waste their humble homes with a hurricane of fire; help us to wring the hearts of their unoffending widows with unavailing grief; help us to turn them out roofless with their little children to wander unfriended in the wastes of their desolated land in rags and hunger and thirst, sports of the sun flames in summer and the icy winds of winter, broken in spirit, worn with travail, imploring thee for the refuge of the grave and denied it –

For our sakes who adore Thee, Lord, blast their hopes, blight their lives, protract their bitter pilgrimmage, make heavy their steps, water their way with their tears, stain the white snow with the blood of their wounded feet!

We ask it, in the spirit of love, of Him Who is the Source of Love, and Who is the ever-faithful refuge and friend of all that are sore beset and seek His aid with humble and contrite hearts. Amen.

Notes

1   We use the term register in its original sense in systemic functional linguistics of a functional variety of language – rather than in the derived sense of the contextual setting of field, tenor and mode in which such a functional variety operates (as in Martin 1992).

2   As already noted, this means viewing functional variation in language 'from above', from the vantage point of register. This view is an ecological one: we are viewing variation in language in relation to the environment in which it operates. Of course, we can also view functional variation in language 'from below' – in terms of how it is reflected in patterns of wording (lexicogrammar) and sounding (phonology) or writing (graphology), and 'from roundabout' – in terms of how it is reflected in patterns of meaning (semantics). Studies of register variation drawing on large corpora have, quite naturally, tended to adopt the view 'from below' since they need to proceed by means of forms of analyses that can be automated with computational tools (such as tagging in terms of word classes). Ultimately, however, all three angles of approach should produce results that resonate with one another.

3   For discussions of this typology and examples of applications based on it, see e.g. Matthiessen (2006); Teruya, (2007); Matthiessen, Teruya and Lam (2010); Halliday and Matthiessen (2013:Ch. 1); Matthiessen (2013; 2015).

4   According to Apple's Dictionary, the term *hybrid* originated in the early seventeenth century from Latin *hybrida* 'offspring of a tame sow and wild boar, child of a freeman and slave, etc.'.

5   The Corpus of Contemporary American English: http://corpus.byu.edu/coca/

6   We also need to recognise indeterminacy between more delicate subtypes within each of the eight primary types set out in Figure 1. For example, documents produced by pharmaceutical companies may appear to be indeterminate between 'promoting' their product and 'advising' readers how to deal with a medical problem.

7   Source: http://www.gutenberg.org/files/376/376-h/376-h.htm (last accessed 1 August, 2013).

8   The positive or negative evaluations in the review may of course be seen as *implicit* recommendations, and this is already a link between exploring and recommending.

9   Source: http://www.goodreads.com/review/show/516821363 (last accessed 1 August, 2013).

10   Source: http://www.goodreads.com/review/show/572330626 (last accessed 1 August, 2013).

11   Some also appear to be blends of advertisements (promoting) and advice columns (advising).

12   Source: http://blogs.hillandknowlton.com/glennschloss/files/2009/10/scmp-rail.jpg (last accessed 1 August, 2013).

13   See e.g. http://www.theguardian.com/technology/2010/jan/11/facebook-privacy (last accessed 1 August, 2013).

14   Source: OZ Talk, a corpus of spoken Australian English compiled by researchers at UTS and Macquarie University in Sydney, Australia.

15   Source: http://www.imdb.com/title/tt0111161/reviews?start=20 (last accessed 1 August, 2013).

16   Source: http://www.imdb.com/title/tt0111161/reviews?start=20 (last accessed 1 August, 2013).

17   Source: http://www.gutenberg.org/files/1080/1080-h/1080-h.htm.

18   Source: http://warprayer.org (last accessed 1 August, 2013).

References

Baker, N. (2009). 'The greatest liar': Is Defoe's *A Journal of the Plague Year* a work of journalism? *Columbia Journalism Review: Second Read.* http://www.cjr.org/second_read/the_greatest_liar_1.php?page=all (last accessed 1 August, 2013).

Bastian, F. (1965). Defoe's *Journal of the Plague Year reconsidered. The Review of English Studies.* New Series, 16(62), 151–173.

Christie, F., and Derewianka, B. (2008). *School Discourse: Learning to Write Across the Years of Schooling.* London, New York: Continuum.

Dunbar, R. (1996). *Grooming, Gossip, and the Revolution of Language.* London: Faber and Faber.

Eggins, S. (1990). *Conversational Structure: A systemic-functional analysis of interpersonal and logical meaning in multiparty sustained talk.* Unpublished Ph.D. thesis, Department of Linguistics, University of Sydney.

Eggins, S., and Slade, D. (2005). *Analysing Casual Conversation*. London: Equinox.

Halliday, M.A.K. (1978). *Language as Social Semiotic: The Social Interpretation of Language and Meaning*. London: Edward Arnold.

Halliday, M.A.K. (1995). Fuzzy grammatics: a systemic functional approach to fuzziness in natural language. *Fuzzy Systems, 1995. International Joint Conference of the Fourth IEEE International Conference on Fuzzy Systems and The Second International Fuzzy Engineering Symposium, Proceedings of 1995 ITTT Int.* Volume 1, 9–26.

Halliday, M.A.K. (1996[2007]). Literacy and linguistics: a functional perspective. In R. Hasan and G. Williams (eds), *Literacy in Society*, 339–376. London: Longman. Reprinted in M.A.K. Halliday (2007), *Language in Education*, Volume 9 of *The Collected Works of M.A.K. Halliday*, edited by J.J. Webster, 97–129. London and New York: Continuum.

Halliday, M.A.K. (2011). *Some thoughts on text and discourse, information and meaning.* Paper given to 'Choice and Text. Institute of Language and Communication, University of Southern Denmark.

Halliday, M.A.K., McIntosh, A., and Strevens, P. (1964). *The Linguistic Sciences and Language Teaching*. London: Longman.

Halliday, M.A.K., and Matthiessen, C.M.I.M. (1999). *Construing Experience Through Meaning: A Language-based Approach to Cognition*. London: Cassell.

Halliday, M.A.K., and Matthiessen, C.M.I.M. (2013). *Halliday's Introduction to Functional Grammar* (4th ed.). London: Routledge.

Hasan, R. (1973). Code, register and social dialect. In B. Bernstein (Ed.), *Class, Codes and Control, Volume 2: Applied Studies Towards a Sociology of Language*, 253–292. London: Routledge and Kegan Paul.

Hasan, R. (1985). *Linguistics, Language and Verbal Art*. Geelong, Vic.: Deakin University Press.

Hasan, R. (2000). The uses of talk. In S. Sarangi and M. Coulthard (Eds), *Discourse in Social Life*, 28–47. London: Pearson Education.

Iedema, R., Feez, S., and White, P. (1994). *Media Literacy*. (Write it right industry research report no. 2.) Sydney: NSW, Department of Education, Disadvantaged Schools Program Metropolitan East.

Lukin, A., Moore, A., Herke, M., Wegener, R., and Canzhong, W. (2008). Halliday's model of register revisited and explored. *Linguistics and the Human Sciences*, 4(2), 187–243.

Lemke, J.L. (1995). *Textual Politics: Discourse and Social Dynamics*. London: Taylor and Francis.

Macnamara, J. (2010). *The 21st Century Media: (R)evolution – Emergent Communication Practices*. New York: Peter Lang.

Mann, W.C., Matthiessen, C.M.I.M., and Thompson, S.A. (1992[2001]). *Rhetorical Structure Theory and Text Analysis*. USC/ISI Report. Reprinted in W.C. Mann and S.A. Thompson (Eds) (2001), *Discourse Description: Diverse Linguistic Analyses of a Fund Raising Text*, 39–78. Amsterdam and Philadelphia: John Benjamins. http://dx.doi.org/10.1075/pbns.16.04man

Martin, J.R. (1992). *English Text: System and structure*. Amsterdam and Philadelphia: John Benjamins. http://dx.doi.org/10.1075/z.59

Martin, J.R. (1993). Life as a Noun. In M.A.K. Halliday and J.R. Martin (Eds), *Writing Science: Literacy and Discursive Power*, 221–267. London: Falmer.

Martin, J.R. (2006). Vernacular deconstruction: undermining spin. *DELTA*, 22(1), 177–203. http://dx.doi.org/10.1590/S0102-44502006000100007

Martin, J.R., and Matthiessen, C.M.I.M. (1991[2010]). Systemic typology and topology. In F. Christie (Ed.), *Literacy in Social Processes: Papers from the Inaugural Australian Systemic Functional Linguistics Conference, Deakin University, January 1990*, 345–383. Darwin: Centre for Studies of Language in Education, Northern Territory University. Reprinted in J.R. Martin (2010), *SFL theory, Collected Works of J.R. Martin*, edited by W. Zhenhua, Volume 1 167–215. Shanghai: Shanghai Jiao Tong University Press.

Matthiessen, C.M.I.M. (1993). Register in the round: diversity in a unified theory of register analysis. In M. Ghadessy (Ed.), *Register Analysis: Theory and Practice*, 221–292. London: Pinter.

Matthiessen, C.M.I.M. (1995). Fuzziness construed in language: A linguistic perspective. *Fuzzy Systems, 1995. International Joint Conference of the Fourth IEEE International Conference on Fuzzy Systems and The Second International Fuzzy Engineering Symposium, Proceedings of 1995 ITTT Int.* Volume 4. 1871–1878.

Matthiessen, C.M.I.M. (2006). Educating for advanced foreign language capacities: Exploring the meaning-making resources of languages systemic-functionally. In H. Byrnes (Ed.), *Advanced Instructed Language Learning: The Complementary Contribution of Halliday and Vygotsky*, 31–57. London, New York: Continuum.

Matthiessen, C.M.I.M. (2013). Appliable discourse analysis. In Fang Yan and J.J. Webster (eds.), *Developing Systemic Functional Linguistics: theory and application*, 135–205. London and Oakville: Equinox.

Matthiessen, C.M.I.M. (2015). Register in the round: registerial cartography. *Functional Linguistics* 2(9).

Matthiessen, C.M.I.M., Teruya, K., and Lam, M. (2010). *Key Terms in Systemic Functional Linguistics*. London, New York: Continuum.

Mueller, A. (2005). Daniel Defoe, Master of Genres. *Worcester Papers in English and Cultural Studies*, 3. http://eprints.worc.ac.uk/312/1/Andreas_Mueller_Defoe.pdf (last accessed 1 August, 2013).

Nanri, K. (1993). *An attempt to synthesize two systemic contextual theories through the investigation of the process of the evolution of the discourse semantic structure of the newspaper reporting article.* Unpublished Ph.D. thesis, Department of Linguistics, University of Sydney.

Shirky, C. (2010). *The Cognitive Surplus: Creativity and Generosity in a Connected Age*. New York: The Penguin Press.

Swales, J. (1990). *Genre Analysis: English in an Academic and Research Setting*. Cambridge: Cambridge University Press.

Teruya, K. (2007). *A Systemic Functional Grammar of Japanese* (2 vols.) London, New York: Continuum.

Watt, I.P. (1987). (1957[1987]). *The Rise of the Novel: Studies in Defoe, Richardson and Fielding. London: Chatto and Windus. Reprinted.* London: Hogarth Press.

About the authors

Christian Matthiessen became Chair Professor at Macquarie University in 2002 and was appointed Chair and Head of the Department of English at the Hong Kong Polytechnic University in 2008. He has worked and published in a wide range of areas, including language typology, linguistics and computing, grammatical descriptions, grammar and discourse, functional grammar for English-language teachers, text analysis and translation and the evolution of language. Among his well-known work is *Lexicogrammatical Cartography: English systems* (Tokyo, International Language Sciences Publishers, 1995), *Construing Experience through Meaning: A language based approach to cognition* (with Michael Halliday, Cassell, 1999), as well as his collaboration with Halliday on the 3rd and 4th editions of *An Introduction to Functional Grammar*.

Kazuhiro Teruya is assistant professor at the Hong Kong Polytechnic University. His research interests include Systemic functional linguistic theory and description, language comparison and multilingual studies, language typology, language logic, discourse analysis, register profiling and advanced second/foreign language learning. He has collaborated on *Key Terms in Systemic Functional Linguistics* (with Matthiessen and Lam, Continuum, 2010). He is also a contributor to the *The Bloomsbury Companion to M.A.K. Halliday*, edited by Jonathan J. Webster, with a chapter on Halliday in relation to language comparison and typology (to appear).

11

Woolf's lecture/novel/essay
A Room of One's Own

Carol Taylor Torsello
University of Padua

11.1 Introduction

Woolf's *A Room of One's Own* (hereafter *A Room*) developed from notes for lectures on 'women and fiction' for the students of two women's colleges. She refers to herself as 'a lecturer', makes repeated reference to her audience, and uses many clear signs of oral discourse. But she says 'I propose, making use of all the liberties and licences of a novelist, to tell you the story of the two days that preceded my coming here,' (6)[1] and she tells that story as the story of her thoughts, using the grammar of projection in a way typical of narrative (Taylor Torsello 2007). Furthermore, she introduces, developing their stories in time and space, several fictional characters. Even more strikingly, she fictionalises the speaker while at the same time making us see her as Woolf herself (see, e.g., Rosenberg 1995:71). But she also (along with many critics)[2] calls this text an essay. The discourse of the text, however, more than being dialogic (writer and her readers), as are the novel and the essay, is triologic (writer, her audience of female students, the readers) (Marcus 1987: 157). So how can we classify this text in terms of genre?[3]

The analysis begins in Section 11.2 with a careful reading of *A Room* to extract all the explicit textual indications of its genre. These are seen to point in different directions, thus confirming the pertinence of our question about the genre.

The analysis in Section 11.3 focuses on generic structure. Seeing how a text is built up by functional phases or elements is an important way of assigning it to one genre or another, since texts of the same genre should have in common a basic generic structure (Hasan 1989:63–67). The structure of *A Room* is analysed and compared with structures proposed for an essay (Martin 1985:86), an academic lecture (Young 1990), and a novel (or other story) (Labov and Waletsky 1967; Eggins 2004).

As a final step in this attempt at classification, in Section 11.4 a contextual configuration (CC) (Hasan 1978:230–244, 1979:381–388 and 1989:55–56) is posited for *A Room*. The CC of a text is the composite set of extralinguistic values for the corresponding Context of Situation, made up of those for each of its three parts, field, tenor, and mode. Its delineation should, therefore, help us to understand the genre of the text by showing us the type of situation it functions in and the role it plays there. CC's are also posited for each of the three genres – lecture, novel and essay – and the CC of our text is compared to each of these. The analyses in this Section involve adapting Hasan's model for CC, applied by her to practical transactions, for use with other types of texts.

In Section 11.5, I reflect on the generic indeterminacy that emerges from the three analyses. Relating it to Woolf's authorial strategies, I conclude that the metaphor of hybridity is appropriate, since it seems clear that Woolf purposely mixes the three genres with the intention of providing her work of verbal art with desired characteristics inherent some to one and some to another of these three genres. As with hybrid breeding, the result is innovation. Woolf's generic innovation is discussed in relation to the connection between text and context and to the notion of genre, with particular reference to Systemic Functional Linguistic (SFL) theory.

11.2   Textual indications of three genres in *A Room*

In this Section I point out what I find in the text that indicates that it is one genre or the other: in 11.2.1 a lecture, in 11.2.2 a novel, and in 11.2.3 an essay.

11.2.1 Textual indications of the academic lecture

The book begins interactionally, with the speaker addressing an audience who has asked her to *speak*: 'But [...] we asked you to speak [...]' (5).[4] She then refers to herself as a 'lecturer' and to the 'notebooks' of her audience: 'I should never be able to fulfil [...] the first duty of a lecturer – to hand you [...] a nugget of pure truth to wrap up between the pages of your notebooks [...]' (5). She refers to the 'presence' of her audience: 'I am going to develop in your presence [...]' (6). She uses the spatial deictics 'come' and 'here' with reference to the place shared with the audience: 'the two days that preceded my coming here.' (6). She refers to the 'audience' and the 'speaker': '[...] give one's audience the chance of drawing their own conclusions as they observe [...] the speaker.' (6). She presupposes familiarity with the university chapel: 'As you know, its high domes and pinnacles can be seen [...]' (11).

The indications of the lecture genre reported so far all appear in the first seven pages of the text. Only very few more will then be found near the middle of the book. See, for example, the following direct addresses to the audiences: 'it is one [...] that you will investigate when you have five hundred a year of your own' (38); 'My aunt, Mary Beton, I must tell you, died [...]' (38); and '[...], for you know [...], for you may have tried.' (39). She also refers to the lecture as 'the problem you have laid on my shoulders' (41) . She addresses directly an audience of female college students with an emphatic 'I can assure you' and reference to 'your grandmothers and great-grandmothers', then speaks to them as 'you, who have got yourselves to college' (57) and uses a deictic for shared time saying '[...] for me to say to you tonight [...]' (66). To this audience she also says: 'I do not want, and I am sure that you do not want me, to broach that very dismal subject [...]' (78).

The remaining indications of the lecture genre come near the end of the text. She refers to the 'promise to give you the course of my thoughts' and to her audience as 'you who have not yet come of age.' (102). The next five pages contain various references on the part of the speaker to the interlocutors' possible criticisms and objections, which give the text the feel of oral interaction. This part of the text contains several instances of *you* which are clearly referred to women and contain recommendations to the audience, such as 'So long as you write what you wish to write, that is all that matters; [...]' (105). On the same page these women are further specified as students through a reference to one of their professors: 'Let me then quote to you the words of your own Professor of Literature, [...]' (105). Explicit deictic reference is made to the time and place of the lecture: 'Otherwise you would not be here tonight, [...]' (106). The speaker also refers to her (lecture?) 'notes' (108) and classifies her text as a 'speech' and 'a paper read by a woman to women' (109). She also points at 'that cupboard there' (109), indicating that the speaker and the audience share the same material context, which is true of a lecture but not of a novel or an essay. Here there are also references to the sound of her discourse: 'make it sound exalted', and 'adopt a sterner tone' (109). She addresses the audience of 'young women' announcing that 'the peroration is beginning'[5] (110). She says that she will put her suggestions 'in the form of fiction' (111), thus specifying that her text is something other than fiction, and refers to the text as 'this paper' (111).[6] Further deictics pointing to the spatial and temporal context of the lecture follow: 'She lives in you and in me, and in many other women who are not here tonight [...]' (111).

We have seen, then, that the majority of the textual indications of an academic lecture, and the most explicit ones, characterise the beginning and the end of this text, although there are some found in the middle as well.

11.2.2 Textual indications of the novel

Now we will consider the textual elements that point to the novel, or at any rate some type of written work of narrative fiction, as the genre. In the first of these there is reference to 'fiction', 'novelist', and 'story', the reality of places and events is denied, and even the identity of the speaker is fictionalised:

> Fiction here is likely to contain more truth than fact. Therefore I propose, making use of all the liberties and licences of a novelist, to tell you the story of the two days that preceded my coming here – [...]. I need not say that what I am about to describe has no existence; Oxbridge is an invention; so is Fernham; 'I' is only a convenient term for somebody who has no real being. Lies will flow from my lips, [...] (6)

The fictionalised speaker is given three possible names, and a novel-like temporal and spatial setting is specified:

> Here then was I (call me Mary Beton, Mary Seton, Mary Carmichael or by any name you please – it is not a matter of any importance) sitting on the banks of the river a week or two ago in fine October weather, lost in thought. (6–7)

At the beginning of the passage about the luncheon, the speaker mentions 'the novelist's convention' of not writing about foods that are eaten, only to say that she will 'take the liberty to defy that convention' (12).

The long central passage between the bottom of page 8, where the first instance of the projecting clause 'I thought' is found, and page 103, where 'I thought' appears for the last time, reads very much like a novel from one point of view, that is, in the way PROJECTION is used. Here I will provide just one passage to exemplify this:

> Walk through the Admiralty Arch (I had reached that monument), or
> any other avenue given up to trophies and cannon, and reflect upon
> the kind of glory celebrated there. Or watch in the spring sunshine
> the stockbroker and the great barrister going indoors to make money
> and more money and more money when it is a fact that five hundred
> pounds a year will keep one alive in the sunshine. These are unpleasant
> instincts to harbour, I reflected. They are bred of the conditions of life;
> of the lack of civilization, I thought, looking at the statue of the Duke
> of Cambridge, and in particular at the feathers in his cocked hat, with
> a fixity that they have scarcely ever received before. (40)

This is a passage of narration of the speaker's thoughts (which pre-
dominate) and actions. Most of it is projected mentally by the two projecting clauses 'I reflected' and 'I thought' in what I call free direct report
(direct report without the inverted commas) (Taylor Torsello 2007:118).
'I reflected' includes in its scope of projection not only the projected idea
that precedes it in the same sentence, but also the whole of the two preceding sentences. 'I thought' follows in the same sentence the idea it projects,
and is expanded by an imperfective enhancement of contemporary time
(from 'looking' to the end of the sentence), which brings the reader back
from the metaphenomenal world of thoughts to the phenomenal world in
which the speaker is moving and acting, but without making explicit the
conjunction (*while*) or the subject (*I*) or information contained in the finite
(*was*). The pattern is typical of novels: the projecting clause is in the middle
or at the end of the projected clause so as to background the narrator's role
and foreground what is said or thought, and it is followed by an enhancement which is most often imperfective, so as to add information about the
speaker and his or her actions, perceptions, or attitudes while keeping the
impression of narrator intrusion to a minimum (Chatman 1978:219). To
indicate how very frequent thought projections are in *A Room*, let me just
say that the projecting clause *I thought* occurs 57 times, and if we add to
these other mental projecting forms like *I reflected, I wondered,* etc. and
thought sequencing forms like *I continued,* we get a total of 85 mental projecting clauses, many of which project beyond sentence boundaries. This
use of PROJECTION contributes strongly to giving much of the work (and
precisely from the bottom of page 8 to page 103) the feel of a novel.

The 'speaker' of our text is clearly writing rather than speaking, and even
plays with her role as writer by referring metatextually, in two places in the
text, to the punctuation she uses (three dots and five dots).

> Why, if it was an illusion, not praise the catastrophe, whatever it was,
> that destroyed illusion and put truth in its place? For truth ... those

dots mark the spot where, in search of truth, I missed the turning up
to Fernham. (17).

And again,

> One went to the counter; one took a slip of paper; one opened a vol-
> ume of the catalogue, and ..... the five dots here indicate five separate
> minutes of stupefaction, wonder, and bewilderment. (28).

Woolf, in the following passage, besides referring to her work as 'fiction',
plays with the narrative convention of temporal setting:

> As I have said already that it was an October day, I dare not forfeit your
> respect and imperil the fair name of fiction by changing the season [...]
> Therefore it was still autumn [...] (17–18).

Despite this premise, the scene in the gardens of Fernham – 'perhaps the
words of Christina Rossetti were partly responsible for the folly of fancy' –
is described as though it were spring (see page 18).

She is also tongue-in-cheek about spatial setting: 'The scene, if I may
ask you to follow me, was now changed. The leaves were still falling, but in
London now, not Oxbridge; [...] (27).

Even more strikingly, Woolf plays with the convention of the narrator. It is true that at the beginning of the book she had left it up to her
readers to decide what name to give the speaker (see page 6). But then,
throughout the book the first person speaker – who seems to stay the same
as no shift is noticeable – makes us feel that she is Woolf herself, as she
expresses ideas which we know to be hers. Nonetheless, near the end of
the book, she surprises and baffles us by saying 'Here, then, Mary Beton
ceases to speak.' (103). If we look back at the three names suggested for
the speaking 'I' – Mary Beton, Mary Seton and Mary Carmichael – in the
light of what we learn from the text about these three fictional characters,
it becomes clear that of the three the one who absolutely cannot be the
speaker is Mary Beton, because this is the aunt from whom the speaker
is said to have inherited upon her death. But the system of grammatical
person used within the text also excludes the other two. Mary Seton is the
science-teacher friend at Fernham with whom the speaker dines and con-
verses, and the paragraph in which Mary Seton's part of the conversation
is expressed (see pages 21–22) is completely within the scope of third person projecting clauses: 'said Mary Seton', 'she told me', 'she said', and again
'she said'. Mary Carmichael is a contemporary writer the speaker comes to
know through her books in the British Museum and to whom she imagines

herself as speaking as she reads her works. None of these three is ever the 'I' of the text.[7]

Finally, *A Room* is divided into chapters, as novels usually are, and as lectures are not. Essays can be divided into chapters, but typically they are rather short and their divisions are more often, I believe, simply paragraphs, or sections or parts.

11.2.3 Textual indications of the essay

The most important textual indication that *A Room* is an essay is Woolf's note to the title of the work:

> This essay is based upon two papers read to the Arts Society at Newnham and the Odtaa at Girton in October 1928. The papers were too long to be read in full, and have since been altered and expanded. (5)

Another indication is the use of footnotes, as lectures certainly do not have footnotes, and novels normally do not either, at least not as an integral part of their original version supplied by the writer, whereas essays quite often do.

Other than these, it is hard to point out specific textual indications that *A Room* is an essay. Yet there are passages – even whole paragraphs of the text – which read like a 'traditional' essay, that is to say, the writer seems to present directly, in an expository mode, facts and her opinions about reality directly as statements with supporting argumentation, and not as projected thoughts! The paragraph which follows is an example:

> And one gathers from this enormous modern literature of confession and self-analysis that to write a work of genius is almost always a feat of prodigious difficulty. Everything is against the likelihood that it will come from the writer's mind whole and entire. Generally material circumstances are against it. Dogs will bark; people will interrupt; money must be made; health will break down. Further, accentuating all these difficulties and making them harder to bear is the world's notorious indifference. It does not ask people to write poems and novels and histories; it does not need them. It does not care whether Flaubert finds the right word or whether Carlyle scrupulously verifies this or that fact. Naturally, it will not pay for what it does not want. And so the writer, Keats, Flaubert, Carlyle, suffers, especially in the creative years of youth, every form of distraction and discouragement. A curse, a cry of agony, rises from those books of analysis and confession. 'Mighty poets in their misery dead' – that is the burden of their song.

> If anything comes through in spite of all this, it is a miracle, and prob-
> ably no book is born entire and uncrippled as it was conceived. (53).

But the beginning of the paragraph that follows this one immediately cancels our impression of a traditional essay style by establishing that the whole paragraph was actually projected thought! It begins: 'But for women, I thought, looking at the empty shelves, these difficulties were infinitely more formidable.' (53–54).

The speaker of the text proposes the types of questions that are posed in essays (or lectures):

> Why did men drink wine and women water? Why was one sex so prosperous and the other so poor? What effect has poverty on fiction? What conditions are necessary for the creation of works of art? (27).

But most often these questions are first person mental projections: 'What were the conditions in which women lived, I asked myself; [...]' (43); 'But what is the state of mind that is most propitious to the act of creation? I asked.' (52). And even the list of questions above (from page 27) is a part of the narrative, as it is preceded by 'For that visit to Oxbridge and the luncheon and the dinner had started a swarm of questions', and it is followed by 'But one needed answers, not questions.'

11.2.4 Conclusions we can draw from the textual indications of genre

As we have seen, *A Room* provides textual indications of each of the three genres – lecture, novel and essay – and thus does not provide us with the elements for a clear assignment of it to any one of these. In my use of the term *genre*, I would expect to be able to say that a text, taken as a whole, is an instance of some genre,[8] and *A Room* is definitely a text, so I will continue my search for an answer to the question about its genre.

11.3 Generic structure

We now turn to another type of analysis from which we can expect to find evidence for the genre of our text: the analysis of its generic structure. For this analysis I re-read *A Room* with an eye to distinguishing its basic structural elements on the basis of the functions carried out in them, as opposed, for example, to settings or to topics. In 11.3.1, I say what I see to be the most obvious division of the text into such structural elements. In 11.3.2, this structure proposed for *A Room* is compared to that of an essay; in 11.3.3, it is compared to one proposed for the academic lecture; and, in 11.3.4, the comparison is with that of a novel (or other story).

11.3.1 Looking at the structure of *A Room*

It seems to me that, in terms of the functions carried out, *A Room* can be divided into three parts:

I   Introduction
II   Story of the 2 days' preparation for the lecture
III Conclusion

The Introduction goes from the beginning of the text on page 5 to the next-to-last line of page 6. The Story of the two days' preparation for the lecture goes from the last line of page 6 ('Here then was I [...]') to the end of the first paragraph on page 103. The Conclusion begins with 'Here, then, Mary Beton ceases to speak.' (103). It ends on page 112, with the last line of the text. The three parts are very unevenly divided, and there is no correspondence with the divisions into the text's six chapters, since the first part is only the first two pages of Chapter 1 and the third is only the last half of Chapter 6. In the Introduction, the speaker announces her subject, purpose, and method, as well as gaining the favour of her audience/readership. The rhetorical mode employed is exposition, including argumentation. In the Story of the two days' preparation for the lecture, the speaker tells the story of her actions and thoughts, and about how her opinion on her subject developed, over a two-day period. The rhetorical mode used for the story is narration, but within the narrative, ideas and opinions are communicated using the rhetorical mode of exposition, with argumentation to show the dynamics of their development. In the Conclusion the speaker summarises, evaluates what she has done in her text, and indicates a course of action. The rhetorical mode is exposition including argumentation.

11.3.2 Comparison of *A Room*'s structure to that of the essay

I am beginning this series of structural comparisons with the essay rather than the lecture as above because the proposed structure for the essay which I have chosen is Martin's (1985:86), which consists in precisely three elements as follows:

I   Introduction – stating the thesis advanced
II Body – consisting of the series of arguments supporting the thesis
III Conclusion – restating the thesis and summing up the arguments

Looking at the part of *A Room* which I have labelled 'Introduction', it is not difficult to see as the 'thesis' of this work the 'one minor point' upon which the speaker says she can offer an opinion: '[...] a woman must have money and a room of her own if she is to write fiction [...]'(6). To make amends for what might be seen as the inadequacy or insufficiency of this thesis, she offers to show how she arrived at this opinion. And this leads us into the part of *A Room* which I have labelled 'Story of the two days' preparation for the lecture'. If we are to consider this central part the Body in Martin's essay structure, then we should be able to interpret it as a series of arguments in support of the thesis. There is, indeed, something very atypical about a Body of an essay which is labelled 'Story'. However, I believe we can easily interpret as arguments supporting the thesis the expository texts projected as the speaker's thoughts. And even the stories told can be seen as arguments, in the form of examples confirming the thesis and expanding on it. This is true both of the fictional ones about Judith Shakespeare, Mary Seton's mother, and Mary Carmichael and the stories of real writers – Lady Winchilsea, Margaret of Newcastle, Dorothy Osborne, Aphra Behn, Jane Austen, Charlotte Brontë, Emily Brontë, George Eliot. The part of *A Room* which I have labelled 'Conclusion', to correspond to Martin's essay Conclusion, should have a restatement of the thesis, and indeed it does: 'She [Mary Beton] has told you how she reached the conclusion [...] that it is necessary to have five hundred a year and a room with a lock on the door if you are to write fiction or poetry.' (103). This is also the beginning of the summary of what (supposedly!) Mary Beton has told the readers and what she has done – 'trying to lay bare the thoughts' of the two days, 'asking you to follow her' in her movements and activities at Oxbridge and the British Museum. But Woolf's own summing up is, I believe, the one that comes in her own voice, within her responses to the 'criticisms' and questions she imagines. It is here that she sums up and clarifies, not what has been said or done (by Mary Beton, she says!), but the conclusions of her own arguments:[9] '[...] It is far more important at the moment to know how much money women had and how many rooms than to theorise about their capacities [...]' (104); 'Intellectual freedom depends upon material things. Poetry depends upon intellectual freedom. And women have always been poor [...]' (106); '[...] When I ask you to write more books I am urging you to do what will be for your good and for the good of the world at large' (108); '[...]When I ask you to earn money and have a room of your own, I am asking you to live in the presence of reality, an invigorating life [...]' (108–109); 'Think of things in themselves.' (109). And the final 'suggestion' (111) – with a function which definitely goes beyond simply summarising – is to work to bring into reality the existence of a female genius on a par with Shakespeare.

11.3.3 Comparison of *A Room*'s structure to that of an academic lecture

We have seen that *A Room*'s structure matches up rather well with that of an essay so long as we accept to consider the long central part as the Body of the essay where the arguments are presented. I believe it is nonetheless useful to go on and carry out the comparison with the other two genres we are considering – lecture and novel.

The structure I am using for the academic lecture is based on Young (1990)[10] and is as follows:

I   Discourse Structuring – alerts students about content to come
II   Contents – concepts and examples
III Conclusion – summary of contents, emphasis on underlying principles, connection to previous lessons
IV   Evaluation (optional) – tells students how to evaluate the material that has been presented, what value to place on various parts of the content
V   Interaction (optional) – dialogue between lecturer and students. Questions posed by lecturer are actually meant to be answered. Students also pose questions and the lecturer answers them.

Here too the obligatory elements are three, with two optional ones also possible. To begin with, I would see no problem in calling the part I have called 'Introduction' a Discourse Structuring: it certainly carries out the function of alerting to the content to come.

> All I could do was to offer you an opinion upon one minor point – a woman must have money and a room of her own if she is to write fiction [...] I am going to do what I can to show you how I arrived at this opinion about the room and the money. I am going to develop in your presence as fully and freely as I can the train of thought which led

me to think this. Perhaps if I lay bare the ideas, the prejudices, that lie behind this statement you will find that they have some bearing upon women and some upon fiction. (5–6).

What I have called 'Story of the two days' preparation for the lecture' can also be seen as the 'Content'. It is, indeed, here that the content is found. The concepts are expressed in the opinions developed in the projected thoughts and the exemplifications are in the stories. The 'Conclusion' I have posited for *A Room* might also be seen to carry out at least most of the functions of Young's 'Conclusion' in the lecture: it sums up the content emphasising the underlying principles (but does not connect to previous lessons).

> She has told you how she reached the conclusion – the prosaic conclu-
> sion – that it is necessary to have five hundred a year and a room with
> a lock on the door if you are to write fiction or poetry. (103).

Interestingly, the two optional elements also seem to occur in some form. Within what I have labelled as *A Room*'s 'Conclusion', there is an Evaluation, but Woolf attributes it to the students!

> While she has been doing all these things, you no doubt have been
> observing her failings and foibles and deciding what effect they had on
> her opinions. You have been contradicting her and making whatever
> additions and deductions seem good to you. (103–104).

Woolf also simulates an Interaction phase. She attributes two criticisms to her audience and produces responses which are careful, elaborate, and emphatic. This element is found in the passage that begins 'And I will end now in my own person [...]' (104), and ends with '[...] I am asking you to live in the presence of reality, an invigorating life, it would appear, whether one can impart it or not.' (109).

11.3.4 Comparison of *A Room*'s structure to that of a novel

We have seen that looking strictly at the functions carried out in its parts, we can associate the structure of *A Room* with that of an essay, but also to some extent with that of a lecture. The structure I will use for the comparison with the novel is based on proposals for narratives or stories (Labov and Waletsky 1967; Eggins 2004:70–74, 348–349, 369–370):

I   Abstract (optional) – a signal indicating the type of story to be told and possibly its theme(s). Labov and Waletsky do not include this element in their framework.

II   Orientation – preliminary information about participants, spatial and temporal setting, initial situation and actions.

III Complication – a problem culminating in a crisis. Of the Complication, Labov and Waletsky (1967: 32–33) say, 'The main body of narrative clauses usually comprises a series of events which may be termed the complication or complicating action.' They also say 'The complication is regularly terminated by a result [...].'

IV   Evaluation – the events, or the predicaments of the characters, are evaluated by the narrator or by a character.

V   Resolution – the crisis is resolved and equilibrium is restored.

VI   Coda (optional) – an overall statement is made about the text. Labov and Waletsky (1967:39) say, 'The Coda is a functional device for returning the verbal perspective to the present moment.'

Eggins gives the order of the elements as listed,[11] and indicates that the sequence Complication – Evaluation – Resolution can be reiterated. Labov and Waletsky (1967: 39) say, 'If the evaluation is the last element, then the resolution section coincides with the evaluation.'

A Room includes many short narrative sequences to which this structure can be applied: the Beadle episode, the exclusion from the Oxbridge Library, the story of Mary Seton's mother, the story of Shakespeare's sister, and many more, but of course the limits of this study make it impossible to analyse all of them. Instead, and more to the point here, I would like to see if it is possible to see a narrative structure like the one outlined above as applying to the work as a whole. So let's try it.

Abstract: 'But in order to make some amends I am going to do what I can to show you how I arrived at this opinion about the room and the money. I am going to develop in your presence as fully and freely as I can the train of thought which led me to think this.' (6). The abstract might be seen to continue to the end of the paragraph.

Orientation: (who, where, when) 'Here then was I (call me Mary Beton, Mary Seton, Mary Carmichael or by any name you please – it is not a matter of any importance) sitting on the banks of a river a week or two ago in fine October weather, lost in thought'(6–7). (what) 'That collar I have spoken of, women and fiction, the need of coming to some conclusion on a subject that raises all sorts of prejudices and passions, bowed my head to the ground' (7).

Complication: The complicating actions along the way to the fulfilment of the speaker's task are the ones through which she develops for her readers a picture of the less than equal opportunities women have, and how these are related to her physical and psychological conditions. The difference in men's and women's educations emerges from the events narrated in Chapter 1. The scarce mention of women in histories and the preponderance of men writers emerges from the research in the British Museum, as does the realisation that men writing about women are angry, and that when women do finally write, they mainly write fiction, and only in very few cases do so well, with 'integrity' (see Chapters 2 to 4). Confirmation that England is definitely under the rule of patriarchy comes from reading the newspaper over lunch, and proof of the importance of money is provided by the ease with which the bill can be paid (Chapter 2). Recognition that today women write almost as much as men and not just novels comes from research done in the section devoted to contemporary writers, but that it is nonetheless almost impossible to find exceptional women writers also becomes evident (Chapter 5).

Evaluation and Resolution: I believe that Woolf gives the narrative we find in *A Room* two alternative (or complementary) Evaluation/Resolution elements. In both cases, Evaluation and Resolution coincide, as foreseen by Labov and Waletsky (see above). One is the episode in Chapter 5 where the speaker discovers and reads Mary Carmichael's *Life's Adventure*. She realises that she actually writes 'Chloe liked Olivia...' (81), presenting women not as men see them but as they are, and says 'she wrote as a woman, but as a woman who has forgotten that she is a woman [...]' (92). The whole episode is a Resolution, since it finally gives the speaker hope for women as writers:

> Give her another hundred years, I concluded, [...] give her a room of her own and five hundred a year, let her speak her mind and leave out half that she now puts in, and she will write a better book one of these days. She will be a poet, I said, [...] in another hundred years' time. (93)

Throughout, it is also Evaluation, some of which is spoken directly by the speaker to Mary Carmichael. The other Evaluation/Resolution element is found in Chapter 6, and is made up of the episode of the man and woman coming from different directions, meeting, getting into a taxi and going off together. The Evaluation is that thinking of the sexes as distinct (as she has done up to this point – and in this sense this second Evaluation/Resolution is an alternative one – see Marcus 1987: 166–167) interferes with the unity of the mind (95), and that 'it is natural for the sexes to cooperate'. But it also continues with the idea that 'in each of us two powers preside, one male, one female [...]' (97). That a Resolution has been reached seems clear from the fact that at the end of the episode the speaker mentions 'crossing over to the writing-table and taking up the page headed Women and Fiction [to write the first sentence of her lecture, which is] that it is fatal for anyone who writes to think of their sex' (102). This opinion emerges directly from the episode of Mary Carmichael, who writes as a woman who has forgotten she is a woman. But less directly it emerges from the taxi episode as well (making this second Evaluation/Resolution element complementary to the first): men and women will be able to function better generally in life if they bring what they have into what they do as best they can, without their sexuality being an issue.

Coda: Perhaps we might consider as a Coda to this work seen as a narrative the final part presented as spoken in the author's own name (103–312). The present perfect is used for recapitulating and discussing what has come before – e.g. 'She has told you how she reached the conclusion [...] (103), while present and future indicative and the imperative are used for addressing the audience in relation to the content. The portion of this 'Coda' which most significantly wraps up the narrative function of *A Room* is the return to the story of Shakespeare's sister, who 'lives in you and me, and in many other women who are not here tonight [...]' (111), and who 'would come if we worked for her [...]' (112).

11.4 Contextual Configuration (CC)

The analyses in this Section are based on Hasan's (1978:230–244, 1979:381–388 and 1989:55–56) model for analysing the CC of a text. I have, however, added subject matter as an element of field, as do Halliday and Matthiessen (1999:320), and rhetorical mode as an element of mode, as do Halliday (1989:12) and Halliday and Matthiessen (1999:321). In this Section I outline what I see as the CC corresponding to Woolf's *A Room*[12] (11.4.1), then I present in the form of a table what I postulate as the CC's of a (prototypical) lecture, novel and essay and examine the match between each of these and the CC postulated for *A Room* (11.4.2).

11.4.1 CC of *A Room*

What follows is my outline of the CC corresponding to Woolf's *A Room*.

FIELD OF DISCOURSE

Kind of activity: Literary and socio-political expression for publication.

Goals: Transmission of knowledge, presentation of thesis and arguments for it to convince her audience and influence their behaviour; finding ways of combining the 'creative' and the 'critical' forces in her writing.

Subject matter: Why women do not have a more important role in literature and how they might improve their role in the future. The invitation to give lectures on women and fiction and the two days of events, thoughts and research that precede the lectures.

TENOR OF DISCOURSE

Agent roles: Writer (an eminent novelist and essay writer) to general public, with particular reference to women, and at points to the young college women who invited her to lecture. The identity of the 'I' is purposely made problematic.

Dyadic relation: Hierarchical, but Woolf uses means to downgrade her own authority.

Social distance: Almost maximal, so somewhat formal, but this does not keep the author from being playful in her treatment of her discourse, and particularly the conventions involved.

MODE OF DISCOURSE

Language role: Constitutive.

Process sharing: Passive.

Channel: Graphic. Book form (paper, now also digital).

Medium: Written, with occasional use of oral forms.

Rhetorical mode: Expositive (including information and argument) and narrative. Woolf in some points creates the impression of conversation as interaction between herself and her audience/readership. Near the end she adopts a persuasive rhetorical mode as she tells young women why they need money and why they should write. We can also speak of an aesthetic rhetorical mode, as there is obviously great attention paid to form and creativity.

11.4.2 CC's of academic lecture, novel, and essay and comparison with that of *A Room*

In Table 11.1, I propose outlines for the CC's of the academic lecture, the novel, and the essay which we can compare with the one given above for *A Room*.

Table 11.1: Contextual configurations of three genres

	Academic lecture	**Novel**	**Essay**
F I E L D	*Kind of activity*: Teaching and learning. Institutional, educational, typical of university classrooms with fixed calendar for time and place of occurrence and lecturer and audience. *Goals*: Transmission of knowledge regarding a particular subject matter, presentation of arguments and reasoning regarding that subject. *Subject matter*: A serious topic set beforehand.	*Kind of activity*: Creative, literary expression for publication. *Goals*: To move the readers emotionally through the created characters and events. *Subject matter*: There is usually a theme – a higher-order subject matter – that the novelist wants to develop, but this is only done indirectly through the story told. The story gives us the lower order field: the time, place, participants and events in the story are all part of the created (lower order) subject matter.	*Kind of activity*: Varied; it can be literary, journalistic (including cultural journalism), academic or scholastic (assignments). *Goals*: To treat the subject matter in a way that will make the general public consider it, possibly in a new light, coming to understand and possibly share the writer's views on it, while being influenced and/or entertained by the writer's treatment of it. *Subject matter*: The subject matter is open and can regard the public or private sphere, but it is based on reality rather than fantasy.
T E N O R	*Agent roles*: Lecturer and students. *Dyadic relation*: Hierarchical. *Social distance*: Near maximal, so style of communication is usually rather formal.	*Agent roles*: Literary fiction writer to readership. *Dyadic relation*: Hierarchical. *Social distance*: Usually maximal.	*Agent roles*: Writer (one who has given particular attention to the subject, and has some authority to write on it, although not necessarily an expert) to readers (general public). *Dyadic relation*: Hierarchical. *Social distance*: Maximal if formal essay, less if informal.

	Academic lecture	**Novel**	**Essay**
M O D E	*Language role*: Mainly constitutive (but may become ancillary momentarily when graphs are presented).	*Language role*: Constitutive.	*Language role*: Constitutive.
	Process sharing: Usually mainly passive, minimally active.	*Process sharing*: Passive. *Channel*: Graphic; book (paper, now also digital).	*Process sharing*: Passive. *Channel*: Graphic; in magazine, newspaper or book, or on the Web, or distributed on its own as a pamphlet, brochure or book, but typically short.
	Channel: Phonic, graphic support possible; face to face oral communication.	*Medium*: Written (with some features of oral discourse in some points, as part of character representation).	
	Medium: Possibly in part written to be spoken.	*Rhetorical mode*: Narrative; also aesthetic, as originality and creativity of language and form are important.	*Medium*: Written. *Rhetorical mode*: Mainly expositive (including argument), but may contain narration (stories, anecdotes, striking illustrations, jokes) to augment the appeal, and elements of persuasion.
	Rhetorical mode: Didactic, expositive (including definition, information, argument), some narrative possible to serve the purposes of the exposition, some conversation.		

I begin by matching *A Room* up with an academic lecture. Due to space limits the focus, for this and the other two comparisons, will be mainly on differences and what is problematic in the match. As far as the field is concerned, the major difference is in the kind of activity: *A Room* is literary and socio-political expression for publication and the time and place are not binding. The lecture, on the other hand, is an activity of teaching and learning. It is institutional and educational, typical of university classrooms, and has a fixed calendar of time and place of occurrence, and the lecturer and (to varying extents) the audience are also fixed ahead of time. As far as tenor is concerned, our attention goes to the agent roles, since in *A Room* these are the writer and readership but also the lecturer and students, whereas for the lecture the roles are simply lecturer and students. Particularly disruptive for the match is the fact that the identity of the 'I' is purposely made problematic, whereas the speaker of the lecture is fixed even from the time of scheduling of the lecture and in case of change is amply announced, so it is unproblematic. But the parameter where there is least fit is mode, since the channel of *A Room* is graphic, while that of a lecture is basically phonic. *A Room* has the form of a book while a lecture has the form of an oral monologue or interaction. The rhetorical mode is also different in that *A Room* has more narrative than we would expect in a lecture. The role of the aesthetic mode is also more prominent than is expected for a lecture.

Now let's look at the match between the CC of *A Room* and that of the novel. Beginning with the field, the kind of activity is literary, and it is for publication, as is the novel, but *A Room* is also socio-political expression, and it is not purely creative as it is also very strongly critical and political. The goals do not match completely either, as *A Room*'s goal is not so much to affect the emotions of the readers as their intellects, and through these their actions. Woolf wants to find ways of combining the 'creative' and the 'critical' forces in her writing,[13] so for her it is very important to convincingly present her subject matter while doing this in a creative manner. Focusing on subject matter, we can say that *A Room* has an overall topic – something like 'why women don't have a more important role in literature and how they might improve their role in the future' – which we might assimilate to the higher-order subject matter in a novel. However, in *A Room* it is much more directly stated than one would expect it to be in a novel. In *A Room*, reality seems more fundamental than fantasy, whereas in the novel the opposite holds. It is true that Woolf plays with multiple identities of the speaker, treating her as a created character, but our impression throughout is that she herself is the 'I' of the text and the opinions expressed are actually hers. For tenor, too, the match is imperfect. In *A Room* the sender of the message is not acting primarily as a literary fiction writer, but as a social and literary critic and analyst, even a polemicist. Furthermore, she addresses not only her readers but also the students who invited her to give a lecture. As regards mode, the most problematic sub-parameter as far as the match between *A Room* and the novel is concerned is rhetorical mode. Although *A Room* contains a lot of narrative, it would be unfair to say that the rhetorical mode is narrative since so much of the text is expository. Yet the narrative frame allows us to follow the process through which the opinion expressed is developed.

Finally, let's see how the CC of *A Room* matches up to that of an essay. When we concentrate on field, the match seems to work quite well as far as all three sub-parameters are concerned. The parameter of tenor also gives us a fair match, although, looking at agent roles, we should note the specificity of the writer as an eminent novelist and essayist, and the fact that, although she addresses the general public, she does at points speak to women, and to the college women who invited her to lecture. Mode also gives us a fairly good match, but with some specificities. The match works very well as far as language role, process sharing, and medium are concerned. The particular type of graphic channel – a book[14] – is one of the possibilities for an essay, although *A Room* is longer than an essay normally is. The parameter of rhetorical mode gives us a combination of exposition and narration, but in *A Room* the narration does not just have the function of providing striking illustrations or humorous insertions to augment the appeal as often happens in traditional essays (Abrams 1999:82–3), but instead becomes the framework within which almost all the exposition is presented. Indeed, the main specificity of *A Room* is the way in which the narrative and the expository modes are combined. The rhetorical mode of exposition is what we find within the narrated thoughts. If we leave out the projecting clauses and skip the contextual asides and elaborations, what we get in these long passages is exposition. *A Room* also has its persuasive passages, as when the speaker encourages women to write. But what can we say about the fact that Woolf in this text includes so many textual indications that it should be classified as three different genres (as we have seen in Section 11.2 above), and about the fact that she seems to give it the structural elements of all three genres (as shown in Section 11.3 above)? If mode is 'how the language is used', then this ambiguity about the genre must certainly be included as part of the mode of this text. But does this fit into the framework we have been using for mode (language role, process sharing, channel, medium, rhetorical mode)? I believe it does, and that its place is under the label rhetorical mode. I am not only convinced that we need to include 'aesthetic mode' as a type of rhetorical mode, but that even artistic creativity of the type exercised by Woolf in relation to the genre of *A Room* – this artistic 'extravaganza' of generic ambiguity – can be accounted for in terms of an aesthetic rhetorical mode, typical of, but not exclusive to literary texts. But a proper investigation and argumentation about the full range of possible rhetorical modes, and if and to what extent texts of verbal art can be accounted for in terms of context of situation (see Taylor Torsello 1994), would take us far beyond the space limits of this article.

11.5 Conclusions

Although we find abundant textual indications in *A Room* that we are dealing with a lecture, and other strong indications that it is a novel, and although we are able to trace the generic structures of lecture and novel as well as that of essay in the work, the analysis of the contextual configuration indicates that the text functions in the context as an essay – albeit a very special one. But simply classifying *A Room* as an essay without taking into account its generic complexity would be disastrously reductive. Woolf composed a text whose structure could be seen as that of three different genres, and she embroidered into it the textual indications that it was each of these. The generic multiplicity we have seen in this work is more complex than the figure-ground relationship of Martin's (1997:33–34) 'contextual metaphor' where (if I have understood Martin properly) 'register variables indicative of a given context' (and genre) become the 'figure' 'to symbolise a complementary genre' (and context) – the 'ground'. As an expression of the complexity of *A Room* the metaphor 'generic hybridity' is appropriate in that Woolf is consciously mixing three genres which pre-exist in her experience, and she is doing this in order to obtain a product which is, from her point of view, a desired innovation.[15] But to try to discover more than this about Woolf's motives or about the effects on the context we must go beyond this metaphor. Genre-mixing is a part of Woolf's authorial strategy in this text. Indeed, I believe it is a key aspect of the symbolic articulation (Hasan 1988:63) of the theme of this text. Women historically have been left without the resources necessary for creativity so they have not participated in the construction of Western tradition (not just literary tradition) with its conventions and its genres. Woolf enacts the frustration of this situation in her text. The use of signs of three genres is a kind of foregrounding (Mukařovský 1964), or patterning of patterns (Hasan, 1988: 63). The aesthetic rhetorical mode operative in this text and important to the realisation of its poetic function (Jakobson 1960)[16] counts substantially on this device. For Woolf, no one single generic 'template' (Hasan 2000:43, 45 n22) among those available would do. It is not hard to imagine why if we think about the complex task she had set for herself. She was writing an important feminist polemic, and for this to have the desired social impact it would need to reach a wide audience, so the most obvious genre for this would be the essay. But the critical exposition and argument of the typical essay, with its distance between writer and readers, was not what she wanted. She wanted to give her text the link to a context and its participants and the interaction of a lecture. But she did not want to give it the exalted tones typical of the academic lecture. To get away from these characteristics she made use of the genre novel. In the economy of *A Room*, couching the exposition in a narrative frame allowed Woolf to trace the development of the opinion she was expressing, presenting it thus as a dynamic process rather than a static result. By fictionalising some of the reality she was writing about, including herself, she avoided presenting herself as an authority figure and her message as 'a nugget of pure truth' (5). The novel was a genre open to women; novels could be written even in a common sitting room (See *A Room* 66–67). Fiction, not being committed to reality, did not require authority, as did the academic lecture and the essay. Throughout the work Woolf diminishes her own authority, she lessens the power of her ideas by projecting them as her thoughts, she deconstructs her own identity as speaking voice, and creates a 'feminine' discourse modelled on conversation among equals, cooperation (Fishman 1992; Maltz and Borker 1992). The text, 'revolutionary' (Marcus 1981b:1) as it is, is full of signs of tentativeness and self-effacement (Taylor Torsello 2012). The indeterminacy as to genre seems to fit very well into Woolf's strategy to deconstruct the discourse models of the male dominated academic world. In *A Room* she dares suggest that even the genre most open to a woman, the novel, might not be 'rightly shaped for her use' and would require some 'knocking into shape', and that it might even become necessary to provide 'some new vehicle, not necessarily in verse, for the poetry in her.' (77–78). Her rebellion against the 'templates' available for text structuring can, I believe, be seen as a generic innovation going in the direction proposed by Conklin (1974:68–69), who suggested that women ought to recognise, legitimise and creatively develop their own speech genres in order to establish their credentials in the public domain.

By defying and deconstructing the culturally learnt templates, Woolf is reconstruing the context (Hasan 2000:43) in the terms proposed by her text. Through the particular choice she makes regarding genre in *A Room*, Woolf might be indicating that for women – who sew, care for children, cater to husbands, entertain, and write in common sitting rooms – contexts of life are more 'permeable' (Hasan 2000:44) than they are for men, and, therefore, so must be their genres. In this book Woolf innovates the literary cannon by tracing a tradition for women writers (Hawkes 1981:42). Just as importantly, she experiments with a new genre (albeit one which as yet does not have a name of its own) which seems more suitable to her purposes than those available in the male tradition.[17] At the same time, she affects the very concept of genre in her culture, making it more dynamic. She also invents a feminine style and shows that it is not just usable for personal letters and fantasy. In *A Room* Woolf contributes to making it possible for women to write forcefully and convincingly about reality without sounding like men.

Notes

1   Throughout this article, quotations from *A Room* are followed by page numbers in parentheses which refer to Woolf (2000).

2   Just to mention a few: Rosenberg (1995:71) considers Woolf's *A Room* an essay and calls it 'her longer critical treatise'; Baxter (1995:7) speaks of 'this fascinating essay', and Gubar (2005:xxxv, xlv, lx) calls it a 'treatise' and 'her most beloved essay'.

3   Throughout this article I will be using the term genre to refer to 'the socially ratified text-types in a community' (Kress and Threadgold 1988:216), but by this I do not mean that they must be institutional in nature. More specifically, I consider genre a cultural abstraction, a generalisation about how texts are organised which is made by people belonging to a given culture on the basis of their experience of situations. These abstractions or generalisations allow the members of a culture to assign texts to text types, or genres, corresponding to similar situations. Situations can be considered similar when they resemble each other in terms of what is going on, who is involved, and how the language is being used. To indicate the genre of a text we must refer to all three of these situational parameters at the same time, otherwise what we get is not genre but something else, e.g., it may be discourse type (medical, economic, etc.), which refers to 'what is going on' and more specifically to subject matter, or it may be speaker attitude (sarcastic, formal, etc.), which is an aspect of 'who is involved', or it may be medium (oral, written) or rhetorical mode (narrative, argumentative) which refer to an aspect of 'how the language is being used'. Hasan (1978:230, 241) and Halliday (1984:89) have suggested that the terms 'register' and 'genre' are basically interchangeable. I agree that they refer to much the same concept, but have noticed that they are contextualised differently: the term 'register' is used even when referring to just one contextual parameter, or even to a part of a text, as when people say that a text, or a part of a text, is written in an economic register, a formal register, or an oral register, whereas I don't see the term 'genre' as suitable in these contexts. (See Taylor Torsello 2000:49–51; see also Taylor Torsello 1997:153–156, 1998: 113–115 and Taylor Torsello and Baldry 2005:315–318).

4   See endnote 1 above.

5   The peroration is the concluding stage in a classical oration (Burton 2007). Hynes (1994) sees *A Room* as having the structure of a classical oration. However, I think we must keep in mind that Woolf introduces the notion of the peroration in order to reject it in favour of a simpler tone and message.

6   See the *Shorter Oxford English Dictionary*, Third edition, entry II, 4 under *paper*.

7   Yet some critics have taken seriously Woolf's joke on the reader concerning the narrator. Barrett (1993:xx) writes, 'In her persona as Mary Beton, the narrator/speaker/protagonist of *A Room of One's Own*, Woolf says that her aunt had left her £500 a year [...].' Fernald (1994:246) simply calls Mary Beton

'Woolf's persona'. Rosenberg (1995:72, 76) is a bit more cautious: she says, 'the speaker takes on the points of view of three characters – Mary Beton, Mary Seton, and Mary Carmichael [...]' and then, 'The essay ends with the illusion of shift in the speaking voice'. Marcus (1987:156) sees the three Mary's as 'the collective "Mary"' or all the voiceless women that Woolf the writer/lecturer provides a voice for.

8   For example, my tendency has been to classify as advertisements (although with special characteristics) those texts that mix information-giving with persuasion to buy a product, because the giving of information, and even the disguising of the text as an informative one, have as their end the promotion of a product. However, today we probably need to recognise the existence of a new hybrid genre – 'infotisement'. In fact, this word now appears as an entry in the online encyclopedia Wikipedia. Genres are not static: they change, they disappear, and new ones appear. It is of course the language users that make this happen, prompted by, and prompting, situation changes.

9   The Conclusion stage in Martin's essay structure would probably do well to have some further specification or some addition, since it is only expressed in terms of restatement of the thesis and summing up of the arguments. Compare Bhatia's (1993:165) four part structure for the academic essay: Presenting the case, Offering the argument, Reaching the Verdict, Recommending action.

10   Young actually gives different generic structures for each of the three disciplines in her corpus of academic lectures – engineering, sociology and economics. For all three disciplines I see three common elements – Discourse Structuring, Content, Conclusion – which I treat as obligatory. Evaluation and Interaction each appear as major elements in the structures of two disciplines, so I have considered them optional. The definition of the phases also differs slightly for Young's three disciplines, so I have chosen the one I see as most representative.

11   In one of her examples (Eggins 2004:251–252), however, Resolution precedes Evaluation. Furthermore, an unfortunate misprint at the bottom of page 70 makes the discussion of the structure's sequence less clear than it might have been.

12   I do this despite Hasan's (1978:244) warning that the schema she presents for the study of texts (i.e., the one for CC) 'is not suited to texts in verbal art'. I am, in fact, convinced that this text is verbal art, although it puts forth a strong political argument. My additions of subject matter to field and rhetorical mode to mode do seem fundamental to my endeavour. I do tend to agree with Hasan, however, that one could probably not derive the generic structure from the CC of a literary text.

13   'We know that Woolf was satisfied with neither the form of critical prose nor that of fictional narrative. The greatest problem for Woolf as a writer was the split she found in her own thinking; there are the 'critical' and the 'creative', [sic] which are, on the one hand, vehemently opposed, and on the other, somehow inextricably linked. [Omissis.] For Woolf, the creative and the critical are related to her sense of inner and outer worlds; for her these terms represent

opposition and difference. Her desire was to find an artistic form that would embrace both modes of thought. [Omissis.] The critical and creative could never be fully synthesized, so she developed forms that could contain the two antithetical modes of thought.' (Rosenberg 1995:69–70).

14 In her letters, Woolf wrote that *A Room* was not really 'a book' (L, IV 102, 104) and that it was 'only talks to girls' (L, IV 101) (quoted in Bisson 1994:198).

15 I agree with Hasan (2000:43–44) that the metaphor of hybridity is not appropriate for the seamless discourse shifts between one and the other of the mothering functions – care-taking and teaching – in her examples of mother-child talk, or for other similar examples of 'con/textual integration' one can find in everyday conversation.

16 I agree with Miller (2012) that both Mukařovský's foregrounding and Jakobson's grammatical parallelism fit well with Hasan's patterning of patterns, and here I not only extend these concepts beyond lexico-grammar to discourse and genre, but also include them as aspects of the aesthetic rhetorical mode.

17 Woolf takes up the experiment again in her other major political work, *Three Guineas*, published nine years after *A Room*. Also an example of generic hybridity, *Three Guineas* combines the letter with the pleading of a case in a courtroom and the essay.

References

Abrams, M.H. (1999). *A Glossary of Literary Terms, seventh edition*, Boston: Heinle and Heinle, http://www.ohio.edu/people/hartleyg/ref../abrams_mh.pdf (last accessed October 15, 2012).

Barrett, M. (1993). Introduction. In M. Barrett (Ed.), *V. Woolf, A Room of One's Own and Three Guineas*, ix–liii. London: Penguin Books.

Baxter, J. (1995). Cambridge literature. In J. Smith (Ed.), *V. Woolf, A Room of One's Own 7*. Cambridge: Cambridge University Press.

Bhatia, V.K. (1993). *Analysing Genre: Language Use in Professional Settings*. London: Longman.

Bisson, L.M. (1994). Virginia Woolf and the university. In M. Hussey and V. Neverow, (Eds) *Virginia Woolf: Emerging Perspectives: Selected Papers from the Third Annual Conference on Virginia Woolf*, 197–203. New York: Pace University Press.

Burton, G.O. (2007). *Silva Rhetoricae*. http://rhetoric.byu.edu/ (last accessed 15 May 2013).

Chatman, S. (1978). *Story and Discourse: Narrative Structure in Fiction and Film*. Ithaca, NY: Cornell University Press.

Conklin, N.F. (1974). Towards a feminist analysis of linguistic behaviour. *University of Michigan Papers in Women's Studies*, 1, 51–73.

Cortese, G. (Ed.) (1992). *Her/his Speechways: Gender Perspectives in English.* Torino: Libreria Cortina.

Eggins, S. (2004). *An Introduction to Systemic Functional Linguistics.* London: Continuum.

Fernald, A. (1994). A room, a child, a mind of one's own: Virginia Woolf, Alice Walker and feminist personal criticism. In M. Hussey and V. Neverow (Eds), 245–251.

Fishman, P.M. (1992). Interaction: the work women do. In G. Cortese (Ed.), 107–120.

Gubar, S. (2005). Introduction. In V. Woolf (Ed.), *A Room of One's Own* xxxv–lxi. Orlando: Harcourt.

Halliday, M.A.K. (1984). Language as code and language as behaviour: a systemic-functional interpretation of the nature and ontogenesis of dialogue. In R.P. Fawcett, M.A.K. Halliday, S.M. Lamb and A. Makkai (Eds) *The Semiotics of Culture and Language, Volume 1: Language as Social Semiotic,* 3–35. London: Frances Pinter.

Halliday, M.A.K. (1989). Part A. In M.A.K., Halliday and R. Hasan, *Language, Context, and Text: Aspects of Language in a Social-Semiotic Perspective,* 1–49. Oxford: Oxford University Press.

Halliday, M.A.K., and Hasan, R. (1989). *Language, Context, and Text: Aspects of Language in a Social-Semiotic Perspective.* Oxford: Oxford University Press.

Halliday, M.A.K., and Matthiessen, C. (1999). *Construing Experience through Meaning: A Language-based Approach to Cognition.* London, New York: Cassell.

Hasan, R. (1978). Text in the systemic-functional model. In W.U. Dressler (Ed.) *Current Trends in Textlinguisics,* 228–246. Berlin: de Gruyter. http://dx.doi.org/10.1515/9783110853759.228

Hasan, R. (1979). On the notion of text. In J.S. Petöfi (Ed.) *Text vs Sentence: Basic Questions of Text Linguistics, Second Part,* 369–390. Hamburg: Helmut Buske Verlag.

Hasan, R. (1988). A framework for the study of verbal art. In N. Mercer (Ed.), *Language and Literacy from an Educational Perspective,* 59–74. Milton Keynes: Open University Press.

Hasan, R. (1989). Part B. In M.A.K., Halliday and R. Hasan, *Language, Context, and Text: Aspects of Language in a Social-Semiotic Perspective,* 50–118. Oxford: Oxford University Press.

Hasan, R. (2000). The uses of talk. In S. Sarangi and M. Coulthard (Eds), *Discourse and Social Life,* 28–47. London: Longman.

Hawkes, E. (1981). Woolf's 'magical garden of women'. In J. Marcus (Ed.), 31–60.

Hussey, M., and Neverow, V. (Eds) (1994). *Virginia Woolf: Emerging Perspectives: Selected Papers from the Third Annual Conference on Virginia Woolf.* New York: Pace University Press.

Hynes, N. (1994). The chameleon voice and classical structure in Three Guineas and A Room of One's Own. In M. Hussey and V. Neverow (Eds), 140–146.

Jakobson, R. (1960). Linguistics and poetics. In T.A. Sebeok (Ed.), *Style in Language,* 350–377. Cambridge, MA: M.I.T.

Kress, G., and Threadgold, T. (1988). Toward a social theory of genre. *Southern Review (Baton Rouge, La.)*, 21(3), 215–243.

Labov, W., and Waletzky, J. (1967). Narrative analysis. In J. Helm (Ed.) *Essays on the Verbal and Visual Arts. (Proceedings of the 1966 Spring Meeting of the American Ethnological Society)*, 12–44. Seattle: University of Washington Press.

Maltz, D.N., and Borker, R.A. (Eds) (1992). A cultural approach to male-female miscommunication. In G. Cortese (Ed.), 171–189.

Marcus, J. (Ed.) (1981a). *New Feminist Essays on Virginia Woolf.* London and Basingstoke: Macmillan.

Marcus, J. (1981b). Thinking back through our mothers. In J. Marcus (Ed.), 1–30.

Marcus, J. (1987). Taking the bull by the udders: sexual difference in Virginia Woolf – a conspiracy theory. In J. Marcus (Ed.), *Virginia Woolf and Bloomsbury: A Centenary Celebration*, 146–169. Bloomington, IN: Indiana University Press.

Martin, J.R. (1985). *Factual writing: exploring and challenging social reality.* Victoria: Deakin. University.

Martin, J.R. (1997). Analysing genre: functional parameters. In F. Christie and J.R. Martin (Eds), *Genre and Institutions: Social Processes in the Workplace and School*, 3–39. London and Washington: Cassell.

Miller, D.R. (2012). Slotting Jakobson into the social semiotic approach to verbal art: a modest proposal. In F. Dalziel, S. Gesuato, and M.T. Mussacchio (Eds), *A Lifetime of English Studies: Essays in Honour of Carol Taylor Torsello*, 215–226. Padova: Il Poligrafo.

Mukařovský, J. (1964). Standard language and poetic language. In P. Garvin (Ed.), *A Prague School Reader on Aesthetics, Literary Structure and Style*, 17–30. Washington, DC: Georgetown University Press.

Rosenberg, B.C. (1995). *Virginia Woolf and Samuel Johnson: Common Readers.* New York: St. Martin's Press.

Taylor Torsello, C. (1994). Approaching even the literary text through field, tenor and mode: a way of giving unity to the language and literature program, *Rassegna Italiana di Linguistica Applicata*, 26(1–2), 187–213.

Taylor Torsello, C. (1997). Linguistic management of shared and unshared information: from the fairy tale through the scientific article to the novel. In F. Gozzi and A.L. Johnson (Eds), *Scienza e immaginario*, 133–158. Pisa: Edizioni ETS.

Taylor Torsello, C. (1998). The linguistic management of information in medical texts. In P. Evangelisti Allori (Ed.), *Academic Discourse in Europe: Thought Processes and Linguistic Realisation*, 89–116. Rome: Bulzoni.

Taylor Torsello, C. (2000). Il genere discorsivo. *Rassegna italiana di linguistica applicata*, 32(3), 49–66.

Taylor Torsello, C. (2007). Projection in literary and non-literary texts. In D.R. Miller and M. Turci (Eds), *Language and Verbal Art Revisited*, 115–148. London: Equinox.

Taylor Torsello, C. (2012). Woolf's non-assertive stance in *A Room of One's Own*. In A. Oboe and A. Scacchi (Eds), *A Garland of True Plain Words*, 139–155. Padova: Unipress.

Taylor Torsello, C., and Baldry, A. (2005). SFL in text-based, web-enhanced language study. In R. Hasan, C. Matthiessen, and J. Webster (Eds), *Continuing Discourse on Language: A Functional Perspective* (Vol. 1), 311–334. London: Equinox.

Woolf, V. (2000). *A Room of One's Own*. London: Penguin.

Woolf, V. (2006). In J. Marcus (Ed.), *Three Guineas*. New York: Harcourt.

Young, L. (1990). *Language as Behaviour, Language as Code: A Study of Academic English*. Amsterdam and Philadelphia: John Benjamins.

About the author

Carol Taylor Torsello retired in 2009 from her position as full professor at the University of Padua in Italy where she taught English Language and Linguistics. Her most recent publications include the volume, *Corpora for University Language Teachers* (co-edited with Ackerley and Castello, Peter Lang, 2008); 'Lexical Density and Grammatical Intricacy in some Varieties of Written Texts' (in *Threads in the Complex Fabric of Language*, in Bertuccelli Papi, Bertacca and Bruti (eds), Pisa, Felice Editore, 2008) and 'Woolf's Non-assertive Stance in *A Room of One's Own*' (in *A Garland of True Plain Words*, Oboe and Scacchi (eds) Padova: Unipress, 2012).

12

Genre and register hybridisation in an historical text

Michael Cummings

York University, Toronto

12.1 Introduction

The historical text is called, in one of its manuscripts, the *Sermo Lupi ad Anglos quando Dani maxime persecuti sunt eos*; that is, 'the sermon of the Wolf to the English at a time when the Danes were oppressing them severely'. It is a classic reading in introductory anthologies of Old English literature. My purpose in discussing it here is to demonstrate two points: first, that approaches and categories from Systemic Functional Linguistics (SFL) can be very applicable to remote historical dialects and remote historical texts; and, second, that in particular Ruqaiya Hasan's discussion of the 'permeability' of register and genre categories is very illuminating for the genre analysis of such an historical text.

12.1.1 Introduction to the text

Despite the Latin of its title, the language of the text is Late West Saxon English, the basis for the literary koine of the last century of Anglo-Saxon England (Quirk and Wrenn 1981:5). Its style is rhapsodic, based on a two-stress phrase rhythm characteristic of the author, and related to the two-stress rhythm of the Old English poetic half-line (McIntosh 1949:114). The text is found in five different versions in five different eleventh- and twelfth-century manuscripts, which can be understood to represent an original version preached in 1014, and two successive authorial expansions (Whitelock 1976 [1939]: 1–6; for a discussion of the relations among the versions and a useful non-linguistic discussion of *Sermo Lupi* structure, see Dien 1975 and Hollis 2002 [1997]).

The author is called *Lupus* ('Wolf') because that was the *nom de plume* of Archbishop Wulfstan of York, the second-ranking prelate of the English church from 1002 to 1023. Like most Anglo-Saxon period names, his is a compound, of *wulf-* ('wolf') and *-stan* ('stone'), hence the logic of the Latin nickname. Wulfstan had come up through the ecclesiastical ranks until his elevation to the see of York. He had become famous as an eloquent preacher, went on to become a legal expert for King Aethelred, authored the king's later lawcodes, kept his place under the conquering King Cnut, and authored Cnut's laws too, dying in office in 1023 (Whitelock 1976 [1939]: 10, 15–16, 23–25).

The last 25 years of the reign of King Aethelred was a period of foreign invasion and domestic disintegration. The government foolishly tried to appease the Viking raiders of the 990s by buying them off from the proceeds of a new tax, the Danegeld, then early in the next century ordered a massacre of people of Danish-descent throughout the kingdom, fearing them as traitors. Svein Forkbeard, king of Denmark, seized the occasion to invade. He and his son Cnut drove Aethelred into exile for a time in 1013–1014. In 1016, the last man standing, Cnut, absorbed England into a Scandinavian empire (Stenton 1971:371, 374–375, 380, 385). In the year of Aethelred's collapse, Wulfstan preached the *Sermo Lupi* probably to the *Witan*, or King's Council, as a call to restore the national moral fibre and the national resistance. The role thus played is consistent with his whole career as a Christian rhetorician and reforming jurist (Jurovics 1978: 203, 209; Rabin 2006:400–402, 414).

The sermon begins with the announcement of four motifs: first, that the end of the world is near; second, that this is evident from the national calamities of the day; third, that these calamities are the result of the great moral decay of the English; and fourth, that God may be appeased by an equally great moral improvement. In the sermon which follows, chiefly macro-Theme (Martin 1992:437) three, the sins of the people, and four, the resulting calamities, are (in terms of the SFL logico-semantic subcategories of expansion, Halliday and Matthiessen 2004:377) elaborated on, enhanced and extended, until the end, where macro-Theme four, moral improvement, is held out again as the only hope.

12.1.2 Introduction to SFL genre and register

My purpose is the mutual illumination of this text and SFL register and genre theory. As is well known, the theory has two main strands, the Halliday and Hasan approach, and the Martin and Rose approach. In her own writings, Hasan presents genre as the verbalisation of a particular set of values selected from the field, mode and tenor potentials belonging to a particular context. Such a particular set of field, mode and tenor options is called a 'contextual configuration' (CC). The genre in question has a 'generic structure potential' (GSP), which can be represented formulaically, and contains both obligatory and optional elements of structure. The structure potential is mainly a construal of field values, and represents a purpose which is mainly a construal of mode. A further question is the relation of genre and contextual configuration to culture. Culture is realised jointly by a social semiosis and by contexts of situation, that is, a semiotic side and a situational side, which correlate and mutually construe. Genre is a verbal instantiation of the social semiosis, and the contextual configuration is an instantiation of the context of situation (Halliday and Hasan 1985:54–69, 97–118; Hasan 1996:37–50; 1999:225–271; 2002:112–126; 2005:57–67).

For Martin and Rose, the relationship between context and language is viewed as a realisational ordering of content-expression planes, based on the notion of the connotative semiotic. Genre as patterning of human activity is such a connotative semiotic system, whose expression is register. Register is a metaredundant connotative semiotic system, whose expression is language, on successive metaredundant planes of discourse semantics, lexico-grammar and phonology. Genre itself is the expression of the ideology content plane, which, as the expression of culture, caters to the variety of cultural resources across human communities. Genre is thus not a verbal expression as such, but a social semiotic which preselects values in field, mode and tenor, which preselect verbal expression. Both the structure potential of a particular genre, and its purpose, thus determine register choices, and not the other way around (Martin 1992:493–508, 546–573; 2000:4–18; 2006:283–287; 2009:11–13; Martin and Rose 2008).

12.1.3 A particular approach to genre and register

Resolving, or even defining, the conflict between these two theories is beyond the scope of this chapter. My sole intention is to utilise some of the techniques of analysis which are common to the two approaches in order to expose the elements of structure in the *Sermo Lupi* and to characterise their registerial differences and similarities. That this is possible is evident from a similarity between the two theories in their treatment of the interface between field, mode and tenor choices and the corresponding genre category. Martin himself makes this point, in suggesting (1992:505) that the difference in theory between seeing genre as a realisation of register and seeing register as a realisation of genre is not crucial to the actual analysis of texts in terms of structure.

Another technique which will prove crucial to the analysis is Hasan's description of generic permeability. Genre categories applied to texts or within texts can have fuzzy boundaries. Depending on perspective, two genres can be distinct, may overlap, or one may be a subtype of the other (Halliday and Hasan 1985:107). Yet another crucial technique will be taken from Martin's description of genre agnation, in which genres systematise themselves in families. The story genre family, for example, includes subgenres such as recount, exemplum, narrative and so forth. Other families include history, report, explanation, procedure and so forth (1992:560–569; 2000:13–16; Martin and Rose 2008: esp. 235–242).

12.2 Genre and subgenre in the Sermo Lupi

The sermon genre has to be distinguished from that of the homily, although the terms are often used synonymously. Strictly speaking, a homily is an analysis of and commentary on a gospel text, that is, an exegesis. The gospel text is properly the gospel reading assigned to the mass of the day in the church calendar. A homily therefore belongs primarily to the genre family of explanation. The sermon on the other hand is not necessarily associated with any scriptural reading at all (Gatch 1977:19). As a subgenre it belongs to the genre family of persuasion. Other persuasion types with which it is agnate would include military persuasions (recollect George C. Scott's rendition of a Patton speech at the beginning of the movie of the same name), sports persuasions ('Win one for the Gipper!'), political persuasions ('… that from these honored dead we take increased devotion to that cause for which they gave the last full measure of devotion …'), forensic persuasions, etc.

12.2.1 Context of situation (field, mode, tenor)

The context of situation to which the sermon genre corresponds has a field of reference which includes at least two participants, a representative of a moral code and one or more other subjects to the moral code. The activities of the former are twofold: first, the blaming of the latter for a lapse from the moral code, and second a persuasion to adhere to the moral code. Tenor relations therefore involve two agent roles, a preacher and an audience.

These roles are hierarchic, with the preacher possessing greater authority than the audience, and a certain social distance from the audience; but the degree of the authority and the social distance may vary greatly. In terms of mode, the language role is constitutive rather than ancillary, which is why a sermon might end up as a work of literature. The medium may be spoken, written to be spoken, or written to be read as if spoken. If spoken it is usually monologic, but may be dialogic in a minimal sense with rejoinders from the congregation.

Typically the purpose of a sermon may be to persuade an audience to refrain from actions ('Thou shalt not ...'). It could be attempting to promote positive actions. It might not even be directing blame and persuasion at the actual audience, but rather at some abstract third-party. Hence the minimal goal to be assigned to the genre is a moral edification, which may or may not have an intended realisation in action.

12.2.2 Structural elements

I propose that the structure formula for sermon genre will have four essential elements: the Opening, the Complaint, the Directive and the Closing. The first and last of these obviously have a fixed place. One instance of the Complaint must come before one instance of the Directive, but both of these elements may recur numerous times, without any further determined order.

Optional elements of structure, on the other hand, can be numerous, recursive and without any predetermined order. Both the essential elements Complaint and Directive, and the optional elements, can be instances of numerous different subgenres from various families – narrative, exemplum, procedure, protocol, histories, explanations, and so forth. At a minimum the Complaint is realised by a subgenre of blaming, and the Directive by a subgenre of protocol or procedure.

12.2.3 Subtextual hybridisation

The subtexts which make up the *Sermo Lupi* sermon text and which realise the structural elements, both essential and optional, are sequentially distinct because they realise subgenres which vary. These subtexts always relate to one another by way of Halliday's logico-semantic categories, elaboration, extension and enhancement, and thus constitute a complex. The sermon then can be looked on, in Martin and Rose's terms (2008:218–224), as a complex of subgenres, that is, a 'macrogenre'. An essential point to be demonstrated is that the subtexts which make up the *Sermo Lupi* are often a hybridisation of some predominant subgenre with one or even more other subgenres. That is, the subgenres often blend into one another to enable some subtext to carry out a complex function.

12.3   Illustration from analysis of the first three sections

12.3.1 Opening

Table 12.1 shows the first three generically distinct subtexts or sections of the *Sermo Lupi* in Old English (adapted from Whitelock 1976 [1939]:47–49) and in present-day English and with comment. The first section announces the first three macro-Themes, the end of the world, national calamities and the people's sins. In order to signal the sermon genre and distinguish the roles of preacher and congregation, it begins with the conventional greeting as the Opening element (*Leofan men*, 'Dearly beloved'). It then realises the Complaint element; but on Martin and Rose's terms (2008: 150) it is also generically an explanation, at one point factorial (multiple causes) and at another simply sequential (simple cause and effect). That is, the first phenomenon is that the world is daily getting worse, for which there are two causes, the imminent end of the world, and the people's sins. A second phenomenon is the sheer horror of the last days to come, for which the cause is the arrival of Antichrist. However this explanatory section also involves an element of procedure, 'know what is true', which frames the explanation. The imperative plural form, as the first word of the body of the text, helps establish the degree of social distance between the two participants.

Table 12.1 Opening of *Sermo Lupi ad Anglos*

Section	Sermo Lupi	Translation	Comment
1	Leofan men, gec-nawað þæt soð is: ðeos worold is on ofste, 7 hit nealæcð þam ende, 7 þy hit is on worolde aa swa leng swa wyrse, 7 swa hit sceal nyde for folces synnan ær Antecristes tocyme yfelian swyþe, 7 huru hit wyrð þænne egeslic 7 grimlic wide on worolde. (lines 4–8)	Dearly beloved, know what is true: this world is in haste, and it is nearing the end, and for that reason it is in this world ever the longer the worse, and so it must necessarily be that things greatly worsen on account of people's sinning before the coming of Antichrist, and indeed it will then be terrible and grim widely throughout the world.	(procedure >) explanation: – modalising imperative in frame – gives way to explanation which is a mixture of factorial and sequential causes and effects
2	Understandað eac georne þæt deofol þas þeode nu fela geara dwelode to swyþe, 7 þæt lytle getreowþa wæran mid mannum, þeah hy wel spæcan, 7 unrihta to fela ricsode on lande; 7 næs a fela manna þe smeade ymbe þa bote swa georne swa man scolde, ac dæghwamlice man ihte yfel æfter oðrum 7 unriht rærde 7 unlaga manege ealles to wide gynd ealle þas þeode. 7 we eac forþam habbað fela byrsta 7 bysmara gebiden, (lines 8–15)	Understand also well that the devil has now greatly deceived this people for many years, and that there was little loyalty among men, though they spoke well, and too many crimes prevailed in the land; and there were never many men who considered the remedy as zealously as one should, but daily one evil was added to another, and crimes heaped up and many infractions all too widely throughout this whole nation. And we have therefore also endured many injuries and insults,	ELABORATION (instance) (procedure >) historical account: – modalising imperative in frame – gives way to historical account in which one episode causes another and causality is foregrounded over time – consequential: deofol […] dwelode > lytle getreowþa […] þas þeode – factorial: lytle getreowþa […] þas þeode > fela byrsta 7 bysmara

Section	Sermo Lupi	Translation	Comment
3	7, gif we ænige bote gebidan scylan, þonne mote we þæs to Gode ernian bet þonne we ær þysan dydan. Forþam mid miclan earnungan we geearnedan þa yrmða þe us on sittað, 7 mid swyþe micelan earnungan we þa bote motan æt Gode geræcan, gif hit sceal heonanforð godiende weorðan. La hwæt, we witan ful georne þæt to miclan bryce sceal micel bot nyde, 7 to miclan bryne wæter unlytel, gif man þæt fyr sceal to ahte acwencan; (lines 15–23)	and, if we are to experience any remedy, then we must merit better with God than we have done before this. For with great efforts we have earned the miseries that afflict us, and with very great efforts we must obtain the remedy with God, if things are to get better henceforth. Lo, we know full well that for a great infringement there must be a great recompense, and for a great fire much water, if that fire is at all to be extinguished.	ENHANCEMENT (result) explanation (> procedure) – conditional cause and effect (2x) – sequential cause and effect (2x)

12.3.2 Elaboration

The second section (see Table 12.1) is an elaboration of the first, that is, mainly an instancing with many particulars of the national sins, but also at the end, a brief instancing of the national calamities. Generically this is not an explanation like the previous subtext, but rather an historical account in which one episode causes another and causality is foregrounded over time (Martin and Rose:134–135). The first episode is the activity of the devil over a long time, which leads to the multiple consequences of disloyalties, hypocrisy, crimes, neglect, etc. These episodes lead to the outcome of national insults and injuries. It is thus a mixture of consequential and factorial causes and effects. This degree of cohesion with the first subtext is matched by the similar framing of the subtext with a modalising imperative: 'Understand also well that …'. Like the first subtext, the real subgenre is thus also nominally a procedure. Despite the generic distinctness of historical account from explanation, it is still a recursion of the Complaint element in sermon structure.

12.3.3 Enhancement

The third section (see Table 12.1) is an enhancement of the first and second sections together, representing a further result of the national sins. Generically it is a return to explanation, in which there is a repetitious series of cause and effect, this time making for an explanation which is first conditional, then merely sequential (Martin and Rose 2008: 150). That is, the national sins have produced a condition as a result: if the English are to enjoy the effect of relief from the national calamities, then they must cause such a relief by improving their behaviour. The condition is repeated and amplified with the qualification that the cause of relief must be proportional to the degree of the original misbehaviour. This is followed by two metaphors (*bryce/bot,bryne/wæter*) in explanatory form, sequential explanations that the degree of remedy required is caused by the degree of distress. The whole section is therefore also the announcement of the fourth and last macro-Theme, that God may be appeased by a suitable moral improvement. It is thus also the first appearance of the Directive element in the sermon structure; hence explanation genre is here permeated with the procedure genre.

12.3.4 The language of persuasion

The persuasion genre has its own set of registerial probabilities. The language of persuasion may be logical, authoritative or affective, or mixtures of these three features. Imperative mood realises authority, conjunction realises logic and a great variety of features on every level are affective. Wulfstan's persuasiveness depends on all of these, but especially on the affective. Affective features permeate the entire sermon text, prompting assent everywhere. Chiefly to be noted in these first three subtexts are the repetitious, at times hypnotic, two-stress phrase rhythm; the extensive parallelism and balance, both structural and semantic; and the fire and water metaphor of subtext 3.

12.4 Further illustration from analysis of the body and the concluding section

12.4.1 Summary of the body

The body of the sermon continues in two further sections (4–5) on the subject of macro-Theme four, moral improvement, and macro-Theme three, the national sins. These are elaborations, the first a further instancing, and the second a generalisation. Generically they are an explanation and an historical account respectively. At the same time, in the call for moral improvement they are generically procedures also. Thus they are two more recursions of the Complaint element and of the Directive element in the sermon structure. The body of the sermon then continues through another eight generically distinct sections (6–13), mostly concentrating on the people's sins with a few reminders of contemporary calamities, mostly elaborations and extensions, and mostly historical accounts alternating with causal explanations. The difference between the realisation of these two genres, historical account and causal explanation, is often little more than variation between past transgressions in past tense and current transgressions in present tense. This series builds to a climax in the three sections 14–16, each of whose beginnings are set out in Table 12.2.

Table 12.2 The *Sermo Lupi* rises to a climax

Section	Sermo Lupi	Translation	Comment
14	7 la, hu mæg mare scamu þurh Godes yrre mannum gelimpan þonne us deð gelome for agenum gewyrhtum? Ðeh þræla hwylc hlaforde æthleape 7 of cristendom to wicinge weorþe, 7 hit æfter þam eft geweorþe þæt wæpngewrixl weorðe gemæne þegene 7 þræle, gif þræl þæne þegen fullice afylle, licge ægylde ealre his mægðe; 7, gif se þegen þæne þræl þe he ær ahte fullice afylle, gylde þegengylde. Ful earhlice laga 7 scandlice nydgyld þurh Godes yrre us syn gemæne, understande se þe cunne; 7 fela ungelimpa gelimpð þysse þeode oft 7 gelome. Ne dohte hit nu lange inne ne ute, ac wæs here 7 hete on gewelhwilcan ende oft 7 gelome, 7 Engle nu lange eal sigelease 7 to swyþe geyrigde þurh Godes yrre... (lines 102–114)	And lo, how may greater shame through God's wrath befall men than it often does us for our own deeds? Although some slave escape his lord and, leaving christendom become a Viking, and after that again it happen that a fight take place between thane and slave, if the slave kill the thane outright, he lies uncompensated to all his kinsmen; and, if the thane kills outright the slave that he had previously owned, he must pay the price of a thane. Very shameful laws and shameful tributes through God's wrath are common among us, let him understand who can; and many misfortunes befall this nation again and again. Nothing has prospered now for a long time at home or abroad, but there has been devastation and hatred in every district time and again, and the English for a long time now have been entirely without victory, and too greatly disheartened through God's wrath...	ELABORATION (result) (exemplum/ explanation): – sequential cause (agenum gewyrhtum) > effect/cause (Godes yrre) > effect (þræla hwylc...) – interruption – story (pres. tense) – judgemental interpretation macro-Theme 2, (3) – consequential effects: (Godes yrre > fela ungelimpa:...) – climax of macro-Theme 2: listing, vivid drama

Section	Sermo Lupi	Translation	Comment
15	Nis eac nan wundor þeah us mislimpe, forþam we witan ful georne þæt nu fela geara mænn na ne rohtan foroft hwæt hy worhtan wordes oððe dæde; ac wearð þes þeodscipe, swa hit þincan mæg, swyþe forsyngod þurh mænigfealde synna 7 þurh fela misdæda: þurh morðdæda 7 þurh mandæda, þurh gitsunga 7 þurh gifernessa, þurh... (lines 133–139)	And it is no wonder although things go wrong for us, because we know very well that now for many years men have not cared very often what they did in word or deed; but this people, as it can seem, has become very corrupt through manifold sins and through many misdeeds: through murders and through crimes, through avarice and through greed, through...	ELABORATION (cause) historical account, factorial causality: ...mænn na ne rohtan [...] hwæt hy worhtan wordes oððe dæde...; ...wearð þes þeodscipe [...] forsyngod [...] þurh morðdæda 7 þurh mandæda, þurh gitsunga 7 þurh gifernessa... etc. beginning of climax of macro-Theme 3: listing
16	7 eac syndan wide, swa we ær cwædan, þurh aðbricas 7 þurh wedbrycas 7 þurh mistlice leasunga forloren 7 forlogen ma þonne scolde; 7 freolsbricas 7 fæstenbrycas wide geworhte oft 7 gelome. 7 eac her syn on earde apostatan abroþene 7 cyrichatan hetole 7... (lines 143–148)	And also are, far and wide, as we said before, through oathbreakings and through pledgebreakings and through various lies lost and perjured more than should be; and non-observances of feasts and fasts widely committed time and again. And also here in the land there are degenerate apostates, and hostile persecutors of the Church...	EXTENSION [continues with more sins] explanation, factorial (later sequential, and consequential) causality: ...syndan [...] þurh aðbricas 7 þurh wedbrycas [...] forloren 7 forlogen ma... etc.

4.2   Rising to the climax

The three sections whose beginnings are shown in Table 12.2 are the culmination of the body of the sermon. Section 14 in Table 12.2 (lines 102–132) represents the climax of the treatment of macro-Theme two, the punishment of God. Sections 15 and 16 in Table 12.2 (lines 133–183) together represent the climax of the treatment of macro-Theme three, the sins of the people. The technique used to effect the climax of each macro-Theme is extreme repetition, and with it, an intended growing affective sense of horror and disgust. Section 14 is an elaboration of the preceding section which has dealt with the people's sins, because this section now deals again with the results in terms of explanation genre. The section opens with a rhetorical question ('... how may greater shame ...') which reiterates a sequential causality: 'our own deeds' have effected 'God's wrath' which in turn has effected 'shame'. What follows to exemplify the 'shame' has all the earmarks of the exemplum. It is introduced by an exclamative interruption and a condemnatory interpretation of events, it tells a little story, and it is followed by another condemnatory interpretation of events. The section continues with consequential effects, 'many misfortunes' which have also proceeded from 'God's wrath'. These misfortunes are represented in a series of further stories, each more shocking than the last, about the humiliations which the English suffer at the hands of the Danish invaders. The preacher's rising indignation ends in another rhetorical question, '... what else is there in all those happenings except Gods wrath ...?' (*... hwæt is ænig oðer on eallum þam gelimpum butan Godes yrre ...?* lines 130–131), which neatly rounds off the section.

Section 15 in Table 12.2, in its return to macro-Theme three, the sins of the people, stands as an elaboration of 14 by offering a causality. As an historical account it proposes a factorial causality for God's anger: '... for many years men have not cared [...] what they did in word or deed; but this people [...] has become very corrupt through manifold sins [...] murder [...] crimes [...] avarice [...] greed ...'. Section 16, an extension, differs minimally from 15 by reverting to explanation genre through its switch to present time. Later on its presentation of causality will become consequential: 'Here are, through the stains of sin, as it can seem, too many in the land sorely blemished. Here there are manslayers and kinslayers, and priest-killers and persecutors of monasteries, and ...' (*Her syndan þurh synleawa, swa hit þincan mæg, sare gelewede to manege on earde. Her syndan mannslagan ꝥ mægslagan ꝥ mæsserbanan ꝥ mynsterhatan, ꝥ ...,* lines 166–168). The climactic effect in both sections is achieved through the accumulating volume of different types of sins and different types of sinners set out in longer and longer lists, often as alliterating pairs of terms, sometimes seemingly chanted in the rhythm of the two-stress phrase. At the end is a call to avoid universal destruction, which is generically both procedure and Directive: '… let us do as is needful for us, protect ourselves as zealously as we can, lest we all perish together' (… *utan don swa us neod is, beorgan us sylfum swa we geornost magan, þe læs we ætgædere ealle forweorðan.* Lines 181–183).

12.4.3 Extension by exemplum and historical account

Finally we get to the conclusion of the sermon, in two final sections found in Table 12.3. The first of these is a very deliberate change of pace, an historical account from the earliest days of the Anglo-Saxons. The interruptive 'once upon a time' beginning and the incipient story-line marks it as an exemplum, but in the same first sentence it soon turns into an historical account with causally related episodes and causality foregrounded over time. It starts out just sequentially, with the British people's sins causing God to be enraged, but then becomes consequential, with the enraged God causing both the loss of the British land and the utter destruction of the British forces. The second and third sentences elaborate the episodes, which now become a factorial account with a multitude of different sins as causes. This historical comparison of the English to the British ends with a return to the moral improvement motif, realised in another recursive Directive element, with the procedure genre realised by imperatives in the form of '… let us …' and '… there is […] need for us …'.

Table 12.3: Conclusion of *Sermo Lupi ad Anglos*

Section	Sermo Lupi	Translation	Comment
17	An þeodwita wæs on Brytta tidum, Gildas hatte, se awrat be heora misdædum, hu hy mid heora synnum swa oferlice swyþe God gegræmedan þæt he let æt nyhstan Engla here heora eard gewinnan 7 Brytta dugeþe fordon mid ealle. 7 þæt wæs geworden, þæs þe he sæde, þurh ricra reaflac 7 þurh gitsunge wohgestreona, þurh leode unlaga 7 þurh wohdomas, þurh biscopa asolcennesse 7 þurh lyðre yrhðe Godes bydela, þe soþes geswugedan ealles to gelome 7 clumedan mid ceaflum þær hy scoldan clypian. Þurh fulne eac folces gælsan 7 þurh oferfylla 7 mænigfealde synna heora eard hy forworhtan 7 selfe hy forwurdan. Ac wutan don swa us þearf is, warnian us be swilcan; 7 soþ is þæt ic secge, wyrsan dæda we witan mid Englum þonne we mid Bryttan ahwar gehyrdan; 7 þy us is þearf micel þæt we us beþencan 7 wið God sylfne þingian georne. (lines 184–199)	Once was a learned man in the time of the Britons named Gildas, who wrote about their misdeeds, how they with their sins so excessively angered God that He at last let the English army conquer their land, and destroy the army of the Britons outright. And that came about, as he said, through plundering by the powerful and through greed for ill-gotten gains, through the people's injustices and through unjust judgments, through the bishops' laziness, and through the wicked cowardice of God's messengers, who kept silent about the truth all too often and mumbled in their chops when they should have cried out. Also through the people's foul wantonness and through gluttony and manifold sins they forfeited their country and they themselves perished. But let us do as is necessary for us, take warning from such things; and true is it what I say, we know of worse deeds among the English than we have heard of anywhere among the Britons; and therefore there is a great need for us to reflect, and zealously to intercede with God Himself.	EXTENSION exemplum (> historical account) – interruption – story – episodes cause another – causality foregrounded over time – sequential (heora synnum > God gegræmedan > he let…) – consequential (here […] gewinnan, dugeþe fordon) – factorial (misdædum/synum: reaflac […] gitsunge…etc.) – procedure

Section	Sermo Lupi	Translation	Comment
18	ꝥ utan don swa us þearf is, gebugan to rihte, ꝥ be suman dæle unriht forlætan, ꝥ betan swyþe georne þæt we ær bræcan; ꝥ utan God lufian ꝥ Godes lagum fylgean, ꝥ gelæstan swyþe georne þæt þæt we behetan þa we fulluht underfengan, oððon þa þe æt fulluhte ure forespecan wæran; ꝥ utan word ꝥ weorc rihtlice fadian, ꝥ ure ingeþanc clænsian georne, ꝥ að ꝥ wed wærlice healdan, ꝥ sume getrywða habban us betweonan butan uncræftan; ꝥ utan gelome understandan þone miclan dom þe we ealle to sculon, ꝥ beorgan us georne wið þone weallendan bryne helle wites, ꝥ geearnian us þa mærþa ꝥ þa myrhða þe God hæfð gegearwod þam þe his willan on worolde gewyrcað. God ure helpe. Amen. (lines 199–211)	And let us do as is necessary for us, turn to righteousness, and to some degree leave off unrighteousness, and zealously make amends for what we previously transgressed; and let us love God and keep God's laws, and zealously observe what we promised when we received baptism, or those who at baptism were our sponsors; and let us order words and deeds rightly, and cleanse our thoughts zealously, and carefully keep oath and pledge, and have some loyalty among ourselves without deceits; and let us often reflect on the great judgment to which we all must go, and zealously protect ourselves from the surging fire of hell's punishment, and earn for ourselves the glories and joys that God has prepared for those who do his will in the world. Let God be our help. Amen.	ELABORATION (instances) procedure (mainly): - imperatives (utan don [...] ꝥ utan God lufian [...] ꝥ utan [...] fadian..., etc.

12.4.4 Elaboration and conclusion

The last section in Table 12.3 is entirely procedural (technically with one protocol). The passage is accordingly another recursion of the Directive element in sermon structure, until the Closing element realised as 'Let God be our help. Amen'. It is an elaboration of the preceding Directive element by instancing the various desirable ways in which we may '... intercede with

God Himself.' The language in which this is realised is full of first-person plural imperatives, 'let us do', 'let us [...] love', 'let us [...] keep', 'let us [...] understand', and so forth.

12.5 Conclusion

At the end we should note that the *Sermo Lupi* is often found to have a difficult and elusive structure. Critics have sometimes felt that its effect depends only on accumulation and repetition (Hollis 2002 [1977]:182–183). The generic analysis however goes a long way towards demonstrating its structure, substructure and reasoned argument. At the same time the prevalent multifunctionality of its hybridised subgenres demonstrates both the usefulness and the necessity of the concept of generic permeability.

References

Dien, S. (1975). Sermo Lupi ad Anglos: the order and date of the three versions. *Neuphilologische Mitteilungen*, 76, 561–570.

Gatch, M. (1977). *Preaching and Theology in Anglo-Saxon England*. Toronto: University of Toronto Press.

Halliday, M.A.K., and Hasan, R. (1985). *Language, Context and Text: Aspects of Language in a Social Semiotic Perspective*. Victoria, N.S.W.: Deakin University Press.

Halliday, M.A.K., and Matthiessen, C.M.I.M. (2004). *An Introduction to Functional Grammar* (3rd ed.). London: Arnold.

Hasan, R. (1996). *Ways of Saying: Ways of Meaning: Selected Papers* (C. Cloran, D. Butt, and G. Williams (Eds)),. London: Cassell.

Hasan, R. (1999). Speaking with reference to context. In M. Ghadessy (Ed.), *Text and Context in Functional Linguistics*, 219–328. Amsterdam and Philadelphia: John Benjamins. http://dx.doi.org/10.1075/cilt.169.11has

Hasan, R. (2002). Semiotic mediation and mental development in pluralistic societies: Some implications for tomorrow's schooling. In G. Wells and G. Claxton (Eds), *Learning for Life in the 21st Century: Sociocultural Perspectives on the Future of Education*, 112–126. Malden, MA: Blackwell Publishers. http://dx.doi.org/10.1002/9780470753545.ch9

Hasan, R. (2005). Language and society in a systemic functional perspective. In R. Hasan, C. Matthiessen, and J. Webster (Eds), *Continuing Discourse on Language: A Functional Perspective*, 55–80. London: Equinox.

Hollis, S. (2002 [1977]). The thematic structure of the *Sermo Lupi*. In R.M. Liuzza (Ed.), *Old English Literature: Critical Essays*, 182–203. New Haven, CT: Yale University Press (reprint of *Anglo-Saxon England*, 6, 175–195). http://dx.doi.org/10.12987/yale/9780300091397.003.0008

Jurovics, R. (1978). Sermo Lupi and the moral purpose of rhetoric. In P.E. Szarmach and B.F. Huppe (Eds), *The Old English Homily and Its Backgrounds*, 203–220. Albany, NY: State University of New York Press.

Martin, J.R. (1992). *English Text: System and Structure*. Amsterdam and Philadelphia: John Benjamins. http://dx.doi.org/10.1075/z.59

Martin, J.R. (2000). Analyzing genre: functional parameters. In F. Christie and J. Martin (Eds), *Genre and Institutions: Social Processes in the Workplace and School*, 3–39. London: Continuum.

Martin, J.R. (2006). Genre, ideology and intertextuality: A systemic functional perspective. *Linguistics and the Human Sciences*, 2, 275–298.

Martin, J.R. (2009). Genre and language learning: A social semiotic perspective. *Linguistics and Education*, 20(1), 10–21. http://dx.doi.org/10.1016/j.linged.2009.01.003

Martin, J.R., and Rose, D. (2008). *Genre Relations: Mapping Culture*. London: Equinox.

McIntosh, A. (1949). Wulfstan's prose. *Proceedings of the British Academy*, 35, 109–142.

Quirk, R., and Wrenn, C.L. (1981). *An Old English Grammar*. London: Methuen.

Rabin, A. (2006). The Wolf's testimony to the English: Law and the witness in the *Sermo Lupi ad Anglos*. *Journal of English and Germanic Philology*, 105, 388–414.

Stenton, F. (1971). *Anglo-Saxon England* (3rd ed.). Oxford: Clarendon.

Whitelock, D. (Ed.) (1976[1939]). *Sermo Lupi ad Anglos*. (Reprint, with additional bibliography, of Methuen ed.) Exeter: University of Exeter Press.

About the author

Michael Cummings has taught English, linguistics and humanities in various departments at York University, Toronto, since 1968. He is currently teaching in the English Department of York University as Professor *emeritus* and Senior Scholar. His latest book is *An Introduction to the Grammar of Old English: A systemic functional approach* (Equinox, 2010). He is also co-author or co-editor, with Robert Simmons, of *The Language of Literature: A stylistic introduction to the study of literature* (Oxford: Pergamon, 1983), *Linguistics in a Systemic Perspective* (Benjamins, 1988), and *Relations and Functions within and around Language* (Continuum, 2002).

13

Hybrid contexts and lexicogrammatical choices: Interpersonal uses of language in peer review reports in linguistics and mathematics

Akila Sellami-Baklouti

Faculty of Letters and Humanities, Sfax, Tunisia

13.1 Introduction

This chapter addresses the functional significance of hybridity for analysing texts, showing that the text is the product of hybrid discursive contexts: genre and discipline, which constitute two cultures interacting in the text. The paper adopts a Sydney School definition of genre as 'a staged, goal oriented social process' (Martin and Rose 2003:7; Martin and White 2005:32; Martin 2009:159). The main argument of the paper rests on the 'activation-construal dialectic' (Hasan 2009:170) between context, meaning and wording. The study aims to show that the text displays lexicogrammatical choices 'activated' by semantic choices, which are, in turn, activated by hybrid discursive contexts. To fulfil this objective, a quantitative and qualitative study is applied to semantic and lexicogrammatical choices realising the interpersonal uses of language in a corpus of 30 Peer Review Reports (henceforth, PRR) relevant to two disciplines: Mathematics and Linguistics. A comparative approach between the two sub-corpora is adopted with the aim of showing points of convergence, determined by the PRR genre, and points of divergence, explained as the effect of the specificities of each disciplinary community and the relations between its members. The first part of this study presents some major theoretic assumptions of Systemic Functional Linguistics (henceforth, SFL) about text, context, genre, and discipline, while the second part investigates the lexicogrammatical realisation of the interpersonal function with the aim of providing some empirical evidence for the hypothesis defended in this work.

13.2 Background

This section starts with the dialectical relation between text and context [13.2.1]; it then overviews the contextual factors that are expected to leave their traces in the corpus, namely, genre [13.2.2] and discipline [13.2.3]. Finally, the reasons behind the choice of the interpersonal function as the focus of the empirical analysis are presented in [13.2.4].

13.2.1 Context and text

Relying on the text as a 'window on the system' (Halliday and Matthiessen 2004:3) has led to the consideration of context as a dimension of analysis. In fact, a text cannot exist outside its context and this context can help understand the meanings of a text; otherwise, 'we cannot use it [text] as a window on the system' (Halliday and Matthiessen 2004:3). Accordingly, similar to text, context occupies an important position for SFL theorists who 'claim quite confidently that there can be no comprehensive scientific linguistics without parole, and no study of parole without context' (Hasan 2009:168).

In this theoretical framework, context is 'modelled as a stratum in the linguistic hierarchy, "above" (i.e., realised by) the stratum of semantics' (Halliday and Webster 2009:240). This higher position in the hierarchy makes it possible for context to affect lower strata (i.e., semantics and lexicogrammar), assuming that context leaves its 'traces' in the text (Hasan 2009:176). The relationship between text and context is dialectical because it works in two directions: going downwards, the context 'activates' semantic choices, which, in turn, activate lexicogrammatical choices; going upwards, 'lexicogrammatical choices CONSTRUE semantic choices, which, in turn, construe contextual ones' (Hasan 2009:170).

This dialectical relationship has two methodological implications: on the one hand, the analysis of lexicogrammatical choices in the text helps construe meanings, hence, context. On the other hand, context, as an activation force, helps explain the motivation behind such semantic and lexicogrammatical choices. This activation-construal dialectic is applied to the corpus under study, to construe contextual factors relevant to both PRR genre and disciplinary genre on the basis of lexicogrammatical choices made in the two sub-corpora.

13.2.2 Context of culture: PRR genre

In order to address the traces of context in the text, the concept of genre can be used 'to describe the staged, structured way in which people go about achieving goals when using language' (Eggins 2004:10). In the present study, this can be done by analysing PRR in terms of generic features, namely, their overall purpose [13.2.2.1] and their rhetorical organisation [13.2.2.2].

13.2.2.1 Communicative purposes of PRRs

PRRs are representative of 'review genres', which may be defined as 'texts and parts of texts that are written with the explicit purpose of evaluating the research, the texts and the contributions of fellow academics' (Hyland and Diani 2009:1). Within review genres, PRRs are considered as a disinterested genre, 'expected to give both positive and negative opinions, if they have both reactions' (Shaw 2009:218). Therefore, using the Attitude sub-system of APPRAISAL SYSTEMS, part of the analysis in this study [13.3.5.] is concerned with exploring how these attitudes are negotiated in the text (Martin and Rose 2003:22).

Another feature of the PRR genre that is expected to leave its traces in the text is its 'occluded' nature. In fact, unlike 'public evaluation of research', as for example, book reviews, PRRs are '"out-of-sight" to outsiders and apprentices' (Swales 2004:47), which means that access to them is restricted to a limited number of participants in the process of evaluation, who are represented as interactants in the text; namely, the reviewer (addresser), the author and the editor (addressees).

Evaluation in PRRs is not limited to pointing out positive and negative aspects of research papers; the role of the reviewer rather extends to requiring changes to be brought to the article evaluated in order 'to secure a manuscript sufficiently revised to be publishable' (Swales 2004:47). Accordingly, PRRs play an important role not only for authors, but also for the whole scientific publication process, because they help improve the 'published papers in terms of both their scientific quality and written presentation' (Gosden 2003:88). Therefore, PRRs have two functions depending on whether the reader is the editor or the author (Fortanet 2008:27). For the editor, the reviewer acts as an adviser as s/he helps him/her to determine whether to publish the paper or not; for the author, the reviewer acts as an evaluator/assessor as s/he persuades him /her to bring changes to render the paper suitable for publication. These communicative purposes that the PRRs are expected to fulfil have led to a common conventional structure.

13.2.2.2 Rhetorical organisation of PRRs

The analysis in this study focuses on the rhetorical organisation of the PRRs as it is of more relevance from the perspective of interpersonal meaning than the text's logic (Martin and White 2005:33). Despite the absence of guidelines by journal editors for a standardised structure of the PRR, some common structural patterns have been identified (Gosden 2003). The present study is based on a 4-Move structure suggested by Fortanet (2008:35), based on her study of PRRs pertaining to Applied Linguistics and Business Organisation:

Move 1: Summarising judgement regarding suitability for publication.
Move 2: Outlining the article.
Move 3: Points of criticism.
Move 4: Conclusion and recommendation.

The claim that is made in the empirical part of this study is that although the PRRs in the corpus share common communicative purposes and common textual structure, the distribution of the moves varies according to the discipline they represent. This claim is based on the assumption that the research discipline is another contextual factor that leaves its traces in the text.

13.2.3 'Disciplinary genre': Linguistics vs. Mathematics

In addition to the consideration of genre in terms of common communicative purposes and textual structure, which may leave their traces in the text, the 'disciplinary genre' (Hyland 2004; Bhatia 2004) may constitute another source of influence on the text. In fact, each discipline may be considered as a culture within which 'individuals acquire specialised discourse competencies that allow them to participate as group members' (Hyland 2004:8). Accordingly, 'disciplinary cultures differ on several dimensions' (Bhatia 2004:32) and each discipline can be seen as constituting a separate 'culture', not only in terms of fields of knowledge, but also in terms of 'specifically favoured discursive practices' (Bhatia 2004:46). The variation between disciplines in their discursive practices is reflected in different lexicogrammatical choices (Bhatia 2004; Fortanet 2008; Halliday 2005; Hasan 2009; Sellami-Baklouti 2011; 2013), confirming Hyland's (2006:39) statement that 'effective academic communication depends on rhetorical decisions about writers' and speakers' deployment of community-sensitive linguistic resources to represent themselves, their positions and their readers'. I seek to provide further support for this statement through showing the impact of disciplinary variation on the text.

A comparison between texts representing different disciplines can be helpful in depicting such variation, and the choice of Mathematics and Linguistics is motivated by the fact that they represent two distant points on 'the hard-soft continuum' (Hyland 2004:34). On the one hand, Mathematics, as an exact science,[1] is representative of hard disciplines, which may be characterised by methodological rigor, full control of variables, and which are 'built on non-contingent pillars such as strict procedures, replication, falsification and rigorous peer review process of publication' (Hyland 2004:34). On the other hand, Linguistics is representative of soft disciplines, which 'need to be more explicit in personal projection in the text and in strategies of reader's engagement' (Hyland and Bondi 2006:9). This disciplinary variation is assumed to overlap across genres (Bhatia 2004:30), which implies that writings representing the same discipline share some features whatever their genre is (Research Article, Book Review, Textbook, PRR, etc.). It is, therefore, worth investigating how lexicogrammatical choices reflect the social behaviours and power relations between the disciplinary community members, namely between the reviewer, the author, and the editor, as interactants in the PR process. The tenor vector of register analysis can be useful in such an investigation.

13.2.4 Interpersonal uses of language in PRR

Although three contextual variables of register (mode, tenor and field) can be explored as far as their traces in the text are concerned (Eggins 2004; Thompson 2004; Hasan 2009), some aspects of the situation may have more impact on language use than others (Eggins 2004). Given the significance of the evaluative dimension, I have opted to focus on the tenor vector defined as 'the role relationships entered into by the interactants taking part in a given context' (Matthiessen, Teruya and Lam 2010:217), which makes it a useful framework to detect the power and solidarity relations between the reviewer, the editor and the author in the PRR interaction. The analysis focuses on the realisations of the tenor vector in terms of MOOD choices, MODALITY choices, and ATTITUDE choices within APPRAISAL SYSTEMS. In this process of analysis, it is hypothesised that these relations would be different in the two disciplines under study.

So far, the PRR genre and disciplinary genre, which are expected to leave their traces in PRR texts, have been overviewed. This review was based on two major assumptions: the first is that genres 'in the real world [...] are often seen in hybrid, mixed and embedded forms' (Bhatia 2004:25); and the second is that texts are hybrid because they display lexicogrammatical choices activated by different factors relevant to hybrid genres.

13.3 Case Study

This section offers some empirical evidence for the hypothesis that the PRR genre and the disciplinary genre are two types of interacting contexts that activate different semantic and, in turn, lexicogrammatical choices, resulting, thus, in hybrid texts that display traces relevant to both of these contexts.

13.3.1 Corpus and methodology

The corpus consists of 30 PRRs: 15 in Linguistics and 15 in Mathematics. The limited size of the corpus is due to the 'occluded' (Swales 2004:47) nature of this genre. Table 13.1 provides a detailed description of the two sub-corpora:

Table 13.1: Corpus description

	Linguistics	**Mathematics**	**Total**
Total number of words	9,992	7,290	17,282
Average report length	666	486	

The corpus was annotated manually using the UAM CorpusTool (Version 2.8.7) and a scheme created on the basis of the system of interpersonal choices (Halliday and Matthiessen 2004:135) adapted to the purposes of the present study (Figure 13.1).

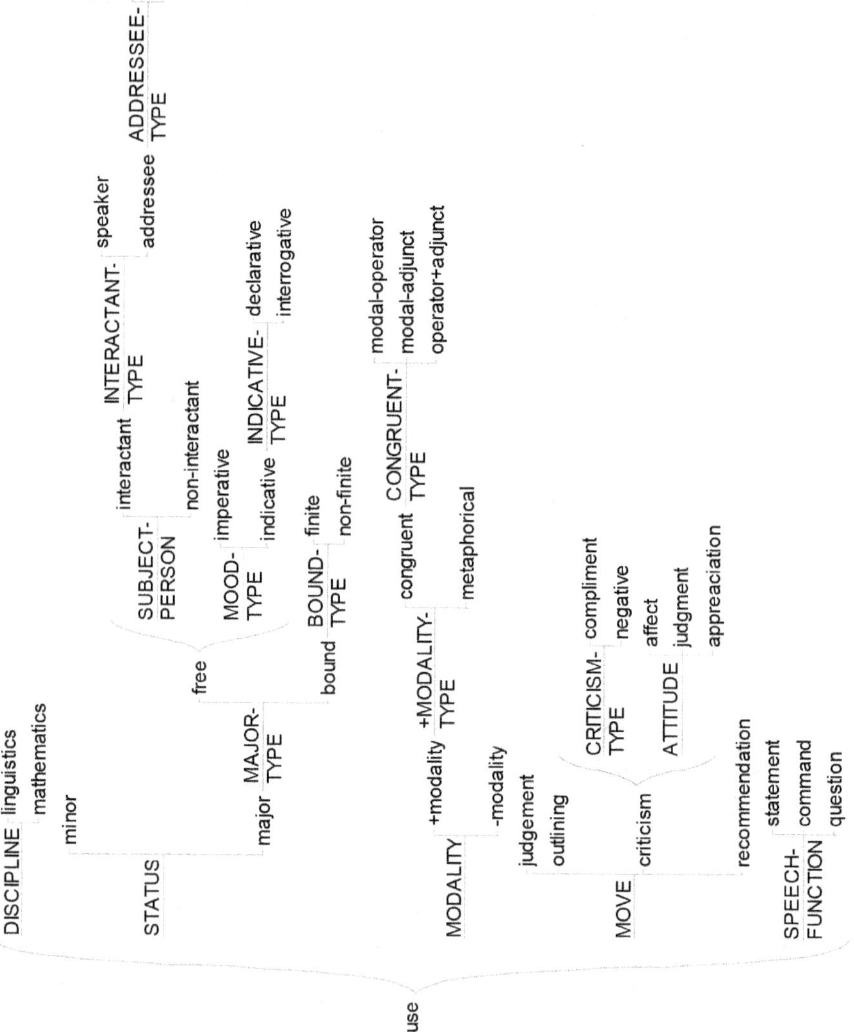

Figure 13.1: CorpusTool scheme for corpus annotation

The study adopts a bottom-up approach, relying on the quantification of semantic and lexicogrammatical choices, which can reveal the meanings construed in the corpus and seeking to explain these choices in terms of contextual factors relevant to both PRR genre and disciplinary genre. The analysis of the corpus, which is based, as is typical in SFL, on the clause as a unit, deals with four angles of the interpersonal function: It starts with identifying the meanings exchanged [13.3.2]; it then analyses MOOD choices [13.3.3] and Modality choices [13.3.4]; and, finally, focus is put on the Criticism move, where the APPRAISAL SYSTEMS choice framework, more specifically the ATTITUDE SYSTEM, is adopted to analyse the attitudes of the reviewers in the two disciplines [13.3.5]. At each level of the analysis, a comparison between the two sub-corpora in terms of the frequency of structural choices is meant to depict similarities and differences. As stated in the Introduction, the assumption underlying this comparative approach is that points of convergences are activated by the PRR genre, while points of divergence are activated by the disciplinary genre.

13.3.2 The meanings exchanged: Generic structure

Following Martin and White's (2005:33) argument, the analysis of generic structure from an interpersonal perspective is 'more interested in the rhetorical organisation of a text than its logic'. This section investigates whether the two sub-corpora follow the conventional structure dictated by the communicative purposes of the PRR genre and whether there is any variation that may be dictated by their belonging to different disciplines. For this purpose, the distribution of moves, based on an adapted version of Fortanet's (2008) 4-Move structure, is studied in the two sub-corpora. Table 13.2 displays the functions of these moves and the percentage of clauses realising them:

Table 13.2: Distribution of moves in the corpus

Move	Function	Example	Ling	Maths
Move 1	Overall judgement statement regarding suitability for publication	(1) RLing10: Overall then I believe this to be case of 'revise and resubmit'	3%	4%
Move 2	Outlining the article's content	(2) RMaths1: In section 6 the authors discuss an orthogonal basis for $L2$ which in some sense play the role of the Hermite functions for the rational Bessel transform case.	38%	41%
Move 3	Points of criticism: meant to include both positive, i.e., compliment (3) and negative criticism (4)	(3) RLing2: I would add that this 'starting point' has considerable news value. (4) RLing1: At time, the formulations are a bit less than clear or correct	34%	23%
Move 4	Recommendation: this move includes clauses that convey suggestions for revision	(5) This inequality should be precisely justified as it is crucial in the proof of theorem 5.1.	24%	30%

Table 13.2 shows that the 4-Move structure is common to the two sub-corpora, which represents a point of convergence. This finding, in conformity with Fortanet's (2008) findings concerning her corpus of Applied Linguistics and Business Organisation PRRs, shows that this distribution is the result of the conventional structure of PRR. A second point of convergence can be seen in the frequency of the clauses realising the first two moves across the two sub-corpora (the Overall Judgement and the Outlining of the article). The existence of the overall (non)-acceptability judgement in all the reports of the corpus can be explained by the editor's expectation from the reviewer to advise him/her to accept/reject the article, thus fulfilling a major communicative purpose of the genre. As for the description of the content of the article, the nearly equal percentages of clauses realising this move in the two sub-corpora can be explained by the fact that this description can serve as a justifying basis for the criticism, as can be seen in example (1), where in the first clause, the reviewer describes the result presented by the paper and in the second, s/he gives his/her assessment of this result. This description endows the report with objectivity, confirming Swales' (2004:47) statement that 'guidelines for reviewers express the need to be collegial in their responses.'

> (1) RMaths1: The authors compute directly the value of the transform on this basis of *L*2, in terms of Wilson polynomials. This is a very nice result.

However, Table 13.2 also shows a variation between the two sub-corpora in the frequency of clauses realising the Criticism and Recommendation moves. While the Linguistics reports display a higher frequency of criticism than recommendation (34 per cent vs. 24 per cent), the reverse pattern is displayed by the Mathematics reports (23 per cent vs. 30 per cent). The Chi-square test shows a statistically significant variation in this distribution ($\chi^2 = 14.64$, $P = 0.01$).

On the one hand, these quantitative results may imply that Linguistics reviewers tend to be more critical, especially that the frequency of negative criticism clauses in Linguistics reports exceeds those in Mathematics ones (73 per cent vs. 67 per cent). This can be confirmed by the Linguistics reviewers' emphasis on negative points, as can be seen in example (2), where the reviewer elaborates on the first clause by clarifying, using positive polarity, what is already stated using negative polarity:

> (2) RLing6: The formatting is not reader friendly; in fact, it is confusing.

The high frequency on negative criticism in Linguistics reports may indicate their tendency to highlight the negative aspects of the reviewed article. This finding is in conformity with Diani's (2009:102) finding on book reviews articles, where, in a comparison with History and Economics, she found that 'linguistics shows a marked preference for negative evaluation'. This tendency on the part of Linguistics reviewers to be 'bluntly' critical is, therefore, determined by the disciplinary culture rather than by the PRR genre. This is confirmed by the fact that, in negative criticism in Mathematics reports, reviewers tend to mitigate their criticism, as can be seen in the following example:

> (3) RMaths1: I think in the e-exponent the sign is wrong.

In Mathematics, due to the more exact nature of this science, the wrongness of a sign is uncontroversial. Despite this, the reviewer mitigates his/her criticism through the use of modality to make it less face-threatening (Kourilová 1996; Shaw 2009).

On the other hand, the higher percentage of recommendation clauses in Mathematics reports can be interpreted as an indicator of more constructive evaluation in this discipline, where suggestions for revisions to improve the quality of the article have more prominence than criticism. This can be confirmed by the fact that, in some instances, the recommendations for change pertain to specific points in the article under review, as the following two examples illustrate:

(4) RMaths4: before the statement of Theorem 1, indicate the fact that the family qX is a partition of $V n X$.

(5) RMaths9: One should say clearly that K is a compact group of automorphisms.

In examples (4) and (5), the reviewer gives precise suggestions for change, which the author will need to make. This is not the case in Linguistics reports, where the reviewer gives general suggestions, as can be seen in the following two examples:

(6) RLing4: I wonder if more could be said about this.

(7) RLing5: The written expression needs attention.

Although in both sub-corpora, reviewers suggest recommendations for changes to authors, given the genre expectation of PRR, Linguistics and Mathematics reports display some variation not only in terms of the frequency of these recommendations, but also in terms of precision. It is to be noted, here, that the author of the Mathematics article will have less difficulty in handling the reviewer's suggestions than the Linguistics article author, especially in example (7), where the reviewer does not give any hints about specific passages having problems of expression. This implies that Mathematics reviewers tend to be more cooperative with authors than Linguistics reviewers and this variation is due to different practices within different disciplinary communities rather than to PRR genre.

This first finding supports the hypothesis underlying this research: that the PRR represent hybrid texts where choices are determined by factors relevant to both PRR genre and disciplinary genre. The next step of the analysis will seek further support to this hypothesis as far as MOOD choices are concerned.

13.3.3 MOOD choices

Table 13.3 displays the distribution of MOOD choices (indicative vs. imperative) in the two sub-corpora:

Table 13.3: Distribution of MOOD in the corpus

	Indicative	Imperative
Linguistics	481	14
Mathematics	354	31

Table 13.3 shows that the indicative: declarative mood largely exceeds the imperative in both sub-corpora (97 per cent in Linguistics reports and 92 per cent in Mathematics reports). This may be explained by the unsuitability of the imperative mood to convey the communicative functions of the first three out of the four/moves of the PRR, namely the Overall Judgment Statement, the Outlining of the article's content and Criticism. In fact, the choice between the imperative and the indicative is relevant only in the Recommendation move, because, in this move, the commodity exchanged is goods and services, as the communicative function is to suggest revisions to the article. Table 13.4 displays the distribution of MOOD in the Recommendation move:

Table 13.4: Distribution of MOOD in the Recommendation move

	LING		MATHS	
Imperative	14	11%	30	26%
Indicative	110	89%	84	74%

Although in both sub-corpora, the indicative mood exceeds the imperative in the Recommendation move, Table 13.4 shows that the choice of the imperative is more than twice as frequent in Mathematics reports as in Linguistics ones (26 per cent vs. 11 per cent). The computation of Yule's coefficient of correlation may help to decide whether this variation correlates with disciplinary variation:

$$Q = \frac{A - B}{A + B} = \frac{(30 * 110) - (14 * 84)}{(30 * 110) + (14 * 84)} = \frac{3300 - 1176}{3300 + 1176} = \frac{2124}{4476}$$

The coefficient obtained is outside the rejection interval, which means that a positive correlation is proved to exist between discipline and MOOD choice. The higher frequency of imperatives in Mathematics reports might be explained by the more exact nature of this discipline. In fact, Mathematics can be considered as an exact discipline because 'accurate quantitative techniques are used and there are accurate means of testing hypotheses and repeating results' (http://www.collinsdictionary.com), which makes Mathematics 'objective, rational, and factual' (Oliveira and Cheng 2011:258). This implies that the content presented in Mathematics articles is subject to binary truth values, where results are either true or false and the assignment of this truth value is uncontroversial as the result is reached after demonstration and logical reasoning. Accordingly, suggestions for changes tend to be more straightforward. This can be an indicator of the reviewer's expertise, which gives him/her more power in making commands, leaving little choice to the author, as the following example shows:

> (8) RMaths4: b) modify the statement of theorem 1 as follows…

Linguistics, however, is subject to relativity as different conclusions can be reached by interpreting the same data from different perspectives. Accordingly, the suggestions provided by the reviewer may just be different perspectives from which the data may be studied. The author is, therefore, given some degree of freedom to choose whether to carry out the reviewer's suggestion or not if s/he has another opinion to defend as the following example illustrates:

> (9) RLing3: However *I would like* the authors to revise the manuscript according to the comments I have given *where possible.*

It can be concluded that the variation in MOOD choices to realise the Recommendation move in the two sub-corpora is due to the difference between the two disciplines as to the strength of the suggestions for change, which, in turn, can be explained by the nature of the discipline. Although in the two sub-corpora recommendations for revisions are made, fulfilling a substantial function of the PRR, each discipline leaves its own traces in the text, making it a hybrid outcome of hybrid contexts.

13.3.4 MODALITY choices

MODALITY is the system that helps to 'construe the region of uncertainty that lies between 'yes' and 'no" (Halliday and Matthiessen 2004:147). All the clauses in the corpus have been classified according to how the reviewer exploited the MODALITY SYSTEM: first whether modality was used or not; whether it is congruent or metaphorical; and in case of congruent modality, whether it was realised through a finite modal operator or through a modal adjunct (See Figure 13.1). Table 13.5 displays the distribution of modality in the different sections of two sub-corpora:

Table 13.5: The distribution of MODALITY in the two sub-corpora

	Move	LING		MATHS	
		Number	**%**	**Number**	**%**
– Modality	Judgement	8	1	5	1
	Outlining	172	33	156	39
	Criticism	130	25	78	19
	Recommendation	40	7	73	18
Total		350	67%	312	78%
+ Modality	Judgement	8	1	13	3
	Outlining	26	5	10	2
	Criticism	46	8	15	4
	Recommendation	88	16	49	12
Total		168	33%	87	22%

Table 13.5 shows that, on the whole, the frequency of clauses without modality exceeds those with modality. Table 13.5 also shows that this pattern is common to both sub-corpora in three out of four moves, namely the Overall Judgement Statement, the Outlining of the article's content and the Criticism. The only point of significant divergence between the two sub-corpora is the Recommendation move. In fact, while in Mathematics reports, the absence of modality is more frequent than its presence (73 vs. 49), in the Linguistics reports, the frequency of clauses with modality exceeds those without (88 vs. 40). With a Yule's coefficient $Q = 0.54$, a correlation is proved to exist between Linguistics reports and the use of modality in the Recommendation move. In fact, the use of modality helps the reviewers make their request for change indirect, as can be seen in the following example:

> (11) RLing7: This is where I *am wondering* whether it *may be possible* to rework the positions that were made relevant in the excerpts in terms of 'membership categories?'

In example (11), the reviewer asks for revision using: (a) metaphorical modality through the use of projection 'I am wondering', which can be considered as a softer, downplayed version of the mental projection *'I think that'*; (b) the modal operator 'may'; and (c) the expansion of the Predicator 'be possible', displaying a metaphor of mood. The lexicogrammatical choices conveying low-value possibility contribute to making the request for change as indirect as possible. The use of such low modality to convey indirect requests is frequent in the Recommendation sections of the Linguistics reports and it suggests that the changes are not substantial, in the sense that the author can do without them, as indicated by the expression, *where possible* in example (9) above.

Even in cases where the reviewer uses a higher value modal, the directness of the request is sometimes attenuated by the use of the Actor-less passive, as for example in:

(12) RLing3: In addition, the relation of the type of referent to be offered to the construction of the action (identification of the referent, explicating the offer) *should be* attended to more clearly.

(13) RLing6: Second, transcripts *needed to be* fewer characters per line with lines and line numbers indented.

It is to be noted here that even with the use of higher-value modality, prescription is less strong than in the case of the imperative form, as for example in:

(14) RMaths5: Page 10: *Explain* why condition (i) on line 2 # implies the integral condition on line 11# for almost every n 2 N.

This variation between the two disciplines may be quite informative about the relations between the three parties in the PRR interaction. In fact, following Halliday and Matthiessen's argument (2004:148), commands conveyed through the use of modality may be said to function 'as propositions, since to the person addressed they convey information rather than goods-and-services. But they do not thereby lose their rhetorical force'. This means that, in the case of the corpus under study, commands in Linguistics reports convey a double function: in addition to commanding the author to perform the suggested changes, they inform the editor about the situation. In Mathematics PRRs, however, the interaction in the Recommendation move takes place between the reviewer and the author, as the reviewer addresses the author directly through the use of the imperative mood. This means that the role given to the editor, the third party in the PRR interaction, varies in the two disciplines: while in Mathematics reviews, the editor is not a part of the interaction that takes place in the Recommendation move, in the case of Linguistics, the editor plays a role in this interaction. In fact, being informed about the suggested revisions to be made, the editor is given the responsibility of deciding, in addition to the author, about the urgency of the suggested changes.

It may, therefore, be concluded that although the two sub-corpora display similar frequencies of lexicogrammatical choices in some sections of the PRR, which can be explained by the impact of genre contextual factors, these choices vary in the Recommendation section and this variation is due to the nature of the roles assigned to the interactants (reviewer, author and editor) in the PRR exchange in the two disciplines under study.

13.3.5 APPRAISAL SYSTEMS Choices

This section aims to investigate points of convergence and divergence between the two disciplines at the level of discourse semantics in terms of appraisal (Martin and White 2005:33). The analysis focuses on the inscribed instances of appraisal in the Criticism move because it is in this move that the reviewers explicitly express their attitudes towards the paper under review.[2] Therefore, all the clauses realising this move are classified according to the ATTITUDE SUB-SYSTEM.[3] The results are displayed in Table 13.6:

Table 13.6: Classification of Criticism clauses according to the ATTITUDE SYSTEM

	LING	MATHS
Affect	21%	9%
Judgement	8%	3%
Appreciation	70%	88%

Table 13.6 shows that the order of frequency of the three types of attitudes is common to the two sub-corpora: Appreciation > Affect > Judgement. The fact that Judgement clauses are the least frequent in the two sub-corpora may be explained by the PRR genre, where the communicative purpose is to evaluate the article and its content rather than its author. In fact, even in instances of Judgement, where an attitude to the authors is expressed, this is done in relation to a point in the article, as can be seen in the following example:

> (15) RLing7: The authors do well when analytically moving into these narratives performed by the interviewee.

A second point of convergence between the two sub-corpora is the highest frequency of Appreciation clauses, illustrated by the following examples:

(16) RMaths13: *No backgrounds section* is drawn, which clearly renders uneasy the study of the paper.

(17) RLing3: *The introductory sections* indicate the authors' good knowledge of the area and serve to profile the study well, and *the analytic sections* provide solid analysis of the phenomena in question.

Although examples 16 and 17, display invoked Judgement (the authors not having drawn a backgrounds section in 16 and the authors' good knowledge in 17), the use of impersonal devices – the use of the passive and the impersonal structure – allow the reviewers to focus on the paper rather than on the authors. This endows criticism with an objective dimension and helps the reviewers abide by the guidelines dictated by the PRR genre which 'typically express the need to be collegial in their responses' (Swales 2004:47).

However, some divergence can be observed in Table 13.6. In fact, although in both sub-corpora instances of Appreciation are the most frequent, their frequency is higher in the Mathematics sub-corpus than in the Linguistics one, where, however, clauses of Affect are more frequent (21 per cent vs. 9 per cent), as illustrated by the following:

(18) RLing 2: *I* was also *bothered* by some seemingly rich narrative information that the author chose to omit.

(19) RLing7: What really *intrigued me* here, was the connection of relating past events.

In both examples (18) and (19), the reviewer presents himself/herself as a Senser in a mental process. It may, therefore, be said that despite guidelines of collegiality dictated by the PRR genre, Linguistics Reviewers tend to be more subjective in their criticism, and this can be seen in the choice of Affect in the Attitude system. This pattern, which was also reported by Diani (2009:96) in her study of Book Reviews in three so-called soft disciplines (Linguistics, History and Economics), can be interpreted as reflecting 'rhetorico-argumentative practices of the soft-knowledge domains in constructing an authoritative discoursal identity'.

This comparison between the two sub-corpora regarding the use of the APPRAISAL SYSTEMS in the Criticism move shows that, while Linguistics PRRs differ from Mathematics ones in some features, they share some choices with other texts in soft disciplines which belong to a different (though related) genre.

13.4 Conclusion

The analysis of interpersonal uses of language in the corpus has shown that the two sub-corpora display some common features. Using the 'activation-construal dialectic', these similarities in the frequency of semantic and lexicogrammatical choices are explained as being the traces left in the text by the PRR genre. However, in addition to these similarities, the corpus analysis has revealed some substantial differences which are motivated by disciplinary culture in terms of research paradigms and community members' relationships.

The findings of this study lead to two conclusions: The first, theoretical, is that each sub-corpus, as a sample of Text, is to some degree a hybrid outcome of the interaction of different genres; and the second, methodological, is that the dialectical relationship between text and context proves to be essential to showing this hybridity at work.

Notes

1   Although mathematics is also classified among formal sciences, my point in this study is that the features observed in the PRRs are due to the exact nature of mathematics and not to its formalism.
2   Given space constraints, the analysis of the appraisal instances is based only on the major categories of the ATTITUDE SYSTEM. This can be justified by the fact that this categorisation is enough to illustrate the main argument of the paper, i.e. points of convergence and divergence between the two sub-corpora.
3   The figures in Table 13.6 are based on instances of inscribed attitude, but invoked attitude may also emerge, often pointing up an overlap between Appreciation and Judgement, as will be shown in the analysis of the examples.

References

Bhatia, V.K. (2004). *Worlds of Written Discourse*. London and New York: Continuum.
Diani, G. (2009). Reporting and evaluation in English book review articles: A cross-disciplinary study. In K. Hyland and G. Diani (Eds), *Academic Evaluation: Review Genres in University Settings*, 87–104. London: Palgrave Macmillan.
Eggins, S. (2004). *An Introduction to Systemic Functional Linguistics* (2nd ed.). London: Continuum.

Fortanet, I. (2008). Evaluative language in peer review referee reports. *Journal of English for Academic Purposes*, 7(1), 27–37. http://dx.doi.org/10.1016/j.jeap.2008.02.004

Gosden, H. (2003). 'Why not give us the full story?': Functions of referees' comments in peer reviews of scientific research papers. *English for Academic Purposes*, 2(2), 87–101. http://dx.doi.org/10.1016/S1475-1585(02)00037-1

Halliday, M.A.K. (2005). *Computational and Quantitative Studies*. London and New York: Continuum.

Halliday, M.A.K., and Matthiessen, C.M.I.M. (2004). *An Introduction to Functional Grammar* (3rd ed.). London: Arnold.

Halliday, M.A.K., and Webster, J.J. (2009). *Continuum Companion to Systemic Functional Linguistics*. London and New York: Continuum.

Hasan, R. (2009). The place of context in a systemic functional model. In M.A.K. Halliday and J.J. Webster (Eds), *Continuum Companion to Systemic Functional Linguistics* 166–189. London and New York: Continuum.

Hyland, K. (2004). *Disciplinary Discourses: Social Interactions in Academic Writing*. Michigan: University of Michigan.

Hyland, K. (2006). Disciplinary differences: Language variation in academic discourses. In K. Hyland and M. Bondi (Eds), 14–43.

Hyland, K. and Bondi, M. (Eds) (2006). *Academic Discourse across Disciplines*. Bern: Peter Lang.

Hyland, K. and Diani, G. (Eds) (2009). *Academic Evaluation: Review Genres in University Settings*. London: Palgrave Macmillan. http://dx.doi.org/10.1057/9780230244290

Kourilová, M. (1996). Interactive function of language in peer reviews of medical papers written by NN users of English. *UNESCO-ALSED LSP Newsletter*, 19(1), 4–21.

Martin, J.R. (2009). Discourse Studies. In M.A.K. Halliday and J.J. Webster (Eds), *Continuum Companion to Systemic Functional Linguistics*, 154–165. London and New York: Continuum.

Martin, J.R., and Rose, D. (2003). *Working with Discourse: Meaning beyond the Clause*. London: Continuum.

Martin, J.R., and White, P.R.R. (2005). *The Language of Evaluation: Appraisal in English*. London: Palgrave.

Matthiessen, C.M.I.M., Teruya, K., and Lam, M. (2010). *Key Terms in Systemic Functional Linguistics*. London and New York: Continuum.

Oliveira, L.C., and Cheng, D. (2011). Language and the multisemiotic nature of mathematics. *Reading Matrix*, 11(3), 255–268.

Sellami-Baklouti, A. (2011). The impact of genre and disciplinary differences on structural choice: taxis in research article abstracts. *Text & Talk*, 31(5), 503–523. http://dx.doi.org/10.1515/text.2011.025

Sellami-Baklouti, A. (2013). A Probabilistic Approach to Choice: The Impact of Contextual Factors on the Tactic System in Research Article Abstracts. In G. O'Grady, T. Bartlett, and L. Fontaine (Eds), *Choice in Language: Applications in Text Analysis*, 215–242. London: Equinox.

Shaw, P. (2009). The Lexis and Grammar of Explicit Evaluation in Academic Book Reviews, 1913 and 1993. In K. Hyland and G. Diani (Eds), 217–235.

Swales, J.M. (2004). *Research Genres: Exploration and Applications*. Cambridge: Cambridge University Press. http://dx.doi.org/10.1017/CBO9781139524827

Thompson, G. (2004). *Introducing Functional Grammar* (2nd ed.). London: Arnold.

About the author

Akila Sellami-Baklouti is Associate Professor of English language and linguistics at the Faculty of Arts and Humanities of Sfax (Tunisia). Her latest publications include 'A Probabilistic Approach to Choice: The Impact of Contextual Factors on the Tactic System in Research Article Abstracts' (in O'Grady, Bartlett and Fontaine (eds), *Choice in Language: Applications in Text Analysis*, Equinox, 2013); 'Deviation of Deviant Themes from a Probabilistic Model: Thematic Choice in Enhancing Hypotactic Clause Complexes' (in Guirat and Triki (eds) *Deviation(s)*,Tunis: Imprimerie Officielle, 2013); 'Projecting Others' Speech: Linguistic Strategies' (in *Academic Research*, 2013); and 'The Impact of Genre and Disciplinary Differences on Structural Choice: Taxis in Research Article Abstracts' (*Text & Talk* 31 (5), 2011).

14

The permeable context of institutional and newspaper discourse: A corpus-based functional case study of the European sovereign debt crisis

Sabrina Fusari

University of Bologna

14.1 Introduction

This chapter offers a contribution to the investigations of the interface between Systemic Functional Linguistics, henceforth SFL, and Corpus Linguistics, henceforth CL (e.g. Thompson and Hunston 2006; Bednarek 2010), for the analysis of newspaper and institutional discourse, especially as concerns the potential offered by SFL's rich qualitative detail to provide a reliable key of interpretation for the typically abundant, but not always easy to systematise, language data that can be elicited from corpus analysis. More specifically, I use corpus tools and Systemic Functional categories to explore and interpret the degree of interdiscursivity or, more precisely, intercontextuality,[1] between the institutional and newspaper discourse of the European sovereign debt crisis, an issue that has recently been shaping national and supra-national policies and priorities, in the EU and beyond, obtaining wide coverage and comment in the news, especially financial and economic. Institutional and newspaper discourse can be considered to be particularly suitable for a study of the 'merger' (Crawford Camiciottoli 2007:9) and lack of 'discrete boundaries' (Gee 2010:37) between public contexts today, due to their shared key role in shaping ideologies and structures of power (Fairclough 1992; Beck, Giddens and Lash 1994). In extreme cases, the blend of news and institutional discourse has been so seamless as to give rise to text types, described as 'mediated political discourse (or hybrid)' (Berlin and Fetzer 2012:6), in which the media and institutional component of the register are so intertwined that they are no longer distinguishable.

This chapter has four sections: first, I provide a brief theoretical background introduction to the interaction between SFL and CL; second, I present and compare the layout of the corpora I assembled for my case study, as well as the main keywords and recurrent key word clusters identified in the corpora; third, I use some of the highest ranking keywords for an analysis of the patterns of transitivity (with particular attention to relational Processes) and modality (especially objective) that emerge from the corpora; finally, I offer some tentative conclusions on the consequences of the 'interpenetration' (Hasan 2004:27) of news and institutional discursive contexts for the reader's/ EU citizen's understanding of the sovereign debt crisis.

14.2 Theoretical background

First of all, some background information on the combination between SFL and CL should be provided. The importance of the interplay between these two approaches is clearly stated in the first chapter of Halliday and Matthiessen (2004:34–35), who claim that 'the corpus is fundamental to the enterprise of theorising language' and even argue that 'there is no excuse now for a grammar of a well-researched language such as English not to be corpus-based'. The strength of this argument, in Hunston's (2006:62) estimation, lies in the fact that both SFL and CL could be seen to be data driven, descriptive, and to share 'a concern to express grammatical choice in terms of social construal'. In addition, at least three other important points of contact exist between SFL and CL, but they should be approached with some more caution:[2] (a) the role of text; (b) the concept of lexicogrammar; and (c) the significance of concordance and collocation data.

First, both SFL and CL accord a central role to text, but their approach to the notion of text is different – sometimes quite radically. SFL views text as 'actualised meaning potential' (Halliday 1978:109), as 'the product of two processes combined: instantiation and realization' (Halliday and Matthiessen 2004:33), both as an 'artefact' and as a 'specimen' (Halliday and Matthiessen 2004:3–5), and it favours in-depth qualitative analysis of whole texts. CL, for its part, does not usually require close readings of whole texts, and tends to replace the concept of meaning potential with that of occurrence, so that 'meaning derives from intertextuality, i.e. from recurrence across a large number of texts' (Thompson and Hunston 2006:2). The direct consequence is that whereas, by text, SFL typically means whole texts, characterised by cohesion patterns, thematic structure, and information structure (in a word: texture), CL has a much broader view of the concept of text, as shown by Sinclair's definition of text as 'a succession of discrete items, those items being words' (Sinclair 2004:24). This view of text in CL therefore implies that individual concordance lines will also fall within its definition of text.

Second, both SFL and CL see grammar and lexis as one, but whereas SFL talks about lexicogrammar, and sees its two components as 'two poles of a single cline'/ 'two ends of the same continuum' (Halliday and Matthiessen 2004:43) or, from a slightly different but complementary perspective, it sees 'lexis as more delicate grammar' (originally in Halliday 1961:267; also in Hasan 1987), CL talks about lexical grammar, and sees it as 'an attempt to build together a grammar and lexis on an equal basis' (Sinclair 2004:164). Although the expressions lexicogrammar and lexical grammar may seem co-representational, this distinction entails a subtle divergence. SFL, as its name reveals, accords absolute primacy to the system, applies the principle of 'metaredundancy' (Martin and Rose 2003:254; Matthiessen, Teruya and Lam 2010:19–23), and has therefore been described as a 'theory heavy' model of language (Thompson and Hunston 2006:1) and 'a system in which everything falls into place' (Thompson and Hunston 2006:3). CL, on the other hand, claims a 'theory light' approach to the study of language (Thompson and Hunston 2006:2), a view which has led some scholars to the conclusion that CL might even be understood as being 'theory neutral' (Römer and Wulff 2010:100). More precisely, in the words of Tognini Bonelli (2001:178), 'there is no such thing as a theory-neutral stance, but in Corpus Driven Linguistics the attempt is made to suppress all received theories'. However, the whole idea that it is possible to dispense with a theoretical description, or indeed that the practice of corpus driven linguistics has actually minimised the role of theory, is challenged by SFL (Matthiessen and Nesbitt, 1996:41; Halliday 2004:24).

One final issue to at least allude to is the role of concordance and collocation. Although it is now widely accepted that 'corpus analysis [...] gives both a paradigmatic and syntagmatic view of language' (Flowerdew 2009:393), it can still be argued[3] that corpus research has traditionally focused on syntagms, seen from the perspective of collocation and word clusters, with a typically horizontal examination of concordance output. As a consequence, traditional concordancers and tagging mainly focus on structure and, for higher level corpus-based SFL investigations, special SFL-supporting software may be needed, without losing sight of the fact that 'automatic analysis gets harder the higher up we move along the hierarchy of stratification' (Halliday and Matthiessen 2004:49).

Despite these caveats, SFL and CL have co-operated through most of their history (as shown, most notably, by the study of collocations in Halliday 1966 and Sinclair 1966, as well as by Halliday's endorsement of Sinclair's COBUILD project in the early 1990s) and in a particularly systematic way in the latest decade, giving rise to such diverse studies as automated or semi-automated investigations of lexical cohesion (Flowerdew and Mahlberg 2009), research on 'emotion talk' (Bednarek 2008), inquiries into the ideologies, rhetorical patterns and several other features of news discourse (Bednarek 2006; Haarman and Lombardo 2009; Bevitori 2010), congressional/ parliamentary debates (Bayley 2004; Miller 2007; Miller and Johnson 2009), language education (Flowerdew 2003 and 2009), and many other areas and aspects of grammar and meaning in discourse.

14.3 The corpora

In the following pages, I provide an example of how the interpenetration of news and institutional registers[4] may be investigated through a synergy between SFL and CL. I do this by comparing two specially created small corpora, one consisting of *Financial Times* articles, and one made up of official statements published in the website of the European Union. The corpora contain all the texts published about the European sovereign debt crisis by the two sources in the week 9–15 December 2011; therefore, they reflect a particular stage in this crisis, coinciding with British Prime Minister David Cameron's refusal to sign up to a new EU treaty designed to enforce greater fiscal discipline and integration[5] in the eurozone.

Within the wider aim to exemplify the synergy between SFL and CL, I pursue two specific objectives: methodologically, to add to traditional corpus techniques by interpreting the behaviour of keywords[6] and keyword clusters through SFL labels; conceptually, to identify the main keywords in the discourse of the EU sovereign debt crisis, and to understand how these keywords may change, change their behaviour, or possibly remain the same, across different registers within the discourse of EU institutions.

The data are articulated as follows:

> News Corpus:
> 135 *Financial Times* articles (91,742 word tokens) published in the selected time span, retrieved from the database *Lexis-Nexis*,[7] with search words *Europe, debt* and *crisis*;

Institutional Corpus:
 25 items (33,331 word tokens) published in the selected time span, retrieved from the on-line Register of Documents of the Council of the European Union,[8] with search words *debt* and *crisis*.

The figures above show that the corpora are not comparable in the stricter technical sense of this term in CL, due to their considerably different dimensions (on the usability of these strictly speaking non-comparable corpora for SFL research, see Halliday and Matthiessen 2004:49–50; Matthiessen 2006:107; Bednarek 2010:238).

Keywords were extracted for each of the corpora by using Wordsmith Tools 4 (Scott 2007), and the BNC World wordlist as a reference corpus (RC) (Table 14.1 and Table 14.2).

Table 14.1: First 25 keywords (in order of keyness) in News Corpus

N	Key word	Freq.	%	RC. Freq.	Keyness
1	Eurozone	396	0.4193	0	5514.50
2	EU	196	0.2076	44	2500.40
3	Debt	347	0.3675	5400	2221.40
4	banks	352	0.3727	6932	2095.00
5	European	456	0.4829	20245	2007.00
6	Crisis	321	0.3399	5862	1956.70
7	Euro	207	0.2192	617	1954.40
8	ECB	142	0.1504	3	1947.80
9	Cent	522	0.5528	38385	1804.30
10	Per	539	0.5708	53693	1564.40
11	markets	227	0.2404	5898	1230.30
12	sovereign	150	0.1588	1061	1183.30
13	summit	168	0.1779	2508	1088.50
14	Bank	279	0.2954	16917	1063.80
15	Sarkozy	72	0.0762	0	1002.40
16	fiscal	131	0.1387	1320	946.50
17	Cameron	104	0.1101	868	788.24
18	financial	226	0.2393	16534	782.70
19	Brussels	114	0.1207	1495	766.71
20	investors	130	0.1377	2714	758.90
21	Europe	211	0.2234	16908	695.33
22	Draghi	46	0.0487	0	640.40
23	bonds	103	0.1091	1949	620.63
24	treaty	125	0.1324	4928	577.92
25	IMF	84	0.0890	1030	575.65

Table 14.2: First 25 keywords (in order of keyness) in Institutional Corpus

N	Key word	Freq.	%	RC. Freq.	Keyness
1	EU	141	0.4076	44	2043.60
2	European	296	0.8558	20245	1633.70
3	Euro	116	0.3354	617	1208.30
4	Fiscal	110	0.3180	1320	977.83
5	Growth	160	0.4626	12800	833.96
6	Member	139	0.4019	17230	607.53
7	Europe	130	0.3758	16908	556.26
8	Crisis	96	0.2775	5862	550.44
9	Commission	109	0.3151	9844	542.49
10	Council	147	0.4250	29138	512.52
11	States	123	0.3556	17873	500.42
12	Economic	125	0.3614	23376	449.29
13	Stability	64	0.1850	2122	442.96
14	Financial	102	0.2949	16534	393.88
15	Governance	36	0.1041	180	378.96
16	ECB	22	0.0636	3	332.10
17	We	339	0.9801	300833	329.78
18	Our	177	0.5117	93455	311.39
19	Barroso	22	0.0636	10	310.70
20	ESM	20	0.0578	8	285.09
21	Union	83	0.2400	17000	284.20
22	Global	51	0.1474	3527	280.05
23	Measures	60	0.1735	6878	271.07
24	President	73	0.2110	15747	242.95
25	EFSF	15	0.0434	0	238.94

A certain degree of permeability between the institutional and news discursive context is immediately detectable from the keywords that are common to both corpora (Table 14.3), and it is at least partly traceable to the high level of shared ideational meaning being construed.

Table 14.3: Common keywords in News and Institutional Corpus

Key word	Keyness News	Keyness Institutional
EU	2500.40	2043.60
European	2007.00	1633.70
Crisis	1956.70	550.44
Euro	1954.40	1208.30
ECB	1947.80	332.10
Fiscal	946.50	977.83
Financial	782.70	393.88
Europe	695.33	556.26

The presence of the item *crisis* in both keyword lists is certainly connected with its being one of the search words used to retrieve the texts from *Lexis Nexis* and from the EC Register of Documents. However, it is still worth noting the very different keyness value that this word obtains in the two corpora, demonstrating its considerably higher relative frequency in the News Corpus.

Perhaps even more revealing are the keywords that are exclusive to each corpus (Table 14.4). These keywords highlight some remarkable, potentially register specific or, to put it more accurately, register-idiosyncratic (Miller and Johnson 2009)[9] features, related to the different discourse communities that are addressed in the two corpora: the *FT*, as a leading business newspaper, exhibits much higher keyness values for items like *bank(s)*, *investors*, figures, and *debt*, whereas the transcription of speeches, memoranda and press releases that the Institutional Corpus is composed of place more emphasis on names of institutions, European identity (*we, our, union*), and general measures used to promote it (*growth, stability, governance*).

Again, the item *debt* appears in the keyword list because it was used as a search word for the retrieval of the texts to be included in the corpora. Interestingly, however, it ranks only thirty-fourth in the keyword list of the Institutional Corpus, for which it was also a search word. This demonstrates that, in comparison with the BNC data, the News Corpus discusses debt much more frequently than the Institutional Corpus.

Table 14.4: Keywords exclusive to each corpus

News	Keyness	Institutional	Keyness
Eurozone	5514.50	Growth	833.96
Debt	2221.40	Member	607.53
Banks	2095.00	Commission	542.49
Cent	1804.30	Council	512.52
Per	1564.40	States	500.42
Markets	1230.30	Economic	449.29
Sovereign	1183.30	Stability	442.96
Summit	1088.50	Governance	378.96
Bank	1063.80	We	329.78
Sarkozy	1002.40	Our	311.39
Cameron	788.24	Barroso	310.70
Brussels	766.71	ESM	285.09
Investors	758.90	Union	284.20
Draghi	640.40	Global	280.05
Bonds	620.63	Measures	271.07
Treaty	577.92	President	242.95
IMF	575.65	EFSF	238.94

14.4 Discussion of some register-idiosyncratic keywords

In this section, some keywords that are exclusive to each corpus are analysed in terms of their degree of register specificity, or register-idiosyncrasy.[10]

14.4.1 Eurozone

An item that can be considered to be largely idiosyncratic to news register is *Eurozone*, which is rare in the Institutional Corpus (12 occurrences) and one of the most frequent (396 hits), and by far the highest ranking keyword in the News Corpus. A close reading of the concordance shows that, in 47.5 per cent of its occurrences, *Eurozone* is a Classifier (Table 14.5).

Table 14.5: Collocations with *Eurozone* as a Classifier (News Corpus)

Collocation	#
eurozone debt	33
eurozone crisis	30
eurozone country(ies)	25
eurozone member(s)	15
eurozone government(s)	14
eurozone sovereign	
debt	8
bond(s)	4
eurozone leaders	11
eurozone fiscal	
discipline	4
treaty	2
crisis	2
compact	1
eurozone rescue	
fund(s)	6
efforts)	1
eurozone economy	6
eurozone bank(s)	5
eurozone bail-out(s)	4
eurozone periphery	3
eurozone peripherals	3

When it performs the function of Thing in the nominal group, *Eurozone* (modified by Deictic *the* or, more rarely, *a*) is frequently construed metaphorically as if it were a person. This discourse strategy is aided, as shown in Examples (1)–(3), by *Eurozone*'s participation in mental, behavioural and relational attributive Processes whose entry conditions imply that the Participants are human.

(1) Behavioural Process involving *Eurozone*

In short, if the eurozone *sneezes*, it is difficult for its neighbours to avoid catching a cold.

(2) Mental Process involving *Eurozone*

To that end, the eurozone should now *focus* minds on swiftly finalising a simple treaty.

(3) Relational Process involving *Eurozone*

The eurozone *has* no credible plan to fix the flaws of the eurozone.

In the Institutional Corpus, the function of *Eurozone* within the nominal group confirms the findings from the News Corpus (it is Classifier in 42 per cent of its occurrences). What makes the findings from the Institutional Corpus significantly different from those in the News Corpus is that, in concordances from the Institutional Corpus that include the item *Eurozone*, the Actor is *we* (identifying the EU), and *Eurozone* is almost always used in circumstantial elements. Therefore, in the Institutional Corpus, the eurozone is construed as remaining in the background of the Actor's actions; by contrast, in the News Corpus, the eurozone is represented as playing a more central and active role, as shown in Examples (1)–(3) above.

14.4.2 Debt

The second highest ranking keyword that is exclusive to the News Corpus is *debt*. This item has strong collocational ties with *sovereign, crisis, eurozone, government, markets* and, in over 25 per cent of its occurrences, it appears in the collocation *sovereign debt* or *sovereign debt crisis*. Therefore, from a frequency-oriented CL perspective, it is worth analysing the word cluster formed by *sovereign + debt + crisis*, rather than taking each of its individual lexical components separately. This nominal group is of significant interest in an SFL perspective, insofar as it belongs to the category of 'strings of lexical words without any grammatical words in between' (Halliday, 1989:169). These nominal groups, characteristic of much specialised writing, are typically difficult to understand, due to their lexical density and syntactic ambiguity, even when the meaning of the individual words that compose them is fairly transparent. The main reason for this ambiguity is what Halliday (1987[2003]:129–130) describes as a 'synoptic' or 'attic' mode of discourse, as opposed to the 'doric' style of everyday communication: this typically nominal style is rooted in 'an "expert" grammar, the kind of grammar that is prepared to throw away experiential information, to take for granted the semantic relations by which the elements are related to one another [...] That kind of grammar shuts the layman out' (Halliday 1987[2003]:133). Bayley (1993:275–276), while not endorsing the view of 'the nominal style as a conspirational device to exclude the intelligent layman from scientific discourse', lists a series of 'problems of linguistic opacity' in the interpretation of multiple Modifier + Head structure of the nominal group (Bayley 1993:273–274).

This potential for ambiguity in the reading of nominal groups is one key reason why the grammatical and semiotic resources that characterise technical discourses impact on the degree of accessibility to the 'discursive resources of power' (Martin and Rose 2008:228) by the wider public. In this specific case, the ambiguity mentioned by Halliday (1989) is reinforced by the fact that, although the term *sovereign debt* identifies, in the terminology of finance, the debt that national governments incur, this nominal group is frequently pre-modified by *Eurozone, European, Europe's* and *region's*, which are often used interchangeably, within the same text, as if they were synonyms. It is therefore less than clear to the non-expert or non-initiated where exactly the *sovereignty* lies. This ambiguity is not, however, a feature of the lexical words constituting the nominal group *sovereign debt crisis*, but of its grammar.

In a similar fashion to the previously analysed keyword *Eurozone*, *debt* is also represented metaphorically in the News Corpus, through the Processes in which it participates. This function is performed by material Processes realised by verbs like *explode, shake, strike* that construe the crisis as a bomb or weapon, as well as by relational Processes construed either by circumstantial verbs that imply a comparison (*intensify/ deepen*), or as relational intensive Processes of time-phase (*continue/ persist*) with markers of objective Modality (*was likely to/ would likely*). This combination between objective Modality and intensification/duration will almost certainly have an ideological impact on the readership, insofar as it construes the crisis materially as a *bomb* (*exploding, striking, shaking*) and relationally as an entity that becomes bigger and bigger (*intensifying, deepening, continuing*), unless austerity measures (described as *fiscal/budgetary/ effective discipline*; *fiscal compact/union/rules/treaty*; *financial/monetary stability*) are enforced. In other words, the writer construes the debt crisis as a catastrophic event[11] that warrants special economic measures systematically represented as entailing a cut in public expenditure. Readers are therefore led to concur with the writer's viewpoint, from which dissident voices are essentially excluded.

A comparison with the Institutional Corpus confirms the strong collocational tie between *sovereign* and *debt* (co-occurring in almost 29 per cent of their occurrences), and it also brings to light the presence of figures of speech like those shown in Examples (4)–(5).

> (4)   Repetition
> (a) We have at the same time a **sovereign debt** *crisis* and a financial *crisis*.
> (b) I understand that because of the **sovereign debt** *crisis*, but also the financial *crisis*, most of the media attention was based in terms of the response to the European *crisis*.
> (c) The European Union is in profound *crisis* – a financial *crisis*, an economic crisis, a **sovereign debt** *crisis*, a social *crisis*.

> (5)   Lexical and Grammatical Metaphor
> (a) We need to be at the same time *firemen* and stop the *spread* of the **sovereign debt crisis**.
> (b) We, the EU, are *manoeuvring* our way through the **sovereign debt crisis**.

These rhetorical devices are not used in the News Corpus, so they might be considered to constitute a characteristic feature of the institutional register, less permeable (see Hasan's Chapter, this volume) with the register of news than those seen so far. However, the ideological construal of the sovereign debt crisis is still comparable with the one in the News Corpus: the pounding rhythm created by the repetition of *crisis* in Example (4), and the nature of the metaphors in Example (5) may be considered to construe the debt crisis as a bomb, an illness, or a disaster, just like the material Processes illustrated above.

14.4.3 Banks

Another keyword worth analysing, not only for its remarkable frequency and keyness in the News Corpus, but also because of its importance for a general understanding of the EU debt crisis, is *banks*. The first feature

Table 14.6: Geographical/nationality Classifiers modifying *banks* (News Corpus)

Classifier	#
European	28
of which	
western European	3
US and European	2
French	11
Spanish	10
Europe's	9
German	7
Italian	6
Greek	6
Foreign	4
Eurozone	4
Western	3
region's	3
Greece's	2
Germany's	2
Austrian	2

that strikes the eye when a concordance of this item is examined is the frequency (31 per cent) with which it enters into a nominal group with a geographical/ nationality Classifier, as shown in Table 14.6.

The frequency and diversity of geographical Classifiers pre-modifying *banks* in nominal groups bring to light a contradiction in the corpus between the insistence on the need for a *fiscal/monetary union* and the quite diversified situations and stances of banks throughout the territory of the EU and its financial partners. Although the corpus consists of articles from a leading UK newspaper, British banks are hardly ever discussed, the priority being given to Europe's[12] banks in general, and to the banks of the countries (France, Germany) that have bought the highest quota of the debt of the most debt-laden countries quoted in the corpus (Greece, Italy, Spain). This is in sharp contrast not only with the BNC, in which UK/British banks are mentioned almost twice as many times as European banks (60 occurrences as against 31) but also with data from the IntUne project[13] 2007–2009, where UK/British banks are mentioned more than twice as many times as European ones (154 hits as against 66). This can perhaps be explained because the UK is not part of the eurozone: therefore, the collocation between *banks* and Classifiers related to Europe can be considered to be register-idiosyncratic not so much to the news register per se, but to the register of news about Europe.

Another remarkable feature of the concordance of *banks* is its association with a wide variety of verbs (173), almost 39 per cent of which construe a relational Process. An important caveat is in order at this stage: although, in unmarked congruent transitivity patterns, it is verbs that construe Processes, *verb* is still a class label (indicating 'in a general way its potential range of grammatical functions', Halliday and Matthiessen 2004:52), whereas Process is a function label (providing 'an interpretation of grammatical structure in terms of the overall meaning potential of the language', Halliday and Matthiessen 2004:52); so, in an SFL perspective, the two should not be confused. CL, on the other hand, has traditionally tended to mix these two levels (Neale 2006:162), assigning priority to the class level over the function one. In this analysis, therefore, because I aim to reconcile CL with SFL methodologies, I am not counting the number of verbs, but trying to associate each verb with the Process it construes, based on the co-text provided by concordances and extended fileviews (aiming for 'disambiguated word senses – rather than just for grammatical categories such as "verb"', Neale 2006:162).

A problem that emerges from this analysis is the difficulty of making a 100 per cent reliable calculation of the frequency of the different kinds of Processes. This largely depends on the fact that several Processes can be labelled in different ways, and in different contexts a Process can be stranded between two or more labels. This is typical of behavioural Processes (see Banks, this volume), but some uncertainty is also possible for relational Processes that express circumstances partially overlapping with mental or verbal Processes (Halliday and Matthiessen 2004:238). For the purposes of this analysis, I have classed as relational all the Processes, be they intensive, possessive or circumstantial, identifying or attributive, that serve 'to characterize and to identify' (Halliday and Matthiessen 2004:210), and I have used as guidelines the tables provided in Halliday and Matthiessen (2004) and Eggins (2004) in which Processes are associated with the most typical verbs that construe them.

Although they are slightly less frequent than in Matthiessen (2006:137), relational Processes are still significant in my News Corpus because of their diversity (there are 62 different relational Processes in this corpus that involve banks). Some of the most interesting in terms of their ideological orientation are shown in Table 14.7.[14]

The data in Table 14.7 appear to reveal, at least to this reader, a contradiction in news discourse, as reflected in this corpus, between banks construed as suffering from the debt crisis (being victims, having a higher

Table 14.7: *Banks* in relational Processes (News Corpus)

Clause/complex	relational Process	of the … kind
If the sovereigns go, Europe's banks *are* front line victims.	intensive	attributive: neutral
Forced to bolster capital ratios at home, the western banks that *dominate* central and eastern Europe are deleveraging fast.	intensive	attributive: quality
Yet the roll call of the foreign banks that *dominate* the region reads like a list of institutions that have suffered most in the eurozone crisis, magnifying the potential disruption.	intensive	attributive: quality
Nowadays, a lot of banks *have* a higher cost of funding than corporates – that makes it very difficult to be a lender to corporates.	possessive	attributive: neutral
These institutions *were not the cause* of 'the Greek problem'.	intensive	identifying: neutral/causation
And if all sovereign bonds are risky to some degree, it follows that the banks *no longer have* a base of risk-free capital.	possessive	attributive: neutral

cost, and being left without a base of risk-free capital, while all the time being wrongly accused of having caused 'the Greek problem') and as holding a dominant position. The contradiction fundamentally lies in the public perception of the crisis as having been largely caused by the banks buying and selling toxic funds, whereas the narrative presented here is different, as shown in statements like 'the roll call of the foreign banks that *dominate* the region reads like a list of institutions that have *suffered* most in the eurozone crisis, *magnifying the potential disruption*'. In just one clause complex, banks are construed relationally as dominant, mentally as suffering, and finally, they are portrayed as the Initiator of the potential worsening of the Eurozone's predicament.

This situation of uncertainty extends to what banks are represented as expected (interpreted as modalisation here, due to cotextual prosody), likely (modalisation), obliged or inclined (modulation) to do to face the debt crisis with the aid they are receiving from the ECB. Table 14.8 illustrates some examples within the realm of objective Modality.

Despite the objectivity conveyed by the use of these expressions, the degree of the modals is located between median and low. This seems to confirm, and actually reinforce the findings related to relational Processes involving banks, which highlight a situation of uncertainty, characterised

Table 14.8: Examples of markers of objective Modality associated with *banks*

are expected to follow/to require EUR115bn	modalisation: probability
are likely to fund their dollar assets	modalisation: probability
are the only institutions allowed to buy gilts	modulation: obligation
are unlikely to buy more government debt	modalisation: probability
aren't allowed to buy bank-issued ABS	modulation: obligation

by a contradiction between banks' strength in the region (e.g. dominate) and their weakness in securing funding (e.g. victims).

The first striking difference with the Institutional Corpus is the absence in it of any geographical/nationality Classifiers modifying *banks*. Relational Processes are the relative majority (44.4 per cent), and they tend to construe banks negatively, for example as *reluctant, facing problems, under pressure* and *slow to deliver*. The strong tension between banks and EU institutions is also evident in expressions like 'I am confident that banks are ready to embrace change' (Almunia, Speech 11/ 889, December 2011, 'A Fair and Open System for Payments in the Single Market') and 'Further progress is needed in these areas so that banks can fulfil their essential role in the economy' (Occasional Papers 88, December 2011, 'Economic Adjustment Programme for Ireland'). The actual speech function of these statements is clearly to exhort banks to follow a certain course of action, rather than to express true confidence that they will do so.

14.4.4 Growth

The last keyword I analyse in this chapter is *growth*, which ranks first among the Institutional Corpus keywords, but does not appear in the keyword list of the News one. Like *banks, growth* can be considered to be one of the most important keywords in order to understand the current scenario of the economic crisis, in Europe and beyond, because it is widely held to be not only the key measure of the economic success of a country, but also a reliable indicator of overall well-being, although this tenet of neoliberal economics has been challenged from different points of view (Krugman 1994; Latouche 2006. See also Halliday 1990[2003]:167, on how even grammar itself 'promotes the ideology of growth, or growthism').

In the Institutional Corpus, *growth* has strong collocational ties with *sustainable, Stability, Pact* (in the expression *Stability and Growth Pact*, which accounts for about 10 per cent of all the occurrences of *growth*), *annual* (in *Annual Growth Survey*), *global, jobs* (in *boost/generate/impact on growth and jobs*), *economic, austerity* (in *austerity-growth deadlock*),

Table 14.9: Nominal group complexes with *growth* (Institutional Corpus)

- Reforms and a growth strategy
- Debt instruments and a growth model
- Austerity and growth/austerity-growth
- Stability and (economic) Growth
- Fiscal consolidation and growth
- Job creation and growth
- Reforms for competitiveness and growth
- Sustainable jobs and growth
- Growth and in particular in services
- Growth and jobs
- Growth and employment
- Growth, innovation and job creation
- Growth and development
- Growth and reflation
- Growth and job creation
- Investment and global growth
- Growth and economic reform
- Growth and also social cohesion
- Growth and competitiveness

potential (in *potential for growth*) and *green*. Even more strikingly, a concordance of *growth* shows that, in about 30 per cent of its occurrences in the Institutional Corpus (if the dash in *austerity-growth* is considered to work as a coordinating conjunction, this figure rises to over 33 per cent), *growth* enters into nominal group complexes, as shown in Table 14.9.

The most straightforward interpretation of the expansion relations giving rise to nominal group complexes above would see the conjunction *and* as construing a paratactic relation of extension: however, the wider co-text shows that, in many cases, the conjunction *and* actually construes an implicit relation of enhancement-causation (X, and [*as a consequence*] growth), which is also detectable in the *austerity-growth* dyad quoted above. The wide variety of nouns that *growth* is linked to via the conjunction *and* also provides answers to a question that is central in the economic debate today, i.e., the actual meaning of the word *growth*, which Table 14.9 shows to be in close association with *jobs/employment* and *reforms*.

The meaning of *growth* in this corpus is also clarified by recurrent Epithets and Classifiers modifying *growth* as Thing (Table 14.10), as well as by the Things that *growth* modifies when it is used as Classifier (Table 14.11).

Table 14.10: Epithets and Classifiers modifying *growth* as Thing (Institutional Corpus)

Classifier	#
Annual	9
Sustainable	8
Global	7
Economic	7
Inclusive	4
Green	4
European	3
GDP	2

Table 14.11: Things modified by *growth* as Classifier (Institutional Corpus)

Thing	#
Pact	13
Survey	8
Strategy	2

Despite the variety of modifiers and expansions that *growth* is associated with in the Institutional Corpus, how exactly the EU plans to bring about this *growth* remains less than clear. Attempts to identify the meaning of *growth* in the corpus include those shown in Examples (6)–(8):

(6) statements by the president of the European Economic and Social Committee, Staffan Nilsson, who describes growth-enhancing measures as including
(a) education and skills, RandD, innovation, networks, energy and transport interconnections; public investment;
(b) effective implementation of innovation, better education and support for SMEs.

(7) speeches by the President of the European Commission, José Barroso, who mentions
(a) key decisions to prepare the relaunch of economic growth, through the development and strengthening of the single market, notably on the e-economy;
(b) green growth, energy security, and fight against climate change;
(c) education, research, innovation, also infrastructure (there is some infrastructure that can generate growth, namely if we address the problems of missing links in the European infrastructure) and energy;
(d) proposals to enhance growth such as support for SMEs, better regulation, tax initiatives, fast-tracking proposals, especially those

> that extend the benefits of the Single Market and, last but not the least, targeted investment at the European Union level, including through project bonds.

(8) a speech by the president of the ECB Mario Draghi, who claims that (a) sustainable growth can be achieved only by undertaking deep structural reforms that have been procrastinated for too long.

What these reforms might consist in, however, is left unexplained in Draghi's speech.

So, despite Barroso's insistence that

> we now have a European strategy for growth – Europe 2020. We have a substantially reinforced Stability and Growth Pact with the so-called Six-Pack, which will come into force today and will apply to all 27 Member States, a Pact which Barroso also describes metaphorically as a *Roadmap* for growth, there still seems to be much confusion as to what *growth* actually means within the context of an exit strategy from the EU debt crisis.

This is confirmed by the Epithets used to modify *growth* in the website of *Europe 2020 Growth Strategy*,[15] referred to above by Barroso: while *growth* is associated with the same Epithets that can be found in the Institutional Corpus (e.g. smart, sustainable, inclusive), proposals on how to achieve these targets are just as generic in the website as they are in the Institutional Corpus.

In the News Corpus, the meaning of *growth* is more clearly GDP-related, and generally connected with other economic data, as revealed by the collocations (*economic, global, GDP, low, outlook, rate, forecast*). The greater importance attached to the economic dimension of growth is confirmed

Table 14.12: Epithets and Classifiers modifying *growth* as Thing (News Corpus)

Classifier	#
Economic	14
GDP/ gross domestic product	7
Global	5
Low	5
Export	3
US	3
Continued	2
Eurozone	2
Income	2
Price	2

Table 14.13: Things modified by *growth* as Classifier (News Corpus)

Thing	#
rate(s)	6
Outlook	4
Bonds	3
forecast(s)	3
Stocks	2

by the Epithets and Classifiers that modify it (Table 14.12), as well as by the Things that *growth* modifies when it acts as a Classifer (Table 14.13).

In the News Corpus, almost no attention is paid to the Stability and Growth Pact, with only two occurrences, from the same text: an editorial criticising Mr Cameron's decision to veto the fiscal compact treaty and portraying, at the same time, the Pact as self-defeating. Examples (9)–(10) illustrate these occurrences.

> (9) The core decision was to strengthen fiscal discipline, so building what Angela Merkel, Germany's chancellor, and Nicolas Sarkozy, the French president, last week called a 'stability and growth union' – or, as I think of it, an 'instability and stagnation union'.

> (10) The decision is, instead, to try still harder with a stability and growth pact whose failures have been both predictable and persistent.

It appears clear, at least to this reader, that the growth that is advocated by the *Financial Times* (and therefore by the City of London) is not the same kind of growth that is pursued by EU institutions, whose discourse as exemplified in my Institutional Corpus lends more emphasis to the quality (e.g. sustainable, inclusive, green, etc.) than the quantity of growth. However, the degree of uncertainty that surrounds the actual implementation of the growth measures put forth in the Institutional Corpus reduces their likeliness to prevail over the more traditionally neoliberal view of growth that the News Corpus upholds.

14.5 Conclusion

To conclude what has necessarily been, due to both space constraints and the still ongoing nature of this study, only a preliminary account of the discourse of the EU sovereign debt crisis, some methodological and conceptual comments should be made. Methodologically, the marriage between SFL and CL meets all the requirements to be a valid and happy one, blessed by Halliday (2006) himself, as pointed out in Miller (2014). If the theoretical differences quoted in the introduction to this chapter are adequately taken into account, there will be a mutual and fruitful exchange between SFL's theoretical depth of detail and the CL (especially in its Corpus Driven strand) empiricist view that theory can, and indeed should, be derived from the data. Both approaches ask us to 'trust the text' – not by chance is Sinclair (2004) dedicated to Halliday – and the different ways in which they ask us to do so are largely complementary.

Directions for future research include:

(a) a substantial enlargement/redesign of the corpora, with a view to making them more systematic (e.g. creating partitions for different text types within the register of news discourse and EU institutional discourse; expanding the News Corpus to include an array of newspapers, and comparing data coming from different newspapers). Although size is not everything, and actually the appropriate size of a corpus depends on the kind of answers we aim to elicit from it, and the phenomena we intend to observe, 'the larger the corpus the more effectively it will reveal the system by which the texts are engendered, and from which they derive their meaning' (Halliday 2006:298).

(b) the use of more recent reference corpora (the BNC being dated 1994).

One viable alternative to the BNC that has been identified for a possible follow-up to this study is the set of British newspaper corpora belonging to the IntUne project, which promises to represent a suitable term of comparison with the News Corpus presented in this study, perhaps even more than the BNC, for a closer analysis of the idiosyncratic features of the news register. However, precisely because of its focus on news discourse, IntUne would perhaps be less readily comparable with my Institutional Corpus. As for the News Corpus, a preliminary comparison with the IntUne corpora of British newspaper discourse seems to confirm the reliability of the findings illustrated in this chapter, insofar as most of the highest ranking keywords remain the same (*eurozone, European, debt, banks, sovereign, crisis, Euro*) when IntUne is used as reference.

Another step to be accomplished is annotation, identified by Wu (2009:133) as 'crucial', but at the same time 'highly technical and complex', due to the necessity of coming up with a standard for annotation that will not only enhance the power of manual analysis needed at higher levels of stratification but also prove the most suitable to reflect, and subsequently retrieve, the association between each lexical item, at various levels of delicacy, and SFL labels. The problem is not a trivial one, and is currently being addressed by scholars involved in various projects, some of which are beginning to yield interesting results in terms of the possibility of performing semi-automated tagging also for systemic functional labels. Some automatic tagging is already possible in the latest releases of the UAM Corpus Tool, which is also perhaps the most popular SFL-aware corpus application, with 8,498 unique IP users as of March 2013 (O'Donnell, personal communication), but research is also progressing in the direction of developing other types of corpus concordancers and parsers (Halliday Centre Tagger, SysAm) specifically designed for systemic functional analysis. In light of these developments, which I explored in Fusari (2014), and despite the fact that much manual work is still required to tag structural functions, annotation is definitely an effort worth pursuing,

> particularly [...] for systemic functional linguistics, where the language is viewed to be multi-dimensional and multi-functional. With the availability of the corpus fully annotated in systemic functional terms, we will be in a very good position to unravel the complexity of language. (Wu, 2009:142)

Despite these limitations, the synergy between SFL and CL seems to offer a qualitatively meaningful and quantitatively reliable methodology for locating and analysing the similarities and differences between registers whose boundaries are not sharply defined. This is clearly the case for news and institutional discourse – news discourse itself having been considered (Van Dijk 2007:20; Montgomery 2011:227) as a particular type of institutional discourse, due to its professional and public nature, and its reliance on official sources (Machin and Mayr 2008:81). The permeability of inter-registerial boundaries becomes even more interesting when the news/institutional discourse involved is the EU's. Indeed, 'the process of making European integration intelligible and communicable in national publics' has been described as 'discursive Europeanization' (Kutter 2007): this expression underscores the centrality of discourse in shaping a true European identity and in solving the dialectic tension between the sovereignty of individual member states and their involvement in a closer integration (Grad 2008). For this and other reasons, the EU itself has been described as 'a hybrid' (Shore 2000:208; Cini 2007:369) giving rise to 'hybrid forms'(Wodak and Weiss 2005:129), both in language and in public spaces, for the analysis of which the marriage between SFL and CL seems to provide a useful methodological tool.

Notes

1   'I suggest the term *intercontextuality*, in an analogy to *intertextuality* and *interdiscursivity*, to refer to the various contexts that intermesh to influence or determine, and be influenced or determined by, texts, discourses, and other social practices' (Meurer 2004:86). Despite its popularity in the terminology of discourse analysis and other areas of language studies, Hasan has argued against the use of the term *interdiscursivity* as 'theoretically unanchored' (Hasan 2004:46). See also Scollon 2008:80–81.

2   As Halliday and Matthiessen (2004:34) have clarified, 'precisely because the corpus is so important it is better to be aware of what is good about it, and also what is potentially not so good'. This shows that SFL is particularly aware not only of the advantages – in fact, of the necessity – of using corpora for studying grammar, but also of its drawbacks.

3   See Bednarek (2010: 239–240) for a survey of the relevant literature and a discussion of this argument.

4   In this chapter, I adopt the definition of register used in Halliday and Matthiessen (2004:27) as a functional variety of language. It should be noted that this notion, unlike Martin's (1992) and Martin and Rose's (2008), encompasses that of genre and text type, in an attempt to 'bring out the way in which genres shade into one another, in a continuous, multidimensional space' (Matthiessen et al. 2010:220). See also Hasan 1995:283.

5   The agreement was described by the president of the European Central Bank (ECB), Mario Draghi, as a 'fiscal compact', an expression that has since become popular in both institutional and news discourse.

6   Keyness here is computed with Wordsmith Tools 4 (Scott 2007), which performs a comparison through a statistical function (log-likelihood) identifying the words that are significantly more frequent in the News and Institutional Corpora as opposed to the BNC, above a minimum threshold level. Therefore, words that are too rare to be representative (below 3 occurrences) are automatically excluded. See Paquot and Bestgen 2009:249.

7   http://academic.lexisnexis.eu/, only available by subscription, last accessed on 17 July 2013.

8   http://register.consilium.eu.int, freely available, last accessed on 14 August 2013.

9   'The term *idiosyncratic* strikes us as being more precise than *specific*, and for at least two reasons: there is always a certain amount of overlap between the material and social contextual variables governing diverse registers;

furthermore, the system, or total meaning potential of a language, may be immense, but it is not infinite. Thus it is predictable that what may be seen as "idiosyncratic" to one register will rarely be the exclusive property of that register' (Miller and Johnson 2009:72).

10 My thanks go to the Donna Miller and Paul Bayley for bringing my attention to this and other concepts and for their valuable advice throughout the editing process. Special acknowledgements to Paul Bayley for his advice and help in using the IntUne corpora for this study.

11 Luporini (2013:169–172) provides an in-depth analysis of the financial press' use of NATURAL FORCE and WEATHER metaphors 'conceptualising economic and financial processes as natural phenomena, following their own rules, and ultimately beyond human control' (Luporini 2013:172).

12 Possessives are best labelled as Deictics (Halliday and Matthiessen 2004:314; Bloor and Bloor 2004:140), but for the exclusive purposes of this analysis we consider their function in context as being semantically contiguous to their respective classifying adjectives (as in, e.g., Europe's banks = European banks).

13 The IntUne project (Bayley and Williams 2012) was a transnational interdisciplinary research project financed by the Sixth Framework programme of the European Union involving 30 European universities from 18 countries to study changes in the scope, nature and characteristics of citizenship in the European Union. It involved political scientists, sociologists and linguists. Among its products was a multilingual comparable corpus of media discourse in France, Italy, Poland and the UK. In comparison with the BNC, IntUne is not only more recent, thus offering a term of comparison for news discourse at a time when the common European currency had already been introduced, but it also provides an entirely different kind of reference because (unlike the BNC) it revolves specifically around media discourse, and it includes a set of British newspaper corpora collected from the *Guardian*, the *Daily Telegraph*, the *Scotsman* and the *Western Mail*, for a total of 49,598,200 words.

14 The labels are taken from Halliday and Matthiessen 2004:238–243.

15 Freely available, last accessed on 20 August 2013.

References

Alsop, S., and Gardner, S. (Eds) (2014). *Proceedings from the 24th European Systemic Functional Linguistics Conference and Workshop: 1st to 3rd July 2013*, Coventry University, UK: Department of English and Languages (DEL). http://curve.coventry.ac.uk/open/items/7b5b94aa-6984-48ad-b29a-9a8e9483fa2d

Bayley, P. (1993). Discourse order in the scientific abstract. In G.G. Castorina and V. Villa (Eds), *La Fortuna della Retorica*, 269–276. Lanciano: Metis.

Bayley, P. (Ed.) (2004). *Cross-Cultural Perspectives on Parliamentary Discourse*. Amsterdam and Philadelphia: John Benjamins. http://dx.doi.org/10.1075/dapsac.10

Bayley, P. and Williams, G. (Eds) (2012). *European Identity: What the Media Say*. Oxford: Oxford University Press. http://dx.doi.org/10.1093/acprof:oso/9780199602308.001.0001

Beck, U., Giddens, A., and Lash, S. (1994). *Reflexive Modernization. Politics, Tradition and Aesthetics in the Modern Social Order*. Cambridge: Polity Press.

Bednarek, M. (2006). *Evaluation in Media Discourse. Analysis of a Newspaper Corpus*. London: Continuum.

Bednarek, M. (2008). *Emotion Talk across Corpora*. Basingstoke, New York: Palgrave Macmillan. http://dx.doi.org/10.1057/9780230285712

Bednarek, M. (2010). Corpus linguistics and Systemic Functional Linguistics: interpersonal meaning, identity and bonding in popular culture. In M. Bednarek and J.R. Martin (Eds), *New Discourse on Language: Functional Perspectives on Multimodality, Identity, and Affiliation*, 237–266. London: Continuum.

Berlin, L.N., and Fetzer, A. (2012). Dialogue in politics. In L.N. Berlin and A. Fetzer (Eds), *Dialogue in Politics*, 3–17. Amsterdam and Philadelphia: John Benjamins. http://dx.doi.org/10.1075/ds.18.03ber

Bevitori, C. (2010). *Representations of Climate Change. News and Opinion Discourse in UK and US Quality Press: a Corpus-Assisted Discourse Study*. Bologna: Bononia University Press.

Bloor, T., and Bloor, M. (2004). *The Functional Analysis of English* (2nd ed.). London: Arnold.

Cini, M. (2007). *European Union Politics*. Oxford: Oxford University Press.

Crawford Camiciottoli, B. (2007). *The Language of Business Studies Lectures: A Corpus-Assisted Analysis*. Amsterdam and Philadelphia: John Benjamins. http://dx.doi.org/10.1075/pbns.157

Eggins, S. (2004). *An Introduction to Systemic Functional Linguistics* (2nd ed.). London: Continuum.

Fairclough, N. (1992). *Discourse and Social Change*. Cambridge: Polity Press.

Flowerdew, L. (2003). A combined corpus and systemic-functional analysis of the problem-solution pattern in a student and professional corpus of technical writing. *TESOL Quarterly*, 37(3), 489–511. http://dx.doi.org/10.2307/3588401

Flowerdew, L. (2009). Applying corpus linguistics to pedagogy: a critical evaluation. *International Journal of Corpus Linguistics*, 14(3), 393–417. http://dx.doi.org/10.1075/ijcl.14.3.05flo

Flowerdew, J., and Mahlberg, M. (Eds) (2009). *Lexical Cohesion and Corpus Linguistics*. Amsterdam, Philadelphia: John Benjamins. http://dx.doi.org/10.1075/bct.17

Fusari, S. (2014). The potential and drawbacks of annotation: what taggers can/cannot do. Contribution to Miller, D.R., Bayley, P., Bevitori, C., Fusari, S. and Luporini, A. *Ticklish Trawling: The Limits of Corpus Assisted Meaning Analysis*. In S. Alsop and S. Gardner (Eds), 100–111.

Gee, J.P. (2010). *An Introduction to Discourse Analysis: Theory and Method* (3rd ed.). London: Routledge.

Grad, H. (2008). The discursive building of European identity: diverse articulations of compatibility between European and national identities in Spain and the UK. In R. Dolón and J. Todolí (Eds), *Analysing Identities in Discourse*, 111–130. Amsterdam and Philadelphia: John Benjamins. http://dx.doi.org/10.1075/dapsac.28.08gra

Haarman, L., and Lombardo, L. (2009). *Evaluation and Stance in War News: A Linguistic Analysis of American, British and Italian Television News Reporting of the 2003 Iraqi War*. London: Continuum.

Halliday, M.A.K. (1961). Categories of the theories of grammar. *Word*, 17, 241–292.

Halliday, M.A.K. (1966). Lexis as a linguistic level. In C.E. Bazell, J.C. Catford, M.A.K. Halliday, and R.H. Robins (Eds), *In Memory of J.R. Firth*, 168–205. London: Longman.

Halliday, M.A.K. (1978). *Language as Social Semiotic: The Social Interpretation of Language and Meaning*. London: Arnold.

Halliday, M.A.K. (1987[2003]). Language and the order of nature. In N. Fabb, D. Attridge, A. Durant and C. MacCabe (Eds) *The Linguistics of Writing: Arguments between Language and Literature*, 135–154. Manchester: Manchester University Press. Reprinted in M.A.K. Halliday (2003) *On Language and Linguistics*, Volume 3 of the Collected Works of M.A.K. Halliday, edited by J.J. Webster, 116–138. London and New York: Continuum.

Halliday, M.A.K. (1989[2004]). Some grammatical problems in scientific English. In *Symposium in Education, Society of Pakistani English Language Teachers*, Karachi: SPELT. Reprinted in M.A.K. Halliday (2004) *The Language of Science*, Volume 5 of the Collected Works of M.A.K. Halliday, edited by J.J. Webster, 159–180. London and New York: Continuum.

Halliday, M.A.K. (1990[2003]). New ways of meaning: the challenge to applied linguistics. *Journal of Applied Linguistics* 6, 7–36. Reprinted in M.A.K. Halliday (2003) *On Language and Linguistics*, Volume 3 of the Collected Works of M.A.K. Halliday, edited by J.J. Webster, 139–174. London and New York: Continuum.

Halliday, M.A.K. (2004). The spoken language corpus: a foundation for grammatical theory. In K. Aijmer and B. Altenberg (Eds), *Advances in Corpus Linguistics. Papers from the 23rd International Conference on English Language Research on Computerized Corpora*, 11–38. Amsterdam and New York: Rodopi.

Halliday, M.A.K. (2006). Afterwords. In G. Thompson and S. Hunston (Eds), *System and Corpus. Exploring Connections*, 293–299. London: Equinox.

Halliday, M.A.K., and Matthiessen, C.M.I.M. (2004). *An Introduction to Functional Grammar* (3rd ed.). London: Arnold.

Hasan, R. (1987). The grammarian's dream: lexis as more delicate grammar. In M.A.K. Halliday and R.P. Fawcett (Eds) *New Developments in Systemic Linguistics, Vol 1: Theory and Description*, 184–211. London: Pinter.

Hasan, R. (1995). The conception of context in text. In P. Fries and M. Gregory (Eds), *Discourse in Society: Functional Perspectives. Meaning and Choice in Language: Studies for Michael Halliday*, 183–283. Norwood, NJ: Ablex.

Hasan, R. (2004). Analysing discursive variation. In L. Young and C. Harrison (Eds), *Systemic Functional Linguistics and Critical Discourse Analysis: Studies in Social Change*, 15–52. London: Continuum.

Hunston, S. (2006). Phraseology and system: a contribution to the debate. In G. Thompson and S. Hunston (Eds), *System and Corpus. Exploring Connections*, 55–80. London: Equinox.

Krugman, P. (1994). The myth of Asia's miracle. *Foreign Affairs*, 73(6), 62–78. http://dx.doi.org/10.2307/20046929

Kutter, A. (2007). Petitioner or partner? Constructions of European integration in Polish print media debates on the EU constitutional treaty. In N. Fairclough, G. Cortese, and P. Ardizzone (Eds), *Discourse and Contemporary Social Change*, 433–457. Bern: Peter Lang.

Latouche, S. (2006). *Le pari de la décroissance*. Paris: Fayard.

Luporini, A. (2013). *Metaphor in Times of Crisis: Metaphorical Representations of the Global Crisis in The Financial Times and Il Sole 24 Ore 2008*. University of Pisa, unpublished PhD dissertation.

Machin, D., and Mayr, A. (2008). News discourse I: understanding the social going-ons behind news texts. In A. Mayr (Ed.), *Language and Power. An Introduction to Institutional Discourse*, 62–89. London: Continuum.

Martin, J.R. (1992). *English Text: Systems and Structure*. Amsterdam and Philadelphia: John Benjamins. http://dx.doi.org/10.1075/z.59

Martin, J.R., and Rose, D. (2003). *Working with Discourse. Meaning beyond the Clause*. London: Continuum.

Martin, J.R., and Rose, D. (2008). *Genre Relations: Mapping Culture*. London: Equinox.

Matthiessen, C.M.I.M. (2006). Frequency profiles of some basic grammatical systems: an interim report. In G. Thompson and S. Hunston (Eds), *System and Corpus. Exploring Connections*, 103–142. London: Equinox.

Matthiessen, C.M.I.M., and Nesbitt, C. (1996). On the idea of theory-neutral descriptions. In R. Hasan, C. Cloran, and D. Butt (Eds), *Functional Descriptions: Theory in Practice* 39–83. Amsterdam and Philadelphia: John Benjamins. http://dx.doi.org/10.1075/cilt.121.04mat

Matthiessen, C.M.I.M., Teruya, K., and Lam, M. (2010). *Key Terms in Systemic Functional Linguistics*. London: Continuum.

Meurer, J.L. (2004). Role prescriptions, social practices, and social structures: a sociological basis for the contextualization of analysis in SFL and CDA. In L. Young and C. Harrison (Eds), *Systemic Functional Linguistics and Critical Discourse Analysis: Studies in Social Change*, 85–99. London: Continuum.

Miller, D.R. (2007). Towards a typology of evaluation in parliamentary debate. *Textus*, 20(1), 159–180.

Miller, D.R. (2014). On negotiating the hurdles of corpus-assisted meaning analysis – while doing appraisal analysis. Contribution to Miller, D.R., Bayley, P., Bevitori, C., Fusari, S. and Luporini, A. *Ticklish Trawling: The Limits of Corpus Assisted Meaning Analysis*. In S. Alsop and S. Gardner (Eds), 100–111.

Miller, D.R., and Johnson, J.H. (2009). Strict vs. nurturant parents? A corpus-assisted study of congressional positioning on the war in Iraq. In J. Morley and P. Bayley (Eds), *Corpus Assisted Discourse Studies on the Iraq Conflict. Wording the War*, 34–73. London: Routledge.

Montgomery, M. (2011). Discourse and the news. In K. Hyland and B. Paltridge (Eds), *The Continuum Companion to Discourse Analysis*, 213–227. London: Continuum.

Neale, A. (2006). 'Matching' corpus data and system networks: using corpora to modify and extend the system networks for TRANSITIVITY in English. In G. Thompson and S. Hunston (Eds), *System and Corpus. Exploring Connections*, 143–165. London: Equinox.

Paquot, M., and Bestgen, Y. (2009). Distinctive words in academic writing: a comparison of three statistical tests for keyword extraction. In A. Jucker, D. Schreier, and M. Hundt (Eds), *Corpora: Pragmatics and Discourse*, 247–269. Amsterdam and New York: Rodopi.

Römer, U., and Wulff, S. (2010). Applying corpus methods to written academic texts: explorations of MICUSP. *Journal of Writing Research*, 2(2), 99–127. http://dx.doi.org/10.17239/jowr-2010.02.02.2

Scollon, R. (2008). *Analyzing Public Discourse. Discourse Analysis in the Making of Public Policy*. London: Routledge.

Scott, M. (2007). *Wordsmith Tools, Version 4.0*. Oxford: Oxford University Press.

Sinclair, J. (1966). Beginning the study of lexis. In C.E. Bazell, J.C. Catford, M.A.K. Halliday, and R.H. Robins (Eds), *In Memory of J.R. Firth*, 410–430. London: Longman.

Sinclair, J. (2004). *Trust the Text. Language, Corpus and Discourse*. London: Routledge.

Shore, C. (2000). *Building Europe: The Cultural Politics of European Integration*. London: Routledge.

Thompson, G., and Hunston, S. (2006). Introduction. System and corpus: two traditions with a common ground. In G. Thompson and S. Hunston (Eds), *System and Corpus. Exploring Connections*, 1–14. London: Equinox.

Tognini-Bonelli, E. (2001). *Corpus Linguistics at Work*. Amsterdam and Philadelphia: John Benjamins. http://dx.doi.org/10.1075/scl.6

Van Dijk, T. (2007). Macro contexts. In D. Scheu Lottgen and J. Saura Sánchez (Eds), *Discourse and International Relations*, 3–26. Bern: Peter Lang.

Wodak, R., and Weiss, G. (2005). Analyzing European Union discourses: theories and applications. In R. Wodak and P. Chilton (Eds), *A New Agenda in (Critical) Discourse Analysis: Theory, Methodology and Interdisciplinarity*, 121–137. Amsterdam and Philadelphia: John Benjamins. http://dx.doi.org/10.1075/dapsac.13.10wod

Wu, C. (2009). Corpus-based research. In M.A.K. Halliday and J.J. Webster (Eds), *Continuum Companion to Systemic Functional Linguistics*, 128–142. London: Continuum.

About the author

Sabrina Fusari is an Associate Professor of English Linguistics at the University of Bologna (Italy). Her interests include corpus assisted discourse analysis, intercultural rhetoric, Systemic Functional Linguistics, English for specific purposes, translation theory and methodology. Her recent publications focus on privatisation discourse: 'Anglicisms in the discourse of Alitalia's bailout in the Italian press' (in *The Anglicization of European Lexis,* Furiassi, Pulcini and Rodríguez González, eds, Benjamins, 2012); 'A miracle. Madonna!': irony in the representation of Alitalia's privatization by the Italian, British and US American press' (in *Discourse & Society,* 2013).

Part IV
A closing statement: Hybridity – or permeability?

15

In the nature of language: Reflections on permeability and hybridity

Ruqaiya Hasan

Macquarie University

> It is ... imperative that we remember what we are doing and how we are doing it, and especially at what level or levels of abstraction and of statement.
>
> [Firth 1968: 199]

> We are all mistaken in our common belief that any word has an 'exact meaning'.
>
> [Whorf 1956: 258]

15.1 Preamble

I wonder if the first half of my title displays some hybridity? Of course I know that both the structure and the words have been deliberately 'appropriated' – everything except the last word comes from the title of the Inaugural Lecture by Mary Douglas (1975:210). Her title had been 'In the nature of things'; I replaced the last word with mine, 'language', realising that the statements here are not as well researched as the material presented in her lecture; and what I have to say is certainly not so widely applicable as to satisfy that sense of universality that she rightly wished to claim by choosing the word 'things'. The problem she explored was why and how, apparently everywhere in the world, we human beings have created 'a boundary between ourselves and animal creation ...', why we reject the idea of the slightest fuzziness between these two categories. My chapter, by contrast, concerns a small matter in the scheme of 'things': it is simply an exploration of certain problems in the description of language that might perhaps raise the same issue of fuzziness. Is there a systemic character to this fuzziness or is it just a random happening? Is it in the nature of language as system to have 'permeable' categories, and is 'hybridity' related to permeability? But of course the reader is entitled to ask: what is permeability, and what is it doing in a volume whose focus is clearly on hybridity?

This introductory section, beginning and ending with questions, indicates the tone of my contribution: throughout, there will probably be many more questions than answers. I will begin with a recount describing how 'permeable' and its formal scatter found their way into my discourse (section 15.2). By presenting some details of the analysis of reasonably well-defined categories of language, I will try to show that permeability is a characteristic of certain categories recognised in language on the basis of principled descriptions. I hope to discuss two examples of permeability active in categories at the stratum of lexicogrammar, at least one in some detail at the more grammatical end of the spectrum (section 15.3), and the other at the more lexical end (section 15.4). There are good reasons for suggesting that permeability is operative not only at the lexicogrammatical stratum but also on the strata of semantics and context: together these three strata cover approximately the area that Hjelmslev referred to (1961) as the 'content plane' of language. The approach to strata and realisation taken here is in keeping with my interpretation of Halliday's modelling of language in SFL (Hasan 2013; 2014a; Matthiessen 2015).[1] Throughout this presentation, I will try to show that, as elsewhere in language, permeability cannot be taken as a licence for crossing boundaries anywhere, anyhow: if language is to function as a communal meaning potential then sign relations will be subject to certain regularities. So while attempting to illustrate how permeability works across categories, I will try also to show how this relation has a systematic basis; it is not just an occurrence, a product of some 'historical accident'. I will suggest (section 15.5) that permeability is predicated by the probabilistic nature of language: it is an instance of 'give' in a tightly held system that comes into being by the myriads of mutual relations (Hjelmslev 1961; Saussure 1966; 2006; Lamb 1999). So, the patterns of permeability most probably inhere in language: it may even be a feature of human modes of thought according to Zadeh, who has suggested that 'fuzziness of granules ... is characteristic of the ways in which human beings granulate information and manipulate it' (1997:111).

In closing the chapter, I will raise a few questions about the relations of permeability and hybridity: do these terms refer to the same/similar concepts? If not, does some other relation hold between them? It is important to enquire what basis there is for recognising hybridity or what it contributes to a linguistic theory; and under what conditions it surfaces in language use. If something is described as a hybrid of 'a' and 'b', does this add to the understanding of the nature of 'a' and/or 'b', or of the hybrid 'ab'? In raising these questions I regret I do not yet hold this volume in my hands at the time of writing; it might hold some answers to these questions. If permeability and hybridity are two names for the same phenomenon, then I fear I am, most probably, carrying coals to Newcastle: at this moment, at least, 'hybridity' is not part of my linguistics vocabulary.

15.2 Permeability

As for 'permeability', I first encountered the word in the late 1960s. In listening to Basil Bernstein use the term, I had a sense that he was talking of a kind of relationship between concepts which, though clearly distinct from each other, appeared not to be totally sealed off – not 'crisp', in Zadeh's terms, as one would expect theoretical concepts to be. I had been working on the final draft of a paper where the aim was to position 'code', 'register' and 'social dialect' *vis-à-vis* each other (Hasan 1973[2005]): naturally the word attracted me. A search of the dictionary revealed that something was 'permeable' if it had the capacity to allow a 'substance' to pass through, to pervade, and so on. It did not specify much detail about the nature of that substance; neither had it occurred to me to pursue those questions. It had seemed enough that in my reading of Halliday, McIntosh and Strevens (1964) at that moment, the mutual relationship of field, tenor and mode of discourse was well described by that word: the authors had assigned the task of defining and identifying register to the three contextual parameters (1964:99, italics added):

> It is as the product of these three dimensions of classification that we can best define and identify register. The *criteria are not absolute or independent*; they are all variable in delicacy, and *the more delicate the classification the more the three overlap*. The formal properties of any given language event will be those associated with the intersection of the appropriate field, mode and style. ['style' was later renamed 'tenor', RH].

It is in this sense that, for some decades now, I have used the term 'permeability' quite regularly and almost exclusively referring to the mutual relations of the three contextual parameters. The permeability of these categories implies that normally each could work efficiently in independence from the others, but there would be occasions when one or both of the others could not be entirely ignored. So long as the three were not 'strongly classified', i.e., their boundaries were not sealed, the three would constitute the necessary and sufficient environment for both the material situational setting and the attributes of the relevant context. (for discussion Hasan, forthcoming). I have used permeability as another example of the fact that 'all descriptions leak at some point', taking note of the fact that the theory had located the parameters *at the same level of abstraction*, i.e., the stratum of context of situation and culture. Each was simply an aspect of the stratum that participated in text activation; from which it follows that in a systemic representation of their description, they would need to be shown as simultaneous vectors.

But to be quite frank, these two facts – one, that the parameters were permeable *and* two, that they belonged to the same stratum of language – had appeared coincidental: I had seen no necessary connection between the two facts until quite recently. The idea that these two facts may be more than coincidental began to dawn on me very slowly and in a rather different context: this happened in the early 1990s in doing some preliminary research for a talk concerning a comparative study of the material and mental process in English and Urdu.[2] This naturally focused attention on the grammar and semantics of two tense choices in the two languages. But even when I began this work, I had no idea that this was the first step in a long and much interrupted journey towards understanding the theoretical significance of permeability in SFL as a linguistic theory (section 15.3–15.3.5).

15.3 Permeability in two grammatical categories

Given the focus of my talk, the two tenses I chose to work on were the 'simple present' and the 'present-in-present'. The resources for thinking grammatically about tense had been available since the mid-1960s in what was to later become SFL (Halliday 1976:136–158): here, seen from the perspective of the logical metafunction, the 'present' tense is a simplex, while the present-in-present, involving serial tense choices, is a 'tense complex'. These two represent just two of the tense types from among the 36 tenses that make up 'system I: Finite' (see Halliday and Matthiessen 2014; Table 6 (13):347, for the entire set; for the underlying system network of the English verbal group, see Figure 6 (19):349). The categories at the stratum of lexicogrammar are the linguistic means of construing meaning, and as Firth reminds (1957:181; *italics original*) 'By means of linguistics we hope to *state facts systematically* and especially to make *statements of meaning*'. At that point, while the resources for making statements about grammar were readily available in SFL, searching for help on the semantics of tense was a different story. There was not much literature on meaning apart from comments interspersed in the grammatical description of tense; these worked well enough as a guide, but at that initial stage of my work, I made use of my fairly basic semantic network (Hasan 1983, mimeo) of English 'time'.[3]

15.3.1 On the semantics of tense

The initial semantic network of time was much inspired by Whorf (1956), who saw time as an abstract phenomenon of nature, not something naturally or directly perceived by the sense. According to Whorf the conception of time that ordinary human beings work with in their work-a-day life was based on 'fashions of speaking'. The idea of time as not a sens-ible phenomenon in the nature of things, that was not by itself accessible to the human senses, is also supported by the logician Reichenbach (1957:115–116, italics original):

> … we never measure a 'pure time', but always a *process*, which may be periodic as in the case of the clock, or nonperiodic as in the case of the moving mass point. Every lapse of time is connected with some process, for otherwise it could not be perceived at all. The measurement of time is therefore based upon an assumption about the behaviour of certain physical mechanisms.

How can we test this assumption? There is only one answer: we cannot test it at all.

The above crisp 'scientific' account of time reminds one somewhat of Whorf's views on time: he thought that the only 'sense' of time human beings could normally arrive at 'sensuously' was that of 'latering' – i.e., getting later and later. In my reading, his discourse about the ontology of cosmic phenomena was often presented in three perspectives: (a) what may actually be sensed as in nature; (b) what language models as nature; and (c) what speakers imagine nature to be. Each of these, according to Whorf, presented a different view of the cosmos. The first, speaking rationally, demanded well-developed, perhaps technological, means for exploring natural phenomena. It follows that only researchers and theorists, with understanding of knowledge and command over technology, could deal with this exotic 'un-commonsense' face of nature: the models of reality that they produced stand in complex relation to the communal ways of knowing; language happens to be the most powerful among these ways of knowing. The second consisted of the many faces of work-a-day reality presented by language. What the members of a speech community work with is a 'common-sense' knowledge as produced by their own language: the habitual behaviours of a community are in this way simply 'language in action'. The third imagined natural phenomena as encapsulated naturally in one's language and revealed to its speaker: this was simply a mirage.

So far as the relations of the first two are concerned, every language according to Whorf produces some 'model' of nature but there is no reason for believing that any of these models is a 'doppelgänger' of the REAL nature. Each of these models must relate well enough to that reality to enable the language to work largely successfully in the living of life. However, as Whorf often said, nature does not stare its beholder in the face; and the faces of nature as produced by language are like so many encrypted messages, requiring a deep understanding of the code: the principles underlying the relation of the linguistic models to nature are different in each case; and these principles, like nature itself, are inscrutable to ordinary speakers much in the same way as the scientists' models are to the 'lay' persons. Whorf believed that the third view – the speakers' image of reality – is not founded on any direct 'natural', 'spiritual relation' with nature, as commonly imagined: instead, their image of nature and their belief in its veracity rely simply on the communal use of language – on what he called 'fashions of speaking'. Speakers see the invisible only as their language chooses to show it to them: like readers of fiction, they universally enjoy a suspension of disbelief with respect to the representations made by their language. So, the arguments used to justify their belief in the imagined knowledge of the world are, in the last resort, based on a circular logic: the images they take as real, believing themselves to better know reality, arise from a misconception of *how their own language works*.

To Whorf, this smacked of both ignorance and arrogance: as he points out (Whorf 1956:144, *capitals original, italics added*):

> We can of course CONSTRUCT AND CONTEMPLATE IN THOUGHT a system of past, present, future, in the objectified configuration of points on a line. This is what *our general objectification tendency leads us to do and our tense system confirms*.

Whorf attempted to demonstrate this particularly with reference to the 'objectification tendency' (134–159), found mostly in Standard Average

European languages: he argued that this 'objectification tendency' is far from universal to language; the adherence to objectification is rooted in the same principles that activate the creation of 'acceptable linguistic patterns' in SAE languages. When other languages are analysed using similar linguistic methodology, the tendency of objectification is found to be missing from them: as an example of this claim, he compared Hopi, an American Indian language, with SAE languages. But Whorf is not alone in his beliefs: we have been reminded by Halliday (2014) of other brilliant linguists such as Sapir (1921) and Mathesius (1964) who have recognised the existence of an over-all underlying principle that gives each language 'a certain cut' not found in others, a design or disposition unique to each language: for Mathesius it was 'linguistic characterology' (1964:59–67); Sapir (1921:120) called it 'a basic plan, a certain cut, to each language'; and Whorf (1956) referred to it as 'fashions of speaking'. A great admirer of Sapir, he attempted to actually show how the basis of such 'a cut' might be established for SAE languages by carrying out a close analysis of the principles governing the 'configurative rapport' revealed in the 'patternment' scheme of a language, which produces its unique web of meanings. It is this 'configurative rapport' in linguistic patterns that creates the representation of a 'real world' for the speakers of a language.

In the history of linguistics there have been many and diverse conceptualisations of semantics, but none is as demanding as that of Whorf: his study of cryptic patterns that determine a language's style of meaning goes beyond lexicogrammatical analysis, to an additional level of analysis whose job it is to establish the 'configurative rapport' that governs the formation of wording-meaning patterns in a language. It is this deepest level of patterning, ignored in most other models, that, in Whorf's view, reveals the principle(s) underlying the meaning making 'cut' of a language. But, exciting as the prospect of this latter kind of analysis is, the semantics of tense that I employed in my analysis did not go beyond the first stage: its aim has been to examine only the semantics of the grammatical categories far enough – i.e., to ask how those meanings are made that in the end construe the speakers' view of the world (Halliday and Matthiessen 1999) – a view of nature created semantically, whose 'naturalness' will be seldom questioned.

There is one very good reason for assigning primacy to such semantic reality. We do not know exactly when that property of human language evolved which Whorf (1956:220–231) referred to as patternment, but it is the unpacking of the patterns that forms *the* secret of that deeper level of meaning making, and this seems to be true for all human language as far as their recorded history shows: languages change across time and given the same 'état de langue' they display principles of synchronic variation. And of course the individual patterns of wording-meaning vary both intra- and inter-culturally. Despite displaying variation across historical time and cultural space, both inside the same culture and across cultures, the method of meaning construal has, in principle, remained the same in human history: any system, that is an instance of language as a semiological system, must make meaning by patternment. Obviously, then, the ability to compare the world views construed by the meanings of the innumerable languages will call for an understanding of how such meanings are actually construed. But the sad fact is that, although the 'science of meaning' is said to predate the publication of Bréal (1964), who invented the word 'semantics', this kind of understanding, especially in its finer details, has eluded linguistics.[4] SFL has assigned the task of representing 'the potential of meaning' to the stratum of semantics: the job assigned to it includes a paradigmatic enquiring into the details of how linguistic meanings are construed, how the units of meaning configure, and how they create the speech community's view of work-a-day reality. Being a stratal theory, SFL offers good resources for such stratified enquiry: semantics primarily exploits the resources provided by stratification and realisation. In pursuing this enquiry it uses the 'trinocular perspective', which allows a view of what systems of meaning are available to the community; how lexicogrammatical categories construe the choices of those semantic systems; how these semantic categories might be related to each other; and how they construe the categories located at the stratum of context. The details of this complex story cannot be pursued here. As for the patterns construing time lexicogrammatically, I will rely here largely on the description of tense presented in Halliday and Matthiessen (2014).

There are, however, other facts to be remembered about tense and time: one was implicit in the above extract from Reichenbach, namely that time can be measured only in the context of some process. There is no way of measuring the present, the past, or the future: what one measures is the *lapse of time*. Of course, the *measurability* of time is not the issue in linguistics; rather, the important issue is the *nature of time* and that, as SFL has suggested, can be construed by tenses and the temporal circumstances, always as they occur *in specifiable textual and contextual contexts*. Strange as this may sound, time is extraordinarily sensitive to a number of co-textual and/or contextual factors. For example, the present tense construes one kind of time if the clause's process type is relational, as in *electron is the first subatomic particle, gold is a precious metal*, or *the baby is asleep*; BUT the same tense will construe a somewhat different time when used in the context of a material process, as in *gold does not rust, they are making a lot of noise* and *it wakes the baby up*. And as I will show below this same simple present tense with the same material process type, may construe a different time as in, *Haneef takes a start, runs in and bowls*. So the meaning of an English tense varies not only across distinct process types but with changing environments. Quoting Whorf (1956:258):

> ... the 'patternment' aspect of language always overrides and controls the 'lexation' (Nama) or name-giving aspect. Hence the meanings of specific words are less important than we fondly believe. Sentences, not words, are the essence of speech, just as equations and functions, and not bare numbers, are the meat of mathematics. We are all mistaken in our common belief that any word has an 'exact meaning'.

The theme of changing environment also recurs in Firth (1957), though he tended to refer to it as 'context'. And an explanatory version of this tendency in language is implicit in Hjelmslev (1961) when he claims that linguistic strata must logically be 'non-conformal': the implication is that there must be some units not in a one-to-one relation with the units on the contiguous strata. The following group of factors specifies the context of the simple present and present-in-present tenses in my earlier analysis (Hasan 2011) as well as in the present one, unless otherwise indicated:

- the tenses occur in a Finite clause, and pertain to System I: 'Finite';
- the clause must be 'mood selecting', specifically 'indicative', so neither 'imperative', nor 'hypotactic';
- 'Process' in clause is 'material': (action) e.g., *run, throw, put, make, give*, (i.e., [+volition]) or (supervention), e.g., *stumble, grow, rot, stink*, (i.e., [-volition]);
- typically 'active' or 'middle' voice.[5]

15.3.2 Time and tense: (a) default meaning in simple present

Beginning, then, with the 'simple present', first, two naturally occurring extracts, one written, the other casual spoken, where those instances of simple present tense which meet the condition just described above have been *italicised*.

> **Extract 1: *Evolution: View from the 21st Century*.** (Shapiro 2011:7). (1) Living cells *do not operate* blindly. (2) They continually *acquire* information about the external environment (3) and *monitor* their internal operation. (4) Then they *use* their information (5) to guide the processes essential to survival, growth, and reproduction. (6) Cells

constantly *adjust* their metabolism to available nutrients, (7) *control* their progress through the cell cycle (8) to make sure (9) that all progeny are complete at the time of division, (10) *repair* danger (11) as it occurs, (12) and *interact* appropriately with other cells.

Extract 2: *Rhetorical Units and Decontextualisation*. (Cloran 1994: Appendix A:13)
[casual conversation: Mother with Stephen 3;6]

Mother: (1) but you might not get mandarins from it
Stephen: (2) why?
Mother: (3) because when you plant seeds from mandarins or oranges (4) sometimes you *get* very strange fruit (5) or sometimes you *don't get* much fruit at all (6) so you have to plant a tree that's been grafted – that's been stuck on (7) they're special trees that they *make* by sticking one tree to another
Stephen: (8) how *do* they *stick* it?
Mother: (9) well I think they *cut* it in a special way (10) and they *put* them together (11) and then they *bind* stuff around the outside (12) to hold them together (13) till they *grow* together … (14) they eventually *grow* together the same way as when – (15) if you cut yourself (16) the skin *grows* back together again, doesn't it? (17) the two pieces of skin *grow* back together again (18) well the tree – the two bits of the tree – *grow back* too (19) so you don't need to use glue or anything
Stephen: (20) why?
Mother: (21) oh you just need to hold it there (22) so the tree *mends* itself …

I have sometimes quipped about the traditional term 'simple present' being an utter misnomer: for the fact is that neither is this tense 'simple' by being 'transparent in its meaning', nor does it refer to 'present time', in the sense of time coinciding with speaker's moment of speaking. In SFL, when this 'present' tense is called 'simple', this is in contrast with 'complex' (as in 'clause complex'): the tense choices, simple or serial, derive from an experiential system oriented to the logical metafunction as applied to the English verbal group; the 'serial tense' could have been called 'tense complex'. In this perspective, a 'simple tense' is one which is realised as having single (tense) element structure, while with 'serial tenses', more than one tense choice is made, each related to the others in the one complex tense structure: thus an instance of a serial tense would be the 'present-in-present', whose structure is $\alpha 0 {}^{\wedge} \beta 0$.[6] The system of FINITENESS is treated in SFL as one of the earliest to announce its centrality in the ecology of the clause: thus the working of the Finite Auxiliary vis-á-vis Subject is central in the system of MOOD ('interpersonal metafunction'), while at the same time indicating relevance to the 'speech event' ('textual metafunction'); given some systemic choices in the verbal group, this element of the clause must fuse with the main verb that realises the element Event in the Process of the clause, e.g., *eats, ate* ('experiential metafunction'); and finally as the 'carrier' (i.e., realiser) of the logical relations of tenses in the verbal group of the Finite clause, the finite auxiliary appears in a fused form ('logical metafunction'). The simple present and simple past typically fuse with the Process (as in *eats* or *ate* respectively), while future tense fuses with the Subject (as in *she'll eat*). It is of some interest that the 'time' associated with the former tenses – present or past – is, in Whorf's terms, 'sensuous', either being sensed as the speaker is speaking or capable of being recalled because of having been sensed earlier; the future tense refers to 'time' which Whorf called 'expective'.[7] The claim is not that fusion is 'obligatory' with simple tenses, only that it is the 'default' principle for realising these tenses. For Halliday, a default principle underlies normal choice which may be over-ridden with 'good reason'. So far as tense is concerned, three 'good reasons' will prevent the principle of fusion from applying: (a) the clause has 'interrogative' MOOD as in Extract 2, clause 8: *how do they stick it?*; or (b) the clause POLARITY is 'negative', as in Extract 1, clause 1 *living do not operate...* (or *don't operate*); or (c) if the Process is 'marked' being emphatic and/or contrastive, (e.g., *cats **do** like milk*).[8]

It is a curious fact that the English 'time' referred to by the English simple present tense does not include time which, in Whorf's terms, could be described as 'actualizing'; it, in fact, relates to time that is in memory and/or expectation, not here and now. This is obvious from the instantiations of this tense in the extracts above: the meaning which comes closest to this tense in the context of material process is that of elapsed or expected 'time', typical of the performance of a norm, some kind of established routine or habitual doing. What it does not do is to construe time concurrent with the present moment. So when in the last clause of Extract 2, the Mother says: *they* (i.e., the trees) *mend themselves*, she is describing something that trees routinely do in that sort of situation; she is not specifying any particular moment of time at all, and much less is she claiming that *the trees are mending themselves in time concurrent with speaking*. Sometimes, a clause with a simple present tense might give the impression that the action referred to by the process is concurrent with the speech time, as for example, in Shapiro's *Cells constantly adjust their metabolism to available nutrients* (Extract 1, clause 6). But, as is obvious on reflection, the 'concurrence' is not construed just by the tense: this clause cannot be simply paraphrased as *at this moment of speaking, cells are adjusting to available nutrients*. To do justice to the meaning of Shapiro's clause, it must perhaps be re-worded as: *cells normally adjust, **as they are doing at this moment**, to available nutrients*. The ***foregrounded*** part of the meaning of the original clause is implied by the temporal Circumstance *constantly*; it adds the meaning 'all the time' to the 'time required routinely' construed by the simple present tense. The concurrence of speech time with a specific process could well happen co-incidentally, but such accidental 'doing' in the real world would bear little relevance to the present debate: what is really at issue is not the once occurring action at any one moment but rather the habitual elapsing of time, and this, logically, entails *recurrence*, not co-occurrence. Had the meaning 'concurrent' inhered in the simple present tense, the interpretation of a clause such as *these cells adjust each month at full moon to available nutrients* would have brought about a sense of contradiction: this is quite obviously not the case; the clause is free of any problem of this kind, though I have no idea if in the real world any cells behave in this way – but that is irrelevant. Semantics is, in other words, not about truth; it is about how the necessary and/or possible meanings can be made by linguistic patternments.

Since in the context of material process, the 'default' meaning construed by the simple present tense is 'time taken in the performance of a normal, or a habitual action', this logically presupposes two related qualities: first, the process must 'recur'; neither is it undertaken just once, nor all of the time, nor necessarily by the same actor; further, it will be contextualised as routine with respect to an individual (or section) belonging to the community. Second, being routine, recurrence raises the expectation of such action to have occurred on some occasions in time prior to speaking; and there is also a high probability of its occurrence in time after the speech event, unless the possibility of future occurrence is explicitly denied.[9] Thus the implication of elapsed and expected time is clear; what is not clear is the claim that the action is going on at the moment of speaking, and this is just as well for otherwise it might be difficult for a speaker to say casually over a cup of coffee *I walk to the office*.

To conclude, the semantics of tense is not about 'measuring' time or necessarily deciding duration of act: but *it simply presents a way of generalising when the action occurred: before, after or concurrently with speech time*. The generalisation may be absolute, as in *John walks to the office*, or universally applicable as in *precious metals do not rust* – but in the latter case, the universality is not simply due to the choice of tense; it is just as much due to the 'class exhaustive' reference to doer and/or the choice of a Circumstance that realises appropriate temporal meaning e.g., *always*. In between these universal and specific ends, are the *conditioned norms* such as *If you prick us do we not bleed?* (note, the implied class exhaustive *you* and *we* – as the gist of racial prejudice). These last differ slightly from others discussed so far, mainly because they are subject to a hypothetical state of affairs. All the same, they do occur in normal discourse as when the Mother claims: *because when you plant seeds from mandarins or oranges, sometimes you get very strange fruit* (extract 2: clauses 3 and 4). Whatever the case, the default meaning of the simple present tense retains the two features: one, that the action, being due to a routine, will be recurrent; a single happening does not make a norm. Second, as routine, the tense will 'implicate' such action undertaken in the past and expectation of its occurrence in the future (see note 9). Further, because the duration of neither the process itself nor the intervals between its recurrence are inherently specific, the tense is likely to attract the co-occurrence of a temporal Circumstance. There is a wide range of these, e.g., *always, often, occasionally, sometimes, typically, continually, constantly* and so on. If exactness is required, time units may be referred to as regulated by communal conventions, e.g., *every now and then; every other day; on Mondays, twice a day before or after meals, four times a day, annually*, and so on.[10]

15.3.3 Time and tense: (b) default meaning in present-in-present

As its name shows, present-in-present is an instance of serial tense: so like other serial tenses, it will have more than one element in its structure. The ideational structure of the present-in-present is α0 β0 (for details, Halliday and Matthiessen, 2014, section 6.3.4; also Figure 6:19). As before, in these naturally occurring extracts the relevant instances of this tense have been italicised.

> **Extract 3:** *Labour row over EU migrants.* Guardian Weekly: 06. 06. 2014:16
> (1) Ed Miliband *is facing* a backbench revolt over immigration policy
> (2) as senior Labour MPs warn of catastrophic consequences for the party (3) unless he seeks constraints on the free movement of the EU workers. (4) The unrestricted entry of EU citizens from eastern Europe since 2004 *is hurting* the 'very communities that the labour party was founded to represent', (5) the MPs claimed in an open letter published in the Observer.

Extract 4: *Music career the X Factor in selling home.* Manly Daily: 07. 06. 2014:5

(1) X FACTOR finalist Christian Anthony is off to the US (2) to study music (3) and his parents *are selling* the family's multi-million dollar home in Seaforth (4) to follow him. ... (5) The teenage musician is in a new band called Chase Atlantic, (6) a song he wrote has been selected to help fight youth depression, (7) and several of his hits *are climbing* the YouTube charts. ... (8) Mr Anthony *is putting together* a television series called School's Out in the US.

Extract 5: *Rhetorical Units and Decontextualisation.* (Cloran 1994: Appendix A:15) [casual conversation: Mother with Cameron 3;8]

Cameron:	(1) mum what*'re* you *doing?*
Mother:	(2) *getting* your lunch
Cameron:	(3) oh, I thought [NOT INTELLIGIBLE]
Mother:	(4) what do you say?
Cameron:	(5) thank you mum ..
Mother:	(6) now what sort of fruit do you want? Mandarin, apple, pear, banana, orange?
Cameron:	(7) Oh .. mandarin you got?
Mother:	(8) yes .. got mandarins
Cameron:	(9) well after I finished this (10) I'll have a mandarin
Mother:	(11) right, there it is
Cameron:	(12) thanks .. (13) but I still haven't finished my lunch
Mother:	(14) yeah, I know (15) but I just put it there ready (16) because I*'m getting* my lunch now (17) so I just put it there ready for you
Cameron:	(18) where will you sit mum?
Mother:	(19) in my usual place
Cameron:	(20) OK I'll put that over there (21) I need to put it over there
Mother:	(22) what're you saying? (23) *are* you *moving* the little bird?
Cameron:	(24) no .. just *moving* the mandarin

What I am calling present-in-present tense here has different names in different models of linguistics: for some it is a tense, for others it is no tense at all but an aspect, though the name 'present continuous' or 'present progressive' may be used in either case – thus whether tense or aspect it does have some reference to time; and some will explain this by saying that aspect always includes tense, for others the two are quite distinct; SFL belongs to the last category. Wikipedia, that self-designated 'public voice', consulted early June 2014, informed that '... as with other grammatical categories, the precise semantics of the aspects varies from language to language and from grammarian to grammarian'. But, while granting that the semantic, lexicogrammatical and phonological categories of one language will differ in some way from those of the others, I would doubt if things are as uncertain as that remark suggests. It may be not too large a claim to make that language abhors only two things in its machinery of patternment – namely, randomness and message-internal contradiction; and there are certain semantic aspects of the present-in-present tense which remain the same for a specific language, no matter what name is ascribed to it. One of these may be put negatively for English: the default function of the present-in-present is definitely not to construe a routine, or habitual doing. Instead, putting it positively, the default semantics of that tense may be described as to construe 'concurrence' between the process and the moment of speech. So on hearing the utterance *Cameron's mother is getting him his lunch*, the very probable interpretation, by a normal speaker of English, would be that the process of getting Cameron's lunch has begun but is not yet completed at the time of speaking. Similarly, Cameron's mother could have said *I am putting the mandarin here so it'll be there when you want it*; no one would have sought a justification for using present-in-present for an 'instantaneous' action; nor would they have asked how long it takes to put down a mandarin somewhere (cf., Huddleston 1984:153–154). The normal reading of the mother's utterance would have been that she was putting the mandarin within reach of her son just as she addressed those words to him.[11] Similarly when the *Manly Daily* (cf. example 4; clause 3) tells us that *his parents are selling their multi-million dollar family home in Seaforth*, normally the assumption would be that the process of selling that property is a-foot, even though the buyer is nowhere on the horizon, so clearly the action of selling is not going to finish any time very soon. But *to sell* cannot be treated as an ambiguous verb simply because selling cabbage is quite a different kind of activity compared with the selling of a mansion. The present-in-present tense (given the properties stated above in 15.3.1) does have a default meaning: it quite unambiguously claims that the action referred to by the main verb is 'entrained' or 'a-foot' at the moment of speaking; moreover, the process is not expected to be accomplished during the speech event. By any standard, 'the moment of speaking' is an absurd unit for 'measuring the time period' by which to establish one's sense of past becoming present or for solving the problem of how far the present can extend before it 'becomes' the future. Grammatical categories are ineffable (Halliday 1985): if naming them solved the problem of determining their semantics, then the best name for the present-in-present tense would have been 'present concurrent incomplete' in the given context of the clause type (cf., 15.3.1); this is precisely the default meaning of the present-in-present tense.

15.3.4 Time and tense: (c) 'conditioned' meaning in two tenses

The above statements about the default semantics of the two tenses as they function in the limited context of material process (section 15.3.1) is clearly far from exhaustive: while listening to a cricket commentary, one might easily come across something like *Haneef takes a start, runs in and bowls*; or one might be drinking a quiet cup of coffee with a friend who suddenly announces *I am going to London*. Most English speakers would agree that here the first example does not refer to any routine or habitual actions – Haneef does other things during the cricket game; nor can the second be interpreted as an action that is 'already afoot' – the most likely response would be *Oh! When?*. The meaning of these two examples is obviously not in keeping with the generalisations made earlier about the default meaning of the two tenses being interpreted by reference to the material processes. If those generalisations are correct, then the tenses in these two examples are some kind of exception: the question is are such exceptions random? I have already suggested that it is not in the nature of language to tolerate randomness: when it comes to the formation of meaning-making patterns, the principle of laissez-faire does not seem to be popular with natural languages. So, if the departures are not random, then it should be possible to demonstrate what exceptions of this kind mean and why. I hope to achieve some explanation of this in the present section on the way to showing what permeability looks like in action. So first the examples of the two tenses with the so-called 'exceptional meanings' in order to establish the conditions in which they apply:

simple present
1: Haneef takes a start, runs in and bowls.
2: (i) you know what happened yesterday (ii) I was just walking to the store (iii) and suddenly this man *comes* out of nowhere (iv) and *snatches* at my bag (v) I was gob-smacked (vi) didn't know what was going on …
3: I leave for London this summer.

present-in-present
4: (i) come to bed, Karen! (ii) you *are going* to school *tomorrow*.
5: (i) I have a big load this semester (ii) so Shirley's *helping* me *out*.
6: I am sending it tomorrow.

Beginning with the simple tense, here example 1 is easily recognisable as part of a radio commentary on a game of cricket. The default meaning of the simple present tense bears no resemblance to the meaning of this example; it is not a routine or habitual act: instead, here it would be normally interpreted as actions occurring at the moment of speaking, so that its meaning is closer to the default meaning of the present-in-present tense as described above. But with two differences: one, that the duration of its continuation is not uncertain, and two, that it seems to construe a pretty precise time. Thus Haneef's acts of 'taking a start', 'running in' and of 'bowling' occur in the indicated order, the performance of each act coinciding almost exactly with the moment of being referred to; the beginning or end of each is precise. That as a well-known bowler in the 'real world', Haneef would actually have a characteristic (habitual?) style of taking a start, of running in, and of bowling is not relevant here: the focus is on the action occurring now, not on any norm. Here the Circumstances *usually, normally, as a rule* are all ruled out, or rather if they occur they would be very clearly distinguished from the example. Thus we may have something as follows: *Haneef normally walks in and throws the ball but this time he is running and now he bowls.* The claim is not that every verbal group occurring in a cricket commentary will have simple present tense, nor that all uses of that tense will have the meaning 'time of speech and of action are concurrent here and now'. It is, in fact, much more restricted: in a radio commentary when the use of the simple present tense is co-selected with material action as described in 15.3.1, then it is very likely to construe 'time in which the performance of the mentioned action and of speech will be concurrent', as an indication, in this function the action cannot be 'modified' by a Circumstance indicating 'usuality'. So, the meaning of the tense, far from being random, is tightly conditioned: the conditions that govern this 'usage' include both the contextual and the lexicogrammatical environment of tense selection; the conjunction of both is called upon in the construal of this meaning. I will refer to this kind of construal of meaning as a 'conditioned' meaning. I had remarked in section 15.3.2 that the simple present does not construe 'present time', but it is obvious from the discussion of example 1 that the tense can actually construe present time – but conditions apply: it must have the environment as specified here.

Example 2 would also be familiar to many ordinary speakers: this use of the simple present tense (*italicised*) is well known as 'historic'/'narrative present', so called perhaps because it occurs typically in a text type that describes past events. But there is an additional requirement: when the material mode of contact is 'phonic', the style of describing past events must be addressed to a familiar addressee.[12] Under these conditions the use of the simple present construes 'time prior to the moment of speaking'. Ignoring here the history of the development of this usage, in some ways it seems to be like the radio commentary such as just discussed: a commentary attempts to 'bring' to the listener the cricket game as it is happening in real time and space. The narrator uses this same tense to transport the listeners to the past events as if the event is actually taking place in situ, here and now. This explains the 'management of time' in something like Placement (Hasan 1984) (or scene setting), where the simple present is sandwiched, typically, between the use of past and present tenses as in example 2: a simple past in clause (i), followed by past continuous in (ii) construes the Placement of the story; this is followed by two simple present tenses in (iii and iv) which describe the Initial and Sequent event, followed again by clauses with past tense which tend to lead to the outcome (Finale). So this 'exceptional' use of the tense and the meaning of 'past time' it construes is tightly conditioned, not at all random.

The kind of clause shown in example 3 is more likely to occur in a conversation where the 'social distance' between the interactants is 'fairly' or 'extremely' 'close' (for the meaning of these terms, Hasan, forthcoming). As the use of the temporal Circumstance *this summer* shows, the simple present here stands proxy to the future tense. Other 'time adverbs' that could have occurred here are those capable of being co-selected with future time only, e.g., *soon, tomorrow, next week, in two weeks, right now, in a few days*, and so on; no time adverb can be used that configures with the past tense only, e.g., *last summer, two days ago*, and so on. And it is not clear if the clause could occur with no temporal Circumstance at all.

What the discussion of these three examples shows is that the simple present tense is capable of construing (a) the 'true' present, i.e., this here and now time coinciding with the time of speaking as in the cricket commentary: this is a present tense true to its name, or (b) the past, as in the use of the 'narrative present', or (c) the future with co-textual support. But these meanings of the simple present (as defined in 3.1) are not 'random': one knows where, when, and how these meanings may be construed by the simple present tense, albeit sometimes with support from temporal Circumstance. All meanings of this kind are 'conditioned': they can be construed by the simple present tense only under specific conditions. These conditions pertain either to the co-text and/or to the con-text of situation: in either case the focus is on meaning; it does not seem possible to specify the properties of the co-text in purely formal terms. This appears to confirm the status of semantics as the interface implicating both the lexicogrammatical stratum and the context of discourse in its process, thus foregrounding the three strata that are concerned with the making of linguistic meaning.

Turning now to the present-in-present tense: here example 4, clause (ii) resembles example 3 in its conditioned meaning: a temporal Circumstance feature occurs in both, referring clearly to time that follows after the speech event. The temporal adverbs are typically univalent: their meaning does not shift with shifting environment; tomorrow is always the day after speaking. So, in clause (ii) of example 4, the present-in-present would be heard as referring to a unit of time that is anticipated by the speaker of that utterance. Given the lexicogrammatical and situational context of this clause, it will, like example 3, reject a temporal Circumstance referring to the past or the present. Thus, (a) *?you are going to school yesterday* clearly has self-contradiction, while (b) *you are going to school right now*, taken as a substitute for clause (ii) of example 4 will be contextually improbable/inappropriate. Supposing it is encountered in isolation and without any idea of its original co-textual or contextual background, its meaning will be ambiguous: either it would be interpreted as construing the default meaning of the tense (as described in section 15.3.3) or as 'an obligatory demand for carrying out the action', i.e., as a 'mandatory command', semantically somewhat close to *you must go to school right now*; in other words, to construe the meaning 'time anticipated at moment of speaking', the present-in-present tense requires appropriate contextual and/or contextual support.

In example 5, we see the semantic 'force' of co-textual information. Here, clause (i) of the example has a temporal Circumstance *this semester*; the deixis of *this* fixes the time of *this semester* as 'extended present', which, normally interpreted, will cover some of the time prior to speaking as well as that to follow the speech event. In this co-text, the present-in-present in example 5 clause (ii) *Shirley is helping me out* is a logical 'sequitur' to clause 5 (i) and the tense in this clause will refer to an extended 'present', as it were, leading into near future. In fact, its time reference is very much like that of routine as discussed in section 15.3.2 with reference to simple present; it can be assumed that Shirley has helped the speaker (in the past), and that she is expected to continue this practice also in the forthcoming days/weeks (as the extent determined by *this semester*). There is, however, one significant difference: unlike the default meaning of the simple present, in example 5 the routine has a temporary quality: the past and future are not indefinitely open, the norm is not an established one; it will last only as long as *this semester*. This conditioned meaning of present-in-present is clearly not synonymous with the default meaning of routine which is construed by the simple present. Further, for the ascription of this conditioned meaning to the present-in-present, there must be a co-selection of some item in its conditioning environment that is capable of construing time of the kind I am here calling the 'extended present'. This would explain the higher likelihood of the co-occurrence of some temporal Circumstance such as *these days, now-a-days, for the time being, this year/week, lately* and so on.

I have not come across any mention of the 'historic present continuous' in the literature on narrative styles, but if there is increasing use of the historic present as the preferred 'literary style' (as discussed with reference to simple present in example 2), it is quite possible that the use of the 'historic present-in-present' has already arrived or it might do so in the future. One can conjure examples such as: *she sees the sturdy figure of her father towering over little William. William **is cowering** in the corner trying to hide. The hard toe of Dad's thick boot hits him hard on the chest; William gives an anguished scream 'aow!'; he **is protecting** his face with hands that tremble ... .* Here the present-in-present tenses (**foregrounded**) would be understood as referring to actions that have already occurred in the 'past' in the same way as the simple present tenses would: what presents them 'as-if happening here and now' is the vividness of the speaker's memory.

It is possible that other semantic options are also open to these tenses (as defined in 15.3.1), but the examples presented here are most probably sufficient for the discussion of the principles underlying the concept of permeability, which is essentially a device for relating linguistic patternments, thereby extending their semantic space.

15.3.5 The concept of permeability

Two terms, default and conditioned, have been used in this discussion to classify the kinds of meaning brought to attention. In general terms, not just meaning, but any aspect of the description of a precisely identified linguistic category, must have some default properties. For example, a declarative English clause may be said to have the following *default structure*:[13]

Subject ^ Finite ^ Predicator (•Complement) (•Adjunct)

This generalisation could be paraphrased using technical words as: it is highly probable that the English 'declarative clause' will have the structure shown above, *unless* there is some good reason for over-riding this general principle; and, 'good', in this context, can *only* be taken to mean 'explicitly specifiable', as for example the categories discussed in section 15.3.2–15.3.4. Taking the same category, declarative, but now viewing its semantic aspect, it might be claimed that the *default semantics* of the 'declarative clause' is 'statement': if there are other meanings that can be attributed to that clause type (as suggested in the Hasan 1983 network), this will require especial conditions. Typically such conditioning over-rides the default principle, thus re-aligning the probabilities of the coupling of that category to those on other strata. Conditioned meanings are regulated by a principle that has, as it were, replaced the default principle. This is how the terms default and conditioned have been used above in the discussion of meanings ascribed to the two tenses (15.3.2–15.3.4): the discussion began with tightly identified categories (cf. 15.3.1) and also presented an explicit and precise profile of those conditions under which both the simple present tense and the present-in-present will regularly construe their conditioned meanings. I am suggesting that, generally speaking, these relations are not limited to any single linguistic stratum.

Now, as the idiom goes, one can count on the fingers of one hand those specific conditions in which non-default uses can occur; by contrast, the categories functioning in the default mode have no such restriction on their use. This leads to the assumption that the latter, able to occur in a much wider set of situational contexts, are likely to be used more often that the former.[14] And, in this perspective, it appears very likely that the awareness of the default meaning would be better foregrounded in memory. This would furnish one reason for the wide-spread belief in linguistics that a one-to-one coupling of wording and meaning is in the nature of language. For example, Antilla (2002:210) reports a comment with implicit acceptance of the position: 'It has been suggested that the form meaning relation in natural language is ideally one-to-one and that this is the principle that languages strive to satisfy (Antilla 1989)'. When the superior value of the ideal is ascribed to default meaning, its alternative, namely conditioned meaning, become 'the other', the non-ideal, the exception. But, as Douglas (1975) has argued, the values typically attached to the 'other' by this implicit separation is often based on a variety of mythology, seldom capable of explaining the real basis.

So far as the nature of language is concerned, as Saussure (2006) argued cogently, 'the morphology of meaning' is rooted in the relations of signs. Excluding everything from the linguistics of *langue* that was not internal to the sign, he suggested that the heart of the linguistics of langue was the study of the multiple relations of signs; but it is best to remember that the existence of this relational web cannot be even suspected, let alone analysed, *unless* the signs are used as a means of meaning. It is also beyond doubt that in the life of every social subject, the use of linguistic signs must happen in social contexts.[15] So it is the analysis of *parole* in social context that, contra Saussure, reveals the nature of the *signified*, allowing the linguist to see through to the signs' myriad of relations. Logically, if language strives for anything, it is very much more likely to be the creation and maintenance of the web of relations that define its being: and so the task of linguistics is most probably not to preclude but to include all those relations that form the basis of meaning – the propagation of which must, in the last analysis, depend logically on communal conventions.

But what have all these issues to do with permeability? I would suggest that the concept of permeability demonstrates the existence of both kinds of relations in the same category, the default – the one-to-one coupling – and also the conditioned – the one-to-many couplings. What I have done so far in this lengthy discourse is to provide evidence that such categories do exist, and this will furnish the basis for claiming that permeability is a viable concept: the careful tense-time analysis was begun originally with no idea of this relation (Hasan 2011). I will now use some aspects of the analysis as reported above, but the concern will no longer be with the tense-time relations per se: they will be used as material for exemplifying how permeability plays a part in creating this relation of one-to-many in linguistic categories. This perspective foregrounds a different order of phenomenon at a higher level of abstraction: it explains how the analysis of categories carried to an increasingly delicate level reveals the intricacy of the relations of linguistic categories – a density which so far we have suspected but not attempted to probe. Below I offer criteria for recognising permeability as well as its scope of operations. Moving step by step, three principles appear notable.

PRINCIPLE 1: *a specific instance of permeability is detected in inter-stratal context*: this primary principle derives from the concepts of strata and realisation. In order to carry out an orderly analysis, the theory suggests language is best conceptualised as a set of interrelated strata, each an individual, representing a distinct orders of abstraction: the five strata recognised in SFL are familiar. But, the experience of actually engaging in acts of meaning by means of language demands the conceptualisation of language as one integrated whole: the concept of realisation in SFL is treated as such an integrative device. Both these concepts had been presented by Hjelmslev (1961), from whom they were first borrowed into SFL, but, by now, the adaptation and elaboration of these concepts has given them a distinct identity to suit the tenets of the theory. I have suggested elsewhere (2009; 2010) that the three higher strata forming the plane of content in SFL are engaged in a dialectic.[16] According to this dialectic, the speakers' interpretation of an instance of context as relevant to a particular social practice which forms the occasion of talk 'activates' the relevant semantic selections, which activate relevant lexicogrammatical selections; whereas for the listener, the perception and recognition of lexicogrammatical choices construes the semantic choices, which construe the speaker's perception of context of situation as being broached by the speaker.[17] The concept of *trinocular* perspective, in my understanding, assumes the analyst's awareness of what the speakers-listeners might sense as the relevant linguistic and contextual possibilities that might bear on 'what is going on here and now': the move up and down the strata, and around the various relations at each, must occur as a necessary part of speaking and understanding. Going back to the earlier examples, it is notable that the phonological shape of the two foregoing tenses does not change whether their semantic realisation is default or conditioned. Had the description been limited to just the formal status of the tenses, ignoring the inter-stratal realisational relation between semantics and lexicogrammar, the idea of 'something being different' would perhaps not have arisen: the inter-stratal relation of realisation is what reveals their permeability, and raises an issue about their grammatical status of the category. It might be thought that the relation of permeability is some variety of 'homonymy' since the latter too is an inter-stratal relation, but this would be an error.[18] Permeability has other characteristics that would distinguish it from homonymy.

PRINCIPLE 2: *a specific instance of permeability is limited to one single stratum.* This principle is logically related to the last point; given the meaning of 'permeable', it is obvious that the process of permeability will involves other categories: one precisely identified category permeates into some other category. So when under some specific conditions a simple present tense is said to be permeable, what this means in practice is that (a) this particular category has abandoned its own default area of operation, say, the construal of routine time lapse (cf., 15.3.2 and 15.3.4); and (b) it has moved to another area, permeating its meaning space, and (c) that this area must always be at the same stratum to which the category itself belongs. That this is the case with the English tenses has been demonstrated above; it is obvious that all the relations involved in this permeability – those that are needed to permeate and those that are permeated – have pertained to the system of TENSE: *no other lexicogrammatical category is involved in the operations that create permeability.* This logically implies that for permeability to come about the permeating category and the permeated one must both belong to one single stratum: the diagnosis depends on inter-stratal behaviour; the permeability itself is a property of some particular stratum.

PRINCIPLE 3: *the realisation of the permeating category does not duplicate an existing meaning.* Axiomatically, language shuns 'absolute synonymy': that on the one hand supports the foregoing generalisation, and on the other, it suggests that the principle cannot be treated as specific to permeability. Nonetheless, it does need to be shown that the principle applies to permeability. I have remarked above in passing that conditioned meaning is a mode of extending language's meaning potential. For example, both the simple present and present-in-present in their conditioned mode construe reference to categories of time; but none of these refer to exactly the same time lapse as any other of the tenses, so it is only in general terms that they may be said to 'wander' beyond their own space, into that of other tenses. An example might illuminate the issue:

> 6:   I'm sending it tomorrow   [conditioned present-in-present: permeating]
> 6a: I'll send it tomorrow.   [permeated tense: default future]

In general terms, both, 6 and 6a refer to future time – the action of sending in both cases will happen after the moment of speaking and from this perspective it is being said that the tense *'m sending* has wandered from its default meaning area of concurrent time into one that may be said to be the legitimate semantic space of *'ll send*, naming a future act. However, it is highly likely that speakers of English – especially those 'brought up' in that language – would perceive a distinction between 6 and 6a. I suggest tentatively that here 6a is likely to be taken as a fairly firm expectation, perhaps announcing a tangible, already considered plan. By contrast, example 6 might be heard as having the 'tone' of a 'plan in process'; and *tomorrow* might be the likely end point for that planning decision to occur: it is something like saying 'I am thinking of sending it tomorrow'. To move these interpretations beyond a suggestion or personal impression towards a degree of certainty, what is needed is access to the results of some corpus based studies of the two verbal groups which might permit evidence leading perhaps to greater certainty; better still, there could be a comparison of what speakers think they would understand and what they actually do understand. But this kind of information is not available. To conclude: if the reading provided here seems plausible, then the conditioned present-in-present does not duplicate the default time associated with it realisationally, i.e., *action afoot during speech but beginning and completion points unknown*; nor does it behave like the simple future. Of course, one might object that it is the temporal Circumstance *tomorrow* that construes the meaning 'future', not the tense *'m sending*; and so there is no permeability in the tense itself. Of course *tomorrow* does refer to a future unit of time, but the reason for referring to the interpretation as 'conditioned meaning' is precisely that the tense's environment has a specifiable co-textual and/or con-textual condition. Besides, it seems reasonable to ask:

if the time is being construed by *tomorrow* alone, what function does the tense choice have in example 6? We know that *I'm sending it yesterday* is not a possibility, but why not? If tense choice is not contributing to making the meaning of time, it should be possible to use just any temporal Adverb as a Circumstance.

15.4 Permeability: The viability of the concept

This entire discussion of permeability is based on the analysis of two out of the 36 tense configurations presented in Halliday and Matthiessen (2014: Figure 6–13:401–403). So, have I been crying 'Summer!' simply on sighting that one single swallow notorious for 'not making summer'? My concern with making the background information easily available in a reasonably precise form has cost a good deal of time and space. However, now, another example of permeability can be offered that, like tense, pertains to the 'verbal group', but this time, unlike tense, it does not open the verbal group; rather, by realising the last element called Event, it closes the verbal group. While in exploring tense, the categories under focus had been 'fully grammatical', now in the study of Event, the concern was with a class of verb whose members were 'fully lexical' items, i.e., lexemes.[19] Here, the aim of the two original studies (Hasan 1985, 1987) had been to enquire into the reality of 'the grammarian's dream' of 'lexis as most delicate grammar' (Halliday 1961[2002]), by pushing the paradigmatic analysis of these lexemes up to the most delicate level of description so that at the terminal point of the analysis each of the paths would be identified as a set of systemic choices, each such path realising one and only one unique lexeme capable of realising some Event.[20] Exceptions there certainly were, and it had seemed very probable that some principles were at work governing the regular relations between the default and what I am now calling conditioned uses. As in the case of tense so here too, during these analyses, the idea had never occurred that the concept of permeability might, in any way, be involved in explaining those 'exceptional' uses of the 'lexical verb'.

The sub-category that I choose here to explore from the perspective of permeability is capable of acting as a specific type of material process: the choice configuration shown below distinguishes this particular material process type from the others; it can thus be taken as constituting this category's precise systemic identity:

PROCESS TYPE material: dispositive: bestowal; BENEFACTION benefactive: inherent

Some examples of lexemes with the above choices would be *give, send, lend, donate, deliver, convey, hand ....*[21] To limit the pattern further, I stipulate now that in addition to the above selections, in system of VOICE, the choices 'effective: active' are to be taken to have been co-selected simultaneously. In that case, the structure of the clause capable of realising the named choices will have four ENTAILED elements: Event, Actor, Goal and Recipient. The default structure of the clause is shown in the example below:

> 7: *the mother* (Actor) ^ *gave* (Event) ^ *a new book* (Goal) ^ *to the child* (Recipient).

Of course, other elements could occur in this clause type, e.g. an instance of some type(s) of Circumstance, but unlike the four shown above, they are just potentially selectable elements, *not entailed* by the clause type identified in 7. As material process, each member of this subclass will conform to the tests proposed in SFL (e.g. Halliday and Matthiessen 2014): given the Voice choice as above, Actor will be conflated with Subject (*the mother*); Event, with Predicator (*gave*), Goal, with Complement (*a new book*); and the element Recipient (entailed by the choices 'benefactive: inherent') will conflate with Adjunct IF realised as prepositional group (as ***to*** *the child* in example 7 above) or with Complement$_2$ IF realised as a nominal group (as in 7a: *the mother gave the child a new book,* then the Recipient *the child* would be Complement$_2$ and the Goal *a new book,* Complement$_1$). With this process type, the element Thing in the nominal group capable of realising Goal must belong to a class of noun with the systemic options 'concrete: alienable', e.g., *gift, book, dog, jacket, flowers ...,* while the Thing element of the nominal group realising the Recipient must be 'animate' (and most often 'human'). Consider in this light examples 7a and 7b and 7c.

> 7a: the mother gave the child a new book
> 7b: Sheila sent her friend congratulations
> 7c: the man gave the door a coat of new paint

7a is a default clause, already described above: it conforms to both the default structures, including the built in constraint on the realisation of Goal and Recipient; but the other two 7b and 7c are departures. In 7b, although, as required for realising the Recipient, the nominal group, *her friend,* is 'animate', the nominal group *congratulations* as Goal departs from the default realisational requirement: the noun here is not 'concrete: alienable'. In 7c *the door* is not 'animate', so its function as Recipient needs more 'work' of analysis though the Goal, in a manner of speaking, can be viewed as 'concrete: alienable'.

The default experiential meaning construed by the clause types under discussion, namely 7 and 7a, may be rendered roughly as follows: Actor undertaking some action at some point in time, that moves the Goal away from the Actor and into the direction of the Recipient. In both examples 7 and 7a, the material action is that of 'bestowal' and the *bestower*, here, is Actor: the intended destination of the Goal is the Recipient. But as 7b and 7c show there are departures from this default meaning: all going well Sheila's friend will receive the congratulations sent to her, but perhaps in the shape of a card with semiological indication to that effect: there is a difference, though a delicate one, between receiving 'books' and receiving congratulations (discussed below, cf. 8n in Table 15.1). No matter how delicate the difference, in the last analysis, the last two clauses represent a departure in terms of their semantics. And, as before, the question arises: are these exceptions, and if so, are there any underlying regularities; and if yes, are they subject to any conditions; and if they are, then is that condition such as to qualify as an instance of permeability. These are the questions I will raise in examining the use of bestowal type Event; and in seeking the answers, the same considerations will be used as above with the tenses, keeping the three principles in mind that were abstracted above (in section 15.3.5).

15.4.1 Does *give* type process have a conditioning environment?

The grammar and semantics of *clauses* 7 and 7a have been presented as the wider context for the category which is specifically under focus from the perspective of permeability: this category is the main verb ('lexeme' or the 'lexical verb') capable of realising the function of Event in the structure of the clause. A majority of verbs in this class are normally used in fairly specific environments – such as *bequeath, donate, convey, hand,* and so on; but the particular lexeme *give* (cf. Tucker, this volume) can occur in the majority of these environments as well as in those where their use might be seen as rather inappropriate; thus, the *give* can realise Event in a clause such as *she gives huge amounts of money to hospitals,* as well as in such ordinary sentences as *the mother gave the child a book,* where it would have been quite odd to say that *the mother donated a book to the child.* In this

Table 15.1: Conditioned uses of *give* type Process: grammar and meaning

Give in conditioning environment	Nearest match for conditioned Process
(A) Pro material: dispositive: bestowal; benefactive	(A) material: nondispositive: nonbenefactive

8a: the mother **gave** the child *a warm hug*
8b: the thief **gave** him *a knock on the head*
8c: my son **gave** me *substantial help*
    Actor   Pro.   Recipient   Goal
	9a: the mother **hugged** the child warmly
	9b: the thief **knocked** him on the head
	9c: my son **helped** me substantially
	    Actor Pro. Goal Circ.

(B) Process presented as in A
8d: he **gave** her *a friendly nod*
8e: she **gave** him *a careless shrug*
8f: Leila **gave** me *a brilliant smile*
    Actor   Pro.   Recipient   Goal
	(B) Process material: somatic
	9d: he **nodded** at her friendlily
	9e: she **shrugged** at him carelessly
	9f: Leila **smiled** at him brilliantly
	    Actor Pro. Range Circ.

(C) Process presented as in A
8g: the decision **gave** them *a great shock*
8h: she **gave** him *her love*
8j: the news **gave** them *serious fright*
    Actor   Pro.   Recipient   Goal
	(C) Process mental: reaction
	9g: the decision **shocked** them greatly
	9h: she **loved** him
	9j: the news **frightened** them seriously
	    Phenomenon Pro. Sensor Circ.

(D) Process presented as in A
8k: she **gave** him *an explicit order*
8m: they **gave** us *a response*
8n: the cuts **gave** us *a warning*
    Actor   Pro.   Recipient   Goal
	(D) Process verbal
	9k: she **ordered** him explicitly
	9m: they **responded** to us
	9n: the cuts **warned** us
	    Sayer Pro. Addressee Circ.

way, *give* is prototypic of the class of verbs which forms the focus of discussion from the perspective of permeability; and from now on I shall simply use *give* whenever referring to the category identified in section 15.4.

Table 15.1 presents four obvious types of departures from the default use of *give*: these are presented in the four distinct parts A–D. The aim is to ask if this 'divergent behaviour' of *give* can be legitimately described here as a permeating category. To begin with, a few basic facts about Table 15.1: each part A–D has three clauses, making up 12 clauses 8a–8n in the left column, and 12 in the right, 9a–9n; in all cases, the item realising Event has been picked out in **bold**. Clauses facing each other in the left and right column form a pair by some points of resemblance. The choices underlying the Event are shown in each part A–D and their structural configuration is clearly presented. In the left column, in each clause 8a–8n the segment realising Goal has been *italicised*: this is where things 'begin to go haywire'. If in these clauses, Goal had been realised by a nominal group following the default principle, i.e., with features 'concrete: alienable', then the clauses would obviously have represented the default clausal category. And in that case, they would have been nothing else but instances of that default clause type whose Event is the verb *give*. But as they stand, these clauses do represent some kind of departure from the default clause type. Clearly the departure is not random, so the search is on as to whether there is a principle to explain this particular departure.

I would interpret the presence of the italicised segment in 8a–n as representing a conditioning environment for *give* type process: it is only when an instance of this italicised type is co-selected with *give* that, in general terms, the *give* clause can no longer be seen as referring to the same type of state of affairs as that referred to by clauses 7 and 7a. This means the default structure assigned to clauses 8a–8n cannot be taken as representing the complete analysis of these clauses: in short, *give* is here not behaving as the default category *give* normally does. This opens two options: (a) the clauses 8a–8n are ungrammatical; (b) this *give* is not the same *give* as used in 7 and 7a – is it perhaps a homonym of default *give*? As for (a), the fact is that speakers of English will normally assign a meaning to all these clauses without any hesitation. And their communal acceptance as meaningful implies that they are just as 'grammatical' as *'m leaving tomorrow* as placing the leaving at some 'time the next day, i.e., after the moment of speaking'. And, there is a considered argument against treating the two kinds of *give* verbs as homonyms: the relation of homonymy tends to be just skin-deep; thus, the animal, *bear* and *bear* the verb, a near synonym of *tolerate* – or, for that matter, of *bear* meaning *give birth* – are homonyms, and like homonyms, in general, the lexemes do not show any regular lexicogrammatical or semantic relation to each other. This is not the case with *give* in 8a–8n: this *give*, on the one hand, bears a regular relation to the *give* in clause types 7 and 7a, and, on the other, it bears a regular relationship to the semantics of clauses 9a–9n in the right column; the meaning of clauses 9a–n appears to be pretty close to that of their counterpart clauses 8a–n. What clinches the issue is that just as the conditioned meaning of present-in-present as referring to future time is echoed by the co-selection, in its conditioning environment, of *tomorrow* as the temporal Circumstance, so also an echo of the principle whereby the conditioning environment of *give* can be interpreted in 8a-n can be found in the formation of the clauses 9a–9n, which, as pointed out, stand in a near equivalence to the conditioning meaning of the clauses 8a–8n. The presence of this regular principle for relating clauses 8a–8n to clause 9a–9n and the significance of this relation to the interpretation of the verb *give* will be explored in the following sections.

15.4.2 The permeating verb *give*: Its conditioning meaning

The question is if the implicit relation between clauses in the two columns of Table 15.1 add up to any proof that permeability is at work in the case of verb *give* as used in the left column, and if this can be demonstrated by unpacking the relation across the column. On the face of it, this may not seem very likely, but the parallels drawn in the previous section between the permeating tenses and the *give* type verb, when it is operating under a condition relevant to 'fixing' its analysis and meaning, do appear quite suggestive: so, in a way, the discussion seems to have already touched upon some of the principles for recognising permeability. I hope to develop this claim, and to achieve that aim, it will be necessary to be more precise about the nature of what is being called the 'conditioning environment'. Pooling the information provided in Table 15.1, the conditioning environment may be stated as follows: *IF with this Process type, the default realisational principles for the element Goal are ignored, this will form a condition under which the clause with give functioning as Event will construe a conditioned meaning.* As a hypothesis, this claim holds good so far as it goes, but does it go far enough?

This generalisation does identify a segment that could play the role of conditioning environment in terms of its own properties, but this is just a possibility: after all, there are occasions when ignoring a realisational principle for an entailed element simply 'results' in creating a pattern that is outright unacceptable; the community does not treat it as having a reasonable meaning. The above definition still fails to explain the precise relations between the conditioning environment and the conditioned meaning so far as clause types 8a–8n are concerned; this is what is needed to clinch the status of the segment. It was pointed out in the last section (15.4.1) that a specific kind of relation exists between the clauses 8a–8n in the left column and those in the right column 9a–9n. An examination of Table 15.1, had revealed a 'semantic echo' between what is being called the conditioning environment of the *give* type clauses 8a–8n and their counterparts clauses 9a–9n: the latter offer a good rendering of the conditioned meaning of 8a–n, so much so that the pairs were described as being 'near synonymous'. It appear most likely that a deeper insight will be afforded if those items which are responsible for creating this 'semantic echo' can be pinpointed. One way of doing this is to abstract such items from both columns: this is what is presented in Table 15.2 with respect to just the three clauses belonging to part A of the two columns; what this abstracts out is

Table 15.2: The permeability of Process *give* in operation

Give with the nominal group realising Goal	The relation leading to the semantic echo
8a: **gave** a *warm <u>hug</u>*	
8b: **gave** a *<u>knock</u> on the head*	
8c: **gave** *substantial <u>help</u>*	9a: **hugged** warmly
9b: **knocked** on the head	
9c: **helped** substantially	
the conditioning environment of permeating *give*	the permeated <u>verbs</u> in conditioned meaning

the nominal group realising the Goal in the clauses 8a–8c, and the verbs that realise the elements (Event) and the Circumstance in clauses 9a–9c. The verb lexemes are foregrounded in both columns; the left column underlines the Thing in the nominal groups; the right column shows the location of the semantic echo: this helps us see very clearly that although the distribution of grammatical functions in the echoing 'bits' of the two clause types is different, the principle underlying the relation is the same.

One aspect of the phenomenon brought to attention by Table 15.2 would be immediately recognised by SFL practitioners as 'grammatical metaphor': this is located in the left column, and its congruent version is unpacked in the right counterpart. This clinches the issue of the status of the italicised nominal group in the clauses 8a–8n. The particular category of grammatical metaphor needed here to create a conditioning environment in the conditioned *give* type Event is well known: Halliday introduced this class of grammatical metaphor some decades back in the context of describing the tenor of the register of writing about scientific experiments. The category particularly relevant to the discussion of a *give* type Event can be easily identified as numbered 2(i) in Figure 2.3 in Halliday (1998[2004b]:41–42): this was succinctly described there as follows: '(2) process – entity (i) Event = Thing.' Table 15.1 shows, the observation is applicable not only to part A but to parts B–D as well. Given this information, the nature of the conditioning environment for this class of *give* may be described more precisely as: *the process type give functioning as Event will be conditioned* IF *the clausal element Goal entailed by this Event type is realised as a nominal group whose element Thing is instantiated by a grammatical metaphor pertaining to category 2(i) of Figure 2.3 in Halliday 2004b:41.* Taking the first clause from each part in the left column, such a nominal group would be exemplified as: (A) *a warm **hug***, (B) *a friendly **nod***, (C) *a great **shock***, and (D) *an explicit **order***; each part differs from the others by virtue of the noun realising Thing, which, though metaphorised, still retains the systemic make-up of the verb as a lexeme. Clearly, the grammatical metaphor forms the basis of the semantic echo across the pairs of clauses in Table 15.2: but the importance of the relation goes beyond this contribution: I will return to this later in section 15.4.3. What is important here is the fact that the conditioning of the permeating verb *give* and the categories permeated by it have been precisely indicated by the lexicogrammatical metaphor which is located in the conditioning environment.

It is perhaps necessary to say quite explicitly that the possibility of describing the relation between the pair of clauses in Table 15.2 in terms of grammatical metaphor does not render the concept of permeability superfluous: in the first place, not enough work has been done in this area to allow a definite claim that underlying every grammatical metaphor there will be the relation of permeability, though it can be stated with certainty that the conditioning environment of permeating categories cannot *always* require grammatical metaphor: this much follows from the acceptance of permeability in the two tenses discussed above. But so far as the potential of a *give* type verb to enter in a relation of permeability with other process types is concerned, the evidence in its favour has steadily become more robust as facts in support of this view have emerged in the two sections above.[22] Below I will use the three principles that were announced on the basis of permeability in tenses (section 15.3.5).

15.4.3 Three principles for recognising permeability: The case of *give*

PRINCIPLE 1: Proceeding directly to the first principle, the stress is on the inter-stratal nature of permeability; *a specific instance of permeability is detected only in an inter-stratal context.* Assigning meaning to any lexicogrammatical pattern is in fact equal to working with (at least) the two strata of lexicogrammar and semantics: the solidarity between them, as also that between semantics and context, is effected by the relation of realisation. The 'fixation' of the relations of context-meaning-wording is a complex matter. And speaking about the relation is even more so: it may be sufficient here to say simply that all proofs of 'same or different semantic value' will always be indirect and inexact. If a particular meaning is the realisation of a particular contextual phenomenon, this raises a problem in meaning exchange: to say what a contextual configuration is like will ultimately require the use of language, in the majority of cases: this implies, in the last resort, that the 'proof' of the similarity of semantic values will have to be co-textual; and the basis for the 'measurement of semantic value' lies in the communal conventions.

The ploy I have used in this chapter is to match a clause type with permeating *give* functioning as Event with one that is widely viewed as being semantically pretty close to it (see Table 15.1). It so happens that the presence of the grammatical metaphor provides quite reasonable textual evidence of semantic affinity between 9a *the mother hugged the child warmly* and 8a *the mother gave the child a warm hug* – and this relation applies invariably to every pair in Table 15.1. But, ultimately, whether with fully grammatical tenses or with fully lexical Event verbs, claims about semantic affinity between matching units have to be taken on trust – and more often than not, this trust is based on the realisational relations conventionally accepted in the community between context, meaning, wording and sound images. And, the other side of every such story is the denial of the existence of absolute synonymy: *girl* and *lass* are indisputably synonyms as are *window* and *casement*, but they are not exactly exchangeable everywhere; and this leads one to ask: what's going on in the occasion of talk? It is understanding based on such communal observations that forms the basis for believing with Halliday (2005[2014]) that 'matter and meaning: the two realms of human experience' are permeable, as scholars founding the SFL modelling of language such as Whorf, Firth and Bernstein have recognised. So, it matters that what the mother actually did when she *gave the child a book* (cf. 7a) differs somewhat both experientially and interpersonally from what she did when *she gave the child a warm hug* (cf. 9a). The closeness of meaning between 8a *the mother gave the child a warm hug* and 9a *the mother hugged the child warmly* seems undeniable; but similarly, the resemblance between 7a *the mother gave the child a new book* and 8a *the mother gave the child a warm hug* cannot be ignored: in both cases the *give* is doing what *give* must do – i.e., passing on a gift to the Recipient. What follows from these patterns of similarity and dissimilarity for the debate on permeability will call for a return in principle 3 below; here I reiterate that issues of semantic affinity cannot be discussed without implicating at least the two strata of meaning and wording; and explanations are very likely to take the analyst to other strata – meaning and context on the one hand and wording and phonology, on the other. Whorf tells us that 'speech is the best show man puts on' and that is true; a part of its wondrous quality lies in the parallel intricate inter-relating up and down the strata, in a unit of time that may be measured as that needed for the twinkling of an eye.

PRINCIPLE 2: Despite this emphasis on the inter-stratal perspective, the second principle foregrounds the intra-stratal nature of permeability: *a specific instance of permeability is limited to one single stratum.* Thus, in order to claim permeability, the three relevant categories of process – the default usage (e.g., 7a), the permeating (conditioned) usage (e.g., 8a) and the conditioned pattern (e.g., 9a) which, as it were, fixes the identity of the semantic space 'entered' by the conditioned *give* – must all belong to the same stratum. The use of the temporal Circumstance, *yesterday*, is not conditioning factor in *he left yesterday*; nor is *tomorrow* conditioning in *he will leave tomorrow*. The reason that *tomorrow* in *he leaves tomorrow* is seen as conditioning, is simply that it conditions the meaning of the tense: the clause *he leaves early* has the default meaning of the 'routine lapse of time'. The relation of the three clauses – *he leaves early*; *he leaves tomorrow* and *he'll leave tomorrow* – is, *mutatis mutandis*, the same for the three clause types just discussed above. Meaning is distinguishing them; but it is their lexicogrammatical form that is used for establishing their identities as distinct types. The form of permeability found in tense or in the lexical verb *give* occurs at the stratum of lexicogrammar: the abstraction at the other two strata on the 'content plane', namely that of meaning or context, are of different kinds. One would expect permeability to behave somewhat differently at those strata. Some evidence for this might be derived from the discussion of permeability in Hasan (2014b).

PRINCIPLE 3: The issue of similarity and difference in meaning is central to the third principle: it states that *the realisation of the permeating category in its conditioned mode does not duplicate an existing meaning*. From the perspective of this chapter, the comment applies specifically to the meaning construed by the permeating tenses and by the clauses 8a–8n in Table 15.1: the claim is that with permeability the conditioned meaning is no longer the same as that in the default semantic zone; and although it can be identified as pertaining to some other semantic zone, the specific meaning it construes is uniquely its own: it does not duplicate any existing semantic category. Now, the resistance of language to the duplication of exactly the same meaning has been repeatedly emphasised in this chapter (section 15.3.5, and also in this section): it is not in the nature of language to tolerate absolute synonymy. Thus, when a lexeme borrowed from another language appears to act as an exact synonym of some native word in the host language, the newly introduced word will, often quite readily, tend to develop some trait that will render it distinct. Take, for example, the French word *petite* (feminine; adjective) and *small*: in English today, one may refer to 'a small chair' or 'a small leaf', but neither of these objects come in a *petite* size in English; you need to go to the source language to be able to talk of 'une petite chaise' or 'la petite feuille'; the word 'petite' in English is now dedicated to female fashions, including the size of female clothes.

That said, in talking about permeability, the issue has not been that of 'the same meaning': rather, the concern has been with two closely related issues: entry into a different semantic domain from the default one, and a semantic affinity – not identity – with some category in that permeated zone. To say that the meaning of *I'm sending it tomorrow* and *I'll send it tomorrow* is similar (in that both fall within the domain of future time) is not to say that their meaning is identical (discussion 15.3.5). And when the conditioned *give* is said to abandon its own default domain, moving into some other that forms the legitimate, i.e., default zone of some other process type(s), this is not to claim that the conditioned *give* has assumed the *identity* of those other process types: every semantic domain is simply a subset of the total potential of a language's meanings. In this perspective, each semantic domain presents a calibrated set of possibilities, and it is choices from amongst these that specify the identity of the various categories of that domain. When a semantic domain is permeated by a permeating category, the latter acquires an identity that is all its own. In talking about language, we use words that make it sound as if language – its concepts and relations – are like material things in the material world, but nothing could be further from reality, and it is worth remembering that semantic space is not like material space that can be competed for. The various tables presented in this section are an attempt to show the relevant relations that hold between the three categories: (a) the default; (b) the permeating; and (c) that category from the permeated domain which is closest in value to the permeating one. The discussion of examples 7 and 7a (in section 15.4) had established the defining features of clauses with the default *give*. Table 15.1 (in section 15.4.1) had been an effort to show the regularity of the principle underlying the relations between the permeating *give* and the closest category from the permeated domain(s). Table 15.2 was an attempt to reveal (in section 15.4.2) the principle underlying that semantic affinity. Table 15.3, presented in this section, shows the extent to which domains pertaining to other process types are permeated by the conditioned meanings of the verb *give*: the evidence concerning this comes from the points of resemblance between the permeating categories (i.e., 8a–8n) and those closest in meaning to it from the permeated domains (i.e., 9a–9n): the former, i.e., the permeating ones thus construe a pattern that is simultaneously reminiscent of the domain from which the permeating category is coming from and where it is moving to (see the left and right columns of Table 15.3, respectively). The distinct identity of the process types permeated by the permeating *give* can be arrived at by examining parts A–D of the right column in relation to the same parts in the left one, i.e., permeating process *give*.

Table 15.3: Some ways of construing process

Part	conditioning environment of permeating *give* semantic equivalence: semantic affinity to default *give*	Part	process type bearing semantic affinity to permeating *give*
A: 8a	gave the child a warm hug meaning as if gave the child something = a **hug**	A: 9a	**hug**ged the child warmly Process type = *material: impactive*
B: 8d	gave her a friendly nod meaning as if gave her something = a **nod**	B: 9d	**nod**ded at her friendlily Process type = *material: somatic*
C: 8g	gave them a great shock meaning as if gave them something = a **shock**	C: 9g	**Shock**ed them greatly Process type = *mental: reaction*
D: 8k	gave him an explicit order meaning as if gave him something = an **order**	D: 9k	**order**ed him explicitly Process type = *verbal*

The right column of Table 15.3 explicitly indicates the areas which according to my research have proved permeable in the specific sense discussed here. This permeability, originating from the permeating *give* type process (8a–8n), extends to other material process types: the first of these in part A is the 'impactive' material process, realised by lexical verbs which in their default form do not construe direct exchange such as is characteristic of the *give* type process. Some examples of this type are *put, paint, measure, kick, walk,* and so on; it is a sub-set of these, such as *hug, embrace, knock, assist,* that participate in permeability of the kind shown in part A (right column). Another class of material process type, which the permeating verb *give* can permeate is that labelled 'somatic': examples of this are given in part B. An action type, physiologically mediated, it has no *material* impact on any entity other than the Actor: thus it is different from *put, kick, knock, help,* and so on, which affect other bodies; but the members of this class of lexical verb are capable of being interpreted as referring to a kinesic 'tone setting' material action. The third permeated area is shown in Part C: here the class suggested by the examples is that called 'reaction', a sub-class of the mental process type.[23] It is possible that its other subclasses 'cognition' and 'perception' might also be permeated; cursory enquiry has failed to produce convincing examples. Finally, part D shows that the permeability of *give* extends to 'verbal' process type. The one main process type that appears to be completely unaffected by the permeating *give* is the relational type.

The above account has presented a quick view of the areas the permeating *give* is able to permeate: just as the tenses had permeated other tenses, the conditioned process type *give* has permeated other process types, following a pattern established in Table 15.2. The left column of the Table has maintained in every case the 'invariability' of the structure of clauses 8a–n; and by adopting a structure suited to clause 7a which is a default example of the default use of *give*, it has emphasised the relation of 7a to 8a–8n. The left column of Table 15.3 is an attempt to present the best gloss for the clause type with the conditioned *give*. But of course, no matter how close the gloss offered in the left column might be to the 'wording', the 'intended' meaning of the clauses, when thus paraphrased, is very far from what an ordinary person might think of as an English way of saying or meaning: the description assigned to them in Table 15.1 is just skin-deep. Lexicogrammatically each clause in the left column may be said to have the same choice of Event as the default clause 7a; but when it comes to construing meaning, 7a and 8a are significantly different. The verb *give* in the latter has only the appearance of having the default function of Event; in fact, it contributes just two elements of meaning: one of these is the fusion of simple past tense with the lexical verb, and so is not intrinsic to the meaning of *give* as a lexical verb. The second presents the most general, non-specific meaning of lexical verb *give*, namely, an exchange of the given between Actor and Recipient. Both the default clause type exemplified as 7a: *the mother gave the child a new book* and the permeating one *the mother gave the child a warm hug*, exemplified as 8a, construe the Event as occurring in the past, and both refer to some 'thing' given as the left column in Table 15.3 shows. In 7a the given is a concrete, alienable entity; so bestowal and benefaction can be taken as the 'natural' outcome of giving. In 8a things are different and that is what gives an indication of how this clause should be interpreted: the given in this category does not have the required attributes, it is simply a 'gift'. Since the given is a verb metaphorised as noun – verb $\Rightarrow$ noun – in the conditioning Goal, it is the meanings implicit in the noun that must be interpreted as given: the metaphorised verb working as noun suggests that the conditioned clause is a nuanced way of saying that hugging has been done. The specific nature of the nuance is implicit in the verb appearing as noun, since lexemes of any kind, in their metaphorised state, retain the evaluation assigned to them communally. This reminds me of a concept introduced elsewhere some years back (Hasan 1999) as 'tone setting': this refers to any kind of saying which, irrespective of its lexical meaning, adds to the saying a nuance, an attitude, that impacts on the tenor relation of Sayer and Addressee. So the permeating *give* has, as it were, forgone most of its experiential information: what it has gained is the specification of a quality that points to interpersonal relations in the action. In the terms of Whorf, this makes the permeating verb *give* a crypto-typic, i.e., a category that does not proclaim its meaning by its shape: instead, the meaning has to be worked out by reference to the relationships of the item.

15.5 Permeability, Hybridity and Linguistics: Concluding remarks

I hope the last two sections have succeeded in demonstrating an orderly linguistic basis for the relation of permeability in categories that would play an explanatory role in a functional linguistic theory. There is some indication that the form taken by permeability at the two remaining strata of semantics and context will be somewhat different, if only because, at this stage, construal beyond context appears rather improbable. But it seems certain that the two general principles will apply: one, the diagnosis of permeability will be assisted by inter-stratal relation, and, two, the permeable categories – i.e., those that permeate and those that get permeated – will be confined to one single stratum. The third principle will depend on how the terms of reference about similarity and difference in meanings would be interpreted. Obviously, such a debate could not have been included within the scope of this chapter, but so far as context is concerned, there is some indication about the relation of permeability across the parameters (Hasan 2014b; forthcoming). And, having introduced the concept of 'text complex', I do feel impelled to say that realisation is best not confused with permeability: realisation is needed to recognise the relation of permeability, but what actually counts is the specific kind of relations characteristic of the permeable categories. It has been argued in some detail (Hasan 1999; 2000) that a text complex is the realisation of a complex contextual configuration (CC); and there is good reason to argue that in the process of a main CC there may arise the need to select one or more subsidiary contexts in order to deal with contingencies. The way the interactants manage these contingencies will contribute to a successful – or unsuccessful, as the case may be – completion of the social practice; and as I have suggested social practice is what in the context of situation functions as the primary activator of the meaning-wording that the interactants produce by way of a text simplex or a text complex.

Is permeability a different term for hybridity? This depends on how the term 'hybridity' is used in linguistics; and, as I admitted earlier, the word has not been part of my vocabulary for doing linguistics, though I may have used it as a step for establishing some kind of contact. Permeability, as this chapter has attempted to demonstrate, is a means of bringing order into what appears on the surface to be chaos, and, in a sense, identifying permeability is equal to identifying principles of regularity, no matter how abstruse they may seem. Could one, perhaps, claim that permeability produces hybrids, for example, such as the clause type 8a–8n in Table 15.1. If the answer is yes, has something more been achieved by this than the labelling of a set of instances? Where is the principle underlying this hybridity, if hybridity it is? And, as a matter of fact, hybridity as used in plant or animal genetics is based on explanatory concepts – certainly it is not a free floating phenomenon that can be reduced to co-location. It is surely not an accidental omission that has prevented us from hearing about some variety of rose being grafted on to a date palm? The principles that underlie the relation of permeability in some linguistic categories is, perhaps, not so very different, in general terms, as the set of complex factors which must be known to raises the probabilities of producing viable hybrids.

A functional linguistic theory such as SFL needs to recognise the concept of permeability: developing this theme fully would requires more than this chapter. Here I discuss just the few aspects of their relation that appear most important. Language, according to SFL, is a meaning potential, thus suggesting that language must be semogenetic (Halliday and Matthiessen 1999): a permeating category is, in fact, a device for creating new meanings. But perhaps what is remarkable is not just that new meanings are produced by the device of permeability, but that subtle distinctions in meaning are introduced such as those between *will send* and *'m sending tomorrow* or between *the mother hugged the child warmly* and *the mother gave the child a warm hug*. Enquiry into permeability demands detailed attention to the relations of linguistic patterns: the description is not simply about default patterns as conventionally foregrounded in a language; it focuses attention on conditioned environments. And whether one explores the default patterns or the conditioned one, the ultimate story is that of the regularity of a set of relations. This draws the analysis some steps closer to Whorf's ideal of studying the 'configurative rapport' – i.e., principles that forge a relation between crypto-typic patterns the decipherment of whose deeper meanings requires a good deal of close examination. Above all, permeability is an eloquent response to the idea of language as a rule governed system: it is a sobering thought that there are regular relations in language, that, as a matter of rule, should have been 'ungrammatical' but that thrive side by side in a language. The fuzziness of language is not a fuzziness of what a category means, how far its domain of reference extends; rather, the web of relations in any language is dense and what is needed is 'most delicate grammar'. In this perspective much remains to be explored. To finish with Whorf (1956:250):

> We must find out more about language! Already we know enough about it to know it is not what the great majority of men, lay or scientific, think it is. The fact that we talk almost effortlessly, unaware of the exceedingly complex mechanism we are using, creates an illusion. We think we know how it is done, that there is no mystery; we have all the answers. Alas, what wrong answers!

Notes

1   Hjelmslev's concept of the different orders of abstraction has been adopted in the SFL theory in general, though the elaboration of the planes and their relations as *developed* in Halliday's SFL modelling of language do differ significantly from Hjelmslev's ideas. I say this in recognition of the two variant models of SFL – Fawcett's, e.g., 2000 and Martin's, e.g., 1992. The statements made here, e.g., about strata, realisation or systems, are made with the present version of Halliday's model in mind; they may or may not apply equally well to the two variant models.

2   The talk was presented to a conference hosted by the Society of Pakistan English Language Teachers (SPELT). The title of the talk was *English Process, English tense: foreign learner, foreign teacher*. An abridged version of the talk was published in the *SPELT Newsletter*, 10[4], December 1995, and a revised version is reprinted in Hasan. 2011:336–79.

3   This system network representing the semantic choices for describing the meanings relevant to the unit 'message' (realised as clause) included the majority of systems in as much as they pertained to that semantic unit – the system of time was a small part of that system network, describing time construal within the various messages types. Some version of these semantic systems have been briefly described in Cloran 1994; includes here is also her revised system network of time which develops and elaborates the 1983 version of the system of time (see, especially Chapter 5:185–221).

4   See back cover of Bréal (1964 edition with introduction by Joshua Whatmough) as well as the Preface by J. P. Postgate, which goes back to 1897. Of course, the study of meaning goes back much further; not only to classical Greece, but also to Panini of India or the 'erya' of China.

5   It seems that the context as described here can be widened, but this needs further research. I have not presented the justification for specifying these

features as essential to the context of the two tenses, as that discussion demands much time and space, but the reasons have to do with the nature of time, whether it is 'sensuous' or 'subjective' in the terms of Whorf (1956).

6   This is not the occasion for discussing the meaning of the term 'serial tense'; the use of this term here is in keeping with the usage in Halliday 1976, 1985, 1994 as well as Halliday and Matthiessen 2004; 2014. The distinction between simple and serial is important: for one thing, the form taken by the same three tenses differs when they function in a serial tense. See, however, Bache 2008, according to whom SFL does not treat tense as 'serial'.

7   Not to make too much of it – clearly further and more intensive research in semantic analysis of tenses as a whole is needed – but it is remarkable in view of Reichenbach's claim that 'pure time' cannot be measured; for Whorf too the 'sensuous' time is time sensed through some process. So it is notable that past/present, both 'sens-ible' time, do fuse with the Process of the clause, while future, being a 'subjective' phenomenon of intention, desire, and expectation, fuses with Subject.

8   Compare *we'll move to the new house* (*before you are four*) with *will we move to the new house* (*before my birthday*); or *we will not* (*we won't*) *move ...* (*before my birthday*); or (*oh yes*) *we will move to the new house ...* (with accent on *will*). Note, I have ignored here (a) the contribution to meaning made in all these cases by the intonation or emphasis; and (b) other constraints on fusion which are phonological and/or morphological.

9   Consider by way of substantiation: ?*I walk to the office though I have never done that before* (past denied) and ?*I walk to the office but not again* (assumption of future excluded); if the tense word *will* is added between *but* and *not*, this will be explicit exclusion, and that utterance would be non-problematic.

10   For a range of interpretations of the simple present see also Huddleston (1984:143–152) and Leech (1989:5–8).

11   In today's security conscious world, opening a parcel can take a good deal of time, certainly more than it does to put something down. The probability of this tense occurring in the context of 'durative' main verb may be higher, but non-duratives such as *close, step, throw, put* and others are not, as it were, prohibited from co-occurring with this tense. (cf., Huddleston, 1984:153–154).

12   Today this requirement has weakened a good deal; often historical fiction, e.g., a novel by Hilary Mantel, might use this tense for substantial parts of the novel using 'tense shift' as an artistic device to identify certain kinds of situation types.

13   It is this kind of generalisation that I extended in Hasan 1978 to the description of text type (or more accurately register type) with the simple innovation of introducing more symbols to account for the options in the relations specific to textual elements, and/or to recursion, one device for the creation of variation.

14   There are other process types and each places some 'constraints' on the default meaning of a tense used with it; most obviously, in native English present-in-present is rare with mental Process. Thus *I like this city* not *I am*

liking this city. The latter would be viewed as a 'conditioned' use requiring specific conditioning environment of use (Halliday and Matthiessen 2014; Hasan 2011).

15 In fact, the earliest forms of communication are by means of kinesic signing and the interpretation of those signals depends almost entirely on the material situational setting (Malinowski, 1923; Trevarthen, 1974; Halliday, 2004a),

16 In my view, the two theories developed their 'plane of content' differently: there is no dialectic at any point in Hjelmslev's model, unless 'solidarity' is a different name for it. The distinction is central: the dialectic of context, meaning and lexicogrammar is, in my view, essential to the kind of functionality that characterises Halliday's SFL; the absence of this dialectic bars Hjelmslev's Glossematics from being viewed as a functional theory.

17 The concept of Maya (the sensible) and Aroopa (the intelligible) are highly relevant at this point: the ordinary speaker's intuitions are intuitions of meaning, not intuitions of lexicogrammar; the wording-meaning connection is, in terms of the Prague School scholars, 'automatized' in native speakers. To appreciate the depth of this observation, much more needs to be specified about who the speaker/listener are and what conditions apply to them to enable exchange. The point that seems important here is that whereas meaning is construed by a lexicogrammatical category, the lexicogrammatical category is not construed by the phonological shape that expresses the category. The relation between lexicogrammatical and phonological categories is established for ordinary speakers-listeners by conventional association of 'meaning' with an 'acoustic shape': the 'acoustic shape' does not construe the lexicogrammatical identity of a category; it simply signals that possibility. This implies that 'linguistic patternments' remain sub-conscious. Which is what makes linguistics an un-commonsense domain.

18 A number of questions arise at this point but will have to remain unanswered as much for lack of background knowledge as for lack of space. However, unlike homonymy, permeability is not a 'sense' relation of any kind.

19 A fully grammatical category has greater generalising power and it can be described exhaustively in fewer systemic steps, whereas a fully lexical item requires a good deal of steps, since each particular lexical item is 'unique': the choice path realising such a unique item contains the range of choices beginning from the primary delicacy to the most delicate choice (Hasan 1971; 1985; 1987). I will sometimes use the term 'lexeme' (Lyons 1968; 1977) to refer to such a lexical item.

20 Much water has flowed under the bridge since this research was done: so the description of the class of verbs can be presented in a more economical way today (and I might use some descriptive terms here that do not appear in the original), but the methodology underlying the analysis remains viable.

21 At that initial stage, I had used the term 'deprivation' for what is called 'bestowal' here, which now seems to me a much better term for characterising the action; 'acquisition' is retained as the other term of the system (see Hasan 1987: figure 7.2:189). Lexemes capable of realising the process type with

choices 'material: dispositive: acquisition' would be such verbs as *buy, collect, receive, steal, take* ...; the choices in the system of BENEFACTION applicable to this sub-class differ qualitatively from those that apply to the 'give' class.

22   I have perhaps tediously repeated '*give* type verb/Event' instead of referring to it as the lexeme *give*, because there are other extensions of meaning of this lexeme, e.g. in uses such as *the material has quite a bit of give in it*, not to forget the more complex cases combining grammatical metaphor with some figure of speech as in *lend me your ears, gave a piece of her mind,* and so on. Everything that has been said here concerns the function of *give* as Event in the identified clause type with its default structure as specified in section 15.4 – and this represents a very small corner of the grammar of English.

23   More recently, e.g., Halliday and Matthiessen (2004), the term 'affection' has replaced 'reaction' in SFL. I prefer 'reaction' to 'affection' since in English, 'affection' seems to construe a much more specific meaning than 'reaction', even though the verb 'affect' from which affect is derived is perhaps as general as 'react'.

References

Antilla, R. (1989). *Historical and Comparative Linguistics*. Amsterdam and Philadelphia: John Benjamins. http://dx.doi.org/10.1075/cilt.6

Antilla, A. (2002). Variation and phonological theory. In J.K. Chambers, P. Trudgill, and N. Schilling-Estes (Eds), *The Handbook of Language Variation and Change* 206–243. London: Blackwell.

Bache, C. (2008). *English Tense and Aspect in Halliday's Systemic Functional Grammar: A Critical Appraisal of an Alternative*. London: Equinox.

Bernstein, B. (1990). *Class, Codes and Control, Volume 4: The Structuring of Pedagogic Discourse*. London: Routledge. http://dx.doi.org/10.4324/9780203011263

Bréal, M. (1964). *Semantics: Studies in the Science of Meaning*. (Translated by H. Cusp, with added Introduction by J. Whatmough). New York: Dover.

Cloran, C. (1994). *Rhetorical Units and Decontextualisation: An Enquiry into some Relations of Context, Meaning and Grammar*. Monographs in Systemic Linguistics, Number 6. Nottingham: Department of English Studies, University of Nottingham.

Douglas, M. (1975). In the nature of things. In M. Douglas, *Implicit Meanings: Essays in Anthropology by Mary Douglas*. London: Routledge and Kegan Paul. (Inaugural Lecture given at University College London, 1971).

Fawcett, R.P. (2000). *A Theory of Syntax for Systemic Functional Linguistics. Amsterdam and Philadelphia*. John Benjamins. http://dx.doi.org/10.1075/cilt.206

Firth, J.R. (1957). *Papers in Linguistics 1934–1951*. London: Oxford University Press.

Firth, J.R. (1968). *Selected Papers of J.R. Firth*, edited by F.R. Palmer. London: Longman.

Halliday, M.A.K. (1961[2002]). Categories of the theory of grammar. *Word* 17(3), 241–92. Reprinted in M.A.K Halliday (2002) *On Grammar*, Volume 1 of the The Collected Works of M.A.K. Halliday, edited by J.J. Webster, 37–94. London: Continuum.

Halliday, M.A.K. (1976). The English verbal group. In G. Kress (Ed.), *Halliday: System and Function in Language: Selected papers*, 136–158. London: Oxford University Press.

Halliday, M.A.K. (1984[2002]). On the ineffability of grammatical categories. In A. Manning, P. Martin and K. McCall (Eds), *The Tenth LACUS Forum*, 3–18. Columbia, SC: Hornbeam Press. Reprinted in M.A.K. Halliday (2002) *On Grammar*, Volume 1 of the The Collected Works of M.A.K. Halliday, edited by J.J. Webster, 37–94. London: Continuum.

Halliday, M.A.K. (1985). *An Introduction to Functional Grammar*. London: Edward Arnold.

Halliday, M.A.K. (1994). *An Introduction to Functional Grammar* (2nd ed.). London: Edward Arnold.

Halliday, M.A.K. (1998[2004b]). Language and Knowledge: the 'unpacking' of text. In D. Allison, L. Wee, Bao Z., and S. Abraham (Eds), *Text in Education and Society*. Singapore: Singapore University Press. Reprinted in M.A.K. Halliday (2004) *The Language of Science*, Volume 5 of the Collected Works of M.A.K. Halliday, edited by J.J. Webster, 24–48. London: Continuum.

Halliday, M.A.K. (2004a). Representing the child as a semiotic being (one who means). In M.A.K. Halliday *The Language of Early Childhood*, Volume 4 of the Collected Works of M.A.K. Halliday, edited by J.J. Webster, 6–27. London: Continuum.

Halliday, M.A.K. (2005[2014]). Matter and meaning: the two realms of human experience. *Linguistics and the Human Sciences*, 1(1), 59–82. Reprinted in M.A.K. Halliday (2014) *Halliday in the 21st Century*, Volume 11 of The Collected Works of M.A.K. Halliday, edited by J.J. Webster, 192–214. London: Bloomsbury.

Halliday, M.A.K. (2014). That 'certain cut': Towards a characterology of Mandarin Chinese. *Functional Linguistics 1*(2). doi:10.1186/2196-419X-1-2

Halliday, M.A.K., McIntosh, A., and Strevens, P. (1964). *The Linguistic Sciences and Language Teaching*. London: Longmans.

Halliday, M.A.K., and Matthiessen, C.M.I.M. (1999). *Construing Experience through Meaning*. London: Continuum.

Halliday, M.A.K., and Matthiessen, C.M.I.M. (2004). *An Introduction to Functional Grammar* (3rd ed.). London: Arnold.

Halliday, M.A.K., and Matthiessen, C.M.I.M. (2014). *Halliday's Introduction to Functional Grammar*. (4th edn, Revised by Matthiessen). London: Routledge.

Hasan, R. (1971). Syntax and semantics. In J. Morton (Ed.), *Biological and Social Factors in Psycholinguistics*, 131–151. London: Logos Press.

Hasan, R. (1973[2005]). Code, register and Social dialect. In B. Bernstein (Ed.), *Class, Codes and Control, Volume 2: Applied Studies towards a Sociology of*

Language, 253–293. London: Routledge and Kegan Paul. Reprinted in R. Hasan (2005) *Language, Society and Consciousness*, Volume 1 of The Collected Works of Ruqaiya Hasan, edited by J.J. Webster, 160–193. London: Equinox.

Hasan, R. (1978). Text in the systemic functional model. In W.U. Dressler (Ed.), *Current Trends in Textlinguistics*, 228–246. Berlin: Walter de Gruyter.

Hasan, R. (1983). A Semantic Network for the Analysis of Messages in Everyday Talk between Mothers and their Children. Department of Linguistics: Macquarie University. (mimeo).

Hasan, R. (1984). The nursery tale as a genre. In M. Berry (Ed.), *Nottingham Linguistic Circular 13, Special Issue in Systemic Linguistics*, 71–102. Nottingham: Department of English Studies.

Hasan, R. (1985). Lending and borrowing: from grammar to lexis. In J. Clarke (Ed.), *The Cultivated Australian: Festschrift in Honour of Arthur Delbridge* 55–67. Hamburg: Helmut Buske.

Hasan, R. (1987). The grammarian's dream: lexis as most delicate grammar. In M.A.K. Halliday and R.P. Fawcett (Eds), *New Developments in Systemic Linguistics, Volume 1: Theory and Description*, 184–211. London: Pinter.

Hasan, R. (1999). Speaking with reference to Context. In M Ghadessy (Ed.), *Text and Context in Functional Linguistics*, 219–328. Amsterdam and Philadelphia: John Benjamins. http://dx.doi.org/10.1075/cilt.169.11has

Hasan, R. (2000). The uses of Talk. In S. Sarangi and M. Coulthard (Eds), *Discourse and Social Life*, 28–47. London: Longman.

Hasan, R. (2009). *Semantic Variation: Meaning in Society and in Sociolinguistics*, Volume 2 of The Collected Works of Ruqaiya Hasan, edited by J.J. Webster. London: Equinox.

Hasan, R. (2010). The meaning of 'not' is not in 'not'. In A. Mahboob and N. Knight (Eds.), *Appliable Linguistics*, 267–306. London: Continuum.

Hasan, R. (2011). English process, English tense: Foreign learner, foreign teacher, (revised version). In *Language and Education: Learning and Teaching in Society*, Volume 3 of The Collected Works of Ruqaiya Hasan, edited by J.J. Webster, 336–379. London: Equinox. First published in *SPELT Newsletter*, 10(4), December 1995, (Karachi).

Hasan, R. (2013). Choice, system, realisation: describing language as meaning potential. In L. Fontaine, T. Bartlett, and G. O'Grady (Eds), *Systemic Functional Linguistics: Exploring Choice*, 269–299. Cambridge: Cambridge University Press. http://dx.doi.org/10.1017/CBO9781139583077.018

Hasan, R. (2014a). Linguistic sign and the science of linguistics: the foundations of appliability. In F. Yan and J.J. Webster (Eds), *Developing Systemic Functional Linguistics: Theory and Applications*, 106–137. London: Equinox.

Hasan, R. (2014b). Towards a paradigmatic description of context: systems, meta-functions and semantics. *Functional Linguistics*, 1(9). http://dx.doi.org/10.1186/s40554-014-0009-y

Hasan, R. (forthcoming). Tenor: rethinking interactant relations. In *Context in the System and Process of Language*, Volume 4 of The Collected Works of Ruqaiya Hasan, edited by J.J. Webster. London: Equinox.

Hjelmslev, L. (1961). *Prolegomena to the Theory of Language*. (Translated by F.J. Whitfield). Wisconsin: University of Wisconsin Press.

Huddleston, R. (1984). *Introduction to the Grammar of English*. Cambridge: Cambridge University Press. http://dx.doi.org/10.1017/CBO9781139165785

Lamb, S.M. (1999). *Pathways of the Brain: the Neurocognitive Basis of Language*. Amsterdam and Philadelphia: John Benjamins. http://dx.doi.org/10.1075/cilt.170

Leech, G. (1989). *Meaning and the English Verb* (2nd ed.). London: Longman.

Lyons, J. (1968). *Introduction to Theoretical Linguistics*. London: Cambridge University Press. http://dx.doi.org/10.1017/CBO9781139165570

Lyons, J. (1977). *Semantics, 2*. Cambridge: Cambridge University Press.

Malinowski, B. (1923). The problem of meaning in primitive languages, Supplement I. In C.K. Ogden and I.A. Richards (Eds), *The Meaning of Meaning* 451–510. London: Kegan Paul.

Martin, J.R. (1992). *English Text: System and Structure*. Amsterdam and Philadelphia: John Benjamins. http://dx.doi.org/10.1075/z.59

Mathesius, V. (1964). On linguistic characterology with illustrations from Modern English. In J. Vachek (Ed.), *A Prague School Reader in Linguistics*. Bloomington: Indiana University Press. (Translated and reprinted from *Actes du Premier Congres International de Linguistes a la Haye* (1928: 56–63)).

Matthiessen, C.M.I.M. (2015). Halliday on Language. In J.J. Webster (Ed.), *The Bloomsbury Companion to M.A.K. Halliday*, 137–202. London: Bloomsbury.

Reichenbach, H. (1957). *The Philosophy of Space and Time*. (Translated by M. Reichenbach and J. Freund, introduced by R. Carnap). New York: Dover Publications.

Sapir, E. (1921). *Language: An Introduction to the Study of Speech*. New York: Harcourt, Brace and Co.

de Saussure, F. (1966). *Course in General Linguistics* (Translated and introduced by W. Baskin). New York: McGraw-Hill.

de Saussure, F. (2006). *Writings in General Linguistics* (S. Bouquet and R. Engler (Eds), Translated by C. Saunders, and M. Piers). Oxford: Oxford University Press.

Shapiro, J.A. (2011). *Evolution: A View from the 21st Century*. Upper Saddle River, NJ: FT Press Science.

Trevarthen, C. (1974). Conversations with a two month old. *New Scientist*, 62 (2 May), 896: 230–235.

Tucker, G. (this volume). Hybridity in transitivity: Phraseological and metaphorically derived Processes in the system network for TRANSITIVITY.

Whorf, B.L. (1956). *Language, Thought and Reality: Selected Writings of Benjamin Lee Whorf* (Edited and introduced by J.B. Carroll). Cambridge, MA: MIT Press.

Zadeh, L.A. (1997). Toward a theory of fuzzy information granulation and its centrality in human reasoning and fuzzy logic. *Fuzzy Sets and Systems*, 90(2), 111–127. http://dx.doi.org/10.1016/S0165-0114(97)00077-8

About the author

Ruqaiya Hasan – who sadly passed away in the final stages of this book's preparation – was Emeritus Professor of Linguistics at Macquarie University, Australia. The life-long research of this extraordinary scholar and generous mentor can be succinctly summarised with the titles of her seven volume *Collected Works,* edited by J.J. Webster for Equinox: *Language, Society and Consciousness; Semantic Variation: Meaning in Society and in Sociolinguistics; Language in Education: Social Aspects of Learning and Teaching; Context in the System and Process of Language; Describing Language: Form and Function; Unity in Discourse: Texture and Structure,* and *Verbal Art: A Social Semiotic Perspective.* The SFL community grieves her loss and honours the legacy she leaves behind.

Index

A

Abrams, M.H., 259

abstract. *See* narrative structure

action process. *See* transitivity

activation-construal dialectic, 4, 11, 286, 287, 303

activity type, 9, 154, 155, 157, 160, 162, 164, 167, 173–174

Adam, C., 135

Adams, J., 156

adjunct, 23, 298, 356, 362

aesthetic mode. *See* rhetorical mode

affect. *See* appraisal

ambiguity. *See* indeterminacy

Antilla, R., 357

appliable linguistics, 86

applied linguistics, 110, 289, 294

appraisal, 101, 288, 291, 293, 301–303, 303 n.2

    affect, 101, 301, 302

    appreciation, 1, 301, 302, 303 n.3

    attitude, 101, 288, 291, 293, 301, 302, 303 n.2, 303 n.3

    judgement, 94, 101, 301, 303 n.3

    valuation, 1

    see also evaluation

appreciation. *See* appraisal

argumentation. *See* rhetorical mode

Artemeva, N., 135

articulacy, 95, 106

    see also literacy

    see also oracy

Arús Hita, J., 7, 45

Arzouan, Y., 70

Aston, G., 61 n.5

asynchronous interactivity, 88, 97

attitude. *See* appraisal

B

Bache, C., 377 n.6

Baker, N., 216

Bakhtin, M.M., 2, 134

Bales, R., 89

Banks, D., 5, 37, 45, 221

Barrett, M., 262 n.7

Bartlett, T., 3

Bastian, F., 217

Bawarshi, A.S., 2, 144

Baxter, J., 262 n.2

Bayley, P., 13, 309, 315

Beck, U., 306

Bednarek, M., 306, 309, 310, 327 n.3

behavioural process. *See* transitivity

Belsey, C., 150 n.2

Berlin, B., 157, 307

Bernstein, B., 89, 110, 114, 135, 339, 369

Berry, M., 27, 189

Bestgen, Y., 327 n.6

Bevitori, C., 309

Bhabha, Homi K., 2, 105, 209

Bhatia, V.K., 263 n.9, 289, 290, 291

Biber, D., 186, 188

Bietsch, W., 182, 184

Bisson, L.M., 264 n.14

Blatt, R.M., 2

blend. *See* indeterminacy

Bloor, M., 24, 328 n.12

Bloor, T., 24, 328 n.12

Bondi, M., 290

Borker, R.A., 261

Bowler, P.J., 156

Brah, A., 156

Bréal, M., 344, 376 n.4

Brumfit, C.J., 86

Bruner, J.S., 149

Burnard, L., 61 n.5

Burton, G.O., 262 n.5

Butler, C.S., 27, 28–33, 34, 43, 61 n.2

C

Caffarel, A., 79 n.1

Callaghan, M., 109, 112

Cardiff grammar (CaG), 6, 14 n.5, 38, 43–44, 45, 48, 51–52, 53, 54, 58, 61 n.1, 61 n.2, 61 n.6

    see also transitivity

Carretero, M., 66

Carter, R., 138, 139, 140, 150 n.2

causality, 55, 168, 274, 275, 277, 279, 280, 281, 282

Centre for Workforce Intelligence, 106 n.2

channel, 93, 191, 201, 208, 212, 218, 225, 255, 257–259

Chatman, S., 244

Cheng, D., 298

Chouliaraki, L., 4, 135

Christie, F., 8, 90, 109, 110, 120, 231

Cini, M., 326

circumstance. *See* transitivity

classifier, 5, 313–314, 317, 320, 321–324

clausal mode of discourse. *See* spoken(ness)

Cloran, C., 346, 350, 376 n.3

Clyne, M., 143, 145

coda. *See* narrative structure

code-switching, 159–160

Coffin, C., 7, 86, 87, 90, 91, 96, 110

cohesion, 97, 275, 308, 309

collocation. *See* corpus linguistics

command. *See* speech function

comparative genre analysis, 140–141, 144, 145, 268

complement, 47–48, 54–55, 57–59, 356, 362

complementarity. *See* indeterminacy

complication. *See* narrative structure

computer mediated communication (CMC), 85–106, 181–201
    see also hybridity and online communication

concordance. *See* corpus linguistics

conditioned meaning, 352–357, 360, 365–367, 370–371
    see also default meaning

congruent meaning. *See* metaphor.

congruent modality. *See* modality

Conklin, N.F., 261

construction of knowledge, 8, 104, 109, 116, 117–118
    guided construction of knowledge, 112, 117–118
    modelling and deconstruction of knowledge, 112, 113, 117–118, 119, 120, 124, 126

setting the context, 112, 116, 117–118, 125

content language integrated learning (CLIL), 109

context of culture. *See* context

context, 3–5, 6, 9, 10, 11, 12, 70, 74, 79 n.1, 134–135, 143, 154, 160, 185, 206, 209, 211, 213, 231, 241, 242–243, 260–261, 270, 286–288, 303, 338, 340, 344, 354, 358–359, 368–370, 374, 378 n.16
    context of culture, 64, 135, 143–144, 146, 148, 154, 288, 340, 359
    context of situation, 4, 90, 135–136, 143–144, 146, 154, 241, 259, 270, 271, 340, 355, 374
    contextual configuration (CC), 10, 241, 250, 254–259, 260, 263 n.12, 270, 368, 374
    contextual variables, 4, 93, 110, 137, 150, 200, 290, 327 n.9
    discursive context, 3, 5, 11, 286, 307, 311
    field, 93, 101, 102, 110, 135, 185, 188, 193, 200, 206–208, 211, 214, 225, 231–232, 235 n.1, 241, 254, 255–257, 258, 263 n.12, 270–271, 290, 339
    field of activity, 206, 208, 211, 214, 231, 232
    mode, 93, 135, 185, 206, 208, 211, 225, 235 n.1, 241, 246, 248, 254, 255, 257, 258–260, 262 n.3, 263 n.12, 264 n.16, 270, 271–272, 290, 315, 339, 353
        see also rhetorical mode
        see also spoken(ness)
        see also written(ness)
    tenor, 93, 135, 136, 185, 200, 206, 208, 211, 225, 235 n.1, 241, 255, 257, 258, 270, 271, 290–291, 339, 367, 374

contextual configuration (CC). *See* context

contextual variables. *See* context

contextualised meaning making, 91, 106
    see also decontextualised meaning making

conversation analysis, 155

conversation, 90, 93, 96, 97, 101, 182, 183, 185, 186–188, 190–193, 195–197,

198–199, 200–201, 225–226, 228, 255, 257, 261, 264 n.15, 354
Coombes, A.E., 156
corpus annotation, 12, 292, 325–326
    Halliday Centre tagger, 326
    UAM Corpus Tool, 291, 326
corpus driven linguistics. *See* corpus linguistics
corpus linguistics (CL), 11–12, 306–310, 314, 318, 325–327
    collocation, 307, 308
    concordance, 307, 308
    corpus based linguistics, 9, 182, 306, 307, 308, 360
    corpus driven linguistics, 308, 325
    keyness, 312, 316, 327 n.6
    keyword, 307
co-selection, 56, 355, 365
Coser, R.L., 163
co-text, 318, 321, 354, 355
Council of Deans of Health and Skills for Health, 87
Crawford Camiciottoli, B., 306
Crystal, D., 95, 186, 201 n.2
Custance, B., 110, 112, 113

D
Dahl, T., 137
Dalton-Puffer, C., 109
Dare, B., 110, 112, 113
Davies, M., 71
Deacon, T., 113
declarative. *See* mood
decontextualised meaning making, 89–90
    see also contextualised meaning making
default meaning, 345, 348–349, 351–353, 355, 357, 360, 363, 370, 377 n.15
    see also conditioned meaning
deixis, 242–3, 314, 328 n.12, 355
Derewianka, B., 90, 110, 231
Derrida, J., 3, 133
Devitt, A.J., 134
dialogism, 92–93, 95, 99, 100–101, 104, 105, 124, 190–191, 193, 196, 198, 199, 200–201, 240, 272
    see also written dialogue
Diani, G., 288, 295, 302
Dien, S., 268

disciplinary genre. *See* genre
discourse analysis, 2, 4, 9, 164, 201, 327 n.1
discourse semantics. *See* semantics
discourse type, 9, 154, 155–156, 160, 162, 165, 167, 168, 170–171, 173–174, 181–182, 262 n.3
discursive context. *See* context
discussion. *See* rhetorical mode
Doidge, N., 114
doing. *See* socio-semiotic process
Donohue, J.P., 86, 87, 91, 110
Douglas, M., 337, 357
Downing, A., 23, 27, 28–33, 34
Dunbar, R., 225
Duranti, A., 154

E
Eggins, S., 25, 27, 28–33, 34, 134, 226, 241, 251, 252, 263 n.11, 288, 290, 318
elaboration. *See* expansion
ellipsis, 184, 187–188, 190, 193, 195
enabling. *See* socio-semiotic process
English for academic purposes (EAP), 134, 136, 139, 148, 150
English for specific purposes (ESP), 133
enhancement. *See* expansion
epithet, 321, 323, 324
Erling, E.J., 87
ethnography, 88, 135
evaluation, 139, 141, 142, 145, 147, 183, 189, 198, 226, 228, 230, 236 n.8, 288, 295, 373
    see also appraisal
    see also narrative structure
event, 347, 361–363, 365, 366, 367, 369, 373, 379 n.22
exclamation. *See* speech function
existential process. *See* transitivity
expansion, 269, 299, 321, 322
    elaboration, 272, 274, 275, 277, 278–279, 280, 283
    enhancement, 244, 272, 275, 276, 321
    extension, 54, 59, 60, 272, 277, 279, 280, 282, 321
experiential metafunction. *See* semantic metafunction
exploring. *See* socio-semiotic process

exposition. *See* rhetorical mode
expository argument genre. *See* genre
expounding. *See* socio-semiotic process
extended present time. *See* time
extension. *See* expansion

F
face-to-face interaction, 98, 99, 199, 208,
212, 225
Fairclough, N., 2, 3, 4, 135, 306
Faust, M., 70
Fawcett, R.P., 5, 6, 14 n.5, 38, 43, 44, 51,
57, 59, 60, 61 n.1, 61 n.3, 376 n.1
Feez, S., 212
Fernald, A., 262 n.7
Ferrara, K.W., 165, 170
Fetzer, A., 2, 307
field. *See* context
field of action, 154
field of activity. *See* context
figurative meaning. *See* metaphor
finite auxiliary. *See* finite
finite, 184, 187, 298, 341, 345, 346–347,
356
finite auxiliary, 346
Firth, J.R., 337, 341, 345, 369
Fishman, P.M., 261
Fløttum, K., 137, 143, 151 n.4
Flowerdew, L., 308, 309
focal event, 154
footing, 162
Forey, G., 8
Fortanet, I., 288, 289, 290, 293, 294
free direct report. *See* projection
Fries, P.H., 183
Fusari, S., 11, 326
future tense. *See* tense
future time. *See* time
fuzziness, 10, 13, 45, 155, 173, 206, 271,
337–338, 376
see also indeterminacy

G
Galton, F., 156
Gatch, M., 271
Gee, J.P., 306
generic structure potential. *See* genre
genre school. *See* genre
generic structure. *See* genre

genre, 2–4, 8, 9, 10, 11, 96, 104, 110–111,
133–135, 136, 137, 138–141, 143–144,
145–146, 148, 149, 150, 217, 222, 240–
243, 247–254, 256, 259, 260–261, 262
n.3, 263 n.8, 264 n.16, 268, 269–271,
272, 273, 276, 277, 280, 281, 286, 288,
290–291, 293–296, 301–302, 303, 327
n.4
disciplinary genre, 288, 289, 291,
293, 296
expository argument genre, 138
generic structure, 114, 240, 247–
254, 259, 263 n.10, 263 n.12, 293
generic structure potential, 270
genre school, 133
hybrid genre, 135, 222, 263 n.8, 291
macrogenre, 96, 273
subgenre, 11, 271–273, 275, 284
see also hybridity, and genre
Gibbons, P., 113, 115
Giddens A., 306
Gilstad, H., 158
Giora, R., 70
Goatly, A., 69
Goffman, E., 155, 158, 160, 162, 164, 165
Goldstein, A., 70
Goodwin, C., 154
Grad, H., 326
grammatical metaphor (GM). *See*
metaphor
Grice, H.P., 155
Gubar, S., 262 n.2
guided construction of knowledge. *See*
construction of knowledge

H
Haarman, L., 309
Hall, C., 165
Halliday Centre tagger. *See* corpus
annotation
Halliday, M.A.K., 5, 6, 10, 11, 13, 14 n.4,
21–23, 26, 28–33, 34, 37, 38 n.1, 38 n.2,
38 n.3, 42, 43, 45, 46, 53, 56, 61 n.2, 61
n.3, 61 n.4, 65, 66, 67, 68, 73, 79 n.5, 93,
94, 95, 105, 111, 134, 135, 184, 185, 186,
201 n.1, 205, 206, 210, 221, 232, 235 n.3,
254, 262 n.3, 269, 270, 271, 272, 287,
290, 291, 298, 300, 307, 308, 309, 310,
315, 318, 320, 325, 326, 327 n.2, 327 n.4,

328 n.12, 328 n.14, 338, 339, 340, 343, 344, 347, 349, 351, 361, 362, 367, 369, 375, 376 n.1, 377 n.6, 378 n.14, 378 n.15, 378 n.16, 379 n.23
Hammond, J., 110, 113, 115
Hammond, P., 155
Harrison, C., 14 n.5
Hasan R., 3–4, 7, 11, 12, 42, 89, 90, 92, 133, 160, 161, 185, 187, 188, 191, 200, 205, 208, 213, 240, 241, 260, 261, 262 n.3, 263 n.12, 264 n.15, 264 n.15, 268, 269, 270, 271, 286, 287, 290, 307, 308, 316, 327 n.1, 327 n.4, 338, 339, 340, 341, 345, 354, 357, 358, 361, 370, 373, 374, 376 n.2, 377 n.13, 378 n.14, 378 n.19, 378 n.21
Hawkes, E., 261
Hedeboe, B., 143
Herring, S.C., 95, 191
heteroglossia, 212
Hewings, A., 87
highbred metaphor. *See* metaphor
Hinds, J., 143
historical/narrative present. *See* tense
Hjelmslev, L., 338, 345, 358, 376 n.1
Hollis, S., 268, 284
homonymy, 78, 359, 365, 378 n.18
    see also polysemy
Huddleston, R., 351, 377 n.10, 377 n.11
Hunston, S., 306, 307, 308
hybrid genre. *See* genre
hybrid language, 2
hybridity
    and genre, 133–151, 240–264, 268–284, 286–303
        see also genre
    and indeterminacy, 205–236
        see also indeterminacy
    and interdiscursivity, 306–328
        see also interdiscursivity
    and metaphor, 64–79
        see also metaphor
    and multilayeredness, 133–151
    and online communication, 85–106, 181–202
        see also computer mediated communication
    and process types, 21–38, 41–60

        see also transitivity, process types
    and professional practices, 154–175
    and/or permeability, 337–379
        see also permeability
    and register 181–201, 205–236
        see also register
    and role, 154–175
    and spokenness. *See* spoken(ness)
    and teaching and learning, 85–106, 133–151, 109–129
    and transitivity, 41–60
        see also transitivity
    and writtenness. *See* written(ness)
    interactional hybridity, 154–175
    kitkat hybridity, 155–156
    lexicogrammatical hybridity, 6, 48, 49, 79 n.3
Hyland, K., 288, 289, 290
Hynes, N., 262 n.5

I
ideational metafunction. *See* semantic metafunction
Iedema, R., 212
imperative. *See* mood
indeterminacy, 10, 13, 206–207, 209, 210–213, 217, 231
    see also fuzziness
    see also hybridity, and indeterminacy
    ambiguity, 10, 157, 206, 210–212, 214–218, 231, 259, 315
    blend, 10, 23, 35, 150, 156, 206, 210, 211, 213, 217, 221–224, 231, 236 n.11, 273, 306
    complementarity, 100, 206, 210
    neutralisation, 10, 210, 211, 213, 231, 225–231
    overlap, 10, 57, 206, 210, 211, 213, 218–221, 231, 271, 290, 327 n.9
indicative. *See* mood
information structure, 308
instance, 4, 5, 68, 135, 144, 150, 194, 210, 212, 221, 225, 232, 242, 243, 247, 272, 301, 302, 338, 344, 345, 346, 349, 358, 359, 362, 363, 365, 368, 369, 375
    see also system

instantiation, 5, 270, 307, 347
interactant reference, 188, 190, 193
interactional hybridity. *See* hybridity
intercontextuality, 306, 327 n.1
    see also interdiscursivity
interdiscursivity, 8, 154, 306, 327 n.1
    see also hybridity, and
        indeterminacy
    see also intercontextuality
    see also intertextuality
interpenetration, 307, 309
inter-permeation, 91
inter-stratal context. *See* stratification
inter-stratal relation. *See* stratification
interpersonal metafunction. *See* semantic
  metafunction
interpretive summary, 165, 170, 171
inter-relationality, 160
interrogative. *See* mood.
intertextuality, 8, 12, 154, 156, 212, 317,
  327 n.1
    see also interdiscursivity
Isaac, A., 2, 8, 150 n.1
Ivanič, R., 181

J
Jakobson, R., 12, 260, 264 n.16
Johansson, M., 2
Johns, A.M., 133
Johnson, J.H., 12, 309, 312, 328 n.9
Johnson, M., 46
Johnstone, B., 136
Jucker, A.H., 195
judgement. *See* appraisal
Jurovics, R., 269

K
Kapchan, D., 2
Kay, P., 157
keyness. *See* corpus linguistics
keyword. *See* corpus linguistics
Khubchandani, L.M., 64
Kienpointner, M., 139
Kilgarriff, A., 61 n.5
Kinn, T., 137
kitkat hybridity. *See* hybridity
knowledge orientation, 86, 91–92, 102,
  105
Kourilová, M., 295

Kraidy, M.M., 64
Krennmayr, T., 144
Kress, G., 96, 114, 262 n.3
Krugman, P., 320
Kutter, A., 326

L
Labov, W., 241, 251, 252, 253
Lakoff, G., 46
Lam M., 110, 206, 235 n.3, 290, 308
Lamb, S.M., 338
Landers, J., 103
Lash, S., 306
Latouche, S., 320
Lauerbach, G., 2
Leech, G., 377 n.10
Lemke, J.L., 212
Levinson, S., 155, 158
lexical density, 94, 98, 315
lexical metaphor (LM). *See* metaphor
lexicogrammatical hybridity. *See*
  hybridity
lexicogrammatical metaphor (LGM). *See*
  metaphor
literacy, 87, 95, 133
    see also articulacy
    see also oracy
literal meaning. *See* metaphor
Littlemore, J., 144
Lock, G., 23
Locke, P., 23, 27, 28–33, 34
logical metafunction. *See* semantic
  metafunction
Lombardo, L., 309
Lukin, A., 205
Luporini, A., 328 n.11
Lyons, J., 378 n.19

M
Machin, D., 326
Macken-Horarik, M., 110, 137, 138, 141,
  146, 150
Macnamara, J., 225
macrogenre. *See* genre
macro-commands, 192
macro-New, 219, 222
macro-scaffolding. *See* scaffolding
macro-theme. *See* theme
Mahlberg, M., 309

Makoni, S., 64
Malinowski, B., 154, 378 n.15
Maltz, D.N., 261
Mann, W.C., 219
Marcus, J., 240, 253, 261, 263
Mariani, L., 114
Martin, J.R., 1, 8, 25, 26, 27, 28–33, 34,
    37, 79 n.1, 109, 110, 114, 133, 135, 136,
    181, 219, 232, 235 n.1, 241, 249, 260,
    263 n.9, 269, 270, 271, 272, 273, 275,
    276, 286, 288, 289, 293, 301, 308, 315,
    327 n.4, 376 n.1
material process. *See* transitivity
Mathesius, V., 343
Maton, K., 91
Matthiessen, C.M.I.M., 1, 10, 14 n.5, 22,
    23, 25, 26, 27, 28–33, 34, 37, 38 n.1,
    n.2, n.3, 42, 43, 45, 46, 53, 56, 61 n.2,
    n.4, 76, 79 n.1, n.7, 110, 184, 186, 201
    n.1, 205, 206, 210, 219, 221, 232, 235
    n.3, 254, 269, 287, 290, 291, 298, 300,
    307, 308, 309, 310, 318, 327 n.2, n.14,
    340, 343, 344, 349, 361, 362, 375, 377
    n.6, 378 n.14, 379 n.23
Mayr, A., 326
McCarthy, M., 182
McIntosh, A., 205, 268, 339
meaning potential, 1, 6, 12, 42–43, 307,
    318, 328 n.9, 338, 360, 375
medium, 92, 94–95, 104, 185, 191, 212,
    255, 257, 259, 272
        see also written(ness)
        see also spoken(ness)
Mehan, H., 164
mental process. *See* transitivity
Merton, R.K., 162, 163, 164
message unit (MU), 186–188, 190, 192–
    193, 195
Mesthrie, R., 2
metaphor, 3–8, 10, 13, 41–42, 45–50,
    55–56, 60, 64–73, 75–77, 79 n.3, n.10,
    160, 189, 209–210, 241, 260, 264 n.15,
    276, 298–299, 314–316, 323, 328 n.11,
    367–369, 373, 379 n.22
        see also hybridity, and metaphor
        congruent meaning, 69, 111
        figurative meaning, 70–72, 76–77
        grammatical metaphor (GM), 46,
            65, 189, 209, 299, 316, 367–369,
            379 n.22
        highbred metaphor, 7, 65, 77–78,
            79 n.10
        lexical metaphor (LM), 46, 65–66,
            71
        lexicogrammatical metaphor
            (LGM), 66
        literal meaning, 7, 64, 70–71, 73,
            75–77
metaphorical modality. *See* modality
metaredundancy, 270, 308
metonymy, 6, 42, 45–46, 49, 53, 56, 59–60
Meurer, J.L., 327 n.1
Michell, M., 113
Miller, C.R., 133
Miller, D.R., 12–13, 14 n.6, 79 n.3, 264
    n.16, 309, 312, 325, 328 n.9, n.10
minor clause. *See* speech function
modalisation. *See* modality
modality system. *See* modality
modality, 291, 293, 295, 298–300
        congruent modality, 298
        metaphorical modality, 299
        modality system, 298
        modalisation, 319, 320
        modulation, 86, 319, 320
        objective modality, 307, 315, 319,
            320
mode. *See* context
modelling and deconstruction of knowl-
    edge. *See* construction of knowledge
modulation. *See* modality
Montgomery, M., 326
mood, 184, 186, 189, 190, 201 n.1, 291,
    293, 296–298, 345, 347
        declarative, 94, 99, 184, 192, 218–
            219, 297, 356–357
        imperative, 166, 192, 198, 218, 254,
            273–276, 281, 283–284, 296–297,
            300, 345
        indicative, 254, 296–297, 345
        interrogative, 99, 184, 189, 192, 195,
            201 n.1, 347
        polarity, 86, 295, 347
        queclarative, 184–185
morphology, 357, 377 n.8
Mueller, A., 217
Mukařovský, J., 260, 264 n.16
multilayeredness. *See* hybridity, and
    multilayeredness
multimodality, 96, 154

multisemiotic resources, 8, 109

N
Nanri, K., 212
narration. *See* rhetorical mode
narrative structure, 147, 252
　　abstract, 252
　　orientation, 252
　　complication, 252–253
　　evaluation, 250–254, 263 n.10, n.11
　　resolution, 252–254, 263 n.11
　　coda, 252, 254
Neale, A., 318
Nesbitt, C., 308
neutralisation. *See* indeterminacy
New Criticism, 138, 150 n.2
Newman, J., 51
New Rhetoric, 133
nominal mode of discourse. *See*
　written(ness)
nominalisation, 53–54, 66, 90, 94, 211
North, S., 87

O
objectification tendency, 342–342
objective modality. *See* modality
offer. *See* speech function
Oliveira, L.C., 298
oracy, 95
　　see also articulacy
　　see also literacy
orderliness, 154–155
orientation. *See* narrative structure
Ortony, A., 79 n.3
overlap. *See* indeterminacy

P
Painter, C., 25, 26, 27, 28–33, 34
Paquot, M., 327 n.6
Parsons, T., 89
participant. *See* transitivity
participant role (PR). *See* transitivity
past tense. *See* tense
past time. *See* time
patterning of patterns, 260, 264 n.16
patternment, 343–345, 348, 351, 356, 378
　n.17
patterns of knowledge, 114, 116

patterns of language, 6, 9, 12, 50, 52–53,
　89, 93–95, 98, 102, 106, 110–111, 115,
　128–129, 135, 139–140, 143–144, 149,
　151 n.4, 183, 185–188, 192, 200, 235
　n.2, 244, 289, 302, 307–308, 318, 343–
　344, 352, 362, 368–371, 373, 375
patterns of semiotic features, 138
permeability, 3–6, 11–13, 64, 91, 96,
　105m 110–11, 134–136, 138, 140, 143,
　209, 213, 218, 261, 268, 271, 284, 311,
　316, 326, 338–40, 352, 256, 358–359,
　361, 363–364, 366–375, 378 n.18
　　see also hybridity, and permability
permeating tense. *See* tense
persuasion. *See* rhetorical mode
phraseology, 6, 11, 41–42, 45–46, 49–50
phonology, 79, 235, 270, 351, 359, 369,
　377 n.8, 378 n.17
polarity. *See* mood
Polias, J., 8, 110, 114
polyphony, 2, 156
polysemy, 78
　　see also homonymy
poststructuralist, 2, 133
pragmatics, 164
predicator, 187, 299, 356, 362
present-in-present. *See* tense
present time. *See* time
problem-based learning (PBL), 158
process types. *See* transitivity
　　see also hybridity, and process types
professional development (PD), 104, 106,
　110
professional practices. *See* hybridity, and
　professional practices
projection, 25–26, 240, 243–244, 247, 299
　　free direct report, 244
prototype, 45, 51–53, 55, 60, 155, 157,
　173, 205, 209
psycholinguistics, 110

Q
queclarative. *See* mood
question. *See* speech function
Quirk, R., 268

R
Rabin, A., 269

Ravelli, L., 66–69
realisation, 43, 46–48, 60, 66–69, 71, 270–271, 77, 287, 291, 338, 344, 358–363, 366, 368–370, 374, 376 n.1
recommending. *See* socio-semiotic process
recreating. *See* socio-semiotic process
re-expression test. *See* transitivity
register, 4, 9–12, 92–94, 135, 137, 160, 181, 182, 185, 186, 188–191, 194, 196–197, 199, 201, 205–206, 210–213, 218, 221, 231–232, 235 n.1, n.2
    see also hybridity, and register
    register-idiosyncrasy, 312–313, 318
    register patterns, 137
    register typologies, 10, 110, 206
    registerial indeterminacy, 211–213, 217
register-idiosyncrasy. *See* register
register patterns. *See* register
register typologies *See* register
registerial indeterminacy. *See* register
Reichenbach, H., 341, 344, 377 n.7
Reiff, M.J., 2, 144
relational process. *See* transitivity
repertoire 136, 140, 181, 217
    see also reservoir
reporting. *See* socio-semiotic process
reservoir, 135
    see also repertoire
resolution. *See* narrative structure
response genre, 138–140, 145, 149
rhetorical mode, 248, 254–255, 257–260, 262, 263 n.12, 264 n.16
    aesthetic mode, 258–259
    argumentation, 87, 144–146, 149, 246, 248, 259
    discussion, 139, 144, 146
    exposition, 139, 232, 248, 257, 259, 260
    narration, 134, 136, 208, 244, 248, 257, 259
    persuasion, 263 n.8, 271–272, 276, 257
rhetorical question. *See* speech function
rhetorical structure theory (RST), 219
role distancing, 162
role embracement, 162
role hybridity. *See* hybridity, and role

role performance, 162, 164
role shift, 164, 170, 172
role type, 9, 154–156, 162, 164–165, 167, 173–174
role-set, 8, 162–167, 171, 173–174
Römer, U., 308
Rommetveit, R., 164
Rosch, E., 45, 157
Rose, D., 110, 269–273, 275–276, 308, 315, 327 n.4
Rosenberg, B.C., 240, 262 n.2, 263 n.7, 264 n.13
Ross, G., 149
Rothery, J., 109–110, 137–138, 145

S
Sacks, H., 155
saliency, 52, 70–72, 74–76, 138, 154, 157, 201
Sapir, E., 343
Sarangi, S., 3–5, 8–9, 134, 154–155, 158, 160, 162, 164–165, 167
Saussure, F. de, 338, 357–358
scaffolding, 90–91, 106, 110–115, 120–121, 123–124, 126, 128–129, 149
    macro-scaffolding, 113
Schleppegrell, M.J., 90
Scollon, R., 327 n.1
Scott, M., 310, 327 n.6
Sellami-Baklouti, A., 11, 290
semantic disposition. *See* semantics
semantic echo, 366–368
semantic metafunction, 21, 210
    experiential metafunction, 75, 135, 189, 315, 346–347, 362, 369
    ideational metafunction, 21, 46, 205, 210, 311, 349
    interpersonal metafunction, 11, 21, 135, 185–187, 205, 208, 210, 286–287, 289–291, 293, 303, 347, 369, 374
    logical metafunction, 340, 346–347
    textual metafunction, 21, 94, 134–136, 138, 150, 185, 187, 210, 240–241, 246–247, 289, 347
semantics, 12, 51, 68–69, 79 n.1, 135, 235, 287, 338, 340–341, 343–344, 348, 350–351, 352, 354, 357, 359, 363, 365, 368, 374

discourse semantics, 270, 301
semantic disposition, 7, 85–86, 89,
 91, 102–103, 106
serial tense. *See* tense
setting the context. *See* construction of
 knowledge
Shapiro, J.A., 345, 347–348
sharing. *See* socio-semiotic process
Sharpe, T., 113
Shaw, P., 288, 295
Shirky, C., 225
signified, 65–68, 358
signifier, 65–68
Silverman, D., 165
Simon-Vandenbergen, A.M., 65–66, 68,
 71–72
simple present. *See* tense
Sinclair, J., 56, 308–309, 325
Slade D., 226
Slembrouck, S., 165
social practice, 2, 327, 358, 374
social semiosis, 270
sociolinguistics, 2, 136
socio-semiotic process, 110, 211, 231
 doing, 110, 116, 206, 208–209, 213
 enabling, 52, 110, 120, 149, 166,
  208, 213
 exploring, 110, 208, 211–212, 218,
  221, 225–226, 229, 231–232, 236
  n.8
 expounding, 110, 207, 211–212, 232
 recommending, 110, 208, 211, 218–
  219, 221–222, 232, 236 n.8
 recreating, 110, 208, 211–212, 214,
  222
 reporting, 110, 208, 211–212, 214,
  222, 232
 sharing, 110, 114, 208, 211, 213,
  225–226, 228–229, 231–232
speech community, 342, 344
speech event, 347–348, 351, 355
speech function, 184, 186–188, 201 n.1,
 320
 command, 186, 192, 197–199,
  218–219, 300
 exclamation, 186, 192, 280
 minor clause, 98, 186–187, 192
 offer, 186, 192
 question, 92, 184–186, 192, 197, 199

rhetorical question, 161, 195, 201
 n.1, 280
 statement, 186–187, 192, 195, 201
  n.1, 297, 299, 319–320, 357
spoken(ness), 4, 92–94, 96, 104–105, 111,
 114, 125, 129, 182–183, 188, 190, 198,
 201 n.2, 212, 257, 272, 345
 clausal mode of discourse, 95–96,
  99–102, 104
 see also medium
statement. *See* speech function
Stenglin, M., 137, 145
Stenton, F., 269
Storey, A.M., 212
stratal continuum. *See* stratification
stratification, 5–6, 12, 21, 43, 48, 79,
 287, 309, 326, 338, 340–341, 344–345,
 354–355, 357–359, 368–370, 374, 376
 n.1
 inter-stratal context, 358, 368
 inter-stratal relation, 359, 374
 stratal continuum, 64, 79 n.1
Strevens P., 205, 339
stylistics, 134–136, 138, 140, 148
subgenre. *See* genre
subject, 48, 57–58, 184, 187, 356, 362,
 377 n.7
Suzuki, S., 90
Swales, J.M., 133, 212, 288, 291, 294, 302
Sydney school, 9, 386
synonymy, 25, 44, 55, 67, 271, 31, 355,
 359, 365–366, 369–370
system, 4, 6, 13, 21–22, 37, 41–44, 48,
 72–74, 77, 93, 116, 134, 163, 185–186,
 209, 212, 221, 245, 270, 287–288, 291,
 293, 298, 301–302, 303 n.2, 308, 325,
 328 n.9, 338, 340, 342, 344–347, 359,
 362, 368, 375, 376, n.1, n.3, n.21
 see also instance
system network, 6, 27, 35–37, 42–43, 45,
 47–49, 56, 60, 340, 376 n.3

T

Taverniers, M., 66, 69
taxonomy, 90–91, 95, 99, 207
Taylor Torsello, C., 10, 240, 244, 259, 261,
 262 n.3
teaching and learning. *See* hybridity, and
 teaching and learning

teaching and learning cycle (TLC), 109–110, 112–120, 128–129
tenor. *See* context
tense, 56, 340–363, 366, 368–370, 373
    future, 254, 347, 351, 354–355, 360, 377 n.9
    historical/narrative present, 353–354
    past, 277, 347, 354, 373
    past continuous, 354
    permeating tense, 366, 370
    present-in-present, 340, 345–346, 349–353, 355–357, 360, 365, 377 n.14
    present perfect, 254
    serial tense, 340, 346, 349, 377 n.6
    simple present, 340, 344–349, 352–357, 360, 377 n.9
    see also time
Teruya K., 1, 10, 110, 206, 235 n.3, 290, 308
textese, 98
textual function. *See* semantic metafunction
thematic structure. *See* theme
thematisation. *See* theme
theme, 183
    enhanced theme construction, 57
    macro-theme, 269, 273, 276–280
    thematic structure, 308
    thematisation, 66
    theme in verbal art, 208, 260
Thompson, G., 9, 24–25, 26, 27, 28–33, 34, 182, 183, 184, 188, 189, 192, 198, 290, 306, 308
Thompson, S., 183
Thompson, S.A., 219
Threadgold, T., 2, 133, 262 n.3
time, 341, 344–348, 350, 352–356, 358–361, 363, 365, 369–370, 376 n.3, 377 n.5, n.7, n.11
    extended present time, 355–356
    future time, 354, 360, 365, 371, 377 n.7
    past time, 347, 354, 377 n.7
    present time, 280, 346, 353, 377 n.7
    time-phase, 315
    see also tense
time-phase. *See* time

Tognini Bonelli, E., 308
transitivity, 6, 41–42, 45, 50, 66, 73, 78, 210, 307, 318
    see also hybridity, and transitivity
    action process, 21, 23, 42, 61 n.3
    and Cardiff grammar, 43, 61 n.1
    behavioural process, 6, 21–28, 34–35, 37–38, 45, 221, 314, 318
    circumstance, 21, 47, 72–73, 318, 344, 348–349, 353–356, 360–362, 365, 367, 370
    existential process, 21–22, 45, 73–74, 78
    material process, 21–24, 26, 37, 43, 46, 48, 50–51, 54, 56–57, 59, 61 n.3, 64, 74, 79 n.7, 221, 315–316, 344, 347–348, 452, 361–362, 372
    mental process, 6, 21–27, 35, 37–38, 42–48, 50, 53–59, 66, 73–74, 221, 228, 244, 247, 299, 302, 314, 318–319, 340, 364, 372, 377 n.14
    participant, 21, 23, 42–43, 51, 56, 61 n.1, n.4
    participant role (PR), 41, 43, 44, 51, 53–54, 57–59, 61 n.1
    process types, 5–6, 21–22, 27, 35–38, 42–45, 47, 52–53, 56–57, 64, 79 n.2, 345, 368, 371–373, 377 n.14
        see also hybridity, and process types
    re-expression test, 43–45, 52–55, 58–59
    relational process, 21–22, 38, 42–46, 51–55, 61 n.6, 64, 70–72, 74–76, 79 n.7, 230, 307, 314–315, 318–320, 344, 373
    transitivity system, 6, 21, 41–44, 73–74, 77
    verbal process, 6, 21–22, 25–27, 36–38, 44–45, 74–75, 318, 364, 372–373
    voice, 345, 362
transitivity system. *See* transitivity
Trevarthen, C., 378 n.15
Tucker, G.H., 6, 45, 52, 79, 363
Turner Strong, P., 2
Turner, J., 144
Turner, S., 144

typology, 10, 110, 139, 206, 210–211, 235
    n.3

U
UAM CorpusTool. *See* corpus annotation

V
valuation. *See* appraisal
van Dijk T.A., 4, 326
Ventola, E., 4
verbal art, 208, 241, 259, 263 n.12
verbal process. *See* transitivity
voice. *See* transitivity
voluntariness of action, 23–24, 26, 35
voluntariness of perception, 23–24,
    35–38
Vygotsky, L.S., 109, 115

W
Waletzky, J., 241, 251–253
Watt, I.P., 217
Weatherall, D., 156
Weiss, G., 327
White, P.R.R., 1, 212, 286, 289, 293, 301
Whitelock, D., 268, 269, 273

Whorf, B.L., 337, 341, 342, 343, 345, 347,
    369, 374, 375, 376, 377 n.5, 377 n.7
Williams G., 328 n.13
Wittgenstein, L., 157
Wodak, R., 327
Wood, D., 110, 149
Woolf, V., 10, 240–264
Wrenn, C.L., 268
written dialogue, 93, 9–96, 105–106
        see also dialogism
written(ness), 92–96, 98, 104–105, 114,
    125, 129 189, 193, 201, 255, 257, 262,
    272
        nominal mode of discourse, 58, 90,
            96, 99–102, 104, 189, 315
        see also medium
Wu, C., 325
Wulff, S., 308, 326

Y
Young, L., 14 n.5, 241, 250, 251, 263 n.1
Young, R.J.C., 1

Z
Zadeh, L.A., 24, 338, 339

CPSIA information can be obtained
at www.ICGtesting.com
Printed in the USA
BVHW042003250520
580200BV00011B/101